the inclusive city

DESIGN SOLUTIONS FOR BUILDINGS,
NEIGHBORHOODS AND URBAN SPACES

the inclusive city

DESIGN SOLUTIONS FOR BUILDINGS, NEIGHBORHOODS AND URBAN SPACES

edited by

SUSAN GOLTSMAN

DANIEL IACOFANO

MIG COMMUNICATIONS

Berkeley, California

Managing Editor: Joyce Vollmer
Jacket design: Ed Canalin
Interior design: Catherine Courtenaye
Printed in China

Library of Congress Cataloging-in-Publication Data

The inclusive city : design solutions for buildings, neighborhoods, and urban spaces /
    edited by Susan Goltsman and Daniel Iacofano.
        p. cm.
    Includes bibliographical references and index.
    ISBN-13: 978-0-944661-31-4 (cloth)
     1. City planning. 2. Public spaces. 3. Universal design. 4. City planning—Case
studies. I. Goltsman, Susan M. II. Iacofano, Daniel S.

    NA9031.I52 2006
    711'.4--dc22

                                                                                    2005053382

MIG Communications
800 Hearst Avenue
Berkeley, California 94710 USA
510-845-7549 phone
510-845-8750 fax
www.migcom.com

This book is dedicated to all those helping to make cities vital and healthy, humane and just.

CONTENTS

x   *Preface*

xi   *Foreword* | *Andrew Altman*

xv   *Acknowledgements*

1   **Introduction: The Challenge of Our Cities** | **Susan Goltsman, Daniel Iacofano**

PROJECTS

15   **CELEBRATING AN INDEPENDENT LIFE**

Ed Roberts Campus, Berkeley, California | **Joan Leon**

This world-class center provides a home for the Independent Living Movement and the organizations that helped found it, demonstrating the principles of universal design atop a rail transit station.

35   **HELPING CHILDREN HEAL**

Edelman Children's Court, Los Angeles County, California | **Susan Goltsman**

The Edelman Dependency Court's child-friendly design contributes to family healing and reunification.

61   **BRINGING NATURE INTO THE URBAN SCHOOL**

Tule Elk Park Child Development Center, San Francisco, California | **Susan Goltsman**

A relatively small space becomes a complex urban ecosystem and learning laboratory in the middle of a diverse neighborhood.

77   **EXPANDING THE LEARNING ENVIRONMENT**

St. Coletta of Greater Washington, D.C. | **Susan Goltsman**

A creative, caring educational program coupled with a nontraditional school design negotiates for space in a dense urban environment.

97   **REDISCOVERING THE TOUCH OF ART**

Musées des Beaux Arts, Valenciennes and Calais, France | **Coco Raynes**

Innovative exhibit design helps people with visual disabilities appreciate sculpture at museums in France.

111   GROWING CARING CHILDREN

Explore! A Child's Nature, Brookfield Zoo, Illinois | *Robin Moore*

A venerable, world-renowned zoo instills environmental responsibility and stewardship through interactive exhibit design and adventure play.

155   ADOPTING A NEW HEART

Chase Palm Park, Santa Barbara, California | *Susan Goltsman*

As mitigation for new development, an oceanfront park recreates city history and aquatic life, attracting city residents and visitors.

173   COMBINING COMMUNITY FACILITIES

Edison School / Pacific Park, Glendale, California | *Susan McKay, Susan Goltsman*

A novel grouping of neighborhood facilities draws diverse communities into one central location in this traditionally underserved area.

193   GATHERING PLACES

Central Park, Davis, California | *Stanton Jones, Cheryl Sullivan*

Community action leads to a new central park and farmers market, strengthening identity and pride in this small town.

211   TRANSFORMING RETAIL SPACE INTO COMMUNITY SPACE

Davis Commons, Davis, California | *Cheryl Sullivan*

Reconfiguring a neighborhood shopping center provides spaces for social interaction and public events.

229   RECONNECTING WITH THE STREET

R Street Urban Design and Development Plan, Sacramento, California | *Daniel Iacofano, Mukul Malhotra*

Pedestrians, bicyclists and vehicles share the road in the innovative redesign of this classic industrial street.

273   CONNECTING URBAN AND NATURAL SETTINGS

Presidio Trails and Bikeways, San Francisco, California | *Larry Wight, Sally McIntyre*

An extensive trail network provides a high level of access to the outdoors for this national park set within an urban area.

295   **SPANNING THE COMMUNITY**
      Alfred Zampa (Carquinez) Bridge, San Francisco Bay, California | *Bart Ney, Daniel Iacofano*
      A major piece of transportation infrastructure becomes a source of pride and reunification for a small suburban community.

313   **REMAKING AN AMERICAN DOWNTOWN**
      Downtown Area, Spokane, Washington | *Daniel Iacofano, Mukul Malhotra, Rosemary Dudley*
      A series of community-based plans and projects revitalizes a major urban center on the edge of decline.

INCLUSIVE DESIGN GUIDELINES

387   **LESSONS FROM THE PROJECTS**

388   **DEPENDENCY COURTS**

399   **SCHOOLS (K-12)**

411   **MUSEUMS**

413   **CHILDREN'S ZOOS**

417   **PLAY AREAS**

423   **PLAZAS**

425   **TRAIL SYSTEMS**

435   **OPEN SPACE PERFORMANCE STANDARDS**

454   **CITYSCAPES**

471   REFERENCES

473   CONTRIBUTORS

PREFACE

In the fall of 2005, as we were working on this book, the Gulf Coast of the United States was devastated by two major hurricanes: Katrina and Rita. We all saw the images of New Orleans, and the small cities of Louisiana, Mississippi, Alabama and Texas. As the winds stripped the land bare, they exposed the hidden underclass that remained: our most vulnerable—the poor, the elderly, the disabled, and the very young. Perhaps it shouldn't have been a shock to see that they were the ones who suffered most, as they have historically, because our city infrastructures do not fully support them.

As we looked at those destroyed cities and torn communities, we saw that they might have to be entirely reconceived and rebuilt—and that offered our country a redeeming opportunity. We can do better.

Cleveland's great equity-planner, Norman Krumholz, said that urban planning is a "perpetual opportunity…a field for those who wish to shape our collective future." As urban planners—and designers, architects, developers, economists, politicians and policymakers—we can build *inclusive* cities. Our built environments can be structured to embrace, welcome and encourage all members of our communities to thrive and prosper. This is the hope for our collective future; this is why we do what we do.

Daniel Iacofano and Susan Goltsman
October 2006

FOREWORD

ANDREW ALTMAN

While the predominant pattern of development in the United States continues to be characterized by relentless sprawl with population and employment decentralization, there are clear signs that cities nationwide are resurgent once again. But what kind of city are we building? Each burst of urban rebuilding begs the question: for whom is the city being built? Further, what does the new form of the built environment say about our values as a society?

Cities at the turn of the 21st century are doing better than they have in decades, but it's not yet clear that we will able to look back at this latest age of urban renaissance as having created a more *inclusive* city. Will changes in the form, diversity, social vitality and health of our 21st century city be more profound than simply having created islands of prosperity and entertainment for a new urban elite? Or will the built environment being constructed in this time of rapid development and expansion create buildings and settings reflective of an inclusive city—an inclusive society—where diverse populations interact and their needs and aspirations are respected and encouraged? This is the central challenge that this book implores us to confront.

City master plans, planning conferences, architectural competitions and political discourse are replete with laudable and sincere aspirations to "build the inclusive city" and there are many success stories. Indeed we have come a long way since the era of Urban Renewal. However, if cities are to succeed in the 21st century, we must sharpen the tools and instructive cases that the shapers of urban environments can use to build the inclusive city. If the aspiration for an inclusive city is to be more than words, the arts of city planning and city building, which so often diverge in practice, will need to join again. Because it is in the detailed act of *building* the public and communal spaces of the city where the translation of an inclusive vision into an actual inclusive city often goes unrealized.

That is why this book is needed now more than ever.

Let us reflect upon this provocative challenge for a moment. If left unchecked, what would the paradox of growth sweeping our country portend for cities? There is evidence that the new information and service economy of the 21st century will favor urban attributes. The timeless assets of successful cities—density, urbanity, compactness and complexity—constitute the ingredients of success in an economy where innovation, the exchange of ideas and the value of environments all become economic imperatives, not just niceties.

Moreover, there is a return to urban living. People are moving downtown again, especially as empty nesters and young professionals seek the dynamism and range of social amenities and interactions that a city offers. Popular culture has signaled a change in our prevalent attitude toward cities. From apocalyptic images of cities in the cinema of the 1970s to the "hip" media favorites "Sex in the City" and "Friends," cities are again described in the media as "hot" places to live, work, shop and visit. As a consequence of this, some of the troubling signs of urban decline seem to have abated and in many cities are being reversed: indices of population decline, segregation and concentrated poverty are, on average, improving.

Yet we must not let these improved times for cities belie the harsh reality that cities continue to house the majority of the poor and segregation continues to persist as the basic form of the city. And while urban downtowns are indeed exciting destinations featuring celebrated new icons of modern architecture and temples of culture, they are often not the places where the diversity of the city intersects and enjoys shared public space. The very meaning and success of the city must be measured not solely by growth statistics or increased tax receipts—although these are both vital to the health of cities—but more importantly, by whether we are in fact creating an inclusive city that overcomes the economic, physical, environmental and social barriers that perpetuate inequality and separation.

But how do we do it? We bemoan our helplessness in achieving an inclusive city because its lofty goal seems too difficult and overwhelming to actually achieve "on the ground." The argument is that the forces that shape the destiny of the city—the economic, market and government policies—are beyond the influence of a city. How can we create an inclusive city in an environment seemingly aligned against it, and that in fact fosters the very conditions of disparity and inequity that this book challenges us to confront, understand and resolve?

I believe we can meet this challenge. Even in the face of federal withdrawal from cities and the hostility of many state governments to the interests of cities, there is increasing evidence that cities and urban communities are seizing control of their own destiny. New models of entrepreneurial urban development are emerging that, while on their own cannot resolve basic urban disparities, offer us hope for seeding an inclusive city that can be replicated on a larger scale.

My own experience as planning director of Washington, D.C., confirms that just such an urban transformation is possible. Under the leadership of a visionary mayor, Mayor Anthony A. Williams, urban planning was empowered to think big again. Through the combination of generating bold ideas for urban transformation, engaging in participatory planning that attempted to bridge economic, social and racial divisions, and planning with—not against—the market so that opportunities are harnessed and created, Washington, D.C., is growing and addressing fundamental urban inequities after decades of steady decline. Its new master plan focuses on balancing growth, equity and a shared sense of community and responsibility across neighborhood, racial and economic fault lines.

But while attention is often given to the "big" programmatic ideas that are prerequisite to building an inclusive city—such as in Washington, D.C.—it is at the ground level where we are often left without sufficient professional guidance and successful examples. This is where *The Inclusive City* makes an important contribution. The public spaces and facilities that have defined the urbanity of cities for millennia can either be spaces and buildings that invite the interaction of diverse populations and encourage serendipitous experiences, or they can be controlled spaces that enforce segregation and sterility. Successful—inclusive—cities are designed to engage divergent and oft times conflicting communities in the civic and public life of the city. Nowhere is this more important than in the design and use of our public spaces—the streets, squares, schools and public facilities—that determine the extent to which the daily life of the city is either inclusive or exclusive.

We desperately need a framework to provoke us, teach us and stimulate our work: what are the building blocks, principles and guidelines that we should look to and measure ourselves against so that values match desired outcomes? This much-needed book offers just such a guide and inspiration. From the scale of planning for downtown and pedestrian corridors, to the design of new parks, and the detailed layout of the interior and external environments of community facilities and schools, this book offers us a toolbox to bridge the gap between theory and action.

Having worked with Daniel and Susan for many years, beginning with my tenure as planning director for the City of Oakland, California, I know their work exemplifies the search for and realization of community and inclusiveness in its most positive and myriad forms. We find this in Daniel's adroit organization of inclusive planning processes that break down the barriers separating communities from each other and planning professionals from the constituents they serve. And we find it in Susan's work designing humane environments for some of the most challenged and vulnerable populations in our society. The concept of the inclusive city, both as process and outcome, are pervasive in every aspect of their work. And importantly, if life is to be lived by example, their indefatigable optimism is simply an inspiration to be around, filling one with the belief that, with the right attitude and commitment, inclusive environments and inclusive cities are possible and within our reach.

Andrew Altman is the former Director of the Washington, D.C. Office of Planning and Anacostia Waterfront Initiative.

ACKNOWLEDGEMENTS

This book began with a vision: an "inclusive city" that fully supports the physical, economic, cultural, and social needs of all people of all abilities, of all social strata and of all income levels. As with all visions, implementing it required the creativity and dedication of a great many people.

All of the book's contributors graciously shared their projects, their time and their enthusiasm. We would like to thank them: Coco Raynes, Joan Leon and Stanton Jones, and those who worked at MIG on projects with us, Robin Moore, Susan McKay, Mukul Malhotra, Larry Wight, Sally McIntyre, Bart Ney and Cheryl Sullivan.

During the course of researching how built inclusive environments are actually being used, we interviewed over 100 community members and planning staff from various cities who generously contributed their time and their insight. We thank all of them for their participation in this project.

We would also like to thank the creative MIG Communications and Media Services team: writer Joyce Vollmer, director Carie DeRuiter, art director Ed Canalin, graphic designer Catherine Courtenaye and production manager Kim Donahue.

This book is funded in part by the National Endowment for the Arts (grant number DCA 01-04/2001-2002) as part of its Universal Design Leadership Initiative. Additional funding has been provided by PLAE, Inc.

NATIONAL
ENDOWMENT
FOR THE ARTS
A great nation
deserves great art.

PLAE inc.

INTRODUCTION

"Concepts such as harmony, beauty, variety, and order have been thought of as attributes of the [physical environment] itself. Designers have unconsciously relied on their own implicit values and perceptions, projecting them on the physical world as if they were inherent qualities. Not so—one begins with the images and priorities of the users of a place and must look at place and person together."

KEVIN LYNCH
A THEORY OF GOOD CITY FORM

THE CHALLENGE OF OUR CITIES

SUSAN GOLTSMAN
DANIEL IACOFANO

THE MOST PROFOUND CHALLENGES FACING CITIES TODAY ALSO OFFER AN EXTRAORDINARY opportunity: how will we confront, understand and overcome the enormous economic, social and physical disparities that now divide our communities? As planners, designers, developers and managers, how can we overcome:

- Neighborhoods with vastly different qualities of life;

- Fundamentally unequal access to education and jobs;

- Virtually impassable physical barriers that cut through many disadvantaged urban neighborhoods; and

- Environmental disasters like toxic waste sites, a lack of parks and open space, and rivers that no longer resemble anything ever seen in nature?

As long as these disparities exist, they will restrict and confine groups of people, limiting their ability to make choices about how and where they live, perpetuating inequity and cutting the social connections that define vibrant and thriving cities. That is the fundamental unfinished agenda for our cities: balancing the physical improvements of urban revitalization with the goals of social equity, economic development and environmental protection for all city inhabitants.

There have been many attempts to understand what makes a good city, good form and good design. It's more than simply stating that a new building or development is "postmodern with urban edginess"—that's just architectural rhetoric. While there are some general concepts that people agree on, it has proven difficult to define the exact typology. We need a way of objectifying criteria of success, some common points of reference so independent observers and evaluators can arrive at conclusions about what needs to happen as we plan and design cities.

Let's take a brief step back: how did we get to this point?

Since the beginning of U.S. cities, we have been challenged to accommodate and serve the multitudes of people living and working in them. Our first zoning laws, in the early 1900s, were actually developed for public health needs: to separate commercial, industrial and residential areas, with the hope of controlling the miasma of epidemics that ran rampant.

After World War II, the U.S. government offered the GI Bill and low-interest loans that allowed so many people to buy their own homes. That became the American dream: the house with the white picket fence on a tree-lined curb and gutter street. It was all very organized and planned. The suburbs had arrived. William Whyte, the great urban sociologist, wrote in *The Organization Man* how men in the 1950s were trained to buy into the social ethic that the organization is superior to the individual. The suburbs were the extension of the organization.

The new Interstate Highway system—a huge national defense project to improve mobility—also allowed cars and trucks to easily crisscross the country. And it did so in a rather unrelenting fashion. Freeways often cut through cities, creating isolated communities and pockets of unused land that later became blighted areas.

Downtowns, meanwhile, were "messy" places: high-density and lower-income, with kids playing on the streets, people living above shops, street vendors, and neighbors running back and forth. It was crowded, and for some—against the backdrop of the new suburban sensibilities—downtowns were considered unhealthy, or even irrelevant to the new way of living. We thought: the suburbs are successful; if we make the downtowns like the suburbs, downtowns will be successful.

The concept was that *physical* planning could solve social problems. Planners embraced the idea that the new architecture itself would save the city, and they called it Urban Renewal. Many neighborhoods were razed to make way for planned public housing. But often the physical planning did not take into account how people actually use space as they live and work. Planners missed the vital community connections that "messiness" provided. In fact, the underlying design standard was based on the auto and the turning radius for fire trucks. Urban Renewal was not a success. Focusing solely on physical planning—on buildings and the spaces that connect them—did not work.

In reaction, the pendulum swung heavily toward a focus on social planning: on jobs, health care and social services—all essential for people's quality of life in the city. But classical city and building design were almost entirely de-emphasized. Cities were left with suburban style buildings and suburban land use patterns placed into an urban context, continued auto-dominance, and an aging physical infrastructure, leading to continued flight to the suburbs by those who could afford it.

But against the trend toward suburbia, there were other lines of thinking that continued to focus on creating urban vitality. Lewis Mumford examined the driving force behind cities, citing four human needs: protection, culture, commerce and ceremony, the need for finding meaning and value. Jane Jacobs wrote *The Death and Life of Great American Cities,* detailing how urban renewal had created isolated, unnatural urban spaces that stripped the life out of cities. She advocated physical planning for dense, mixed-use neighborhoods. In his seminal book, *A Theory of Good City Form,* Kevin Lynch, one of our most prominent urban theorists, put forth a series of concepts for measuring the quality of the urban environment, called "dimensions of performance." Many planners also looked back to the great cities of Europe, that had never planned to accommodate cars, and retained vibrant and thriving downtowns.

When New Urbanism burst on the scene in the late 1980's, it was a breakthrough in re-integrating the social and physical aspects of planning, and allowing communities to participate in planning their own futures. New Urbanism emphasized people rather than cars, with a human scale "grid" that reduced the amount of space given to cars and increased opportunities for walking and gathering. It reintroduced the concept of the mixed-use, higher-density "urban village" and neighborhoods that activate the public realm. New Urbanist principles aimed for restoring urban centers, creating real neighborhoods, conserving the environment and preserving the built legacy.

But what about the new environments built under the rubric of New Urbanism? Do they take the principles far enough—are they truly meeting the needs of all residents?

Physically, there are well-designed projects in many cities: vibrant streetscapes, interesting architecture, housing on top of retail, people walking and sitting in cafes. But a closer look reveals that many of these isolated projects often don't connect to anything. They are usually designed, still, with cars in mind—surrounded by acres of parking with no transit connections. The housing is expensive, the shops even more expensive. The people who live there don't work there. The people who work there can't afford to live there. And the shoppers just come and go. Where are the urban parks, the true gathering places, the grocery stores, the shoe repair—where are the functional services for real people? Chic boutiques on the corners don't make a social community.

And as people are attracted back to areas with new housing options, more interesting architecture and more vitality, what's becoming of the people who already live there?

The pendulum seems to be swinging once again to an over-reliance on a physical design approach—a set of formulaic design responses, which, when examined closely, do not address the needs of all people.

We need the pendulum to stop its swing right in the middle, if we're to achieve this. So how do we proceed?

The solution is inclusive planning based on economic, social, environmental and culturally sensitive policies that allow everyone to improve economically as the physical area improves. Cities need planning that recognizes that every individual has the right to full and equal participation in the built environment—and that through their direct involvement they can shape their own environment to meet their own needs.

HEALTHY HUMAN HABITATS

Let us examine for a moment a simple ecological principle: every living thing on earth is part of an ecosystem. All successful habitats are uniquely adapted to the species that inhabit them. Our task is to design healthy human habitats. The habitat has to meet the human needs for:

- Physical comfort and safety;
- Community, connections and identity;
- Stimulation and discovery;
- Fun and joy; and
- Meaning.

How do we design the physical environment to provide for those human needs? Again, we can examine basic ecological requirements:

- *Sustenance:* We need resources to sustain us, such as food, shelter, water and sunlight.
- *Diversity:* We need a range of variation in the habitat that allows adaptive potential.
- *Adaptability:* We need the ability to adapt to variations in environmental conditions.
- *Complexity:* We need a richness of stimulation in the environment to promote healthy development.
- *Range:* We need to be able to move through the habitat to acquire resources.
- *Connectivity:* We need safe pathways for mobility to find needed resources throughout the entire urban region.

PROJECT DESIGN CRITERIA

We can translate those ecological principles for a healthy human habitat into inclusive design criteria for the built environment.

Successful inclusive design projects support our unique physical, social, cultural and economic needs with clear philosophies, strategies and tactics. From the outset, these projects aim for inclusiveness in all phases. They push the boundaries of creativity and innovation, energizing and regenerating a community. They result in functional, high-quality and aesthetically pleasing environments that manage impacts and add value to cities, providing residents

with opportunities and choices to thrive and reach their full potential.

We propose three criteria that can help us systematically analyze how well environments incorporate ecological principles, and how people are affected by and can shape development projects.

1. *Functionality.* Designs are functionally based, incorporating the physical inclusiveness of universal design, which supports the unique

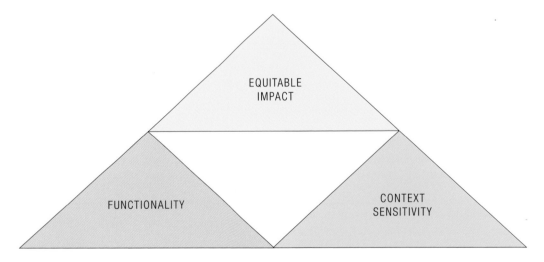

Inclusive design projects must meet three criteria: fulfill functional needs, emerge from the context of the community, and mitigate their own impacts.

physical needs of all types of people, and makes places and programs accessible to the widest possible audience. Universal design assumes that humans have a diverse range of abilities, that this range is ordinary, not unique, and that the range is dynamic—it will change during our lifespan. Friendly, accessible and easy-to-use environments benefit everyone: a mother holding a baby, a very short or tall person, a senior with low stamina or a visual impairment, or a child with a broken leg.

Successful projects support the functional needs of their users such as health, safety and sustenance. There must be good transportation and communication, access to goods and services, and everything must be available to all inhabitants regardless of age, income, power or rank.

It is sized and positioned correctly, or, as Lynch says, the "form and capacity of spaces, channels and equipment in a settlement match the pattern and quantity of actions that people customarily engage in." There must be a match between the environment and cultural constructs such as values and vision. And finally, communities must be able to influence and mana ge the space and activities themselves.

2. *Context Sensitivity.* Inclusive design translates the vision of an inclusive city into the physical; it enables people across the entire economic and social spectrum to participate in and receive value from the project.

The first step is helping the client and the community understand and take an active role in early strategy and project planning. The critical thinking about the real source of a problem and potential solutions is participatory, involving the entire community in hands-on planning and leveraging resources. The projects are always context-driven, emerging from the needs, assets and culture of the communities and the environment in which they exist. With extensive participation, communities then feel strong ownership and commitment to the project.

Successful designs are aesthetically pleasing and in harmony with the surrounding community fabric; people want to live and work there. They provide a sense of place that people identify with and an environmental consciousness that respects our stewardship of the earth.

People can grasp and understand the design; it's navigable. In the organizational sense, the project leaves the community with the capacity to accomplish more than before sthe project was started— the process of doing the project provides people with the tools they need to manage or control their environment.

3. *Equitable Impacts.* Every project has consequences, both intended and unintended. Successful projects mitigate the social and human

impacts, especially on the most vulnerable members of society.

A successful project manages it own impact by ensuring that the design addresses the entire environment, including the externalities beyond the project area. It ensures that there are minimal or no negative impacts and, often, that the impact actually becomes a net positive. For example, transportation infrastructure projects that increase the flow of people, goods and services, are notorious for leaving residue such as a patchwork of left-over land areas, cut-up streets that disrupt social patterns and cultural resources, and increased noise and pollution. And those impacts are far more prevalent in low-income areas.

INCLUSIVE PROJECTS

While it is difficult to find all elements of an inclusive city all in one place, we can find many successful projects in many cities. Here is just a sampling.

■ A transit village in Oakland, California, is stimulating economic development and environmental improvement in an inner-city, moderate- to low-income Hispanic community. The Fruitvale Transit Village above a multi-modal transit station is the result of the neighborhood coming together and insisting that a new development include affordable and senior housing, offices, neighborhood-serving retail, a childcare facility—right there, for parents commuting to jobs—a library, senior center, health clinic, multi-lingual human services offices, and a public plaza. Fannie Mae calls it one of the ten "Just Right" affordable housing markets in the country.

The Fruitvale Transit Village in Oakland, California, provides functional human services while stimulating economic revitalization in an inner-city community.

Pioneer Courthouse Square in Portland, Oregon, is an active community gathering space in a fareless transit zone.

■ Portland, Oregon, has one of the best public spaces in the country. Pioneer Courthouse Square was the community response to a planned ten-story parking lot in the middle of town. There's a transit mall right next to it, featuring a fareless zone—several square miles with *free* bus, street car and light rail service. If you want to commute to work by driving, you'll pay steep parking fees.

■ In Seattle, Washington, downtown property owners have partnered with low-income housing providers. The City changed the development code to increase the housing height limit. Builders buy the extra height and that money goes toward affordable housing. And Seattle's Housing Resources Group, formed by the Downtown Seattle Association, helps property owners or businesses build housing for people who work in their businesses. This partnership has created thousands of units of affordable housing for people of all ages.

■ Vancouver, British Columbia, offers a model of true high-density urban living with activity 24 hours a day. The City created pedestrian-scaled streets with three-story town homes closest to the street. Behind them are fifteen 30-story high-rise condos.

That design allows light and views with transitions to older, single-family residences and commercial office towers. And everything is within walking distance.

- In Southern California, Interstate 710 carries trucks out from the huge ports of Los Angeles and Long Beach. Trucks are jammed up, belching out pollution, a serious health problem. Even worse, trucks go on local streets to connect with Interstate 5 because there's no other connector. Community members came up with a solution: let's not build a connector because it would take homes and a much-needed park. Instead, let's widen the freeway with truck-only lanes and create a new truck-only off ramp that routes them onto a commercial street to the freight yard.

- The University of California in San Francisco offers economic mitigations for its huge new campus in a long-time economically disadvantaged area

Vancouver, British Columbia, offers tree-lined residential streets within walking distance of the commercial center.

just south of the City. It reserved eight acres for usable public open space, with recreational facilities open to the public. It created high school and college programs for local residents to train for well-paid staff positions. It helps local businesses become vendors. It's planning affordable housing for staff, adjacent to the campus. And, noting that over $35 million in tax refunds go unclaimed in the Bay Area, it now offers a free tax service to low-income community members.

- In Washington, D.C.—where disenfranchised areas like the low-income Anacostia Waterfront have borne the brunt of political wrangling for years—an innovative new comprehensive plan is adding jobs, education, arts and culture elements. Based on its "Vision for Growing an Inclusive City," the plan is being built on a monumental community outreach program, benefiting from the ideas of thousands of community members.

INCLUSIVE POLICY FRAMEWORK

These successful projects offer choices and opportunities to all city inhabitants. To set the stage for formulating projects that embody inclusive design, we need a broad, inclusive policy framework that guides urban area decision-making. We need to be sure that cities provide:

- *Economic Development*—
  Opportunities for everyone to participate fully in the economy of the city, with access to a variety of quality jobs. Land use decisions must encourage locally owned, neighborhood-serving businesses and focus on catalyst projects that generate investment and stimulate further development. Cities must insist that new developments hire locally first, develop local vendors and develop courses at colleges or high schools to train community members. New or expanding companies must provide a net gain to the community, both in

terms of numbers of jobs and quality of jobs (wages, choices, opportunities for advancement and ability to spend earnings in the community). Cities can explore the use of zoning overlays, square footage caps, business improvement districts, parking assessments, and other creative, stimulating policies.

- *Housing and Neighborhoods*—*Safe neighborhoods with a range of housing types and price levels to accommodate diverse socio-economic backgrounds and lifestyle choices.* Cities can modernize housing and building codes to focus more on health, safety and community quality of life. They can also adopt in lieu fees, tax credits, Individual Development Accounts, developer incentives, zoning changes and public infrastructure development to stimulate private investment—ensuring a mix of affordable and market rate housing in scale with the surrounding neighborhoods.

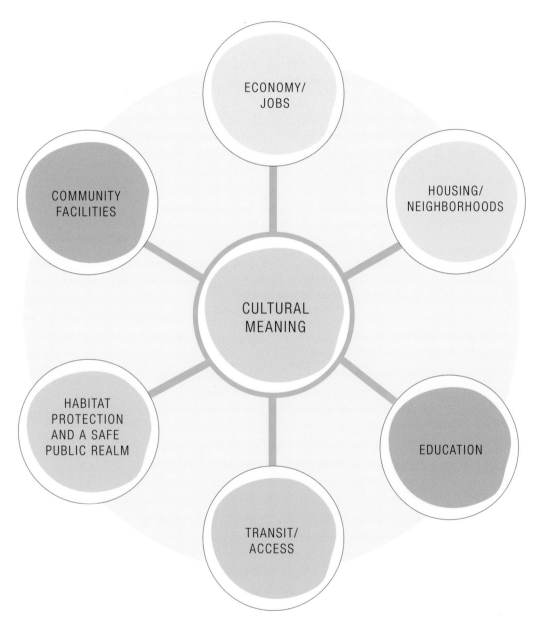

ECONOMY/
JOBS

COMMUNITY
FACILITIES

HOUSING/
NEIGHBORHOODS

CULTURAL
MEANING

HABITAT
PROTECTION
AND A SAFE
PUBLIC REALM

EDUCATION

TRANSIT/
ACCESS

Urban decision-making should be guided by a broad, progessive policy framework.

■ *Education*—*Full access to quality education choices.* The physical condition of a school does have an impact on a child's ability to learn—and defines the social and economic characteristics of a neighborhood. Developers can contribute to renovation, although not in return for usable open space. Cities need to build schools near where children live, explore shared use between schools, parks and community facilities, maintain those facilities, and put their full weight behind any bonds or taxes needed to properly fund them.

■ *Access and Mobility*—*Viable, multimodal and interconnected public transit systems.* Cities can create incentives to promote transit and disincentives to discourage single occupancy car commuting. They can promote transportation demand management measures and funding policies that favor transit.

■ *Habitat Protection and a Safe Public Realm*—*Connected, safe, functional and green connections.* Cities can reintroduce the human scale to create pedestrian-friendly and bike-friendly streets that reactivate the public realm. They can reintegrate land uses, rather than maintaining separation.

■ *Community Facilities and Gathering Spaces*—*Well-maintained and usable open space.* Gathering spaces are virtually the only urban places where people of all socio-economic levels have equal access. Parks and open space are key tools for improved air and water quality and preserving rivers, wetlands and urban forests. In return for development rights, cities can ask for park impact fees, open space, pocket parks and plazas, green roofs, and private green space (property frontages). Cities should consider changing operating procedures to allow capital improvement dollars to be used for landscaping and maintenance and promote expanded roles for private citizens and community groups in maintenance.

■ *Cultural Meaning*—*Spaces and places to create and display social and cultural rituals and symbols that have meaning for all residents.* Public events, such as street fairs and parades, contribute to vibrant neighborhood life. Cities can incorporate one-percent set-asides for arts, provide space for grassroots and community organizations in non-traditional settings and create arts districts—including culinary arts.

These progressive policies require us to go beyond the traditional land use emphasis of city planning, to integrate all the elements of inclusive design. Planners must balance community good with the "right to develop." In return for that right, cities must require that developers deliver certain benefits, in certain ways, in a certain amount of time. Each project must be critically examined:

■ Is this contributing to a real neighborhood?

■ Has the community been involved; does the project actually fulfill the community's vision?

■ Does it respect social and cultural preferences?

■ Does it enhance community connections?

■ Is it environmentally sustainable?

■ Will it allow all residents to improve economically?

■ Does it mitigate its own impacts?

■ Is it truly inclusive?

INCLUSIVE DESIGN: PROJECTS AND GUIDELINES

This book provides a practical look at a range of successful inclusive design projects with positive social impacts in urban environments.

This eclectic mix has one important result in common: doing the project has added value to the world beyond the project itself. For example, building a new bridge with community involvement led to new ways of aligning off ramps that recreated long-lasting community connections—in addition to a stunning new bridge. Taking a fresh look at children's zoos resulted in a nationwide movement toward involving the entire family in experiential learning. And designing the Ed Roberts Campus led to new ways that the philosophy of the Independent Living Movement for people with disabilities will inform design and architecture in the future.

All the projects demonstrate the belief that every individual has the right to full and equal participation in the built environment.

The book also offers a set of inclusive design guidelines that build on lessons learned from the projects. Reading through those guidelines will help provide an intuitive sense of how to achieve inclusive design in other, similar settings.

Since every well-designed project grows out of its own context, it's impossible to find models that transfer exactly to other projects. But it is our hope that the reader will find some of this information useful enough to take to the next project, so that, someday, all built environments and all cities are fully inclusive, welcoming and engaging. The basic fact that we are all connected compels us to do so.

As we continue to search for innovative solutions to creating inclusive environments, we welcome feedback from planners, architects, landscape architects, policy makers and, most of all, from community members who share our passion for great urban places. We hope to create a clearinghouse to share ideas and successes from which others may benefit. Please contact us: www.inclusivecity.com.

ED ROBERTS CAMPUS | BERKELEY, CALIFORNIA

"We propose to build a new building, one that does not look like buildings of the past. We are hoping to change history and move to a brighter future."

BOARD MEMBER, ED ROBERTS CAMPUS

CELEBRATING AN INDEPENDENT LIFE

JOAN LEON

IN 1995, ED ROBERTS, A HERO OF THE INDEPENDENT LIVING MOVEMENT FOR PEOPLE WITH disabilities, died. The movement had begun in Berkeley, California, in the 1970s and it forever changed the lives of people with disabilities. After Ed died, leaders of the movement, the City of Berkeley, and the University of California, Berkeley, gathered to discuss a suitable memorial to his legacy, and the idea for the Ed Roberts Campus (ERC) was born. The campus will be the world's foremost disability service, advocacy, education, training and policy center. It will also be the embodiment of inclusive design, integrating the principles of independent living, universal design, sustainable design and transit-oriented development.

Ed Roberts, a founder of the Independent Living Movement.
LYDIA GANS

PROJECT Ed Roberts Campus   **LOCATION** Berkeley, California   **DATE DESIGNED** 2002   **CONSTRUCTION COST** $35 million   **CONSTRUCTION COMPLETED** 2008   **SIZE** 80,000 sq. ft.   **ARCHITECTS PRE-DESIGN:** Siegel Diamond Architecture   **DESIGN:** Leddy Maytum Stacy   **DESIGN PROGRAMMING** MIG, Inc.   **DEVELOPER** Equity Community Builders   **PROJECT MANAGER** Calib Dardik   **CLIENT** Ed Roberts Campus Partnership

Ed Roberts was born in 1939 and became disabled in 1952 as a result of polio. In 1962, he was the first severely disabled student admitted to the University of California. He was an early leader of the Independent Living Movement, a struggle by people with disabilities to control their own lives. The movement began in reaction to the dehumanizing processes people with disabilities were subjected to, and it championed the need for equal access and equal opportunity. It recognized that the struggle for independence was not a medical or functional issue; it was a matter of civil rights. At a rally in front of the federal building in San Francisco, which ultimately resulted in a major change in federal disability policy, Ed defined the problem as the system's view that disabled people should have a "separate, but equal world." He captured the sentiments of the disability movement when he declared, "Integration is the key word. People with disabilities have to come back into our society."

The Independent Living Movement changed the old paradigm by developing a consumer-directed approach to services—people who use services could have control over the choices and options available to them. Instead of a presumption of charity and dependence, the movement successfully empowered people to become productive members of society.

One of Ed's favorite stories was about how his rehabilitation counselor, employed by the California Department of Rehabilitation, refused to serve him and opposed his desire to go to UC Berkeley. He was "too disabled to work," so what was the point of an education? Ed went to the director of the Department and convinced him to reverse the decision. "You don't let people walk all over you; you do something about it. You fight for what you believe is right," Ed commented. Ed earned a Master's Degree in Political Science and had completed all the course work for his Ph.D. when he left campus to work in the nascent Independent Living Movement. Years later, he became the director of the Department of Rehabilitation for the State of California, the same agency that had tried to refuse him an education.

Ed traveled throughout the world promoting the concept of independent living and firmly believed in the strength

People with disabilities have always known that a simple architectural design change can make all the difference in being able to self-sufficiently navigate and use a building. Their input drove the design process for the Ed Roberts Campus.

of collaborative efforts—he called it "working toward our preferred future." In 1984, Ed was awarded a John D. and Catherine T. MacArthur Fellowship for his work championing the right of people with disabilities. When he died in 1995, the concept of developing the Ed Roberts Campus became a memorial to him.

The Ed Roberts Campus is being developed by eight partner organizations who are board members and co-owners: Bay Area Outreach & Recreation Program (BORP), Center for Accessible Technology (CforAT), Center for Independent Living (CIL), Computer Technologies Program (CTP), Disability Rights Education and Defense Fund (DREDF), Through the Looking Glass (TLG), Whirlwind Wheelchair International (WWI), and the World Institute on Disability (WID). Several other non-profit and government organizations will also be located on the campus.

The founding board agreed on basic requirements for the campus—that it easily accommodate hundreds of people with all types of disabilities at any one time, that it be situated at a transit hub to make it easy for people to obtain the services the organizations offer, and that it be located in Berkeley, the home of the Independent Living Movement. The 80,000-square-foot complex on a 1.5-acre site will house the partner organizations and other tenants, exhibition space, meeting rooms, a fitness center and a café. Construction of the $35 million facility is scheduled to begin in 2007; it is scheduled to open in 2008.

USER GROUPS

- People with all types of abilities
- People of all ages
- Students, researchers and policy-makers from around the world

The Ed Roberts Campus presents a sweeping plaza on Adeline Street, an embracing civic gesture that expresses its important role in the community (artist's rendition).

The Ed Roberts Campus will be the home of eight trailblazing disability organizations; by collocating they will provide services, share resources and expertise, and collaborate on the continued development of improved services for people with disabilities.

People with disabilities in the Bay Area, the nation and many other parts of the world have relied on the ERC organizations for as many as 35 years. Their services and programs offer assistance with all aspects of a person's life, from legal advocacy and computer training to parenting support and wheelchair basketball. In addition, their work in public policy research, advocacy and program development has had a major impact on people in other countries. Many of the programs and services provided by these organizations cannot be found elsewhere.

The ERC will take the popular "one-stop shopping" concept a step further, grouping services in one place. People will come to the campus for a wide range of health, education, recreation and vocational services, and for social, educational and professional programs. Many of the programs will be new collaborative efforts by the participating organizations and other government and nonprofit entities.

One collaborator is the University of California, Berkeley, where, according to former UC Berkeley Chancellor Robert Berdahl, "faculty members have begun to work closely with the ERC and its partner organizations on ways that we can collaborate so that our students will benefit from the vibrant atmosphere, extraordinary accessibility, and talents that will be located at the campus."

TRANSIT-ORIENTED PRINCIPLES

The ERC site is a Bay Area Rapid Transit (BART) parking lot next to a BART station in a diverse neighborhood of single-family homes, apartment buildings and larger commercial structures. Half of the project site is located in a commercial zone facing Adeline Street—a busy commercial boulevard —and a large urban open space created by another BART parking lot to the west (home to a popular flea market on weekends). The other half of the project is located in a residential zone facing the remaining portion of the existing BART parking lot and single-family homes beyond. As a result, the building presents two different, but related, faces to the surrounding community, respecting its diverse context while offering a vitalizing presence to the neighborhood.

Transit agencies in California and the U.S. Department of Transportation have recognized the ERC as a model of transit-friendly development that maximizes the value of accessible public transit. People with disabilities from a multi-county area, who have had little or no access to these services before, will be able to travel easily and inexpensively to the center. The transit

The transparent lobby provides a welcoming view of the helical ramp and covered courtyard for gatherings (artist's rendition).

Project design committee members reviewed the building design concepts to ensure it followed a simple equation: move people with disabilities from being dependent to independent.

DESIGN PROCESS

The relationship between access and design will become ever more important as the population ages and the demand for accessibility grows. Most people who design buildings and public spaces do not have a disability. It is people with disabilities who know what they need and who are beginning to inform design and architecture as direct participants and co-designers.

In designing this campus, members of the disability organizations carried the concept of universal design for large buildings to a new level of innovation and effectiveness. People with disabilities have always known that a simple design change—often at little or no cost—can mean the difference between being able to do something themselves and needing help from someone else. The planning team advanced a simple principle: move people from being dependent to independent. A woman in

location of the ERC is one of its most important innovations and is likely to be replicated in other urban areas. U.S. Congressional Representative Ellen Tauscher, in written testimony for a joint hearing convened by the House Committees on Transportation and Infrastructure and Education and the Workforce in May 2003, said that the ERC "will maximize Bay Area human services and, by locating at a BART station, reduce the need for costly and sometimes unreliable paratransit services."

a wheelchair changes the placement of the hinges on her oven door—now she can bake. Put kickpads on an elevator— she doesn't have to wait until someone comes who can push the button. A beeping light on a traffic signal allows people without sight to cross the street. Perhaps the most well-known example, and the one that people most associate with disability rights, is curb cuts: change the landscape so that people in wheelchairs can navigate sidewalks and walk to the store. And, by the way, that helps mothers with strollers, seniors with walkers and kids on tricycles, too.

The disability organizations started working with the City of Berkeley in 1995 to find a suitable location for the campus. Berkeley is a small, densely built city with little room for new large-scale developments. But in 1996, with the City's help, an ideal site was found: a parking lot co-owned by the City and BART. The City held the air

Wood screens on the Adeline Street main entry integrate warm, natural materials that also control light and add expressive detail (artist's rendition).

The eastern entrance, facing a residential neighborhood, is more compact and enlivened by a colorful mural celebrating people with disabilities, landscaping and an irregular rhythm of projecting bays in harmony with the residential scale of surrounding properties (artist's rendition).

rights to the lot (BART runs underneath) in an agreement executed when the transit system was built. The lot had been slated for development for some 25 years, but no agreement had been made about what to build.

In 1997, ERC held community meetings, neighborhood associations meetings and meetings with local merchants associations. The ERC was agreed on as the only project that was both economically feasible and satisfac-

tory to the neighboring community, the City and BART. The way was cleared for ERC to buy the site from BART at the original 1968 price.

The partner organizations then developed a design program for the campus to visualize how it might fit on the site. They organized design charettes to develop fundamental concepts and principles to incorporate in the design. They

addressed the unique challenges of designing a transit-oriented facility to accommodate hundreds of people with all kinds of disabilities.

The Metropolitan Transportation Commission of the San Francisco Bay Area provided a grant that paid for a series of community meetings on the design and the development of a newsletter so that neighbors could be brought into the process in a meaningful way. At these meetings, the architects presented a facility that occupied 110,000 sq. ft. (including a 13,000 sq. ft. gym and fitness center and a 5,500 sq. ft. Early Head Start Program). It also included a 10,000 sq. ft. conference center and 4,500 sq. ft. of meeting rooms, catering kitchen, library and computer and media resource center. The project provided parking at the ratio of two spaces/1,000 sq. ft. of building (estimated to be 220 spaces), as well as replacement parking on a 1:1 basis for parking displaced on the BART lot.

This plan turned out to be very costly, especially the BART and ERC parking requirements. It also generated considerable controversy in the neighborhood because of concerns about traffic and scale. During the next year, the ERC design went through many iterations as the partners struggled to balance space needs, costs and the concerns and wishes of the neighbors with the organization's fundraising capability. Finally, it was decided that 110,000 sq. ft. was simply too large and, reluctantly, the gym was dropped and other reductions were made in the development program.

FINDING THE FUNDS

As a newly formed organization, the ERC did not have an endowment to tap or a long-standing Board of Directors to support its desire to build a campus. It is a community-based, consumer-led organization very much like the non-profits that founded it. These organizations place the greatest value on having consumers on their boards. They focus

The final design—a transit-oriented facility—will accommodate hundreds of users with a wide range of disabilities (artist's model).
ZD MODELS

so strongly on using their resources to meet the need in the community that they do not have the time to build an endowment. And, of course, as non-profits operating continuously at full throttle, the organizations could not stop their own fundraising efforts while developing the ERC.

The ERC reached out to community leaders to form a campaign committee and decided to approach government sources that support health and economic development and foundations that support disability issues. A major early

supporter was the City of Berkeley. Proud of Berkeley's history with the Independent Living Movement, City officials recognized that the ERC would not only benefit the people living in its boundaries but would also be of major national and international significance, both as a collaborative model for non-profits and as a beacon for independent living for people with disabilities.

One of the other important early donors was NEC Foundation of America, which provided the funds for the design of a comprehensive technology system to make the campus fully accessible with state-of-the-art equipment and facilities for people with disabilities. NEC made the award in commemoration of its 10th anniversary. An NEC-funded report, "Technology and Universal Design Assessment of the Ed Roberts Campus," describes the ways technology is used now by the partner organizations and presents strategies for its use in the future. It recommends technological solutions and an information technology

action plan, and presents a newly created Universal Design Tool. (The report is available from the ERC.)

The ERC developed a long-range financial plan to support planning for the new organization, as well as designing, building and operating the facility. The plan was laid out in phases so that each phase of work could proceed as funds are raised. This approach is working. The ERC raised more than $2 million in public and private funds for the planning. This money was used to incorporate, secure the site and develop the design to the level needed for the City's permit process. While ERC carried out Phase 2—the schematic design—it continued fundraising for Phases 3 and 4, the construction drawings and construction.

Once built, the ERC will be a self-sustaining entity, with partners and tenants paying rents and fees that are adequate to pay off the debt and maintain and operate the facility.

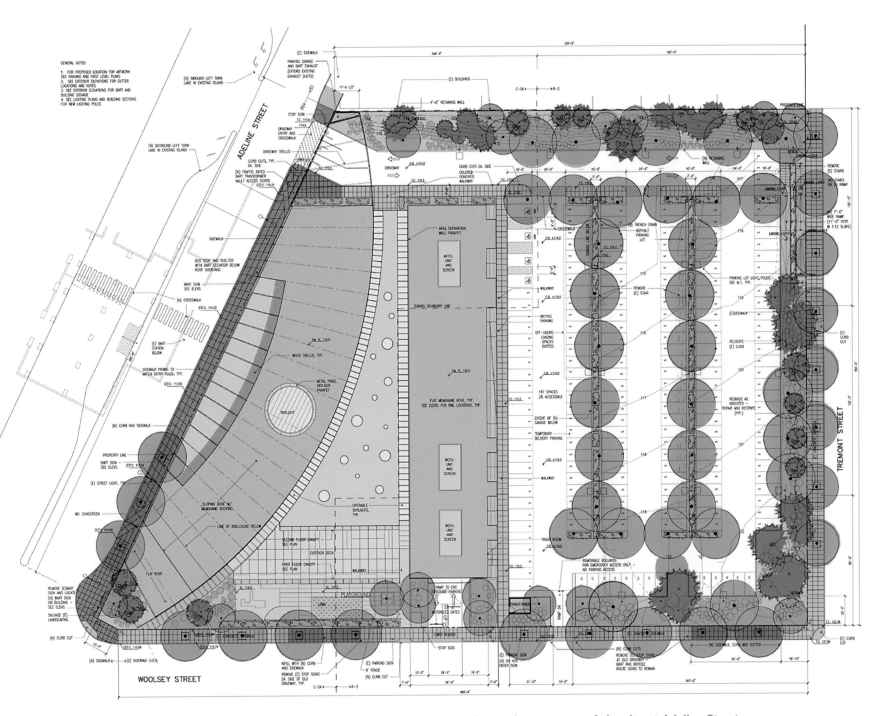

The site plan shows access for BART patron parking via a new driveway at the northwest corner of the site at Adeline Street.

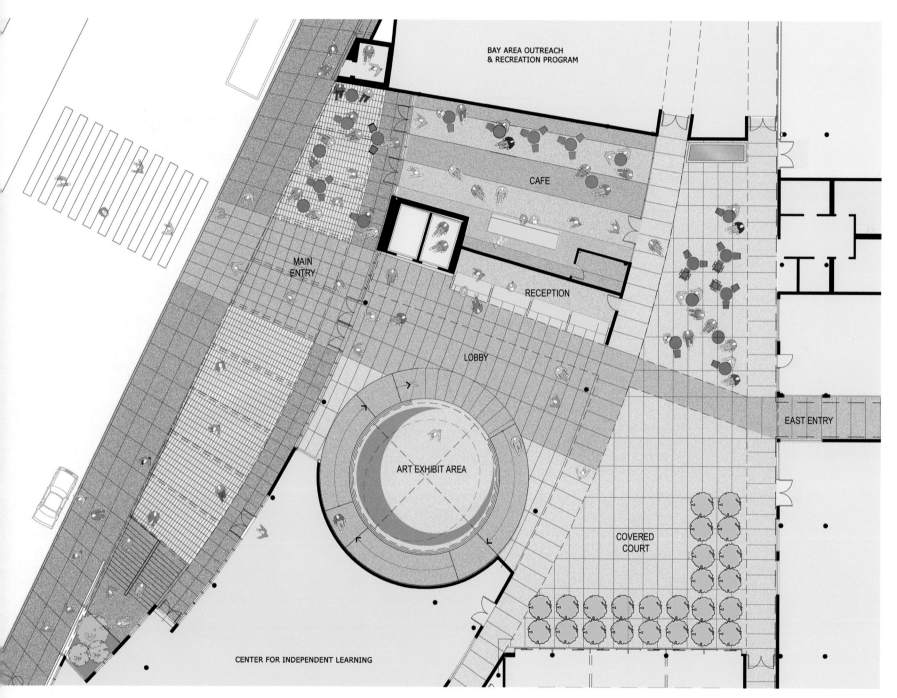

BAY AREA OUTREACH
& RECREATION PROGRAM

CAFE

MAIN
ENTRY

RECEPTION

LOBBY

ART EXHIBIT AREA

EAST ENTRY

COVERED
COURT

CENTER FOR INDEPENDENT LEARNING

This detail of the floor plan shows the entrance to the reception area and ramp, café with both indoor and outdoor seating and the covered atrium. Glass paving blocks at the entrance allow light to enter the BART station below.

Inclusive Design Features and Settings

The design of the ERC integrates advanced elements of universal and sustainable design in a transit-oriented development that serves people of all abilities at many scales of engagement. At the scale of the City, the ERC is designed as a community building with a distinct civic presence that celebrates the collective values of its partner organizations. The building acts as both community center and urban threshold—a gateway to Berkeley—simultaneously positioning the partner organizations on a prominent thoroughfare and at a major regional transit portal.

PLAZA

The building presents an embracing, semicircular plaza to the City on Adeline Street. This serves as a drop-off and clearly identifiable entry for the ERC; a major transit plaza for bus, taxi, bicycle and BART riders; and a public gathering space. A variety of features, including a café, a bus shelter with interactive transit kiosk, a fully accessible public elevator to the BART station below street level and public art, will help create a vibrant new urban space for the City of Berkeley. The transparent entry façade of the ERC borders the plaza, revealing a monumental helical ramp inside. The ramp, itself a work of public art, is placed beneath a large skylight, and serves both functional and symbolic roles, providing inviting access to the upper floor of the ERC for all users, while offering a dramatic symbol of universal design and independent living to the public.

LOBBY

Upon entering the Center through motion-activated automatic doors, the building offers visitors a simple, easily understandable organization. To the left, two large-capacity elevators with sophisticated, accessible controls connect the two floors of the Center with a sub-grade garage and a separate BART station lobby. A large reception and information desk offers human, graphic, Braille, and accessible audio information about Center services. To the right, the skylit helical ramp winds upward to the second floor, encircling a public exhibition area devoted to issues of the Independent Living Movement.

COURTYARD

Beyond the lobby, the two 2-story wings of the building form a central, covered courtyard that will provide natural daylight, ventilation and community gathering spaces to occupants and visitors. The courtyard also serves as a simple orienting device, providing clear access to the ERC's various services and organizations. The café, a fitness center and two levels of shared, flexible meeting rooms open onto the space, fostering a sense of community and ensuring easy wayfinding.

BART STATION ACCESS

A separate lobby serves the sub-grade BART station level, opening directly onto the station concourse. ERC patrons will ascend from the train platform by way of escalators and accessible elevators to the concourse level and then proceed via a short ramp to the new lobby. A curving, skylit gallery below the plaza—displaying a striking "Disability Mural" created by local artists—connects BART patrons to an elevator and landscaped stair to the street. The stair design features an integrated "wheel channel" that allows cyclists to negotiate the stairs without lifting their bikes. The adjacent ERC garage provides secured parking for staff and visitors who must arrive by car, including 18 accessible spaces directly adjacent to the BART-level lobby.

UNIVERSAL DESIGN

The design of the ERC incorporates additional universal design features to ensure equal access and service to all:

- Specially designed, high-contrast audio wayfinding devices
- Automatic, motion-activated doors at major exterior and interior entries

- Abundant natural daylight incorporating glare reduction strategies in all spaces to enhance visibility
- Seven-foot-wide corridors throughout to allow easy circulation and adaptability of pace
- Restrooms designed for a range of ability levels, including private rooms for assisted individuals
- Localized temperature controls within each space for the thermally sensitive
- All light fixtures controlled by hands-free occupancy sensors and timers
- Secured garage access provided by hands-free electronic transponder technology
- Building life safety systems incorporating visual and audio notification and accessible alarm stations
- Acoustical control to foster maximum voice intelligibility
- A fully accessible, south-facing children's play area

SUSTAINABLE DESIGN

The ERC will incorporate a range of sustainable design techniques to serve the diverse needs of the occupants as well as the larger environment. These include:

- Maximum use of natural daylight and sun control strategies to reduce energy consumption and enhance visibility
- Natural ventilation and radiant, hydronic heating in all public spaces
- Rooftop solar water heating system for common space heating and hot water pre-heat
- Energy-efficient, specially filtered heating and cooling systems with localized temperature control in office areas
- Operable windows with easily operated hardware
- Enhanced indoor air quality throughout construction, post-construction and occupancy phases
- Use of non-toxic, recycled and sustainably harvested materials
- On-site recycling center

The Ed Roberts Campus embodies a set of design responses to the diverse needs of the community, the missions of its partner organizations and the varying

The 36-foot-wide landscape buffer along Woolsey Street respects the adjacent residential neighborhood. It also provides a play area for the Daycare Center, which can be used by nearby residents as well (artist's rendition).

The ERC design process evolved through an extensive user participation process.

abilities of the many individuals it will serve. Through the collaboration of many, it will create an environment that embodies the spirit of Ed Roberts and "our preferred future."

User Feedback

Although the campus has not yet been built, the design process itself led to some breakthrough thinking.

Susan Henderson, ERC Board Member and Director of Administration

"It's a beautiful design—functional and beautiful. Accessibility is integrated so well that it is just another part of the design. It shows what can be achieved if an architect starts out with the idea of accessibility rather than incorporating it as an afterthought. We were fortunate in our choice of architects; the design firm understood the importance of accessibility right away and used it as a design

theme. Integration in design is like integration of people with disabilities in society—it's actually easy if it is a part of your thinking from the beginning.

"Working closely with the community in an open process has worked very well for us. Unlike your typical developer, we are nonprofits and we serve the community. So we were willing to take the time to meet again and again with neighbors. As a result, the neighbors are happy, the City is happy, and we have a wonderful building."

Mark Krizack, Whirlwind Wheelchair International

"For several years, as a Hastings College of the Law student, I walked from my

flat to the Ashby BART station to make the trip to San Francisco. From these walks I came to know the Ashby BART neighborhood well. It is now 13 years later and there has been relatively little change in that area, although it has long been in need of an economic stimulus…. The Ed Roberts Campus can be the economic anchor for a revitalization of the Ashby-Adeline Corridor…. As it is now, BART patrons do not stop and linger in the neighborhood either before or after their workday. The Ed Roberts Campus will give them a reason to pause and linger before they continue on their way.

"The Ed Roberts Campus will be architecturally pleasing. It will make the area safer because there will be good street lighting and many more people on the streets. Surely other businesses will see an advantage in relocating to this area."

Ken Stein, Former ADA Unit Manager, Disability Rights Education and Defense Fund

"As a seven-year member and chair of the City of Berkeley's Landmarks Preservation Commission, I am aware of how important it is for new developments to be respectful of the existing physical, architectural and cultural landscape of the surrounding neighborhood and larger community. The effort that the project partners have made to involve the community in the planning process has resulted in a facility that is both sensitive to and respectful to the fabric of the existing community, both programmatically and architecturally."

Jane Berliss-Vincent, Director, Adult and Senior Services, Center for Accessible Technology

"The ERC will be an ideal setting for serving seniors with disabilities. The location at the Ashby BART station will make the ERC agencies easy to find and visit. The one-stop-shop nature of the ERC will provide them with easy access to a wide variety of services related to computer access, grandparenting, exercise and many other areas of interest. I have spoken with many seniors about the potential of the ERC. Their response has been overwhelmingly positive towards both the concept and the location of the campus."

Dmitri Belser, Executive Director, Center for Accessible Technology

"Too often, services for people with disabilities are in remote or hidden locations, kept on the sidelines and out of the mainstream of society. By building

the ERC, the disability community will have a major resource at a highly visible and central location. This sends an important message: people with disabilities are a key part of the community, not an adjunct to the community."

*Stephanie Miyashiro,
Board Chair, Through the Looking Glass;
Board Member, ERC*

"We propose to build a *new* building, one that does not look like buildings of the past. Those buildings did not ever have us in mind. I expect our building will become a historical building—a part of the history of the disabled community and of the City of Berkeley, which is the birthplace of the Independent Living Movement. Buildings of the past, even the recent past, have been part of our oppression. We are hoping to change history and move to a brighter future."

EDELMAN CHILDREN'S COURT | LOS ANGELES COUNTY, CALIFORNIA

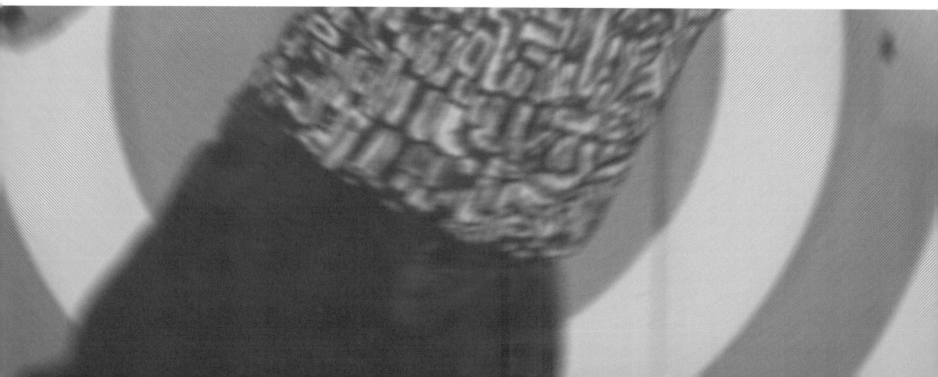

"If spaces are designed around children, adults never forget
why they are there."

CHILD ADVOCATE, CHILDREN'S INSTITUTE INTERNATIONAL

HELPING CHILDREN HEAL

THE EDELMAN CHILDREN'S COURT IS THE FIRST COURTHOUSE IN THE COUNTRY DEDICATED solely to children in the dependency system. The entire courthouse is based on inclusive design principles for children and their families: to help ease their fears, feel less intimidated and begin a healing and family reunification process.

This is the Juvenile Dependency Court for the County of Los Angeles, handling child abuse and neglect cases. It has 25 courtrooms with facilities for supporting services and a jail beneath. Through the legal process, the court protects children from dangerous or imminently dangerous situations. About 300,000 cases of child abuse were reported in the County in 2002, and nearly 100,000 children attended at least one hearing in Dependency Court. Some children remain with their families during the court process; others stay in foster care and may or may not see their families. In addition, a higher than average percentage of these children—about one-third—have disabilities.

The court's objective is to work with families to overcome problems and develop a stable and healthy home environment that will allow the child to return home—or find a viable alternative home environment.

PURPOSE

It is hard to imagine a more traumatic experience for a child than attending a hearing in court in front of a judge. They may have been removed from home and placed in protective custody. A parent may be in jail, leaving the family struggling to maintain itself. Overnight, the children may have lost their support system, with no idea about what will happen next. Children and parents are upset, angry and scared. Worse, the physical environment of the old courthouse added to the trauma. Children were literally housed in cells, waiting for their hearing. They had nothing to do all day other than sit and watch television. They often felt that they were the ones who had done something wrong and were being punished.

The new facility is sensitive to the needs of children and parents, communicates a serious message to abusive parents, and provides comfortable and functional workplaces.

USER GROUPS

- Children in protective custody
- Families with children
- Parents alone
- Parents in jail
- Foster Care parents
- Judges
- Attorneys
- County Counsel
- Dependency Court administrative staff
- Department of Children's Services (DCS) caseworkers and administrative staff
- Sheriff's department
- Court Appointed Special Advocates (CASA)
- Shelter Care staff
- Child advocates/Guardian ad Litum

PROJECT Edmund D. Edelman Children's Court   LOCATION Monterey Park, California
DATE DESIGNED 1990   CONSTRUCTION COMPLETED June 1992
CONSTRUCTION COST $59.6 million   SIZE 275,000 square feet on 4.2 acres
CLIENT County of Los Angeles ARCHITECT Kajima Associates   DESIGN PROGRAMMING
AND ENVIRONMENTAL DESIGN MIG, Inc.   STRUCTURAL ENGINEER Brandow &
Johnston Associates   MECHANICAL ENGINEER Eli Solon & Associates
ELECTRICAL ENGINEER Frederick Brown & Associates   GENERAL CONTRACTOR
Kajima Associates   SIGNAGE AND GRAPHICS CONSULTANT Wayne Hunt Design, Inc.

The teen conversation area in Shelter Care has age-appropriate furniture.
WAYNE THOM

Older children can quietly study or read books while they are waiting in Shelter Care.
WAYNE THOM

DESIGN PROCESS

The key to the entire design process was to view the building through the eyes of the children who are brought to the facility and the parents who need help from the system. It was assumed that if the building accommodates those with the least "power," everyone else would also be accommodated. People who work in the facility are there because it's their job. The families are there because they are in serious trouble.

At the time the project began, there was no research on children in a court environment; the most applicable research addressed children in hospitals. Although children experience stress in both situations, children in court are not ill. The design team needed to define child- and family-sensitive design in the context of a court of law.

To gather firsthand information, the design team conducted focus groups, interviews, surveys and field observations (see table on facing page). The team followed people with different jobs to see how they interacted with children, families and the court system. Workshops were conducted with judges, children and youth in foster care, parents, attorneys and social workers.

Research revealed two terms that would convey the best atmosphere for the court: dignified and friendly. It had to be a serious and dignified place so parents would remember why they are there. Yet, the court also had to empower children, foster education and promote family healing. A 30-person committee, representing all user groups, articulated what "dignified and friendly" meant in spatial terms. "Dignified" translated into a design language of clean, simple lines, geometric symmetrical spaces, gateway entrances, subdued colors, familiar symbols, and strong, durable building materials.

"Friendly" translated to a human scale with extensive indoor plants, warm materials, windows and daylight, incandescent, shaded and non-glare lights, and a view to the outdoors.

The next step was the design and constuction of a full-scale mock courtroom to test hearing room layouts and configurations. The new courtrooms were designed to be one-third smaller to create a more intimate setting. A 30' by 30' bare room was used as the prototype

User Groups and Survey Methods	open-ended interviews with key individuals	questionnaires	focus groups	field workshop observations
Mediator	■			
Foster Parents		■		
Shelter Care Children	■		■	■
Parents	■			
County Counsel	■	■		■
Dept. of Children's Services/Social Workers	■		■	■
Judge	■	■	■	■
Child's Advocate	■	■		
Shelter Care Staff	■			■
Children/Youth in Foster Care			■	■
Panel Lawyers			■	
Clerk of Court	■			
Court Officer		■		

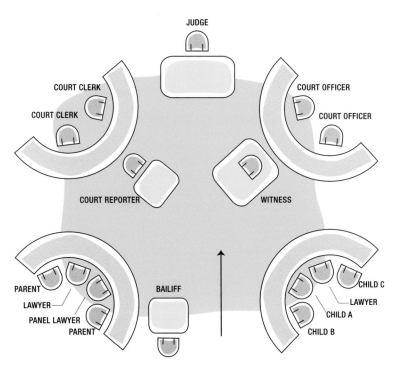

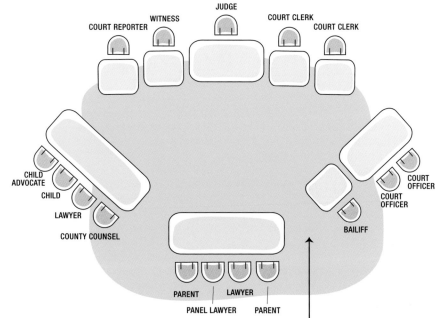

Configuration 1. Four semicircular desks face the center of the room with the judge at the head. This creates separation and provides privacy, ensures children don't have to look directly at their parents and offers clear sightlines. However, the setup feels adversarial with each party in a corner and may not provide the bailiff appropriate access.

Configuration 2. This closed semicircle provides clear sightlines, locates the bailiff in a solid control position, ensures that parents and children are in non-confrontational positions and locates the court reporter for easy listening distances. However, it places the public entrance to the side rather than the middle.

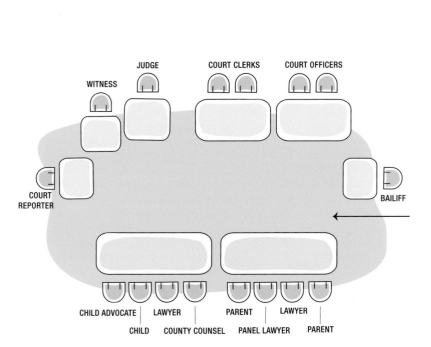

WITNESS
JUDGE
COURT CLERKS
COURT OFFICERS
COURT REPORTER
BAILIFF

CHILD ADVOCATE   LAWYER   PARENT   LAWYER
CHILD   COUNTY COUNSEL   PANEL LAWYER   PARENT

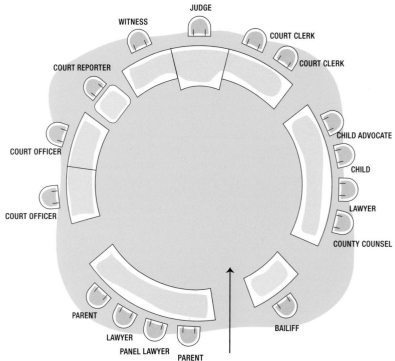

JUDGE
WITNESS
COURT CLERK
COURT CLERK
COURT REPORTER
CHILD ADVOCATE
COURT OFFICER
CHILD
COURT OFFICER
LAWYER
COUNTY COUNSEL
PARENT
LAWYER
PANEL LAWYER
PARENT
BAILIFF

Configuration 3. The parallel conference table places the child and parent in non-confrontational positions and locates the bailiff and court reporter well. However, it's quite formal with little flexibility.

Configuration 4. A circular configuration provides clear sightlines for all parties and a more collaborative, less confrontational environment, while locating the bailiff and court reporter in good positions. However, this may be too informal and non-traditional.

During focus groups, children worked with graphic shapes to help determine who sits where in the courtroom.
WAYNE THOM

space. Cut-out plywood furniture with different shapes was arranged in four different test configurations.

During a three-hour block of time, mock trials were conducted with people representing all user groups, and everyone's actions and comments were recorded. Participants decided that a circular arrangement of furniture,

with the judge included in the circle (Configuration 4) would be most conducive to personalizing the courtroom for children.

However, since the mock trials did not include the children who would really be in the courtroom or the real court personnel, this decision needed to be verified. Otherwise, 25 courtrooms would be built with very little research on whether the arrangement would work the way the design committee expected it would. A full-scale, circular courtroom was built in an existing courtroom and evaluated during a six-week period. Six different judges and their entire staff and court docket each used the room for one week.

As it turned out, the circular arrangement actually did not work for children or the judges. For children, there was too much eye contact between them, their parents and everyone else, which was very intimidating. They thought everyone was staring at them. The judges felt the arrangement was too egalitarian, making their position less authoritative.

The design team used the research findings to produce the final solution for the hearing room design (as shown in the photograph on page 50). The final arrangement of the furniture is semi-circular, placing the judge in front on a raised platform.

Based on the research, the team developed design programming criteria and a set of design guidelines on which the entire building was based. All settings were designed with inclusive design principles; many of the resulting settings may be applicable to other building types.

Inclusive Design Features and Settings

BUILDING ENTRY/LOBBY

Every morning at 8 a.m., over 2,500 people arrive and enter the court building. No one knows what time their case will be called, so everyone must arrive when court begins and wait their turn. That means 2,500 people must enter the

The building looks less intimidating than a traditional courthouse, yet is still dignified.

lobby, pass through security, find their way to the correct courtroom and waiting area, and wait there for up to eight hours.

The building does not look like a traditional courthouse; it's more like an office building. It's on a smaller scale, with more "house-like" features and symbols such as arbors, vegetation and awnings. There is a partially covered outdoor area near the entrance that may be used for sitting and waiting for someone, or just to get some air.

Families arrive by bus or car. The covered bus stop is near a covered entry, with bollards separating pedestrians from vehicles. The bollards are far enough apart for wheelchairs or strollers to pass. People coming from the parking garage are led to the entry through a series of arbors that function like outdoor rooms.

Visitors enter the building through a gabled roof—again, to convey a more "home-like" feel. The covered entry area has long, generous open spaces to accommodate all people trying to enter,

The lobby area is spacious and filled with friendly artwork.
WAYNE THOM

The metal detector is part of the archway. Light fixtures are in the shape of clouds.
WAYNE THOM

including strollers and wheelchairs, without pushing or squeezing. Enough room is provided for kids to move around and fidget.

The lobby is welcoming and friendly, with light, artwork and natural construction materials to soften the feel of the building. Everyone must pass through a metal detector, located at the lobby entrance, surrounded by stylized palm trees so it does not feel threatening. Lighting fixtures in the lobby are shaped like clouds.

Visitors stop by reception to find out to which of the 25 courtrooms they have been assigned. The elevator lobby features a floor-to-ceiling mural of self-portrait tiles created by children who were in the child welfare system and used the court—a vivid reminder of why the court exists.

A tile mural, produced in an art therapy program, shows self-portraits of children in the system—reminding everyone why they are in this building.

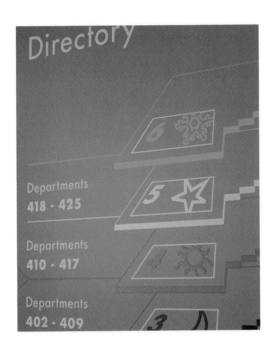

The directory is not language-based; instead it uses colors, numbers and symbols.
CHARLES ALLEN

Signage for each floor has a unique color and symbol.
CHARLES ALLEN

WAYFINDING

Wayfinding and circulation have been combined. The courtrooms are situated on three different floors, with other support services and staff on two additional floors. Since over 150 languages are spoken in Los Angeles, wayfinding cannot be simply language-based. Each floor has a number, a color and an easily recogniz-

able symbol (star, moon, sun, cloud and snowflake). Colors and symbols are also a homey element for children. In addition, symbols and numbers are raised for blind and sight-impaired people to feel.

Visitors use oversize elevators that accommodate large numbers of people, strollers and wheelchairs. The aim is to get people out of the lobbies and into

family waiting areas as quickly as possible. When the elevator doors open, visitors see the wayfinding colors and symbols carried on throughout each floor, in sculptures and on columns.

Children coming from Shelter Care (those in protective custody) have their own elevator that brings them directly to the courtroom; they don't need to share elevators with parents or the public. Judges also have their own elevator, as do prisoners coming from the jail below.

FAMILY WAITING AREA

There are 25 courtrooms on three separate floors. Each floor has a large, 5,000-square-foot waiting area outside the courtroom. In the morning, parents go into their assigned courtroom at the same time as all other families assigned to that courtroom. They receive an introduction, then go back out to wait for as long as eight hours. The area is organized so each courtroom has its own waiting space, but all areas are open so they can be monitored from a single point. The courtroom doors, viewed from the waiting area, look residential, with incandescent light and home-like architectural details.

Waiting areas are open and airy, with panoramic views out the windows. Ordinarily, judges would have these coveted views. But this building recognizes that children and families will especially benefit from not feeling cooped up. The

windows also provide natural light in addition to the overhead lighting. Wide, carpeted aisles accommodate wheelchairs. The soft, cushioned sofas and chairs and small tables can be moved to fit each family's size, creating opportunities for small group inter-actions. Children who are with their parents can eat, sleep and play in that area. There are also areas with facilitated play where a CASA social worker models child/parent play behavior—an opportunity for teaching parenting skills.

The L shape of the building provides the waiting areas with maximum views and natural light.

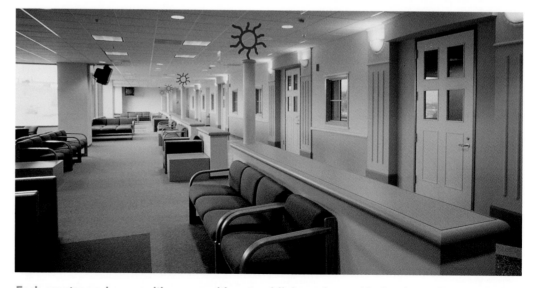

Each courtroom has a waiting area with natural light and movable furniture. The wayfinding colors and symbols are carried on throughout the floor.
WAYNE THOM

Families attending court are often confused about the entire process, so a substantial effort is made to convey vital information. Television monitors located throughout the waiting areas offer multilingual programming about the court process and what to expect during the day. Children's programming is also available. Service desks on each floor allow parents to quickly and easily sign up for services the court may order, such as parenting, anger management or drug treatment.

Bathrooms are separated: men, women, children (with child-size toilets and sinks) and an infant changing area that can be monitored.

MEDIATION/INTERVIEW ROOMS

There are two types of consultation spaces where attorneys can consult with families or children before their hearing begins. *Mediation / Interview Rooms* located off the public waiting area offer privacy—a great improvement over the previous situation, which

Mediation/interview rooms allow attorneys to consult with children in privacy.
WAYNE THOM

forced attorneys to conduct private consultations in public waiting areas. These rooms are also used when a judge orders mediation during a hearing and puts the family and counsel in a room to come to an agreement on a course of action. Attorneys can also meet separately with children in the *Interview Rooms* off the Shelter Care area, which are set up for children to talk privately with their attorneys.

Family visiting rooms have interior windows for easy monitoring. The furniture is homey and comfortable.
WAYNE THOM

FAMILY VISITING ROOMS

After a court appearance, a child in protective custody may visit with parents and relatives they might not have seen since they were removed from their home. Although these visits must be monitored, it's essential to make children feel as comfortable as possible. A series of visiting rooms off the lobby, connected to the Shelter Care area, are designed like home living rooms and can accommodate three to twelve people. They have comfortable chairs, couches, plants and incandescent lighting. Each has a large picture window with shutter details that opens onto the hallway so a monitor can view several families at the same time without intruding into the room.

HEARING ROOMS

Hearing rooms where court is held are scaled down to feel less intimidating; they are about half the traditional courtroom size and ceilings are lower. Colors are neutral and the symbology subdued so people are the focus of the room. The seal of the State of California, a required element in the courtroom, is softly etched in glass. Lighting is directed upward to prevent glare. There is a deep contrast between the floor, furniture and walls. Wainscoting gives the illusion of wood and protects the walls.

The judge is at the front of the room. The bench is raised 12 inches to provide authority, but is lower than a standard 18-inch bench. The judges enter the courtroom through their own separate entrance. When they enter the building

The final design of the hearing room places the judge facing a semicircular arrangement of key participants.

to go to their chambers, they pass by the children in the Shelter Care area, so they are always reminded of why they are conducting hearings. The presiding judge's office is located over the outdoor children's play area to provide a continual reminder that this building is about children.

Families and lawyers sit in a semicircle facing the judge. Children and their advocates sit on one side and parents on the other. Or, the seating arrangement

can be changed depending on the needs of the child: they can sit with parents if they wish or be separated by attorneys and advocates. The key is that children may choose where to sit.

The witness stand is not raised and is on rollers so it can be moved up to accommodate a wheelchair or turned around to the judge if a child witness only wants to face the judge.

The court reporter, who usually sits in the "well" space between the judge's

The state seal is softly etched in glass to convey dignity, without being intimidating.

bench and attorney's table, now sits at the edge of the semicircle. During the research phase, children perceived the person sitting in the middle of the courtroom as staring angrily at them, not realizing the court reporter stared to concentrate on taking down what was said at the hearing. As long as the court reporter can hear all the parties, where they sit isn't critical to the hearing, and they were moved out of the middle. At some point, court reporting may be done remotely though improved electronic communications.

SHELTER CARE AREA

Shelter Care is where children ages 4 to 17 who are in protective custody (those taken from their homes) wait to go to court. It's often the first impression children have of the court system; it sets the tone for the entire court experience and is one of the most important environments in the facility. Children may spend up to 8 hours here, waiting for their hearing—which may take only 20 minutes—and then waiting for the bus ride back to foster care.

Children under stress do not play. The goal of Shelter Care is to help children to understand the court process, play, visit or take classes—and begin their healing process.

This Shelter Care provides more than a waiting area. It is 10,000 square feet of programmed space, accommodating as many as 130 children at a time, with a

Children are taken out of school every six months to spend an entire day at the courthouse. The library provides a place for schoolwork.
WAYNE THOM

There are small spaces for solitary play.
WAYNE THOM

Children can choose from a variety of activities.
WAYNE THOM

staff ratio of 1:4. The entire space, activities and all programs are completely accessible.

Children enter the building through the same back entrance the judges use. To prevent parents from entering the area, it is unmarked, with no signage at all. The entry area provides room for decompression; children can be comforted by staff. There are bathrooms and access to the eating area where healthy snacks are always available. A series of small rooms allow children to meet privately with their attorneys, who must check in with staff first and then take a child out of Shelter Care to the private room.

The main area is divided, but not separated, with younger kids (4–12) on one side and older kids (13–17) on the other. The eating area is in the middle

so that family members of different ages can visit. Children can choose what they want to do, and when and what to eat, which gives them back a little sense of control.

Younger children can choose games, reading, facilitated art and science projects, movies and dress-up or role-playing activities. Older kids choose from aerobics, music and dance, quiet study, conversation pit, foosball, pool, ping-pong and video games. There are low walls separating areas, which also provide some intimate spaces for kids to be alone (although those spaces are always observed). The outdoor area offers hangout space, a giant chessboard, basketball, play equipment, open grassy areas and a covered eating area.

This space and its program are designed to help children process the information

Comfortable conversation areas allow children to form groups or sit alone.

WAYNE THOM

Kids can create their own games, too. There is a Velcro wall for throwing soft cushions.

WAYNE THOM

Kids choose to play on traditional play equipment or some unusual games like giant chess.

WAYNE THOM

The indoor eating area allows siblings of different ages to eat together.

WAYNE THOM

An outdoor eating area is a buffer between indoor and outdoor play areas.

WAYNE THOM

A comfortable spot in the shade is sometimes the best way to relax.

WAYNE THOM

they obtain in court, receive services, satisfy their material needs, and begin to heal. A comprehensive program guide was created as the basis for the Shelter Care program.

Management and Operational Issues

It was apparent to everyone involved in the court system that the previous system was not meeting the needs of children and needed to be changed. The inclusive design approach brought everyone—including children—into a discussion of critical operational and management issues. Designing the building became a catalyst for change because everyone who used the building was forced to think about what he or she did and new ways to do it.

For the first time ever, the court closed for one business day so all staff, including judges, could be trained in how to interact with and be sensitive to children.

- The new furniture arrangement brought the judge physically closer to the children, encouraging better communication between them. Judges now address children by name, instead of referring to them as "the minor," and include them in conversations.
- Because there is a space dedicated to attorney-child conferences, attorneys now take the time to bring children to private rooms to confer, rather than discuss private, intimate details in a public setting.
- Shelter Care staff use play to interact with children and now see the court experience as part of the healing process. Rather than allowing children to watch television, staff and volunteers encourage art and science projects and model good adult-to-child behavior.
- Because there is a place where children can express their needs or their frustrations, and there are adults with authority to intervene, caseworkers can be more responsive to individual children.
- Building staff learned how to use the building: new ways were devised to move children, parents and prisoners

separately through the building, to maintain the building, and to provide places where people can give and receive services.

When children who have been taken from their families arrive in Juvenile Dependency Court, they have no control over their situation, are not living with their families, and have little or no idea what will happen to them. Coming to court is now part of the healing process. Children will have to attend several hearings before potentially being reunited with their family or placed in permanent foster care. Each time they come to court they can be helped in some way, whether it's by participating in an art project in Shelter Care, having an intimate visit with their family, or requesting necessary services to support their life.

The physical environment of the building became the container for change. It locked in the operational and management changes through new spaces that housed services—no one could use the old organizational systems in the new building. It became a place where new

behaviors could be learned and old ones discouraged. It became a place where new life could begin for children and their families.

User Feedback

How spaces are actually used can sometimes be different from original intentions. The following quotes are taken from people who have used the courthouse building for three years.

Presiding Judge Gerald Nash

"This building expresses the value that we want the court to convey: children are important. The Children's Shelter Care area is the largest part of the court—it's also the most unique and best part of the court. It reduces the anxiety children feel when they come to court; they feel welcome. There's also a bright, expansive, open, public waiting area. The hearing room environment is warmer and more comfortable, which reduces the anxiety

of the adults as well. It's not a dehumanizing environment that devalues people; it does just the opposite.

"Strangely enough, the problem is that we've outgrown the building. It would be an improvement to have even more services available to families on site. The courthouse is also a meeting place for many, many different groups and committees—we're now meeting in the Judge's Lounge or Department of Children and Family Services conference room. We could use more office and large meeting places.

"But, without a doubt, this is still the best facility of its kind in the world."

Randall Henderson,
Dependency Court Administrator

"There are 31,105 children currently under jurisdiction of the court, about 10,000 filings a year. About five years ago, the system started providing more services to families to prevent removing children, and also pursuing adoption

The spacious outdoor area provides room to run and lots of choices.
WAYNE THOM

more actively. Both programs have resulted in fewer children coming through the courts." (Five years ago the court had over 50,000 children in jurisdiction at a time.)

"This building sends a message that children matter. It's overwhelmingly successful and a showcase for the Superior Court. It's child-friendly and not intimidating. The functionality is excellent. It's so much better than having children in criminal courts and superior to anything I've seen anywhere else.

"The separate corridors and elevators for children coming up from Shelter Care are much more respectful to the child. They don't have to go through the public areas. And there's a separate child waiting area by the courtroom in case there's a wait once they go upstairs.

"The courtroom configuration is very successful. The layout works well in this situation where we don't have a lot of spectators, but we do have a lot of attorneys. The courtrooms now have

live video available so children can testify from the judge's chambers, away from their parents. Many judges believe that seeing children on a screen has a vivid impact on parents, and moves them more than seeing children testify live. Parents often say, 'I see it now, I see what has happened.'

"One aspect that has not worked so well is the areas in the waiting room for eating. People just eat anywhere, they don't go to the tables. And the furniture choices were not practical. The upholstery started to look grungy quickly. There are just too many people. So the second generation of furniture is more practical.

"This is a multi-agency building. Right after the building opened, the judges decided they wanted the County's centralized adoption unit here. So we had to fit them in. I like that the building allows us to evolve and adjust. Many different agencies need office space and you just can't get enough of it. I'd put in more

conference and office space if I could. You have to be rigorous about allocating and controlling space to avoid compromising space for children's programs.

"Families can get many types of services here. We have Free Arts for Abused Kids, Children's Book Service, a teddy bear program, parenting services, drug and alcohol services, Parents Beyond Conflict, mental health services. It's a huge list."

Supervising Judge Emily Stevens

"Kids and parents who are out of the system now often come back to talk with me and show me how well they're doing. The court seems positive and accessible—I don't think they would come back to the old criminal court.

"The less formal structure of the courtroom lends itself to closer physical contact. I can talk with the kids, there's more interaction between us. Sometimes they want a hug, and I can easily reach them."

"Many more people come to court now than before and they bring more people with them. We encourage that, and I think people find it a comfortable place to be and to wait; it's open, airy and light yet still conveys the serious work we do here. That's a very positive aspect of the building; it's family-friendly.

"The Shelter Care is very good. It's 500 percent better than what the kids had before. The kids love it.

"The building itself is holding up very well. We maintain it very carefully so it still looks fresh and new. We had to make some changes; we used a higher-gloss paint to prevent so many scratches, and we needed tougher furniture.

"However, in designing the building for children, I think they didn't give quite enough consideration to the adults who have to work here. The courtrooms are now too small on a regular basis. Sometimes there are siblings and multiple parents, each with an attorney. There's just not enough space.

"They also didn't expect anybody to keep anything in the courtroom and that's just not practical. We put built-in cabinets in the smaller courtrooms and metal cabinets in the larger. It was just impossible to work without storage. Employees feel they were given very little personal space, so we had to find them some space.

"There was not enough thought given to where the court reporter would be. They didn't have a desk, just a little table and chair. So I had to buy them desks. They sit in different places in each courtroom.

"The courtrooms don't take into account incarcerated parents and security. In my courtroom, the bailiff has to walk in with the custody through the courtroom and there's no barrier between the custody and me.... I have had as many as three custodies in the courtroom at the same time. You can imagine the security and space issues.

"I was appalled at some of the concepts of this building. For instance, the judge's secured corridor is not very secure. There are no stairs from lockup. So in an emergency, custodies have to be taken through the judge's corridor. And bringing in children through the judge's corridor is also problematic. They go off in there. Some of these kids are very upset and they're in the hallway screaming. Sometimes I have to go out to talk them down and get them back down to Shelter Care.

"And it's not practical to have judges go through the areas where children are to get to the courtroom. If they know me, they want to talk to me. But I'm not allowed to have ex partite communications with the minor, so I can't talk. That sometimes upsets them."

TULE ELK PARK CHILD DEVELOPMENT CENTER | SAN FRANCISCO, CALIFORNIA

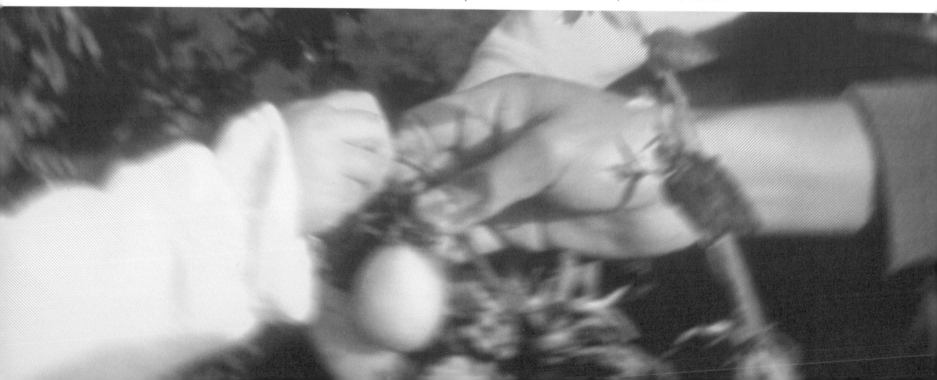

> *"Imagine if this whole asphalt playground were one big garden."*
>
> FORMER DIRECTOR, TULE ELK PARK CHILD DEVELOPMENT CENTER

BRINGING NATURE INTO THE URBAN SCHOOL

SUSAN GOLTSMAN

ONE DAY, A GROUP OF PARENTS AND SCHOOL STAFF LOOKED OUT AT A LITTLE PATCH OF bare dirt and a lot of black asphalt and imagined it all as a big garden. Through a huge collaborative effort, the community transformed dirt, asphalt and an uninspired play structure into a nature-based outdoor learning environment that offers children a wide variety of choices: vegetable and flower gardens, bike paths, sand and water play, construction area, sculpture and an art terrace.

The Tule Elk Park Child Development Center is a public school in the Marina District of San Francisco. The Center is a fully integrated learning environment for

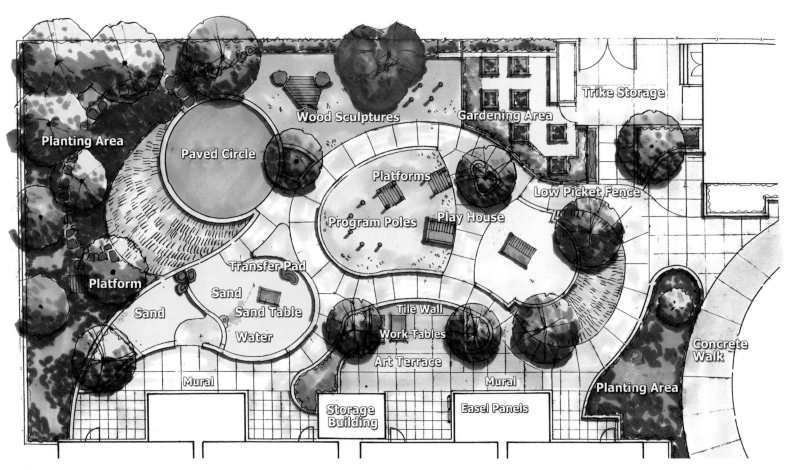

The site plan transformed asphalt into a natural environment.

PROJECT Tule Elk Park Child Development Center   **LOCATION** San Francisco, California
DATE DESIGNED 1990–1997   **CONSTRUCTION COMPLETED** 1998
CONSTRUCTION COST $350,000 **SIZE** 2 acres   **LANDSCAPE ARCHITECT** MIG,
Inc.   **CLIENT** Lynn Juarez (former director), Alan Brossard (current director), Tule Elk Park
Child Development Center, San Francisco Unified School District   **DESIGN TEAM** Frank
& Grossman Landscape Contractors, Inc.; Michael Olexo; Magrane Associates; MIG, Inc.

children with and without disabilities. It serves about 360 children in preschool (ages 3–5) and in kindergarten through third grade in an after school program (ages 5–8) in eight classrooms. The children are primarily from low-income families, and many are learning English while they learn math and reading.

The renovated play area supports the tenets of inclusive design in multiple ways. Where there were once obstacles to mobility (stairs to temporary classrooms), the new design of the space promotes uninterrupted accessibility from the classroom to the playground and among the variety of play areas. The new play areas also make play and learning accessible to a wider spectrum of children because there are now a variety of options that speak to children with different interests, abilities and learning modalities.

The school integrates nature and the garden with standard subjects such as science, math and art.

The outdoor area includes sculpture and artwork.

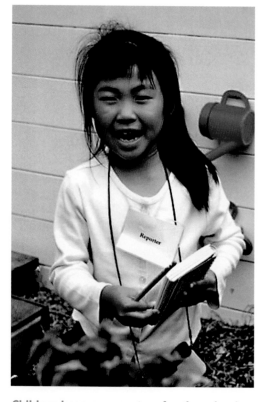

Children become reporters for the school newspaper.

PURPOSE

The project intent was to develop the schoolyard both as a resource for community use and to support school programs. The new master plan aimed to improve physical accessibility, increase staff morale and student engagement in learning, and amplify the connection between the school and its surrounding community.

The school sought meaningful ways to address a diverse population's needs and use the different outdoor elements to address literacy. For example, students now use the garden as an authentic context for dictation, writing and reading. They publish a regular newsletter to educate parents about activities in the garden. The students

Homemade compost becomes a lesson about the "Lasagne of Life."

focus on their schoolwork in a different way. Outdoor settings also allow students to express themselves in sensory ways in addition to the logical ways that are emphasized in the academic curriculum.

The current school director, Alan Brossard, says that children are more engaged in learning when they can see something that has a beginning, middle and end. The garden presents a multitude of projects like this. Children study birds, watch nests being built, see the eggs hatch, and watch birds begin to fly. Or they create compost, plant corn, watch it grow, and eat it.

The physical design reflects the inclusive philosophy of the school. The outdoor area has been a community-builder among all user groups. The staff work together to implement the curriculum; children work together in the outdoor setting; and parents see their children getting interested and become involved in the programs themselves.

observe the garden, interview each other and the garden teacher, transcribe notes, and write articles for their parents and peers to read.

Teachers and staff have noticed that the outdoors has become a place where students who have trouble concentrating inside the classroom become focused and calm. Tying the activities in the schoolyard to classroom curriculum addresses those different learning modalities and allows these children to

Kids are encouraged to dig in and get dirty.

For example, a recent schoolwide project focused on the subject of "tea." All classes and their families learned about the cultural aspects and rituals of tea, conducted tea surveys, had tea in the garden, and involved parents and families in the activities.

Neighborhood residents and surrounding community members also visit the school and want to know what's going on. This community building creates connections for the school and supports the school's belief that relationships are the core of education: people don't learn in isolation, they learn with each other. The outdoor yard is a vehicle for that to happen.

USER GROUPS
- Preschool students (ages 3–5)
- After school students (ages 5–8)
- Teachers
- Staff
- Community members

Community members and parents often come to the school to work on art projects.

The curriculum merges art and seasonal plants, such as pumpkins.

DESIGN PROCESS

Dedicated staff, parents, community members, foundations, and businesses pooled their resources to transform the asphalt schoolyard into a play and learning garden. During the visioning process in 1990, then-director Lynn Juarez and a group of staff and parents looked out at that single, fenced, patch of dirt within the asphalt playground and imagined a huge, open garden.

During the master plan phase, the neighborhood and community were heavily involved in contributing design ideas. A landscape architect was engaged to draw a plan.

Accessible paths link all areas. The white picket fence adds a homey touch around the vegetable garden.

The school staff then built a living model on wheels to use as a community development tool. They brought it to street fairs and used it to educate people about the project. Through this process, they gained monetary donations as well as community connections and commitments of voluntary labor and in-kind donations such as carpentry and concrete work. The school enlisted AmeriCorps workers to remove the majority of the site asphalt.

A contractor donated earth-grading services to the school. There were some grading problems that needed to be solved for accessible pathways. The portable bungalow classrooms were not accessible from the playground grade, and the school wanted continuous accessible circulation rather than separate ramps leading to each classroom. A grading plan was prepared that would achieve this goal and serve as the master plan to further develop areas for outdoor learning.

Inclusive Design Features and Settings

PLAY STRUCTURE

The manufactured play apparatus is accessible to persons with disabilities and provides an opportunity for active play and gross motor development.

OUTDOOR CLASSROOM PATIOS

Outside each interior classroom is a concrete patio that serves as a transition to the playground. The patios are concrete with trees nearby. This patio helps children make the psychological transition between play and work, and serves as additional workspace for large and messy projects.

ACCESSIBLE PATH

The school has universal circulation throughout the site—linking the play area, elevated portable bungalow classrooms, and amphitheater through accessible pathways that provide a continuous, uninterrupted play area for

Insects found in the garden also provide learning opportunities through scientific observation.

tricycles and rollerblades (allowed during community use hours of operation, not during school hours).

AMPHITHEATER/ OUTDOOR GATHERING AREA

The amphitheater is a small concrete circle, edged with turf. This serves as an outdoor gathering area as well as a theater for classes and theater productions.

GARDEN

The vegetable garden is a primary educational resource of the outdoor learning environment. It promotes

Children learn about vegetables by growing and eating them.

accessibility to learners of all languages and ethnicities. Raised beds and accessible, stabilized decomposed granite surfacing ensure that persons with disabilities may use the garden.

CONSTRUCTION AREA

The construction area is designated as a flexible space where children can manipulate their environment and build things. "Program poles" (four vertical columns at the corners of a wood platform) serve as a structure for activities. Children have used the poles as play props for imaginative play during recess (a boat! a house!), as a stage for dances and plays, as armatures for Japanese teahouses during the curriculum unit on tea, and as Sukkahs to celebrate the Jewish harvest holiday of Sukkot.

Children decorate platforms and poles with corn stalks to celebrate a harvest holiday.

The platforms also provide small areas for social interaction.

PLAY HOUSE

The play house provides an opportunity for dramatic play. It is located adjacent to an accessible path and the entry is large enough so that a person with a wheelchair can enter. It is located at ground level so there are no barriers to entry.

SAND AND WATER PLAY AREA

This play area is located so that it does not conflict with any other uses. It is one of the most popular and engaging play areas. There are transfer pads that allow a person to transfer from a wheelchair down into the sand play area.

STORAGE AREA

The storage area for wheeled tricycles allows children to take on responsibilities for their environment. The area also serves as a shed for garden supplies.

A large tree stump in the sand play area is a natural play element: a lily pad, a vantage point, or a throne.

Children work on art projects in the classroom and outdoors.

ART PATIO

The art patio is a large concrete area equipped with a sink, hose bib and drain. Here, students can work outdoors on large projects, such as murals.

ART/DINING TERRACE

This area accommodates large groups and is equipped with a number of picnic tables for outdoor eating or group projects.

Management and Operational Issues

More complex outdoor designs require more maintenance than the standardized asphalt surface, although some design elements actually assist with maintenance. For example, a sand play area is edged with a low concrete curb that keeps the sand from spilling over the edges onto the pathways. The outdoor

Children often work in teams on large projects such as this garden-inspired mural.

Tile murals are mounted outdoors and children are encouraged to touch.

A large painted quilt reflects nature and the seasons.

storage area provided for wheeled toys minimizes the clutter on the play-ground. A raised curb protects the planting. However, ongoing maintenance and care is still a major consideration.

The largest operational issues are overall education and maintenance. Operating the site as an environmental education resource costs about $35,000 to $40,000 per year. This pays for an environmental educator three and one-half days per week to develop curriculum and teach lessons, and for a gardener one day per week.

At the beginning of the project, the City had high hopes that families, staff and the community would be able to maintain the schoolyard through organized "work parties." This approach has not resulted in the consistent level of on-going maintenance that is required for operation. Since the school district has limited available funding and staff to maintain additional vegetation, Tule Elk Park must include funding for maintenance as part of its fundraising efforts (about $5,000 per year). Tule Elk Park also maintains relationships with community organizations and generous individuals who assist through in-kind donations of irrigation maintenance and specific items such as nursery stock.

Another operational issue is the school's need to respond to academic standards and regulations. While some parents and administrators believe this approach meets children's needs, others ask questions: "How do we know that this will translate into academic and lifelong success?" and "Will an investment in this approach yield results?" Tule Elk Park has therefore developed the program into a full environmental science program and has hired an outside evaluator to observe and analyze the program to obtain quantitative data. The environmental education specialist is charged with multiple tasks: integrate outdoor learning activities to align with what children are learning in the classroom; develop schoolwide learning activities that can be performed with the children, their families and the community; and maintain the garden. The school will measure and evaluate the outcomes, institute a curriculum framework and formalize the standards of environmental education.

User Feedback

Tule Elk Park Child Development Center has been in use for almost six years.

Alan Brossard, Director

"One of our biggest challenges has been program development—how to inte-grate the outdoor curriculum with what students were learning in the classroom. At first, the pieces weren't working in synchronicity. Then, we hired an environmental educator to coordinate and formalize the integration of these pieces using state curriculum standards. This has been the key to our success, and now the classroom learning is supported and inspired by the garden.

"At the beginning of the project we met with resistance from the school district, which is understandable because it's hard to have vision when you're trying to survive day-to-day. So we proceeded with a grassroots effort, taking risks and dreaming. We made presentations and reached out to the community. They saw value in the project and supported our school. Once we achieved success, there was visible support from the school board and Superintendent; the Mayor even came to unveil the new park and garden.

"A unique aspect of our school is that the environmental educator, artist-in-residence and classroom teachers form a collaborative team to integrate the curriculum within the context of the outdoor environment."

A leaf can be whatever a child makes of it.

ST. COLETTA OF GREATER WASHINGTON, D.C.

"These children are not sick, they're not broken. They're who they are and how they are....Schools should be shrines to children."

EXECUTIVE DIRECTOR, ST. COLETTA OF GREATER WASHINGTON, D.C.

EXPANDING THE LEARNING ENVIRONMENT

SUSAN GOLTSMAN

ST. COLETTA SCHOOL'S MISSION STATEMENT IS THE ULTIMATE EXPRESSION OF INCLUSIVE design: "At St. Coletta we believe in the immeasurable value of the individual human spirit and the right of each individual to live as full and as independent a life as possible ...our goal is to serve them in an atmosphere that encourages their talents, celebrates their successes and builds their self-esteem."

But the relationship between St. Coletta and its surrounding community has not been inclusive; it has been a clash between two critical but competing needs.

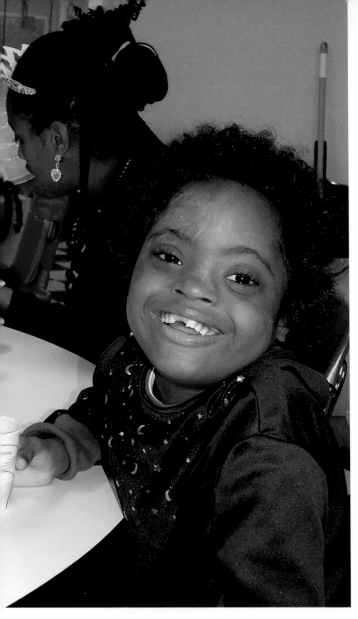

Halloween is one of the students' favorite holidays.

Founded in 1959, St. Coletta of Greater Washington is a private, independent nonprofit school and adult day support program for children with severe mental retardation or autism and multiple physical disabilities. Many have been abused; most are in foster care. The director's vision was to create a jewel of a place for people who usually get nothing—to show these children they are valued and give them the kind of self-esteem they need to survive in the world. Although the school was designed by a renowned architect, this is not a school for rich kids. It exists because public schools don't have the facilities, staff or programming to serve these children. The school had been operating out of two former bank buildings in Alexandria, Virginia, and looked to the new Washington, D.C. site to expand the number of children it could serve. About 85 percent of students at the new site come from the District, referred by their Local Educational Agency.

The community did not want the school and they did not feel included in the planning process. The neighborhood, located in the District's Anacostia River area, is home to a jail, an armory, an abandoned hospital, dilapidated schools and aging row houses. Residents wanted housing and neighborhood-serving retail that could stimulate economic development. They believed that while St. Coletta may have laudable goals, a fancy new school for children with disabilities wouldn't do much for them. They would look over at a beautiful school, while their own children attended schools that are substandard. Once again, they felt, their needs were not taken into account

PROJECT St. Coletta of Greater Washington   **LOCATION** Washington, D.C.
DATE DESIGNED 2003–2004   **BUILDING CONSTRUCTION COMPLETED** 2006
CONSTRUCTION COST $350 million   **SIZE** building: approx. 96,000 sq. feet;
outdoor classroom and recreation areas: approx. 1.5 acres **ARCHITECT AND INDOOR PROGRAMMING** Michael Graves Architect   **LANDSCAPE ARCHITECT AND OUTDOOR PROGRAMMING** MIG, Inc.   **CLIENT** St. Coletta of Greater Washington, D.C.

through the political process of the nation's capital.

St. Coletta received the land through an act of Congress because it receives appropriations from the U.S. Senate. The federal government gave the District a 67-acre site, called "Reservation 13," with the proviso that St. Coletta would get a spot there, along with other government services. The General Services Administration ruled that the land could not be used for retail. St. Coletta took a vacant site, which also happened to be an excellent site for retail, on a corner and near the Metro. The community had no say in what would be built on the site. In addition, St. Coletta will pay the District just $1 a year in rent and the District is required by law to provide schooling for students with disabilities—that could cost about $30,000 a year for each student at St. Coletta. The community was very upset.

To build connections with the community, the school's director had many

meetings with community members, asking for input on usage, site design, school bus routes, and even the height of fences. The school offered to build and maintain a community park and offered the community use of the grounds, community room and gymnasium after school hours. The community refused to accept the park because of maintenance concerns, but the building facilities will be made available to community-serving organizations.

As construction began, the relationship remained a work in progress. St. Coletta continued to reach out to the community and remained dedicated to creating better relations. The school opened in September 2006—a 96,000-square-foot facility that supports 250 students a day and almost 200 staff members.

PURPOSE

St. Coletta's students have severe disabilities and physical challenges that limit their mobility, learning and social skills. Students must meet the admis-

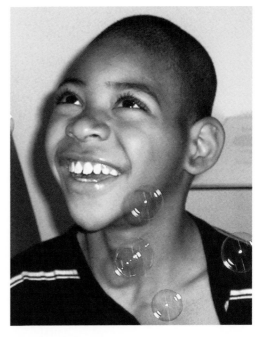

St. Coletta student enjoys activities at school.

sions criteria of "significant cognitive delay." This can be coupled with secondary orthopedic, health, hearing and speech and language impairments.

Over 50 percent of St. Coletta's students live in foster care or group homes. For this reason, St. Coletta serves as more than just a school for these individuals—it is a home custom-tailored to their needs, a place where they celebrate birthdays and holidays, take special trips and make friends.

The staff focuses on the students' abilities, not their limitations. St. Coletta's executive director Sharon Raimo's expression of the school's respect for the students is refreshingly candid and straightforward: "These children are not sick, they're not broken. They're who they are and how they are—they're people."

Students are taught in classes with additional individualized and personalized instruction given to address a student's particular needs or skills. Therapists and educators work together to integrate physical therapy into the students' daily routine—in the classroom, in the lunchroom and in their excursions into the community.

St. Coletta practices an emergent curriculum—one that "emerges" from the interactions between the learners and their environments—both the built envi-

Student interests are incorporated into lessons—from picture books to computers.

ronment and natural areas. The immediate school environment, both indoors and outdoors, and the school's surrounding community therefore play a very important role in the students' education.

Staff often assist students with self-expression through nonverbal means. These methods are not limited to traditional assistive technology; teachers direct students to take photographs (visual documentation and expression) and practice representation and simula-

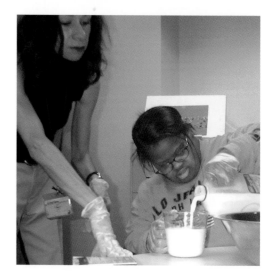

Students learn practical skills, such as cooking, and celebrate birthdays!

tion with models and art. For example, after a field trip to the marshlands, teachers encouraged students to draw or make a model of what they saw. Students simulated the marsh by using a plastic bag laid out on the ground. The wrinkles in the bag formed "rivers" and "marshlands" and when water was poured on the model, students saw how the water runs through the marsh environment.

The new learning environment will expand the settings in the school that can provide experiences like the marshlands. Student learning opportunities are expanded because the new outdoor classroom will provide a safe, enclosed area where students can be supervised. Students and teachers can use the outdoor classroom frequently and therefore experience an outdoor environment more often than they can on a limited number of field trips in a given year. It allows students to engage with the environment in a way that supports their learning.

USER GROUPS

- Children (ages 4–8)
- Youth (ages 9–17)
- Adults (ages 18–22)
- Teachers
- Staff
- Parents
- Board members and guests

DESIGN PROCESS

In the existing former bank facility, many of the current design choices such as paint color have evolved through trial

A workshop with teachers helps designers gather information for the new school environment.

and error over time, resulting in an environment that works. For the new facility, St. Coletta hired skilled architects and landscape architects who folded St. Coletta's gathered knowledge into the design of the learning environment.

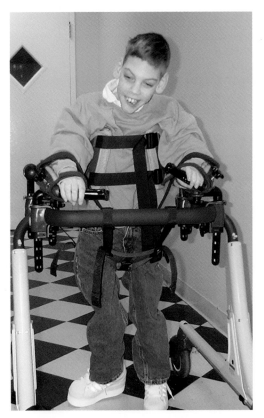

Visiting the school helped designers understand student abilities and design an environment they will can enjoy fully.

Reading with a teacher provides social interaction while learning.

Existing classrooms are painted light green, a calming color.

There are few design standards or guidelines on environments for students with special needs, and each group of students and staff is unique. Therefore, programming workshops with the school's staff and users, along with multiple site visits for observation of use has been a priority for the architects and designers. They have worked very closely with the school during the design process.

For the outdoor environment in the new building, designers first visited the school to observe the typical classroom and activities. A workshop was conducted with staff and teachers to gather ideas about the outdoor space. Teachers expressed their learning goals for the students and described specific behaviors or needs that should be accommodated in the design such as practicing mobility in wheelchairs or walkers, or having the option of being in a quiet natural space versus a group setting.

Inclusive Design Features and Settings

The new building design is multifunctional. It includes classrooms, kitchens, speech and occupational therapy rooms, group rooms, a full-court gymnasium with locker rooms, an infirmary, a hydrotherapy room, administrative offices, conference rooms and a "village green"—a sky-lit atrium hallway that runs the center length of the building's interior.

St. Coletta also plans to make some spaces available for community use outside of school hours, including the gymnasium, kitchen and community room.

A key design element of the new facility is the outdoor classrooms that expand the learning areas for the students. The outdoor context allows for hands-on activities such as gardening and dramatic play, as well as studying nature, wildlife and the seasons.

SITE ELEMENTS

The physical environment reflects how St. Coletta values its students. The school itself tested many elements over many years, which will be continued in the new building and expanded to the outdoors.

■ *Art.* Framed artwork and whimsical sculptures are strategically placed on walls and in rooms. Student artwork is framed and hung on the wall alongside professional art—reflecting that their work is valued and important. In addition to the emotional and psychological

Students hang their artwork on school walls.

benefits, art also serves an interesting educational purpose for this student population. Many of St. Coletta's students are very visual, but don't speak. Staff observe many students staring at the art, especially the autistic children. They note that the art affects their mood and that color also has a tremendous effect on them.

- *Color.* The school's preferred colors are secondary and tertiary colors, rather than primary colors; they are bright and appealing, but not jarring. Currently, yellow is used in public hallways. The director believes it is an "alert" color, which is the behavior St. Coletta wants students to have in public areas. The classrooms are painted green and orange. Quiet Rooms are pink and violet and "under the sea" colors, which seem to have a calming effect.

- *Lighting.* Incandescent light is preferred to fluorescent, which can create a glaring and harsh environment. Autistic children see and hear the "strobe" effect that fluorescent lights have.

- *Social spaces.* Hallways can promote socialization. People cross paths, pass each other in the hall and come together, greeting each other. The school provides spaces where people can be together in big groups and small groups. One of the major goals of coming to school for these students is to learn how to be in a group setting and interact socially with others.

- *Private spaces.* At the same time, people need private areas for reflection. St. Coletta provides alcoves, window seats and places for kids to be alone and look out the window.

ARCHITECTURE

The new building by architect Michael Graves is designed to fit in with its urban community context in Washington, D.C. There are five 3-story pavilions along Independence Avenue. The geometric shapes, evocative of children's blocks, relate to the Armory building across the street and help establish the school's identity along this urban street. Along the 19th Street frontage, the character of the

Rooms are painted and furnished in a single color.
MICHAEL QUILL/ST. COLETTA OF GREATER WASHINGTON

This state-of-the-art kitchen was designed to be functional and calming.
MICHAEL QUILL/ST. COLETTA OF GREATER WASHINGTON

Geometric shapes bring to mind children's blocks and relate to buildings across the street, while establishing the school's unique identity.
MICHAEL QUILL/ST. COLETTA OF GREATER WASHINGTON

buildings mimics the character of the residential neighborhood to the east of the site, appearing as a row of prototypical stylized houses.

CLASSROOMS AS HOUSES

Not only does the architectural character reflect the program and specific nature of the site and its surrounding context, it takes into account the needs and response of the building's users. The house-like façades along 19th Street allow students and teachers to identify with their classrooms in a home-like manner, a compositional strategy that reflects the school's functions through form.

VILLAGE GREEN

Perpendicular to this frontage is a central three-story, sky-lit atrium hallway. This hallway organizes the classrooms in a single axis, like an interior street or "village green." The interior design of St. Coletta reinforces the idea of individual houses, as each classroom adjacent to the village green is designed as a separate "house." Each house corresponds to a different age group and contains several flexible classrooms, various offices, tutoring rooms and elevators.

Above: The "village green," a sky-lit atrium, is a gathering place for the St. Coletta community (artist's rendition).
MICHAEL McCANN AND MICHAEL GRAVES ARCHITECT

Below: The 19th Street building elevation mirrors the character of the adjacent residential neighborhood. Classrooms are like "houses," both in character and function (artist's rendition).
MICHAEL McCANN AND MICHAEL GRAVES ARCHITECT

COMMON ROOMS

Each "house" is composed of two class-rooms that flank a common room. The common room has a special purpose such as horticulture, sensory integration therapy, physical therapy, weaving, art and music. The horticulture room will be set up like a greenhouse with potting tables, a sink and a large table for looking at plans and making charts. The sensory therapy room is designed to contain elements such as changeable colors of light, sound devices, water features that have a calming effect and swings and balls for bouncing. The physical therapy room has a balance beam, steps, balls, bars to hold on to and a removable swing.

The sensory therapy room has changeable light colors, auditory devices and water features that have a calming effect.
MICHAEL QUILL/ST. COLETTA OF GREATER WASHINGTON

OUTDOOR LEARNING ENVIRONMENT

The outdoor environment often becomes the basis of themes in the curriculum at St. Coletta. Students talk about what they see and experience in their surroundings. From these discussions, teachers formulate a curriculum. For example, students recently studied the house. They explored their own houses and animal houses, built models of houses, studied industries that support houses, visited a home supply store to buy nails and shingles to make bird houses, and visited a construction site down the street to study the people who make houses. Math, science, read-

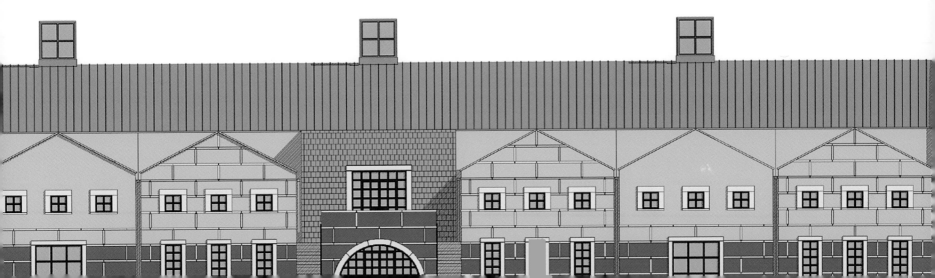

Decorative metal work and landscaping along the wall will provide an attractive buffer to the community, while the building echoes neighborhood architecture.
MICHAEL QUILL / ST. COLETTA OF GREATER WASHINGTON

ing, writing and arts are all woven into the curriculum—and teachers make the children's social experiences with people in the community part of the curriculum as well.

The curriculum of St. Coletta requires outdoor program areas. The new building was designed with a number of outdoor settings to enhance classroom activities. These settings are well-integrated with the school's program needs and have a strong relationship with the architecture and overall site layout.

The outdoor program areas will border the school's east and west sides, adjacent to each classroom "house" and will be enclosed for the safety of the students. A fence along the street will shield these outdoor classroom areas from the street. The full length of the wall includes decorative metal work and trellises, along with ornamental landscaping on the pedestrian side of the fence to offer an attractive buffer to the community.

OUTDOOR CLASSROOM PATIOS

Each patio space will be large enough to accommodate 25 people (including wheelchairs) at one time. This allows for two classrooms to gather for a shared lesson or event. The outdoor classroom patios will be equipped with long tables, a sink, a storage cabinet, an overhead shade structure and a back-drop wall that includes a blackboard for writing and drawing.

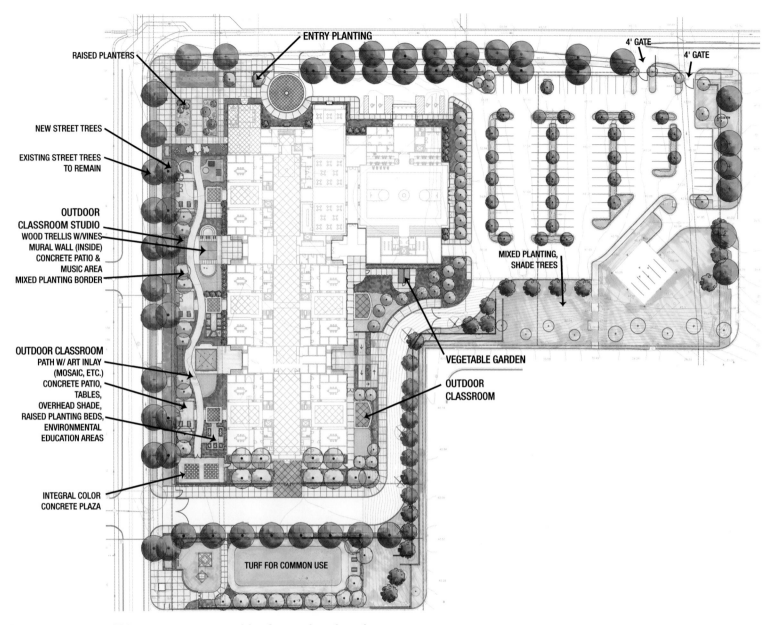

RAISED PLANTERS

ENTRY PLANTING

4' GATE

4' GATE

NEW STREET TREES

EXISTING STREET TREES
TO REMAIN

MIXED PLANTING,
SHADE TREES

OUTDOOR
CLASSROOM STUDIO
WOOD TRELLIS W/VINES
MURAL WALL (INSIDE)
CONCRETE PATIO &
MUSIC AREA
MIXED PLANTING BORDER

OUTDOOR CLASSROOM
PATH W/ ART INLAY
(MOSAIC, ETC.)
CONCRETE PATIO,
TABLES,
OVERHEAD SHADE,
RAISED PLANTING BEDS,
ENVIRONMENTAL
EDUCATION AREAS

VEGETABLE GARDEN

OUTDOOR
CLASSROOM

INTEGRAL COLOR
CONCRETE PLAZA

TURF FOR COMMON USE

The new campus will have many opportunities for outdoor learning.

HARD COURT AREA

The loading and unloading area is a wide driveway that is fenced at either end for security. During school hours, these gates are closed and the driveway serves as a multi-purpose hard court area for play. During peak drop-off hours, the gates are open and the driveway serves that function.

GARDEN

Raised garden beds will be located adjacent to the Horticulture Therapy room and in additional locations throughout the outdoor classrooms.

House-type façades help students identify with their classroom in a home-like manner.
MICHAEL QUILL/ST. COLETTA OF GREATER WASHINGTON

Planting, tending and harvesting plants are core activities in the curriculum for science, math (measuring growth) and art. Growing vegetables and cutting flowers teach students life skills. Plants will be selected to arouse the senses: fragrance, bright color, soft touch, rattles in the wind, and edible herbs and vegetables. A Pizza Garden, located adjacent to the older students' classroom, will allow 17–22-year-olds to grow vegetables and herbs, and cook and eat their own pizzas in outdoor areas.

PLAYHOUSE

The playhouse village will provide dramatic play opportunities for young students, ages 4–8. The props in that area (houses, dress-up clothing, cars) inspire and aid role playing and dramatic play, which are typical activities for young children.

SAND AND WATER PLAY

Sand offers a medium for creative play and social interaction. Students with

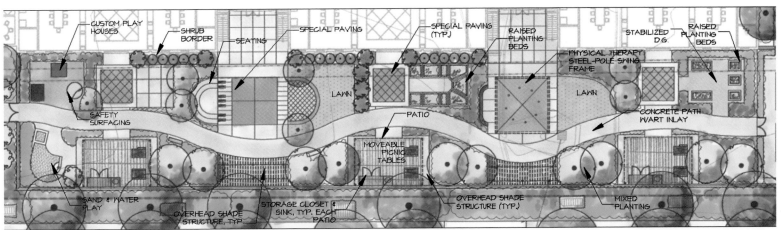

CUSTOM PLAY HOUSES

SHRUB BORDER

SEATING

SPECIAL PAVING

SPECIAL PAVING (TYP.)

RAISED PLANTING BEDS

STABILIZED D.G.

RAISED PLANTING BEDS

PHYSICAL THERAPY STEEL-POLE SWING FRAME

LAWN

LAWN

SAFETY SURFACING

PATIO

CONCRETE PATH W/ART INLAY

MOVEABLE PICNIC TABLES

SAND & WATER PLAY

STORAGE CLOSET & SINK, TYP. EACH PATIO

OVERHEAD SHADE STRUCTURE (TYP.)

MIXED PLANTING

OVERHEAD SHADE STRUCTURE, TYP.

OUTDOOR CLASSROOMS - ENLARGED PLAN

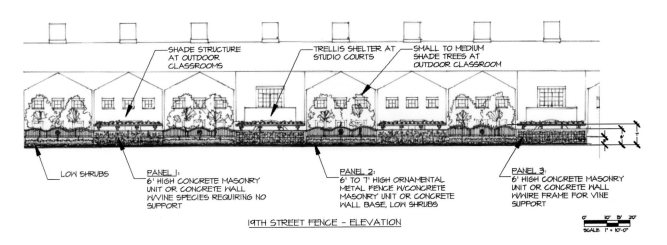

SHADE STRUCTURE AT OUTDOOR CLASSROOMS

TRELLIS SHELTER AT STUDIO COURTS

SMALL TO MEDIUM SHADE TREES AT OUTDOOR CLASSROOM

LOW SHRUBS

PANEL I:
6' HIGH CONCRETE MASONRY UNIT OR CONCRETE WALL W/VINE SPECIES REQUIRING NO SUPPORT

PANEL 2:
6' TO 7' HIGH ORNAMENTAL METAL FENCE W/CONCRETE MASONRY UNIT OR CONCRETE WALL BASE, LOW SHRUBS

PANEL 3:
6' HIGH CONCRETE MASONRY UNIT OR CONCRETE WALL W/WIRE FRAME FOR VINE SUPPORT

0   10' 15'   20'
SCALE: 1" = 10'-0"

19TH STREET FENCE - ELEVATION

Outdoor classrooms are planned immediately adjacent to indoor spaces.

The outdoor classroom environment will support lessons and activities.

physical limitations can mold, form, and shape sand and water. The sand and water will also provide sensory stimulation for students who rarely have contact with natural materials or elements. There will be two sand play areas: one for 4–8-year-olds and one for 9–12-year-olds.

ACCESSIBLE SENSORY PATH

An accessible path will run through and link the outdoor classrooms. The path will be wide enough to accommodate two wheelchairs or one wheelchair and one ambulatory person side by side. The path will be relatively flat, so slope is not a mobility constraint.

The path provides more than just a circulation route. During the design process, teachers requested that a series of elements be placed along the path to attract students and motivate them to be mobile. The sensory path will have mirrors, wind chimes, moving sculptures, and engaging features along the way to encourage students to move.

AMPHITHEATER/ OUTDOOR GATHERING AREA

A small semicircle will provide an area for small concerts or presentations. Teachers and students can pull off the main pathway and gather in a somewhat private area, or a performer could stand on one side and an audience on the other.

Management and Operational Issues

The primary management and operational issues of outdoor learning environments at a facility like St. Coletta are the staffing and ongoing maintenance required to keep up the landscape areas. Since the student population at St. Coletta requires nearly a 1:1 student to teacher ratio, staffing is less of an issue in the outdoor classroom than it is at typical public schools. Some minimal amount of planting and tending will be

Opening celebrations honor the student gardening activities that will expand at the new facility.
MICHAEL QUILL/ST. COLETTA OF GREATER WASHINGTON

taken care of by the students themselves as part of their classes, recreation and therapy. In order to afford and maintain

a facility like this, additional fundraising is required. This is an ongoing task that is critical to ensuring its usability.

User Feedback

Doreen Hodges, parent, as quoted in The Washington Post, *September 6, 2006*

"Truthfully, I just wanted to cry. It's so beautiful and you could just feel the love in the building….You never thought anything like that was ever going to be available to kids like this in D.C."

Chip Henstenburg, parent, as quoted in The Washington Post, *September 6, 2006*

"Everything is really well thought out and designed to minimize disruption in the classroom, and to be able to deliver all the services the kids need in the classroom."

Sharon Raimo, Executive Director, St. Coletta of Greater Washington, D.C.

"People get a sense of what you think and feel about them by their surroundings. Standard school classrooms have four walls and are warm, but that's not good enough.

"St. Coletta's philosophy is to look at the people around you and share experiences together. From experiences you share together—the experiences a person has—will emerge what the learner needs to know. You discern how learners learn best because you know them, and the curriculum will evolve (based on experiences). For example: What's the point of memorizing all the colors, if the kid doesn't perceive colors? There's a different way to go about teaching that.

"We rely on theme-based, hands-on activities that emerge from shared experiences and interactions with people and the environment. That's why the physical things around the building are so important. This generates what the themes are going to be, what we are going to talk about, what we see, what we do together.

"Our students feel valued and important. We hang *their* pictures on the wall. Beautiful work is framed and hung on the wall (with respect). These students are the best they can be and deserve being around things that are beautiful. Autistic kids stare at paintings; paintings provide food for the imagination. Many students are very visual, and don't speak. They're like little cameras, taking it all in. Art affects their mood. And color has a tremendous effect on them."

St. Coletta welcomed students to its new facility in September 2006.
MICHAEL QUILL/ST. COLETTA OF GREATER WASHINGTON

MUSÉES DES BEAUX ARTS | VALENCIENNES AND CALAIS, FRANCE

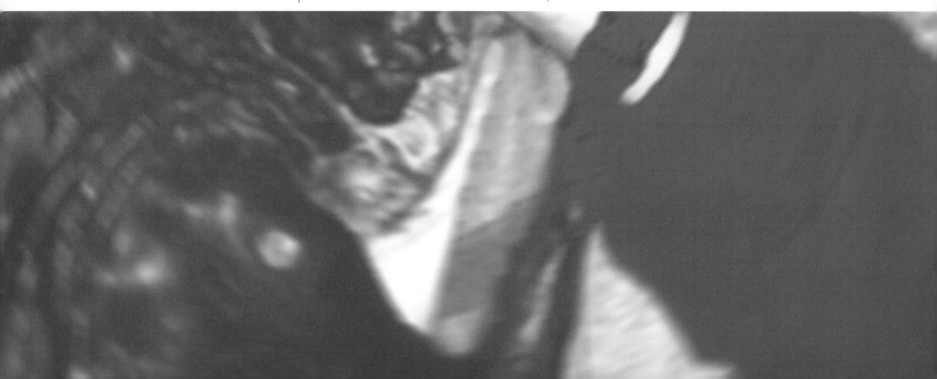

"It is not a question of asserting a right, but quite simply, of a humane step towards equality."

MUSEUM VISITOR WHO IS LOSING HER EYESIGHT

REDISCOVERING THE TOUCH OF ART

COCO RAYNES

ALLOWING VISUALLY IMPAIRED PEOPLE TO EXPERIENCE AN ART MUSEUM MIGHT SEEM paradoxical: how can you appreciate what you can't see?

"The Museum at Your Fingertips" program in the Musées des Beaux Arts in Valenciennes and Calais is a tactile journey for visually impaired visitors. It is planned for all the national museums in the north of France by the Ministère de la Culture— Direction des Musées de France. The tactile program, which is incorporated into the general visit without needing an appointment, allows blind visitors to touch selected sculptures and other pieces. In some museums, audio commentary further describes the artworks. Visitors follow the precise tactile and audio information to move through the museum autonomously and at their own pace. By visiting different museums throughout the north of France, visually impaired visitors can discover the history of sculpture from medieval times to the 20th century.

DESIGN GOALS

The long-term goal of the program is to overcome problems of exclusion by opening France's national art collections to visually impaired visitors, including blind children. It has been widely covered in the press and became the subject of a documentary sponsored by the

Department of Cultural Affairs, which aired on national television.

Although France lacks regulations such as The Americans with Disabilities Act (ADA) in the United States, the Direction des Musées de France had already established many accessibility projects in its national museums. The client wanted to test accessible design concepts in the museum environment. It was understood that access would have to be universal—physical, cultural and social.

ADA regulations regarding signage for visually impaired travelers are fairly simple. In addition to letter size and

The Raynes Rail provides continuous Braille information.

All visitors can press buttons to hear audio information.

PROJECT "The Museum at Your Fingertips" (Le Musée au bout des Doigts)   **LOCATION** Musées des Beaux Arts in the cities of Calais and Valenciennes, France   **DATE DESIGNED** 1996, 1998   **CONSTRUCTION COMPLETED** 1996, 1999   **CLIENT** Ministère de la Culture—Direction des Musées de France and Fédération des Amis des Musées du Nord Pas-de-Calais   **DESIGNER** Raynes Associates

color contrast, they require that rooms be identified with Braille by the doors. However, they do not require any means to find the rooms.

To broaden the ADA standard, the design team developed several approaches to navigation for blind travelers, including the Raynes Rail, a patented Braille and audio handrail system. The rail provides the missing link from a point of arrival to a desired destination. Braille messages on the inner face of the handrail describe open areas and traffic patterns, warn of stairs and ramps and announce turns. Tactile maps and diagrams on glass have also been incorporated.

USER GROUPS

- General public
- Visually impaired adults
- Visually impaired children
- Visitors with reduced mobility

Visually impaired visitors in Valenciennes can touch selected sculptures.

The 19th century sculpture gallery includes works by Auguste Rodin that visually impaired visitors may touch.

Musée des Beaux Arts et de la Dentelle, Calais, France

The 19th century sculpture gallery at the Museum of Calais, which houses Rodin's original bronze studies for the Burghers of Calais, was designated the first "Museum at Your Fingertips" project. The design team worked in conjunction with the nonprofit Féderation du Nord de la France des Sociétés d'Amis des Musées (the Society of Friends of the Museums in the Calais Region), the Lions Club International District 103, and the museum curator.

DESIGN PROCESS

The first step was to inventory the sculptures. Bronze and marble works that could be touched were identified. The more fragile pieces were to be placed in cases along the walls. Works were then rearranged into two rows of sculpture with enough space between each pedestal to allow visitors with seeing-eye dogs or wheelchairs to navigate through the sculptures comfortably.

This simplified floor plan could be easily memorized and would prevent visitors from bumping into the sculptures. Beyond aesthetics, several factors were considered in the new museography, including chronological order, scale and contrast.

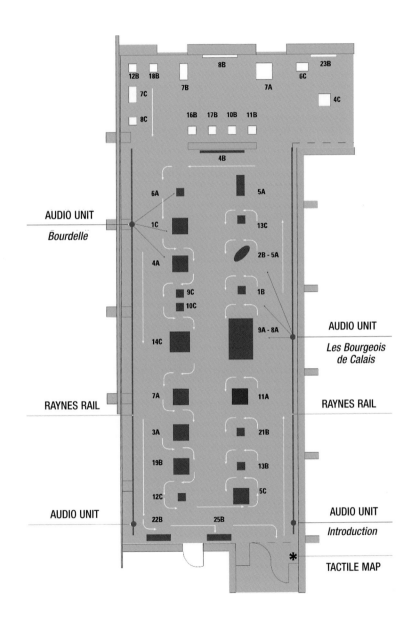

AUDIO UNIT
Bourdelle

AUDIO UNIT
Les Bourgeois de Calais

RAYNES RAIL

RAYNES RAIL

AUDIO UNIT

AUDIO UNIT
Introduction

TACTILE MAP

Statues are arranged in two rows with enough room for wheelchairs and seeing-eye dogs to maneuver between them.

Visually impaired visitors may touch the bronze sculptures.

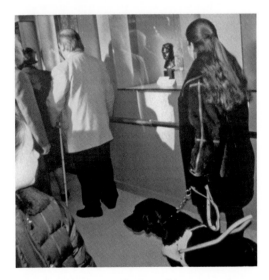

Fragile pieces are displayed in cases along the wall, with information in Braille along the railings.

Inclusive Design Features and Settings

ENTRANCE

At the door of the sculpture gallery, an audio message, triggered by a photo-sensor positioned on the Raynes Rail, introduces the overall concept of the tactile itinerary and the collection.

WAYFINDING

The Braille and audio handrail system runs along both sides of the room. The Braille information allows the visitor to select the sculptures they wish to discover. The messages direct visitors to specific statues they may touch, giving the distances in paces and angles. For example, it may state: "The Burghers of Calais, first study, is on your opposite side, five steps."

Visitors read the information on the pedestals of smaller pieces.

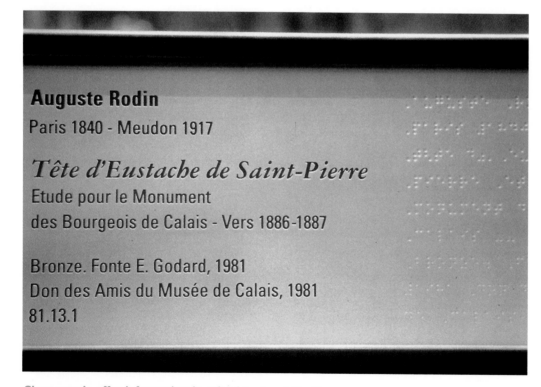

Auguste Rodin
Paris 1840 - Meudon 1917

Tête d'Eustache de Saint-Pierre
Etude pour le Monument
des Bourgeois de Calais - Vers 1886-1887

Bronze. Fonte E. Godard, 1981
Don des Amis du Musée de Calais, 1981
81.13.1

Glass panels offer information in raised text and Braille.

All visitors can have a similar satisfying museum experience.

The room layout allows for groups of children of all abilities to experience the art.

DESCRIPTIVE INFORMATION

Three additional audio units along the rails, also activated by photosensors, address all visitors. The audio commentary describes the characteristics and evolution of masterpieces by Auguste Rodin and Antoine Bourdelle.

The heights of the pedestals were adapted to each sculpture to guarantee ease of exploration. The pedestal incorporates a glass panel, tilted at 30 degrees to facilitate Braille reading. The glass is sandblasted to obtain a non-glare surface and includes both Braille and large raised descriptive text for those who are visually impaired but do not read Braille. For budgetary considerations, the pedestals were designed to be manufactured by the in-house carpenters.

Musée des Beaux Arts, Valenciennes, France

The Musée des Beaux Arts in Valenciennes displays works from the 15th to 20th centuries. It has eleven galleries, featuring bronze and marble sculptures, paintings, a café and a library. Workshops and administrative facilities are located at the lower level. In this museum, visually impaired visitors move through the entire museum independently, at their own pace. An invisible information system guides visitors to selected sculptures throughout the museum.

DESIGN PROCESS

Because the museum is a classified monument, no railing could be installed within the galleries. The existing museography could not be modified; every piece had to remain where it was. The guidance system had

Selected marble and bronze sculptures may be touched.

The main directory is a tactile map that can be used by all visitors. It shows the itinerary as a raised path on the glass surface, with additional information in Braille on the inner side of the rail.

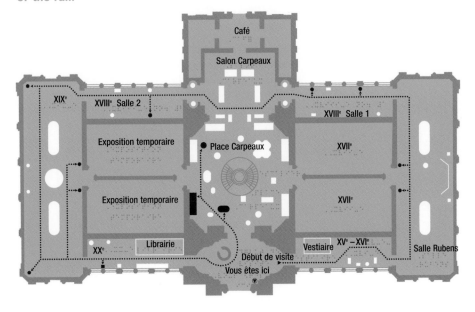

The main map shows the simple route through the entire museum.

to lead visitors down the staircase to the lower level. And, at the curator's request, the system had to be invisible.

The major challenge was to select representative sculptures that could be touched—within every gallery and from each historical period—forming a pathway that would be simple enough to be remembered when presented on a tactile map. Visitors would need to remember the path through a gallery, which pieces they could touch, and how to get to the next gallery.

Inclusive Design Features and Settings

ENTRANCES

At the museum entrance, a main directory made of a tactile glass slab with a Raynes Rail segment introduces the itinerary. Braille information on the inner

A detailed tactile map shows the route through each gallery and into the next gallery.

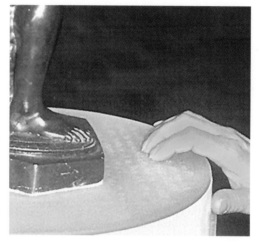

Raised letters and Braille can be incorporated onto the pedestal.

side of the rail provides direction to the information desk and to the start of the tactile visit.

At the entrance of each gallery, a more detailed map is mounted consistently on the right side and at the same height. This map presents the position of the sculptures within the space and the route to the next gallery. Raised dots on the glass maps guide visually impaired visitors to the works they may touch.

Visitors can touch and explore a sculpture, then navigate to the next one.

A discreet glass plaque with a Braille description raised on the blasted surface was positioned between the pedestal and the sculpture.

STAIRCASES AND FLOOR MARKINGS

At the lower level, in staircases, landing areas and in the main corridor, seg-

Visitors follow a series of raised dots to navigate difficult areas.

ments of the Raynes Rail were installed, with Braille messages only. In addition, in areas difficult to navigate, a series of raised dots were installed on the floor about six inches apart. The TacDots, which are made of fiberglass and hollow inside, make a distinctive sound when tapped with a cane.

Management and Operational Issues

To support "The Museum at Your Fingertips," the museums have trained attendants, guides and lecturers. Educational programs have been created in conjunction with the schools to address sighted and non-sighted children who learn from one another—all equally delighted by the exchange. Programs feature artists and storytellers and include sculpture workshops.

The Braille and audio handrails do not require any special maintenance. They are cleaned like other surfaces. In the event of changes in the museography, the Braille inserts can be easily updated. Audio messages can be recorded on site.

In some museums, visitors are instructed to wear surgical gloves to protect the marble statues.

User Feedback

"The Museum at Your Fingertips" program received extensive coverage. The following users were quoted in newspapers and magazines (translated from French).

Pierre Houiez, Blind Visitor

"I was shocked when I came in and the docent told me to touch! I rediscovered an appreciation for beauty and I spent three hours there (Palais des Papes)....The interactions between those who can and cannot see multiply the worth of the art. We are at the beginning of a change in the vision for works of art in museums. Even for those who can see, it is another approach to art." (Mr. Houiez had stopped visiting his favorite art museums after losing his eyesight.)

Docent at the Musée des Beaux Arts

"He came to us and wanted to rediscover the museum he had known.... When you work with people with poor eyesight, you completely lose your frame of reference. We are used to seeing things, and when you approach a piece by touching it, your points of reference change completely."

Depending on the height of the sculpture, sometimes visitors can explore only the lower parts.

Visitor Who Is Losing Her Eyesight

"I understand a piece of work much faster by touching it than by seeing it. You also understand the approach of the artist since he worked with his hands! When the Rodin Museum organized the modeling workshop in addition to the tactile tours, the program enriched our group, allowing us to open up, leading people with new motivation. After a visit, it is a question of reproducing what you have memorized, but also the feelings that you have come away with from discovering a piece of work.

"You touch someone else's work and so enter into a relationship with him. For me, art gives me a lot; it is a means of sharing, of exploring.

"For me, it is not a question of asserting a right, but quite simply, of a humane step towards equality."

EXPLORE! A CHILD'S NATURE | BROOKFIELD ZOO, ILLINOIS

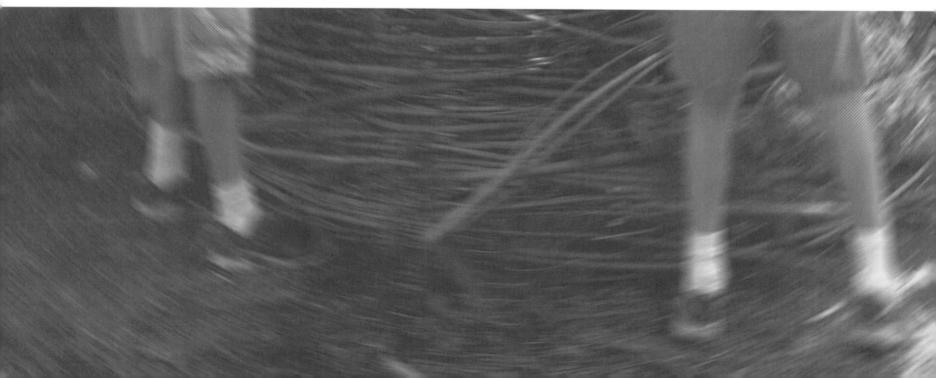

> *"One visit to the Hamill Family Play Zoo affected one of my children enough that she not only learned to love the animal (a lemur), but believed that she could make a difference in its life!"*
>
>

CHICAGO AREA PARENT

GROWING CARING CHILDREN

ROBIN MOORE

NOTHING LIKE THIS PROJECT HAD BEEN TACKLED BEFORE IN THE WORLD OF ZOOS: A ZOO created as a place where children can connect to nature emotionally, through play. Explore! A Child's Nature/the Hamill Family Play Zoo and Play Gardens, part of Brookfield Zoo, is the first children's zoo in the country to adopt adventure play as a core concept of its program. The mission of the Hamill Family Play Zoo and Play Gardens embraces the assumption that children's experiences at a zoo can make a difference in their lives and in the world. Children role-play as animals, create animal

The Hamill Family Play Zoo entrance announces immediately that children are here to play.

habitats with natural materials, search for bugs, and participate in animal care, feeding and grooming—exciting and appealing ways to learn about animals and nature.

The two primary physical components of the zoo are:

- *The Play Zoo,* located in the redeveloped and expanded former Small Mammal House (which dates from the 1950s).
- *The Play Gardens,* surrounding the Play Zoo building and easily accessible from it, providing a broad range of outdoor experiences in both programmed and non-programmed spaces.

The Play Zoo and Gardens are the first phase of Explore! A Child's Nature. When completed, the entire Children's Play Zoo will encompass ten acres of diverse play settings for children and youth.

PROJECT Explore! A Child's Nature, Hamill Family Play Zoo and Play Gardens **LOCATION** Brookfield Zoo, Brookfield, Illinois **DATE DESIGNED** 1998–99 **CONSTRUCTION COMPLETED** June 2000 **CONSTRUCTION COST** $6.7 million **SIZE** 10 acres when completed **CLIENT** Chicago Zoological Society, Brookfield Zoo **DESIGN TEAM** Brookfield Zoo; MIG, Inc.; Wheeler Kearns Architects; Douglas/Gallagher **ENGINEERING** Hanscomb Associates, Inc. **PROJECT MANAGEMENT** McClier Corporation

Children can strut like peacocks.

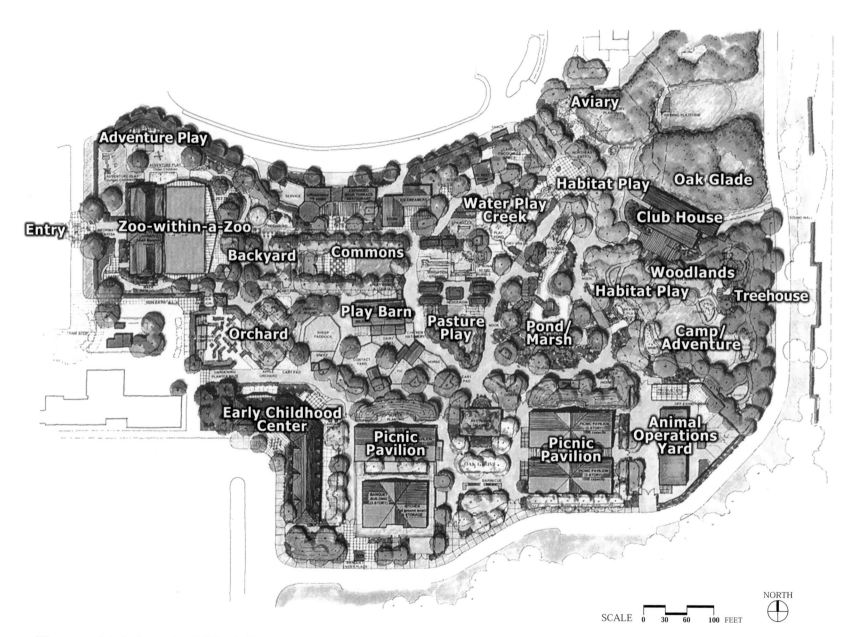

Adventure Play

Aviary

Habitat Play

Oak Glade

Water Play Creek

Club House

Entry

Zoo-within-a-Zoo

Backyard

Commons

Woodlands Habitat Play

Treehouse

Play Barn

Pasture Play

Pond/Marsh

Camp/Adventure

Orchard

Early Childhood Center

Picnic Pavilion

Picnic Pavilion

Animal Operations Yard

NORTH

SCALE 0 30 60 100 FEET

When completed, the entire Children's Play Zoo will encompass ten acres of diverse play settings for children and youth.

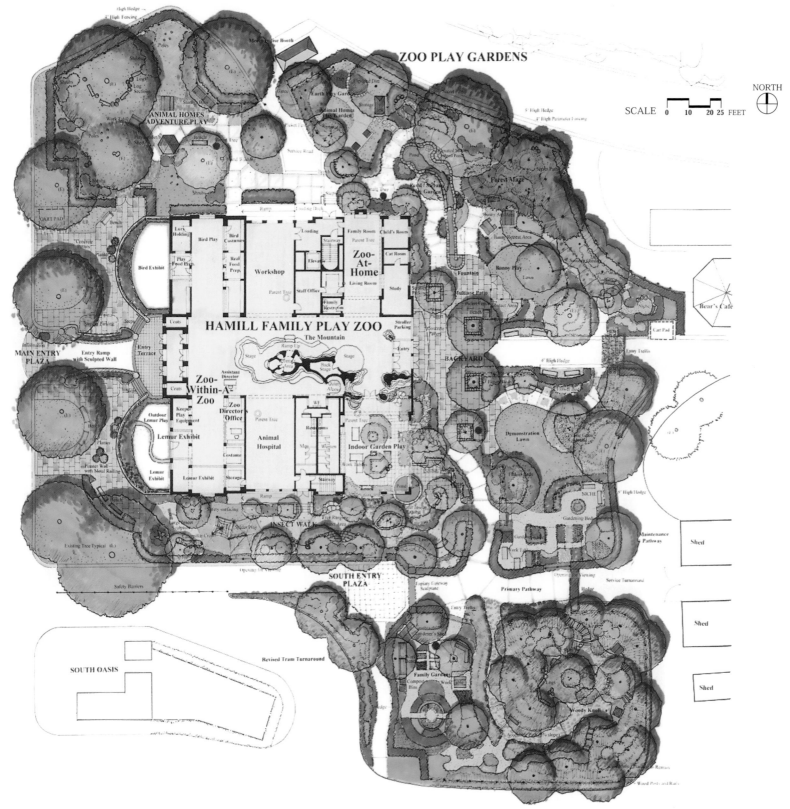

ZOO PLAY GARDENS

NORTH

SCALE 0 10 20 25 FEET

HAMILL FAMILY PLAY ZOO

ANIMAL HOMES
ADVENTURE PLAY

Forest Maze

Bird Exhibit

Lory
Holding

Bird Play

Bird
Customs

Loading

Stairway

Family Room

Child's Room

Parent Tree

Cat Room

Zoo-
At-
Home

Living Room

Study

Bunny Play

Lawn

Bear's Café

Workshop

Play
Food Prep.

Real
Food
Prep.

Parent Tree

Staff Office

Elevator

Family
Restroom

Cart Pad

MAIN ENTRY
PLAZA

Entry Ramp
with Sculpted Wall

Coats

Entry
Terrace

Zoo-
Within-A
Zoo

Coats

Assistant
Director

Entry

Stroller
Parking

BACKYARD

The Mountain

Ramp Up

Stage

Stage

Outdoor
Lemur Play

Keeper
Play
Equipment

Zoo
Director
Office

Parent Tree

Arena
Area

Back
Stage

Demonstration
Lawn

Lemur Exhibit

Costume

Animal
Hospital

Resrooms

Parent Tree

NICHE

Lemur
Exhibit

Lemur Exhibit

Storage

Men

Women

Indoor Garden Play

Work Tables

Gardening Beds

Existing Tree Typical (E)

Ramp

Maintenance
Pathway

Shed

INSECT WALK

SOUTH ENTRY
PLAZA

Primary Pathway

Service Turnaround

Shed

SOUTH OASIS

Revised Tram Turnaround

Family Garden

Woody Knoll

Shed

Phase 1 of the Children's Play Zoo Master Plan is the Hamill Family Play Zoo, consisting of interactive animal exhibits and play settings.

Newspapers are used to wrap "treats" hidden by the zoo keepers for the lemurs to discover and eat, to the great delight of children.

The adventure play concept has three essential components:

■ A team of trained play workers, or as they are called at the Hamill Family Play Zoo, "Play Partners." These professionals work with children and families in an educational role of facilitation rather than traditional instruction.

■ An interactive, participatory environment designed to support experiences by children and families with the physical settings and features of the play zoo.

■ An indoor-outdoor environment designed to offer attractive and varied activities year round.

The zoo provides settings in which all members of the community, of all ages, abilities and cultures, can participate and share experiences.

The Play Zoo opened in the spring of 2001, and rapidly became a popular, repeat visit destination for families, schools and youth organizations from the Chicago region. The target audience is families with children up to 10 years old and their siblings.

Explore! A Child's Nature/Hamill Family Play Zoo is located within a private institution (Brookfield Zoo);

The exhibit design lets children sit on the same rock as a lemur, separated by a glass panel.

nonetheless, it provides an unmatched opportunity for assessment within the broader frame of reference of universal and inclusive design.

DESIGN GOALS

The overall goal of Explore! A Child's Nature is to foster a love of animals and nature by:

- Offering children and their families year-round, hands-on, open-ended opportunities to play with, work with, and care for animals and plants;

- Setting a context that encourages families to experience animals and nature in their everyday lives, wherever they are; and

- Providing the materials, ideas and experiences that help adults rediscover the magic and importance of childhood, play and nature; and encouraging them to integrate these elements into their everyday lives.

The philosophy embodied in this last goal focuses on allowing children to playfully explore their environment and to make their own discoveries. This approach assumes that the environment can be designed to stimulate children's intrinsic motivation to explore and learn about their surroundings through play. The philosophy also recognizes the practical reality of an environment that can attract thousands of visitors on a midsummer's weekend. With such high levels of use, the environment must be appropriately prepared and managed for sustainability, while at the same time

Play Partners work with children and families in an educational role of facilitation rather than traditional instruction; here children are pretending to be lemurs, complete with tails.

engaging users of all ages and abilities to play and learn.

USER GROUPS

- Families with children 10 years old and under
- Older accompanying siblings
- School-aged children on field visits and their teachers
- Children from preschool centers
- Children with special needs from specialized programs
- Children enrolled in summer or vacation programs and accompanying staff
- Children's birthday groups
- College students conducting research

DESIGN PROCESS

A key to the success of the Play Zoo was the preparatory work the zoo staff project team completed before the design consultants were hired. For two years, the Brookfield Zoo Southeast Section Planning Team (SES) organized a series of seminars and workshops with a broad

The zoo provides relaxing time-out settings for parents, such as this parent resource space in the Zoo-At-Home area.

Children's ideas are integrated into many aspects of the zoo's design and programming.

along with other zoo staff and the design consultants. Together, this group participated in the design process for over one year.

The design team included representation of all major functions of the zoo pertaining to the new project, including exhibit design and fabrication, veterinary science, groundskeeping, water quality, docent and volunteer programming, education, safety, development, operations, communications and animal curatorship.

A series of design workshops carried the design team from general considerations of alternative site development concepts to detailed layout, materials selection, lighting, acoustics, air conditioning and plant materials.

The concept of behavior or activity setting was used throughout the design process as the common framework for investigating alternative programmatic themes, functional requirements, detailed features of the space, and the match with user needs.

variety of consultants and stakeholders to pin down the core purpose of the project. The final outcome of this process was the decision to base the Play Zoo on children's play as a vehicle for emotional development in relation to animals and nature.

In this regard, Brookfield Zoo was a "perfect client," meaning that a fully

articulated mission and purpose for the new children's zoo was used as the basis for hiring a design consultant aligned with these core values. For this reason, the match between client and consultant worked well.

The design process engaged a project team composed of selected members from the original SES planning team

Activity Setting Structure of the Play Zoo and Play Gardens

Indoor Settings: Play Zoo

ZOO-WITHIN-A-ZOO

Animal Exhibits
- Lemur Exhibits
- Reptile Run
- Bird Exhibit/Aviary
- The Mountain

Zoo Director's Office

Animal Hospital

Workshop

Indoor Garden Play

ZOO-AT-HOME

Family Room
- Small Pet Display
- Contact
- Habitat-Making Area

Living Room
- Grooming
- Demo

Dramatic Play Area

Study
- Information
- Resource Area Stories
- Pet Memories Area
- Nature Crafts
- Cat Room/Storage

Bath Room
- Dog Bathing
- Grooming
- Fish and Aquaria
- Demonstration Area

Child's Room
- Swap Shop

INDOOR SUPPORT FACILITIES

Stages

Adult Resource Station

Parent Trees

Quiet Alcoves

Restrooms

Base Office

Real Food Preparation

Basement

Carts
- Visitors Services Cart
- Life Safety Cart
- Research Cart

Outdoor Settings: Play Gardens

MAIN ENTRY PLAZA

SOUTH ENTRY PLAZA

INSECT WALK

Willow Tunnel

Insect Exhibits

Dress Up

Storage

ANIMAL HOMES ADVENTURE PLAY

Building Material Storage

BACKYARD

Patio

Animal Homes Play Garden

Woody Knoll

Earth Play Garden

Pet Play Garden

Pond/Stream Play Garden
- Forest Maze
- Demonstration Lawn
- Family Gardens
- Parent Resource Area

CIRCULATION

Primary Pathways

Secondary Pathways

Secret Pathways

Maintenance Pathways

Ambulance and Fire Dept. Access

OUTDOOR SUPPORT FACILITIES

Niches

Cart Pads and Vending Carts

A key component of the participatory design strategy was the early involvement of children. A "Kid's Council" was formed with children of the Zoo's member families. At Saturday morning meetings, the Phase I schematic design was introduced and discussed. Many of the key components of the design program were strongly validated, which was not surprising as so much prior research and expertise had been devoted to the front end of the design process. The most significant Kid's Council contribution was the detailed ideas children presented for activities with animals and nature.

In the first phase of the design process, a schematic design program and concep-

Through the "Kid's Council" children presented detailed ideas for activities with animals and nature.

tual master plan were developed for the entire ten-acre site of Explore! A Child's Nature. The physical boundaries of the project, as well as the extent of the Play Zoo and Play Gardens, were defined.

The Play Zoo contains two main indoor settings and twelve subsettings. The outdoor Play Gardens contain eight main settings and seventeen subsettings. The complete setting structure is presented on the facing page.

The large majority of settings and subsettings were conceptually defined early on in the design programming process as a reflection of overall project goals. However, as detailed functions, adjacencies and characteristics became more and more clearly defined, many iterations and refinements were added. This phase of the project was conducted, in essence, as a collaborative investigation of design options by everyone on the design team.

In the second phase of work, the design program and designs for the Play Zoo and Play Gardens were developed. Once the draft design program and schematic

design of building renovation and landscape were complete, a rough cost estimate was produced. It indicated that the project was substantially over budget.

Understandably, as the team knew that the running cost of the Play Zoo would be greater than the existing children's zoo, some team members remained skeptical of the "play concept." They still had difficulty envisioning the concept in practice and needed reassurance that it would work.

At this point, the team suggested the idea of prototyping—a common approach in the development of zoo exhibits. A one-week prototyping program was set up with zoo visitors, covering both outdoor and indoor settings, using spaces available in and around the building. Prototyping involves setting up a temporary exhibit or experience to test a design before it is actually built. Based on the prototyping results, the design is modified as appropriate, or it is not built because it did not meet expectations.

The prototyping program was the turning point of the project. The public reaction was extremely positive, as documented by the zoo research staff. The enthusiastic smiles and visitor comments were strong indicators of encouragement to proceed. Observations of user response helped refine the design of several settings and articulate programmatic requirements. The size of the building and the scope of some settings were value engineered. An acceptable cost estimate eventually emerged. Design development was completed. Construction documents and building construction followed. After painful cost-cutting and a strenuous fundraising period, the project opened in 2000.

Settings are designed to include all ages, from infants to adults.

UNIVERSAL DESIGN AND ADA REQUIREMENTS

In a family-focused facility, should *all* settings be usable by all age groups—even infants? The design team concluded, "yes." Any other arrangement would inevitably segregate family members from each other; whoever is "looking after the baby" is going to get left out of the action. For that reason, accommodations for infants and toddlers were designed into each setting.

By the same token, care was taken to design each setting as a family-friendly environment. This was achieved on the one hand by making sure opportunities for adults and children to *play together*

Access requirements mandated by the Americans with Disabilities Act (ADA) were applied as a design variable or were interpreted for situations not covered by the ADA.

Within the realm of the ADA, changes in level presented the greatest design challenge. For example, design of a "tree-house" setting was explored early on. An elevated ramp would have made the tree-house accessible. However, the amount of space occupied and installation cost in relation to its capacity (i.e., number of playing children at any one time), value-engineered it out of the program.

But in its place, at a much lower cost, came a miniature "forest maze." This element was added not to comply with ADA, but because of the commitment to universal design principles. The forest maze was installed connecting directly to the accessible route via a narrow, wood mulch path—more challenging to access by wheelchair but potentially usable by all visitors. The maze was scaled to preschool children and placed

Parents get involved in the action, too, such as making habitats.

were provided (supporting the third goal of the Play Zoo). On the other hand, accommodations were made to ensure that caregivers (a weary grandparent, for example) could withdraw from the action for a while, stay on the sidelines, and enjoy observing children playing. Provision of choices for both engagement and disengagement is a key inclusive design principle in family settings.

in the same vicinity as other settings for this age group, easily accessible by caregivers, and more usable than the treehouse by a broader range of visitors. In addition, while many caregivers would have been apprehensive about allowing young preschoolers out of sight playing in a treehouse, they could keep tabs on them more easily in the maze.

Other design variables not discussed here, but nonetheless important, include issues of management, maintenance, consumables, materials selection and staff training. All these issues presented trade-offs which needed to be resolved through the design process.

Inclusive Design Features and Settings

Any place that embraces the broad community has great value, especially at this point in human history, when it has become imperative for global human society to understand its dependency on the biosphere. Design that supports that aim is truly inclusive. The broader the spread of shared experience through the community and the deeper the meaning, the greater the possible impact on conserving the planet for future generations.

Inclusive design is a powerful concept that looks beyond accessible design and the prevailing disability focus to embrace the broader realm of social equity and inclusion in design. Fundamentally, inclusive design is design that meets the basic tenets of democracy, which in public environments means social access that does not discriminate between users. This is the function of the great public open spaces and the role of the world's greatest parks and children's learning environments. They share the same social trait: openness to all comers.

PLAY ZOO MAIN ENTRY

The Play Zoo faces the broad lawns of Brookfield Zoo's main axis. The approaching visitor sees the Play Zoo facility from afar and notices immediately an active area in front, enclosed by open railings, festooned with colorful signs and banners. "This must be something special, something different," the new visitor might muse. Signs announce "family," "children," "nature," "learn" and "play!" Closer in, animated children can be seen looking intently at two bulbous, transparent enclosures on each side of the main entrance. The entry message is simple and direct. It says, "all welcome."

A small, natural timber booth has a friendly feel, welcomes visitors, and perhaps even reduces the painful surprise of having to pay extra to enter the Play Zoo. From the entry booth, broad paths sweep around a central "Stroller Park" bringing the visitor to the main doors. The old, stepped entrance plaza was redesigned to accommodate strollers and at the same time provide a generous sloping entrance—easily navigable by all. No more icy steps to tumble down, no more pedestrian "traffic blocks" outside the main door.

The renovated Play Zoo building is surrounded on all four sides by outdoor settings. The building entrance is on the west end just beyond the site entrance and stroller park. The "rear" building entrance is at the other (east) end facing the more extensive outdoor settings. The narrow, sunny, south side is designed as a Bug Walk, full of perennial flowering plants. The north side is the site of Animal Homes Adventure Play, under huge elm and maple trees.

Animal settings, enclosed with light steel netting, bulge out on each side of the main building entrance—on one side, playful lemurs; on the other, noisy Lory birds. Entering visitors receive immediate live animal cues about the essence of the Play Zoo.

For security reasons, all visitors enter and leave the building at one of two points (of course, additional emergency

The attractive boundary fence expresses a sense of security as parents with young children approach the entry.

exits are available). What is the social effect of few entries and exits versus many? Perceptually, single nodal entry and exit points produce a clear mental image connected to the rest of the zoo. Socially, all visitors share the same spaces and the comings and goings of each other. While waiting or taking a rest, all have the same possibility of making conversation with a neighbor sitting on one of several sitting walls near the entrance. An open site without a boundary fence would not afford these social opportunities. Psychologically, parents feel safer knowing their children are in a bounded space and can be easily tracked.

INDOOR PEDESTRIAN SETTINGS

The design team hotly debated the stroller issue. The fact is, strollers take up lots of space inside zoo buildings—space that could be used by visitors and programs. Indeed, they were not allowed in other Brookfield Zoo exhibit buildings. The design team argued that a Play Zoo would attract so many families with strollers that the quality of the experience of all would be lessened by navigating through bunches of strollers. A positive consequence of this policy has been that all children who can walk or toddle do so, in a fully bounded safe environment with varied floor surfaces, innumerable small cul-de-sac spaces to explore off the main circulation routes,

and visual interest at low eye level.

As the Play Zoo design was executed before the issue of children's increasingly sedentary life styles hit the national press, this benefit was not appreciated until later. Now, the Play Zoo can be viewed as contributing to the solution of this health problem. Emphasizing pedestrian activity of toddlers and preschoolers is essential, instead of encouraging "wheeled mobility" habits by unnecessarily keeping young children in strollers at an early age. What could be more universal, equitable and democratic than an environment where everyone who can must walk?

WAYFINDING

Wayfinding is crucial for new visitors to a complex environment. Immediately after entering the Play Zoo's main entrance airlock, visitors face three choices: left, right or straight ahead. Only once, for the first visit, are the sensory circumstances of this choice relevant and important. Wayfinding success helps define the first impression of the

Bold, colorful graphics, created by Brookfield Zoo staff, add playful expression.

place for, at least, the adult visitor. Parents who have a successful first visit will return.

Signs reinforce the choices: left ("Reptile Run" and "Bird Play") and right ("Lemur Leap"). Straight ahead the "Mountain" rises up, dominating the central, glazed roofed area. Here, wayfinding offers three choices: into the Mountain or along either side of it.

Signage reinforces the identity of each setting. As visitors move around, uniquely styled signs and expressive

Words are recognizable as objects (differentiated by word shape, color, texture and material) and serve as a system of landmarks that help guide visitors through the space.

This sign simply announces a grove of trees.

Signage is part of the identity of each setting.

Signage incorporates expressive children's drawings.

What child hasn't drawn in the mud?

The rustic pet play area holds bunnies and guinea pigs.

custom graphics identify each setting. The "Garden Play" sign looks very different from the "Workshop" sign. Bold and easy to read, these words are recognizable as objects (differentiated by word shape, color, texture and material) and thus serve as a system of landmarks that help guide visitors through the space. This attribute of identity helps children with learning disabilities and partially sighted children by increasing the perceptual function and reducing the cognitive burden of wayfinding.

ZOO-WITHIN-A-ZOO

Zoo-Within-A-Zoo presents children with opportunities to experience aspects of running the bigger Brookfield Zoo—it's not called the "real" zoo, because the Play Zoo is also real. The universal message throughout is "anyone can do it."

In the Zoo Director's Office, children sit behind the director's desk pretending to give and take calls, and issue instructions.

In the Workshop, children and adults can collaborate on construction and exhibit design projects—making signs, animal sculptures, cultural artifacts linked to the zoo, and other imaginable items.

In the Animal Hospital, children can care for plush animals, invent illnesses and cures, conduct surgical procedures, check x-rays, and look up computer animal health records. Everyone is included as a participant.

Even the insides of animals come alive for older children.

A child becomes a zoo worker.

Collectively, in their dramatic play and imaginations, the children are running the zoo. Each of these settings—Director's Office, Workshop and Hospital—is universally appealing and inclusive because of the setting flexibility of movable features and loose parts. These characteristics provide many dramatic play options for all types of children regardless of developmental level, physical ability, personality, mother tongue and gender. In a corner of the Animal Hospital, a four-year-old is quietly examining a plush rabbit with a stethoscope, while a group of girls scurry around organizing a "surgical procedure" on one of the operating tables. In the Workshop, half a dozen children from different family groups are making masks for an "animal parade."

The most universally expressive, dramatic play activity is pretending to be an animal, which also most directly supports the Play Zoo educational

In the Workshop, children can make all manner of zoo-related artifacts.

mission. Prepared loose part props (lemur tails, bird wings and the face-painting station) stimulate young children's animal role-playing.

The lemur exhibit takes inclusive design into a new domain of integration of exotic animals and children. The concept was solidified in the prototyping phase when children expressed great enthusiasm for being in the cage with the animals. Glazed panels subdivide the outdoor enclosure of Lemur Leap—one for lemurs and the other for children

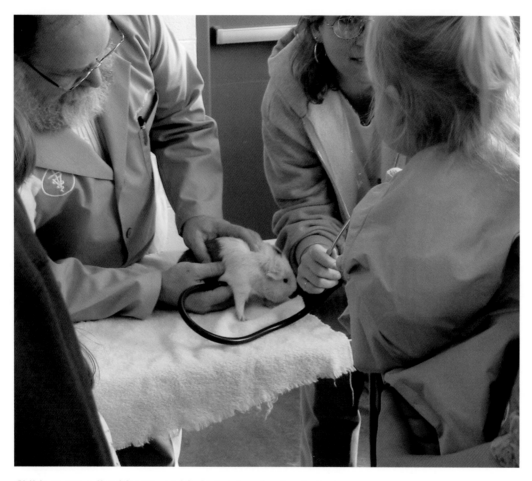
Children can talk with vets and help treat real animals, too.

playing like lemurs. At feeding time, little food treats are hidden by the keepers for the lemurs to find. This always attracts crowds of curious children and stimulates fun lemur play.

Dramatic play activity with loose parts provides special opportunities for adults and children to play together creatively, bolstered by an ambience that gives adults permission to step outside the constraining frame of reference of everyday life at home. Some families come to the Play Zoo every week and always find or invent something new to do. Part of the attraction is the emphasis on full-body play, like the nest building at the Lory bird exhibit. A permanent nest-shaped armature is turned into a "real" nest with loose parts that simulate nest-building materials. Giant bird eggs liberate imaginations as children play mommy and daddy bird, sitting on the eggs, hatching young chicks, teaching

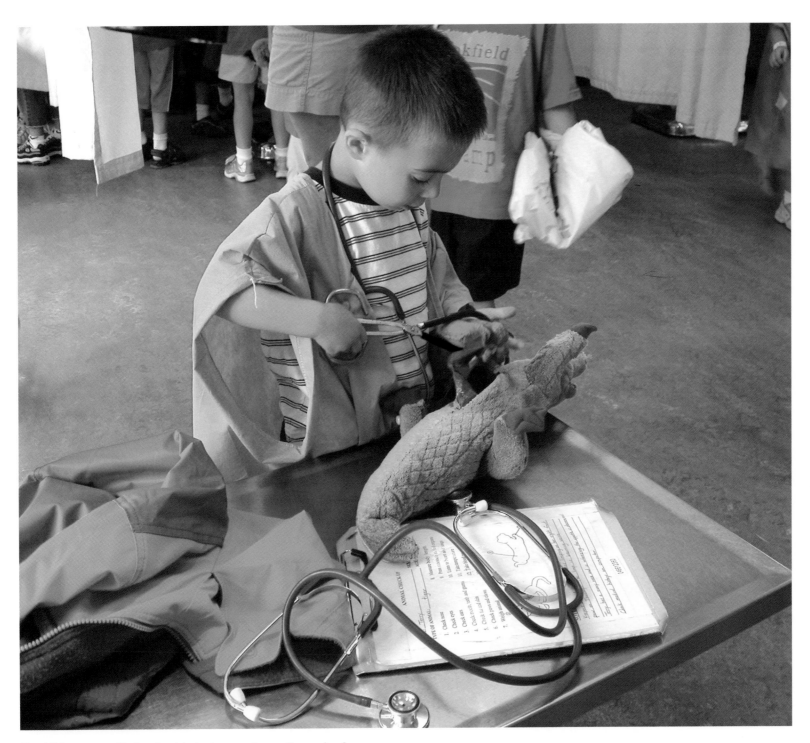

To children, a stuffed animal is just as real as a live animal.

Children can climb into the nest and help "hatch" eggs.

Parents feed "worms" to the "birds" in the nest.

first flight, and away we go! A child using a wheelchair joins in the nest building. Helped out of her chair, she becomes the mother bird in the nest. Another child lets friends bind his chair up like a nest, an egg in his lap.

Full-body play is more participatory and inclusive than traditional tabletop games or games of physical skill that inevitably discriminate against the less skilled. All children have imagination. This is the key ingredient that brings them together.

Inside the Mountain, behind-the-scenes, children experience the backside of animal tanks and cages. They can sweep the floor and begin to appreciate what's involved in creating the public view of animal exhibits. Again, the setting is inclusive. All can participate and define their own role, their own level of comfort. The other end of the Mountain terminates in a small gathering and demonstration setting, which is open to all.

Children get a taste of behind-the-scenes work in animal cages.

Children make packages of "food" for the animals.

fireplace provide glimpses of the outdoor settings, beckoning further fun.

During the design process, this setting took the longest time to resolve. The design team agreed unanimously that linking the Play Zoo and home was fundamental. But how to do it? What style of house? Inner-city apartment? Townhouse? Suburban ranch? Working-class or middle-class, or both? And what about ethnic expression? These fundamental questions of inclusive design were difficult to resolve. The final décor is best described as an eclectic, uncluttered background to the real action: children's play.

Architecturally, the front of the home has an attractive inclusive design feature, the quintessential, classless element of North American domestic architecture—a porch. Here, parents can rest their feet and chat with a neighbor while children enjoy pet play indoors. The

ZOO-AT-HOME

As its name implies, Zoo-At-Home is all about domestic pets. A front porch and rocking chairs welcome visitors. Inside, cats and dogs visit. Children can build habitat trails for gerbils on a large, low, edged tabletop. A walk-in play aquarium invites children to play like fish while playmates on the outside interact. Cats play behind a screened backdoor to the kitchen. Windows on either side of the

Zoo-At-Home looks like a home, with a quintessential American porch.

Domestic animals link the zoo to animals at home.

Inside the living room, children design "habitrails" for gerbils.

A walk-in aquarium invites children to become fish.

The Nature Swap area is designed like a child's bedroom.

Older children classify and collect natural items in the Nature Swap area.

The Greenhouse offers fun-filled warmth on a cold Chicago day.

The Greenhouse extends to an outdoor garden where children can help grow plants and take seedlings home.

Nature Swap is a subsetting of Zoo-At-Home, added later after a member of the design team saw it at another institution. For the upper age level of the Play Zoo target audience, the Nature Swap responds to a desire to collect and classify the natural world—like all good scientists. In this case, natural objects become the universal medium of curiosity that brings children together to share knowledge. The Swap Shop décor is arranged like a child's bedroom, carefully assembled with a non-gendered style.

THE GREENHOUSE

In response to the harsh Chicago winter, part of the concept of Indoor Garden Play was to attract winter visitors to the Play Zoo by providing a warm green place. This spot is open to all, especially those without time or money for a winter trip to southern latitudes.

How to make a garden setting functionally accessible and usable by all? Care was taken to ensure plants were installed at various heights above the floor level so visitors from preschoolers to adults could make tactile contact. To accommodate infants and toddlers

Children are encouraged to touch and water plants.

whose parents were apprehensive about them putting soil and vegetation in their mouths, a play deck was installed in one corner near the Garden Play entrance, furnished with appropriate play objects fashioned from natural materials. Families were thus accommodated in a way that allowed older siblings to play freely.

Spray bottles are very popular. Varied heights of tabletops provide access for children of different heights and those in wheelchairs.

Functional access for children participating in planting and other tabletop activities with plants was accommodated by a wonderful feature invented by the zoo staff: a great slab of thick particle board cut into a fun, amoeba-like shape and supported on a slice of old tree trunk. The height is suitable for wheelchairs, which works fine for most standing children (or they stand on boosters).

One loose part universally enjoyed by children of all ages is a simple spray bottle. Some children do nothing else in Garden Play except go around spraying every plant in sight. How can this behavior be explained? The answer most likely is a combination of factors: the cause-and-effect delight of the spray bottle function, the sensory stimulation of the interaction of misty water and light, the intriguing change in state from liquid to mist, the further intrigue of mist turning to droplets on the shiny leaves, the sense of control over the whole process, and the satisfaction of caring for the plants by watering. Any child whose index finger is strong enough can participate in bottle spraying. And if not, ball-like spray devices are available that can be squeezed with the whole hand. They are especially useful for participants in the zoo's intergenerational playgroup when preschoolers and seniors play together in the Greenhouse.

PARENT RESOURCE AREAS AND QUIET ALCOVES

Two settings, Parent Resource Areas and Quiet Alcoves, are repeated throughout the Play Zoo and serve several purposes. Both function as gathering points, as minor nodes.

Parent Resource Areas are located at seven indoor and outdoor settings and serve as informational landmarks where parents can read permanent graphics

The Backyard of Zoo-At-Home offers information for families...

...and a resting place.

about the importance of play and tips for playing at the zoo.

As this base information is fundamental to the philosophy of the Play Zoo, repeated outlets reinforce a sense of shared meaning of the place among the adult visitors to take away and continue to work with at home. Shared, universal experiences and meanings tie communities together, and increase our understanding of the interconnectedness of life. The broader the spread of shared experience throughout the community, the greater the likelihood of shared environmental values.

Quiet Alcoves have a more modest aim: rest and recuperation, a universal need. These are places where families and small groups can get away from high-level activity, places to nurse a baby or feed a toddler. Open to all, Quiet Alcoves offer additional visitor opportunities for building shared

values that come from positive social contact in an environment that symbolizes those values.

ZOO PLAY GARDENS

Outdoors, the Zoo Play Gardens comprise six main settings and fourteen subsettings. There are four entrances. From the Main Entry Plaza, visitors can bypass the Play Zoo and go directly to Animal Homes Adventure Play (left) or Bug Walk (right). Alternatively, one can enter from the other end of the Play Zoo or directly via the South Plaza Entry.

Wayfinding outdoors at either end of the Play Zoo building is direct. At the front (west) end, visitors can go left or right. At the back (east) end, the same choices are offered plus a central pathway (which eventually will connect with Phase 2 of Explore! A Child's Nature).

ANIMAL HOMES ADVENTURE PLAY

This setting supports the play philosophy of Explore! A Child's Nature in its most classic form: adventure play using loose materials to construct shelters, in this case for animals. Since this is an open-ended activity, anyone can join in and lead it wherever collective desires go. Above all others, this is the setting that became better understood by the design team through prototyping. Once the team saw the adventure play process in action, they understood the potential for engagement and inclusion. Anyone can join in, like a barn-raising—the more the merrier. The only limit is human imagination. Three children roof one of the cubicles used to store building materials with tree branches. They are making a tiger cage. One, her face painted with tiger whiskers (from the indoor face painting), puts on her fiercest expression and growls. She "eats" a small wooden log in the cubicle and paces back and

Building animal homes encourages cooperative play.

Children enjoy inhabiting the new animal homes.

There's no limit to materials that can be used.

Even the youngest visitor can enjoy pounding away.

Children can find secret places for a moment of calm.

forth on all fours, tiger-like. Almost nothing is required to set such imaginative processes in motion, except a few rudimentary props. Adventure Play is not a new idea, but for the first time, it has been applied in a children's zoo. (The Playgrounds for Children with Special Needs in the United Kingdom have applied the adventure play approach successfully for more than 40 years.)

BUG WALK

On the other (south) side of the Play Zoo, a richly planted perennial garden offers a sensory walk replete with insects of many types, depending on the season. "Lift-ups" (boxes planted in the raised bed with lids that house the bug collection) offer critters that like damp, dark places underground. An elevated pool offers dragonflies and their cousins that love damp places. A curvy, living willow tunnel engulfs

Spiderman is spotted in the willow tunnel!

Ladybugs bring good luck—the more the merrier.

Children investigate leaf litter on the ground, looking for bugs.

The dark cavity of a "Lift-up" offers insects in their natural habitat.

And why not *be* a butterfly in the garden?

children in vegetation. The Bug Walk is a quiet spot for reverie, where children are engaged by the colors, fragrances, textures and movement of a myriad of flowers. Because of its quietness and sensory richness, the Bug Walk is a favorite destination of autistic children and their caregivers.

BACKYARD

Eight subsettings comprise the Backyard, which is intended to have a domestic feel so that caring behaviors can be transferred and modeled at home. "Backyard" means different things to different people. Casual observation on a warm, sunny afternoon indicates happy, family enjoyment. A grandfather, his pant legs rolled up, is padding back and forth in the stream with his granddaughter, perhaps recalling similar childhood pleasures—a beautiful example of universal design spanning the generations. The feel of running water

The Backyard stream is a favorite setting on hot summer days.

Children can wade in the water and play with small rocks.

Parents sit on boulders while children play in the Earth Play Garden.

The dirt is a mix of peat moss and sand so children don't get too muddy.

on naked feet is elemental. At one and the same time, it is a delicious sensory experience, perhaps experienced for the first time by a very young child. Sharing across generations adds immeasurable value.

Meanwhile, on the Demonstration Lawn, a group has been called together by one of the Play Partners to "celebrate life." Adults and children lie on their backs in a circle, stand up, move to a tree and stand around it holding hands. It is a beautiful sight. Strangers ten minutes ago, children and adults now trust each other's affirmation of life. The Play Partner receives an affirmation as well: that the risk she took to lead this activity paid off. Participants feel enriched and empowered with an increased sense of shared Play Zoo values. Maybe they will be stronger protectors of the planet.

Along one side of the Demonstration Lawn, zoo staff installed a series of small window boxes (6" x 6" x 12") at different heights on a lattice fence to create a raised garden accessible to seniors and preschoolers doing planting activities together.

In the Earth Play Garden, parents sit on a circle of large boulders while their toddler-aged children play in the enclosed "play soil" (a specially concocted non-soil mix of peat moss and sand to prevent very young children from getting too muddy). An elevated wheelchair accessible play table is part of the installation.

Pet Play is another universal experience for young children; what more needs to be said? Everyone can be involved. The main problem is not to overstress the animals. For this reason, a holding pen where the bunnies and guinea pigs can rest is located alongside the public enclosure where the playing takes place.

A pre-existing natural feature of the Play Gardens is the Woody Knoll, a tree-covered hillock on the eastern boundary of the site. Invasive shrubs were cleared off to reveal the form of the hill, and a circle of logs was installed on the summit. There are two ways up: a direct climb up a large log laid on the side of the hill with steps notched out, and a longer, ramped pathway, winding around the back of the hill. Liz Heller, a wheelchair-using zoo intern, noted that she could access the pathway to the top of the hill using a manual wheelchair with help and with a power chair independently.

PROGRAMMING ELEMENTS

In association with the Illinois Autism Society, Ann Roth, Access Coordinator,

A collection of fall leaves becomes a work of art.

helped design a Visual Schedule Book for families with autistic children as a tool to help with communication. Autistic children are nonverbal, but can communicate visually. The book looks a bit like a stamp album, with movable icons representing each play setting. Child and family members use the book to plan the Play Zoo trip, as well as for deciding changes in the schedule once there. As autistic children often have difficulty transitioning from one activity to another, the toolbook is used as a reference to keep things on track. For the Reptile Run setting, for example, there are photos of all the items needed to build a "herp home," so the activity can be reviewed pictorially step-by-step beforehand. Similarly, the toolbook is used to introduce putting on a tail at Lemur Leap or doing things in the Animal Hospital. The idea is to use the book for practice a few times, then wean individual children away from it into a more independent realm of behavior.

Management and Operational Issues

During the initial stages of the master planning process, Brookfield Zoo made an impressive commitment to supporting a Play Partner Troupe because it was seen as an essential component to implement the Play Zoo mission. The operational economic equation was a challenge, one side of which must be measured by the number of admissions. The books must balance. The Play Zoo enhances the larger zoo's reputation and visibility, which is an added value. Most importantly, the Play Zoo appears to be addressing its mission. This is indicated by visitor behavioral research conducted during the summer of 2003. Preliminary results show child visitors exhibit significant levels of "caring behavior."

Nursing the new landscape was a management challenge at Explore! A Child's Nature. Because interaction with nature is fundamental to the mission, the installed landscape contains many more horticultural species than is typical in other Brookfield Zoo exhibits (even though they are well endowed with attractive landscape treatments). The zoo has a fine professional horticultural staff with decades of landscape management experience, who enthusiastically rose to the challenge of nursing the establishment of the new Explore! A Child's Nature landscape. Existing plantings were conserved in the new play settings or moved from other locations to provide a foundation of older plantings.

The south side of Bug Walk was more challenging, as the landscape was completely new. But after two growing seasons, the perennial gardens were well established. Lack of shade was a major problem in the hot Illinois summer. This was addressed by adding two large shade trees on the south side of the walkway. The original design had included a number of wide arbors over the walkway as shading devices, but these were omitted as a cost-saving measure. They could still be installed to add further shade and extend the diversity of Bug Walk plantings.

Consumables can easily become a significant cost factor in play-based programs. During the design-programming phase, this issue was carefully monitored, so that only essential consumables were designed in. For example, plush animals had to be available as play props in the Hospital. Although not strictly a consumable, they wear out fast and have to be replaced. In Animal Homes Adventure Play, only scrap materials are used, including recycled prunings from the horticulture department. The Workshop uses paper and paint that must be purchased, but also all manner of recycled "scrap" (cardboard, cans, plastic bottles, lumber, etc.). Greenhouse consumables include seeds and planting mix that children take home in (recycled) pots.

The most substantial management issue by far is the use of live animals with children. The main considerations are the health and safety of both children and animals. Having operated a children's zoo since the 1950s, the Play Zoo staff had extensive experience in these areas. That history helped enormously to deal with these issues during the design phase, but still much time was required to make final decisions about specific species and their environmental requirements. For example, sanitation requirements for Pet Play meant using concrete that could be hosed down each day as a substrate with straw.

Play Partners are trained to handle the floor animals in Reptile Run, Zoo-At-Home and Pet Play. Partners walk or carry animals around on a regular schedule, so that hands-on animal experiences are always available on the floor as well as in the permanent exhibits (Lemur Leap, Lory Bird, Reptile Run and the Mountain).

Play Partners will help plan a family's visit and provide tools they'll need.

Liz Heller: "It's useful for people to see someone in a wheelchair working...."

User Feedback

The zoo has been open for four years, with many visitors making multiple visits—some even come every week.

Dave Fuentes, Chicago Area Parent

"…The whole project sounded silly. An exhibit without a lot of animals? Who wants to see that? How is that going to help children understand the importance of nature?

"I took my wife and children to the exhibit's employee premiere…My children played away, uninterested in what the adults thought. Leia, my three-year-old, began talking about lemurs. We bought her a play lemur tail from the zoo and she wore it all the time…When relatives and friends asked her what she was, she would yell, 'A lemur! I made it better!' When asked to explain, she would simply restate, 'I made it better!'

"(On another visit) Leia began working with a stuffed owl. After several minutes she yelled, 'Dada! I made it better!' That's when it clicked…There, in my snapshots (from the first visit), was a photograph of Leia wearing a lab coat and holding a stethoscope to a stuffed lemur's heart. Although it had been over a year ago, she remembered that she had indeed 'made it better.'

"That one visit to the Hamill Family Play Zoo affected one of my children enough that she not only learned to love the animal, but believe that she could make a difference in its life! She never had to hear the words 'endangered,' 'extinct,' or 'killed.' In a two-year-old's world, a stuffed animal is as alive as a real one is. Through her play she had felt empowered and was not made to feel helpless, as a lecture on animal endangerment might have made her. I am a true convert."

Liz Heller, Intern

Liz Heller started volunteering at Explore! A Child's Nature as a high school student when the facility opened in 2000. Earlier, she was a manual wheelchair user but now uses a power chair. Asked about the working environment at Explore! A Child's Nature, she was mostly very complimentary. She mentioned the low cabinets that were easy to use. Even in a manual chair she said it was "easy to get around," including the outdoors, which she said was "well done, with flat, easy grades."

She made specific mention of the occasional drop in level where concrete path and lawn come together as a problem. She noted the woodchip ground surface in Animal Homes Adventure Play that she could not access in a manual chair without help. "I can live with that," she said, recognizing that the setting needed to feel natural (the pervious surface was also critical for the health of the mature trees in that zone).

She commented that, "Everyone is so caring here, and willing to help—but are subtle about it." Heller also reflected on her experiences as a worker at the zoo. "It's useful for people to see someone in a wheelchair working, it's good exposure. It helps counter their preconceptions."

Summing up, Heller noted that "Explore! A Child's Nature has taken the concept of universal access further than most places. It is open to everything. I love working here, it is so great."

Ann Roth, Brookfield Zoo, Access Coordinator

"As all the basic ADA-type access issues were already covered in the design of the Play Zoo, I have been able to devote my energies to responding to the special needs of specific audiences in different program areas.

"The Play Zoo is built for all the senses, so some of the classes we do are very attractive to children with sight disabilities." Roth mentioned a class called "How Things Are Wrapped," which deals with all types of animal coverings. Children handle samples, as well as live animals (snakes, turtles, bunnies). The class is open to all children. "Sight-impaired kids love it," she said.

"Hard of Hearing Days" is a zoo-wide event for which zoo staff are trained in basic sign language. This means signing is going on in the Play Zoo with the Play Partners, which makes it more attractive and comfortable to the deaf culture. "The Play Partners love that stuff," Roth comments. She describes the "Good Works Program," which enables students with disabilities to volunteer at the zoo. Some have cognitive impairments; some are deaf. "Job Coaches" help participants train to get jobs (at the zoo and elsewhere). "The Play Zoo is an ideal place for children with disabilities," Roth emphasizes, "because there is so much going on."

David Becker, Play Manager

"The Play Zoo has developed a strong internal partnership with the Zoo's access programs. Several factors make this possible. Because principles of universal design have been applied to the space itself, it is user-friendly for a variety of visitors including families. The space encourages open-ended exploration, which creates a powerful context for program development and facilitation of learning. In the world-renowned Reggio Emilia schools, the educators refer to the built environment as 'the third teacher.'

"Similarly, the Play Zoo functions in collaboration with the Play Partners, who are equally important in enabling a growing collaboration with the zoo's access programs. It is the staff that activates the space and pushes it beyond the surface potential. Beyond creative programming, Play Partners are committed to creating relationships. To this end, they facilitate interactions between families and nature, support family interactions with each other and become a part of the place attachment that families develop with the Play Zoo. This highly individualized process extends equally to families who have children with disabilities because they know their child will be valued when they visit. This is incredibly empowering for everyone."

The Play Zoo is built for all the senses.

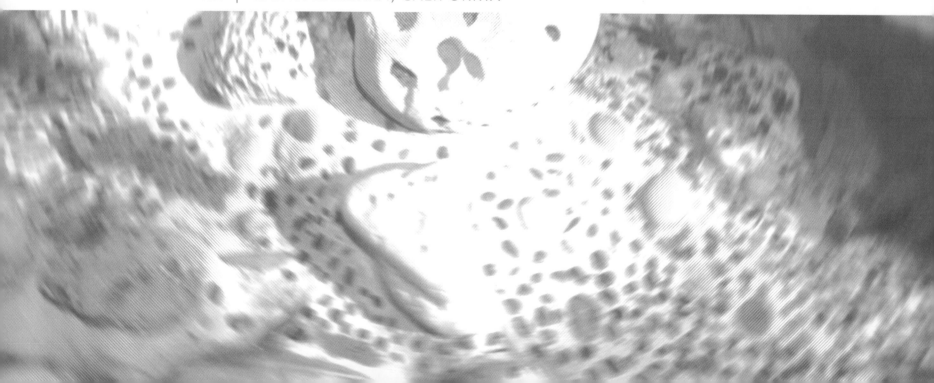

CHASE PALM PARK | SANTA BARBARA, CALIFORNIA

"This park has been adopted into the community's heart....it's a town square right on the waterfront."

CITY OF SANTA BARBARA LANDSCAPE ARCHITECT

ADOPTING A NEW HEART

SUSAN GOLTSMAN

THIS HIGHLY USED PARK WAS ONCE A DERELICT PIECE OF UNUSED LAND, THE LAST BIT OF open space in the City of Santa Barbara, California. Chase Palm Park is now a nine-acre linear park with a one-acre children's play area. It's located across the roadway from the beach, adjacent to railroad tracks, with views of Santa Barbara's golden hills. The park land was given to the City as a trade-off for an expanded development at the nearby resort and conference center.

The City wanted a play area that would serve as a community focal point and link to the ocean. The new play area setting contains an underwater garden of sea life, a full-size pod of anatomically correct whales spouting water, sea caves, a marooned village, a large shipwreck, a lighthouse with kaleidoscope, fishing pier, and docks with the façade of a child-sized City of Santa Barbara in the background.

The park includes many community uses such as a gathering plaza adjacent to a restored historic carousel, a lawn area, a small stage for community events and a park support building (for storage and rentals) across from the play area. The play area and park are linked by a pedestrian path (the paseo) and stream "creeklets" that wind through. The creeklets are a unifying design element of the park and are part of the overall drainage system.

DESIGN GOALS

The play area facilitates recreational programming and stimulates children's imaginations. Thematic settings help children learn about the general context and character of their city through play. Play elements have a strong marine character and are tied to local historical and cultural events.

Park and recreational programming is integral to the project. The play area is more than just play equipment. The recreation staff have support facilities adjacent to the play area, especially needed for public attendance at summer day camps. The entire park provides a great setting for play programming, imaginative play and community gathering. For example, summer evening concerts draw 4,000 to 5,000 people to hear music and play in the park.

USER GROUPS
- Children
- Adults
- Schoolteachers (local field trips)
- Tourists

PROJECT Chase Palm Park—Children's Play Area   LOCATION Santa Barbara, California   DATE DESIGNED 1997–1998   CONSTRUCTION COMPLETED 1998   CONSTRUCTION COST $500,000   SIZE 9 acres (entire park); 1 acre (play area)   CLIENT City of Santa Barbara   PLAY AREA LANDSCAPE ARCHITECT AND DESIGN PROGRAMMER MIG, Inc.   PARK DESIGN George Girvin Associates   ARTISTS Susan Jordan and Scott Peterson   CIVIL ENGINEERS Penfield & Smith

The children's play area in Chase Palm Park is based on a marine life theme and includes elements such as this giant nautilus and the wave wall behind it with a fish emerging.

Children developed the idea of including a shipwreck to play on.

The design team worked with local artists to develop a design concept for the park that reflects the City and the site's history, including a shipwreck that once occurred off the coast. The artists developed sculptural elements that are both artistic and functional.

During one brainstorming session, a desire to create a whale quickly became "an entire pod of whales swimming through the park."

Recreational programming was considered throughout the design process. The design team worked with the Parks and Recreation Department to develop an activity program for recreation leaders to use during summer day camp sessions. The park lends itself to creating theme-based programs and activities such as making treasure maps, dressing like pirates for a day, and making telescopes to explore the shipwreck play area.

DESIGN PROCESS

The design team was selected through a design competition. The project included design programming, conceptual design, participation by children as well as community members, and play area design and development. Santa Barbara's Parks and Recreation Department went into classrooms to talk with schoolchildren about their ideas for the park. Based on the input from these children, the play and learning environment was designed with the theme of life in and by the sea.

Inclusive Design Features and Settings

Accessibility and connections are integrated and expanded in a thematic way throughout the park. For example, the blue "ocean" rubberized safety surfacing serves as a context for the whales and provides an accessible pathway through the play area. This design element provides more than a walkway or ramp up to a play element. It integrates access for everyone into the theme of the play area. Transfer platforms are more than single-purpose assistive devices; they are integrated into the theme and the sitting areas and are usable by all kinds of people.

OCEAN PATHWAY AND A POD OF WHALES

A pathway of blue rubberized safety surfacing meanders through the play area to define the ocean. The pod of sculptural whales flows through the park at various points throughout the ocean pathway. The whales are realistic and true to form and size, but the materials are expressed artistically and creatively. The whales swim in the ocean around the shipwreck, enhancing the theme. They breach and curve throughout the play area and sporadically spray water through their blowholes, adding an interactive element of surprise.

Full-size whales swim through the area.

Randomly timed water spouts add a surprising and entrancing element as whales swim through blue rubberized safety surfaces.

features: a raised nautilus with tide pools and a fish head fountain that spouts water into a basin. The nautilus simulates a tide pool experience and is completely accessible because the tide pools and water are raised. A concrete wave wall curves up overhead like the curl of a wave and provides seating for parents.

The starfish is a three-dimensional, oversized sculpture in the sand, coated in rubberized safety surfacing. It serves two purposes: it is a play element that supports the theme, and it is a place to sit and play in the sand. The starfish offers back support for small children with limited upper body strength, or a slightly elevated place to sit for parents who don't want to sit in the sand.

PLAY VILLAGE/FISHING PIER

The play village and fishing pier serve as a reference to the City. Located on the side of the park adjacent to the community, they add the look and feel of Santa Barbara. The play village, based on tradi-

Children wait by the whales to catch the water spray.

The whales serve as climbing objects and as transfer points onto the grass. They're integrated with seat walls to provide points of access and transfer. Some whales are not accessible but still add to the variety of experiences. The whales also tie the play area into the rest of the park, because some of the whales actually sit on the turf, entering and exiting the play area.

SAND AND WATER PLAY AREA

In this area, children explore and manipulate sand. There are two water

This whale is about to breach as a mother sits on the back of the wave wall.

The nautilus is completely accessible.

Rocks in the nautilus are similar to those found in tidepools.

A spouting fish is an interactive water element.

An oversized starfish provides opportunities for climbing and sitting and to play in the sand.

Local artist Susan Jordan painted a mural of the Santa Barbara mountains and foothills.

The child-size play village is based on the architecture of Santa Barbara.

tional Santa Barbara building façades, is like a stage set: stucco building façades are set at angles so children can imagine their own settings. Local artist Susan Jordan also painted a mural on the adjacent sound wall to create a backdrop to

the play village that looks like the mountains behind Santa Barbara. The setting inspires imaginative play—children pretend the buildings are storefronts and homes while interacting with parents and play leaders.

CREEKLETS

The creeklets are veins of boulder-lined channels that run through the park. They are especially popular in the summertime for small children and parents who sit nearby and talk. They are closely linked

to the play village, enhancing their programmatic contributions. During summer day camps, play leaders seed the creeklets with "gold-plated" rocks. They set up an assay office in the play village where the children trade in their gold for some other prize. It encourages children to explore and discover their environment. The play village façades are wheelchair accessible through relatively flat surfaces.

A wood fishing pier extends into the shipwreck play area; it is suggestive of the real pier in Santa Barbara. The pier is wide enough to accommodate wheelchairs. Play leaders put metal fish in the sand around the pier, and children use fishing poles with magnets on the end.

SHIPWRECK PLAYGROUND

The strong theme enhances the opportunities for universal design. From the play village and lighthouse, a ramp

Children love the creeklets and often pan for gold like the '49ers of early California.

Children and play leaders use the play village to role play, such as exchanging gold for prizes at an assay office.

The fishing pier is wide enough to accommodate wheelchairs.

The back of the shipwreck is a wide inclined plane for going down—and climbing up.

slopes down into the play area and a swath of ocean-blue rubberized safety surfacing connects the ramp to the sinking ship. The theme transforms this

entrance route from a single-purpose accessible ramp to an imaginary boat ramp leading into the ocean that everyone can use for play.

The shipwreck climbing structure is the central element of the play area. The play apparatus is tilted to give the impression that it is sinking into the sand. This slanted ship stern is the most active portion of the play structure. Groups of five or six children often work together to form a human chain, holding hands so they can climb up the

slant. Ramps, bridges and ground plane elements are located at multiple levels so children can transfer to the ship from seating areas and from the ocean, and access a variety of play experiences on different parts of the ship. All levels of the ship are wheelchair accessible.

WOODEN POLE FOREST

A quieter area is nestled among eucalyptus trees across the ocean pathway from the shipwreck. Here, a series of vertical wooden poles of varying heights can serve as a framework for construction games and theater sets to be used by the play leaders in summer day camps. The ground surface is engineered wood fibre—an accessible loose fill material that accommodates wheelchairs.

LIGHTHOUSE AND SEATING AREA

Between the play village and the shipwreck playground is a seating overlook area. Here, parents and caregivers can rest on a bench or steps while they watch their children play. There is also a transfer plank that children can use to access the shipwreck play structure. The lighthouse is designed with enough space inside to accommodate wheelchairs, and children of varying heights can access the handle to turn the light on top.

Children can enter the lighthouse and cooperatively turn the pole to rotate the light.

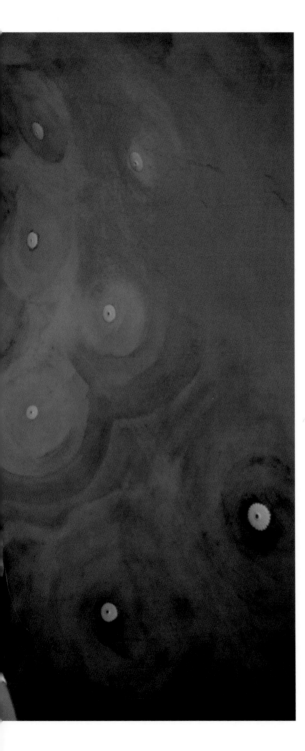

The lighthouse has a prism light, visible from the inside.

Management and Operational Issues

IMAGINATIVE PLAY

Settings that support fantasy play and physical gross motor development present several management and operational challenges if play value is to be maximized. The same regular maintenance and attention to safety is required as a typical playground. However, the park works best with play leaders who engage children in activities and programs that relate to the theme. Play leaders place "gold" in creeks, perform roles and talk with children to inspire play. It can be a challenge to get the play leaders to fully use the settings. The play village, for example, is not as active as other areas. Young children play hide and seek, but without play leaders, the play doesn't progress much beyond that.

DESIGN ELEMENTS

The wooden pole area for younger kids has not functioned as originally intended. The design intent of the forest of poles was to be a flexible retreat space that play leaders could modify by stringing cloth or ribbons from one pole to the next. Now, the poles are more of a curiosity. The balance beam, cargo net and platforms are de facto picnic tables, and places for parents to sit and stash their belongings.

PLAY EQUIPMENT

The designers worked with a play equipment manufacturer to develop the custom shipwreck apparatus. This ensures that the structure complies with current accessibility and safety laws. Two spring play elements have become a problem. The buoy rocker was removed because the spring was too soft

Parents can use the whales for back support while children hitch a ride.

and it was hazardous, while the escape raft spring benches in the shipwreck area are too stiff and don't get enough motion to be an exciting play element.

WATER

Water always presents a management and operational issue in play areas. In Chase Palm Park, some of the water features were experimental. The whale spray needed to be realistic and evocative of real spouting, and still be safe and workable. The plumbing required intricate engineering to adequately handle the water flow so it would not be too forceful.

The expectation was that a park with so much community focus, pride and visibility could afford this higher level of maintenance. Water features need to be tested over a long period of time. The lesson learned is to assume that all maintenance will be performed in-house, and to design with that in mind by specifying parts and maintenance methods that are consistent with a

The spouting fish, by local artist Scott Peterson, is a favorite with small children, and located within easy reach of children using wheelchairs.

maintenance department's operations. Another lesson learned is that a park like this will be so popular and well-used that the normal level of maintenance must be increased.

WORKING WITH ARTISTS

Including artists on the design team adds unique elements to the park. In the design and construction process, working with artists differs from working with trade contractors. Artists' work requires both creative design and fabrication processes beyond typical construction. The City also needed to provide special contracting procedures, insurance and liability for the artists.

For the elements designed by artists to be acceptable in a children's play environment, they must meet all safety, accessibility and maintenance requirements. A greater level of engineering detail (including consideration of maintenance, service and parts required to keep the elements functioning) should be an intentional part of the design process. Ideally, artists will have creative input and then work with an engineer to design the mechanics and prepare the technical drawings required to build and maintain the element.

User Feedback

The following comments are from staff who have used the play area for over three years.

Billy Goodnick, City of Santa Barbara Landscape Architect

"This park has been adopted into the community's heart: family celebrations, weddings, tree dedications to commemorate special events in peoples' lives, and as a destination to show off to visitors. The park provides a needed venue for many daily activities and special events, both public and private. The well-executed design and high caliber of maintenance are a source of pride; a top-notch project creates a higher standard for other community improvements. This park has become the benchmark.

"The community-based design charette was invaluable.... The community's insight was the impetus for a workable design and they got it right. The community process also asked for integrating art into the design, which was successfully achieved by local artists who created a strong sense of place and conveyed Santa Barbara's unique location and character. Santa Barbara is a beach community, but we never had a place to celebrate our strong coastal character. Chase Palm Park provides the equivalent of a multi-use town square, right on the waterfront.

"The totally unique, art-filled play area is a source of hours of play and exploration for children. The summertime creeklets are a huge hit with toddlers and young kids. And there are clutches of kids hanging by the whales, waiting for the spout to go off, which makes the place exciting. There's a lot of fun, wet sand play by the nautilus. Most of the play centers on the sand areas and the shipwreck; not a lot of kids go to the end of the pier, and the wooden poles haven't really worked out.

"The style is a perfect fit with the rest of the distinctive architecture of Santa Barbara and has a timeless feel. All the materials seem to have sprung from one design vision and integrate well with the givens of the site. The final key is that the designers and City staff truly collaborated down to the minute details that allow the park to remain well-maintained without overburdening our perennially tight budgets."

Terri Brown, Assistant Parks and Recreation Supervisor, Youth Activities

"We have programming for ten weeks in the summer. We set the stage up as a frontier village and use the creeklets as part of a frontier village to pan for gold. We trade for play money and set up frontier businesses. The shipwreck lets us create a treasure quest, telling the story of a pirate who left buried treasure. Kids find the map, find treasures and paint their faces like pirates. We can also turn the stage into a circus. During the year, we have other special events, like an egg hunt for thousands of kids."

EDISON SCHOOL/PACIFIC PARK | GLENDALE, CALIFORNIA

"This facility feels like a park, not just a typical school. It's a joy to see kids running and playing tag...just being kids."

PRINCIPAL, EDISON SCHOOL

COMBINING COMMUNITY FACILITIES

SUSAN MCKAY
SUSAN GOLTSMAN

THE NEW EDISON SCHOOL/PACIFIC PARK IS THE RESULT OF A UNIQUE COLLABORATION between the City of Glendale, the Glendale Unified School District and residents of the Edison-Pacific neighborhood. The concept, design and construction were all guided and sustained by local community energy. The school is a community focal point, bustling with activity fifteen hours a day, seven days a week. Residents now enjoy using a new elementary school, library, community center, and a completely renovated and expanded park.

The park facilities include a little league ballpark, multi-purpose field and hard court, children's playground, group picnic area, water play area, and outdoor theater in the

The new community center and public library share many common facilities.
CITY OF GLENDALE

PROJECT Edison School/Pacific Park Revitalization   LOCATION Glendale, California
DATE DESIGNED 1994 (community process began); 1996–1997 (design process)
CONSTRUCTION COMPLETED 2003   CONSTRUCTION COST $26 million
(including land acquisition)   SIZE 9.5 acres   CLIENT City of Glendale and Glendale
Unified School District   NEIGHBORHOOD PLANNING Community Involvement and
MIG, Inc.   DESIGN ARCHITECT Siegel Diamond Architects   ARCHITECT OF
RECORD Leidenfrost/Horowitz & Associates, Inc.   DESIGN LANDSCAPE ARCHITECT
MIG, Inc.   LANDSCAPE ARCHITECT OF RECORD Takata Associates

school playground. The community center also incorporates a special area for youth and teens.

DESIGN GOALS

The City of Glendale faced a set of critical community needs: an old, over-crowded school, the lack of libraries and a park needing renovation. The student population at Edison School is very diverse. Enrollment for the 2002–03 school year was over 800 children in grades kindergarten through 6, with approximately 54 percent Hispanic, 33 percent Caucasian (mainly Armenian immigrants), 6 percent Filipino, 5 percent Asian, and 2 percent African American. About 72 percent of students are English language learners and almost 84 percent are eligible for free or reduced-price meals.

The City decided to enlist the whole community through neighborhood planning, a comprehensive approach that involved the community in the entire planning process. As a result of the three-

Building the new elementary school was fueled by the passion of parents, the school principal and staff.
CITY OF GLENDALE

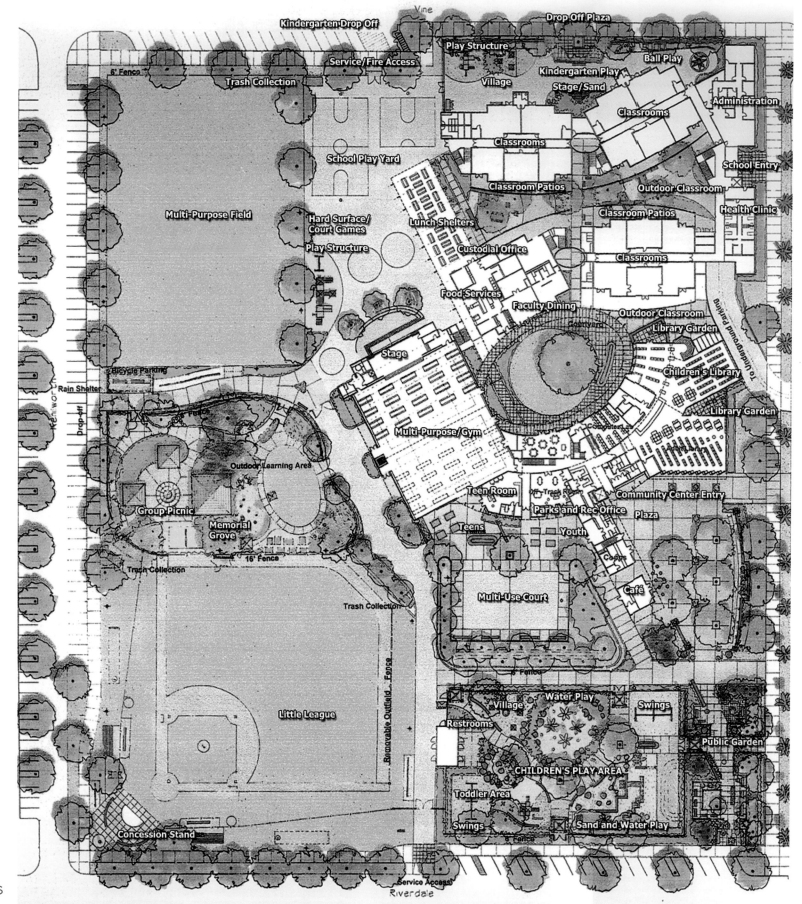

Kindergarten Drop Off
Vine
Drop Off Plaza
Play Structure
Ball Play
Kindergarten Play
Village
Stage/Sand
Service/Fire Access
Administration
Trash Collection
Classrooms
6' Fence
Classrooms
School Entry
School Play Yard
Classroom Patios
Outdoor Classroom
Multi-Purpose Field
Classroom Patios
Health Clinic
Lunch Shelters
Classrooms
Hard Surface/
Court Games
Custodial Office
Play Structure
Food Services
Outdoor Classroom
Faculty Dining
Library Garden
Courtyard
Children's Library
Stage
To Underground Parking
Library Garden
Bicycle Parking
Rain Shelter
Kenilworth
Drop-off
Fence
Outdoor Learning Area
Multi-Purpose/Gym
Group Picnic
Teen Room
Community Center Entry
Memorial
Grove
Parks and Rec Office
Plaza
16' Fence
Teens
Youth
Café
Trash Collection
Multi-Use Court
Trash Collection
Removable Outfield Fence
Water Play
Village
Swings
Restrooms
Public Garden
Little League
CHILDREN'S PLAY AREA
Toddler Area
Swings
Sand and Water Play
Concession Stand
Service Access
Riverdale

176

The school is surrounded by dense urban area. Final siting of buildings and park elements reflected community input.
CITY OF GLENDALE

The fully equipped computer lab is used by the school during the day and by the community in the evenings.
CITY OF GLENDALE

year planning process, the City and the Glendale Unified School District embarked on the joint project. Neither the City nor the school district had enough funds to create two separate facilities. But by pooling and leveraging City and school resources, they achieved sufficient financial capability to create a shared-use facility that could serve the

entire community. The school and adjacent park now share the library, a multi-purpose cafeteria and gymnasium, hard court and turf play areas, and parking. Separate entrances and designated access for the school and for the community facilitate shared use. The mixed-use facility is now the "focal point of identity and activity for

the surrounding residential neighborhood," as stated in the Pacific-Edison model neighborhood plan.

The new Edison Elementary School replaced the existing building with a fully modernized facility. School resources are expanded during school hours with student and staff access to

The conceptual master plan contained a rich and diverse array of community facilities, spaces and amenities.

Many children and youth visit the park after school hours.

Neighborhood residents take advantage of the toddler area, which is open at all times.

the shared-use facilities such as the library, gymnasium, indoor/outdoor stage, athletic fields and food services.

The shared-use Pacific Community Center is designed to serve every age group in the community, from infants to elders. The facility itself includes a multi-purpose gymnasium, game room, computer lab, arts and science room, conference room, and meeting rooms—all of which are used by the school and open to the public during non-school hours. Community members can take a variety of classes and participate in programs such as driver education, English as a second language, parenting and computer classes. Babysitting services are available during class times to encourage participation.

The project also includes a new neighborhood branch of the Glendale Public Library. The Pacific Park Branch Library is open to students during school hours and to the community during non-school hours. Materials at the library are available in the languages represented in the community, including Armenian, Spanish and Korean. Library use is extremely high. In addition to basic reading and book-related services, the library provides a place for children to study after school, job-seeking assistance for community members and health-related materials for seniors.

All areas indoors and outdoors are fully accessible. Buildings and park areas were sited and designed at grade to avoid ramps and stairs. Play areas were designed with accessible play equipment and safety surfacing so that wheelchair users or persons with mobility impairments have access to all play elements.

USER GROUPS

- Preschool children
- Schoolchildren (K–6)
- Teachers
- Staff
- Community members (children, teens, adults, seniors)

Young people use the community center after school and on weekends.

All paths are fully accessible.

The school operates on a year-round calendar so students use the community facilities throughout the year.

DESIGN PROCESS

Neighborhood-based planning brings together all points of view to develop a shared vision for community development. The City of Glendale adopted this inclusive approach for its Strategic Plan process to revitalize neighborhoods Citywide. This process required the active participation of local residents through a neighborhood task force. The City, the school, businesses and community organizations committed their resources to the process. In this case, two usually underrepresented minority communities (Armenian and Mexican) formed a strong coalition. Teachers spoke with students, who in turn got their parents involved. A dynamic principal and staff made parents feel included and involved, and

Armenian and Mexican design motifs on the building façade reflect the ethnic make-up of the neighborhood.
KATE DIAMOND

the community soon became the driving force behind the project. All outreach materials were produced in English, Spanish and Armenian.

The City identified the Edison-Pacific area as a model neighborhood in its Strategic Plan. The City coordinated the project financing and property acquisition, acquiring new parcels within the

A new water play feature replaced the outdated (and expensive!) swimming pool.
CITY OF GLENDALE

This mature heritage oak tree was preserved, becoming a focal point of the courtyard. Some classrooms and labs, as well as the library and outdoor eating area, surround the courtyard and are connected by a covered arcade.

An accessible ramp leads to play equipment in the children's play area.

The interior of the library reflects the colors and design of the exterior.

The plaza contains sitting areas with a lion's head fountain and shade trees, and serves as the public entry to the library.

two-acre block and relocating 150 residents. The Neighborhood Task Force, City departments and school district planned the project. Broader community participation occurred at neighborhood workshops and community festivals.

The design team provided drawings and renderings of the park to help community members visualize this large, complex development project. The illustrations showed how the existing park would be enhanced, and its relationship to the new school. The workshops galvanized the community and gave voice to its ideas and needs.

The architect played a strong role in shepherding the community and City through the process, explaining the complicated project to each City official, including the operational details of how the library, school district, and City would share responsibility and benefit from the project. City officials and school district staff produced the

The school playground includes amphitheater-style seating that is fully accessible by a gently sloping walkway.

program for the site, as well as operations and maintenance plans, through a series of intensive working sessions.

As with any design process, existing conditions and constraints influenced the design. The existing school on the site needed to remain open during construction of the new school. The new school was located on the other side of the street in the existing park, so the old school could stay open. The old school site will eventually become new, badly needed housing.

Land use issues also greatly influenced the design. The mixed-use community facility required a significant effort to purchase the land and relocate about 150 residents, resulting in the entire project being contained within one block. A major benefit of this scheme is that children do not need to cross busy streets to get from place to place as they would if uses were dispersed throughout the neighborhood.

Legal issues also played a role as contracts were negotiated to bring together the school district and the

The group picnic area is used by the school and is open to the public after hours.

A large shade structure keeps eating areas cooler.

City to determine responsibility for property maintenance. This established where the shared-use facilities and fences were located. Now that the school district and the City have a joint use agreement, the stage is set for additional projects and opportunities throughout the City.

This process illustrates the power of inclusive design as a framework for planning that precedes actual design: involving all users in creating an environment results in a project that is usable by the greatest possible number of people.

Inclusive Design Features and Settings

ARCHITECTURAL USE

The school operates year round so there are always children using the shared facilities (park, library, ball fields). The site is flat and designed for convenient access with wide stairs, a visible elevator and gentle slopes. Spaces flow smoothly

The kindergarten play area includes a "village" for fantasy play.

from one area to the next. The site is planned for age-focused activities while still being viewable and accessible to all ages. Fences are transparent, which helps with security issues and prevents groups from being completely segregated from each other.

Spaces throughout the site will eventually be filled with public art. A com-munity center lobby project by an Armenian youth group is in the works.

SCHOOL BUILDINGS

The school has an intimate feeling that is achieved through design. Classrooms have peaked ceilings, rather than the traditionally flat ones prevalent in most schools. Rooms are not entirely rectangular; there are built-in nooks and other "hidden" places. Ground floor class-rooms open directly to outdoor patios. Second floor rooms open to bridged corridors that orient students to the ground level areas below.

The courtyard between building wings is a landscaped outdoor space that supports instructional programs.

Classrooms have peaked roofs and built-in nooks.
KATE DIAMOND

The design of the reading and story area within the library is based on a round building architectural feature found in Armenia.

A poured-in-place, tilt-up construction method was used to form the community center and school buildings. This allowed for relief motifs expressing community cultures on exterior walls.

COMMUNITY CENTER

The Community Center has a large, shared lobby and courtyard space for a café, a future police substation and other community activities. Community members are comfortable with all ages interacting. Senior activities are on the second floor, overlooking adolescents below. There is one entry which everyone uses.

MULTI-PURPOSE FIELD

The multi-purpose field is a large rectangular turf area (approximately 200

The gymnasium opens onto an outdoor stage with amphitheater seating for community events.

The community uses the gymnasium during non-school hours.
CITY OF GLENDALE

feet by 300 feet). Students and community members use this field both for organized and free play sports.

GROUP PICNIC AREA

The group picnic area is located between the field and the little league ball field. Surrounded by pine trees, it contains tables and barbecues underneath shelters, plus benches and trash receptacles. Users can access the picnic area either by the adjacent parking lot or by a gently sloped concrete path connecting the rest of the park and the schoolyard.

BALL FIELD

The renovated ball field is a standard size little league field. It is located adjacent to the picnic area and the restrooms and concession stand. An accessible entrance connects adjacent streets and parking area to the ball field.

MULTI-PURPOSE HARD COURT

The multi-purpose hard court is sized for volleyball and basketball. It is adjacent to the community center entry and youth and teenage area to be convenient for after-school programs.

SCHOOL PLAY YARD

Children have access to the multi-purpose turf field, a composite play structure and hard court asphalt area during recess and lunchtime. After school, all children are welcome to use the area with adult supervision.

CHILDREN'S PLAY AREA AND WATER PLAY

The children's play area has several different settings, including a water spray area (in which sprinklers in the guise of life-sized palm trees rain down on children), swings, and a village with small play houses. All areas are accessible; safety surfacing is either rubberized surfacing or engineered wood fiber.

PUBLIC GARDEN AND PLAZA

The public garden has benches, a lion's head fountain and shade trees. This garden is located at the corner of the site and serves as the public entry to the community center and library. This space was designed to accommodate large community-wide events.

Management and Operational Issues

The project is heralded as a template for a successful joint venture between a city and school district.

After just the first year of operation, the public library circulation matched other established branch libraries. The school principal reports this is partially due to an influx of more children reading after school hours.

No additional staffing has been required at the school. The City's Parks and Recreation Department has an affiliation with a neighborhood church and they have developed a joint use agreement to help maintain the property. This has resulted in additional community involvement and support. Since the school is open from 5:30 a.m. to 11 p.m., wear and tear is higher than most schools, further evidence of the project's success.

Lively building colors and an articulated façade contribute to the vitality of the new community project.

User Feedback

Linda Conover, Principal

"The project is a great success. The collaboration with the City has been very good and a growth experience for everyone involved. There is an overall feeling that the facility serves the community well. The increased number of on-site programs in the family center and library brings parents to the school.

"Students are so proud to be at the school. The first few weeks after it opened, students came up to me in the hallways and said, 'Thank you for the school!' They are excited about all the new facilities: the computer lab, library, field and play apparatus.

"The outdoor spaces, such as the sloping grass courtyards between buildings, make the facility feel like a park, not just a typical school. It's a joy to see kids running and playing tag on the multipurpose field, just being kids."

The second level corridor overlooks the school's landscaped courtyard.
KATE DIAMOND

Colorful mosaic tiles on the school's façade enhance the students' daily experience.

CENTRAL PARK | DAVIS, CALIFORNIA

"Coming to the market is like being part of the hustle and bustle of a large city...everyone's talking, the colors, the people....But it's a small town. I feel comfortable."

DAVIS RESIDENT

GATHERING PLACES

STANTON JONES
CHERYL SULLIVAN

IN 1986, A DEVELOPER PROPOSED TURNING A LARGE GRAVEL PARKING LOT INTO A SHOPPING mall, right across the street from a quiet downtown park. That proposal generated a popular uprising among the residents of Davis, California, and resulted in a one-of-a-kind park that has become the family room for the community of Davis.

Public squares and central parks are not uncommon elements in the fabric of cities and towns across North America; in many cases, cities have found great success in creating a pleasant, vibrant place where members of that community can play, rest and celebrate in a venue that elevates the pride that individuals have for their home town. What is rare, however, is the creation of a place that is so intensely interwoven

A lovely grove of sycamore trees provides shady spots for picnics in the summer. The trees date from the 1930s and the community won't allow them to be touched.

PROJECT Davis Central Park   **LOCATION** Davis, California   **DATE DESIGNED** Phase 1: 1987; Phase 2: 1991   **CONSTRUCTION COMPLETED** Phase 1: 1990; Phase 2: 1992   **CONSTRUCTION COST** $1 million   **SIZE** 5 acres **DESIGN** CoDesign, Inc. (now part of MIG, Inc.)   **CLIENT** City of Davis

into a community's fabric that its residents can't imagine their city without it. Even more rare are places that have been designed for the broadest spectrum of park users imaginable, where programmed and unprogrammed activities abound, and where outside nongovernmental agencies and city park staff cooperate in the development, management and care of the place. Add to this a design process that offered the community a meaningful, participatory role in developing concepts and designs for the park, and the result is a truly special place. Central Park in Davis, California, is just such a place.

The original park, located along the old Lincoln Highway between the heart of Downtown Davis and the campus of the University of California, Davis, was one square block. (Central Park is four blocks from Davis Commons, described in the chapter "Transforming Retail Space into Community Space.") Over time, the park had evolved into a sacred place for the community, a relatively quiet downtown park with a large grove

The park on market day is a bustling place, voted as the best place to picnic in Davis—and to see and be seen.

of sycamore trees where families gathered for reunions, picnics and barbecues. Every Saturday morning, the park bursts with activity when one of the most successful farmers markets in the State of California sets up its trucks and booths on the adjacent street.

In 1986, the proposal to turn the large gravel parking lot directly adjacent to Central Park into a shopping mall led to the creation of a grass roots group called Save Open Space (SOS). Rather than build a mall, the group's counter-proposal was to make one large park by incorporating the gravel lot and eliminating the street between the park and the lot. Their efforts ultimately led to a ballot measure that offered all of the residents of Davis a choice: mall or park. Voters turned down the mall in June of 1986 and design began on the new park.

Reminiscent of a large barn, the pavilion at Central Park is the first permanent covered market structure of its kind in California.

Locally grown flowers are also a big draw.

DESIGN GOALS

From the outset the purpose of Central Park was to provide a truly inclusive, vibrant and adaptive public space that would reflect the soul of the community now and in the future. It also needed to include several critical elements, the most notable being the Davis Farmers Market, which continues to draw up to 10,000 people to the area every Saturday. But the park is more than just an improved venue for the market. Other uses were also incorporated into its fabric, including a teen center, a large picnic and play lawn, a small plaza for performances, a preserved historic grove of sycamore trees, and special features such as an interactive fountain and a community-installed garden. Several public art projects add yet another layer to the park, increasing its appeal to an extremely large spectrum of the population. While this sounds like a long list of concerns to be organized in the park, the key to its ultimate success was the way in which the list, the plan and the design were developed.

The farmers market bustles with activity and seasonal produce.

On Wednesday evenings "Picnic in the Park" draws thousands of people to their community living room, Davis Central Park.

Today, the park serves as the living room for the City of Davis. In addition to the Saturday morning market, on Wednesday nights the "Picnic in the Park" market and food bazaar draws 3,000 to 6,000 people. "Picnic in the Park" runs from May to October. An ongoing list of programmed activities organized by Third & B, the teen center located at the corner of the park, draws 7th through 12th graders to the park during both days and evenings. The large at-grade fountain and its surrounding hardscape (called The Beach by Davis residents) offers children and adults a place to hang out, stay cool and play among the water jets in the hot summer sun. The large lawn area is a place for picnics, dog shows, Frisbee games and all sorts of child's play. Also located in the park is the Hattie Weber Museum, the City's first library. The building was relocated to the park and remodeled as a community meeting hall and museum, with exhibits depicting the history of Davis (which used to be called Davisville) and a pedal-powered carousel donated by the Davis Education Fund.

All sorts of community groups perform on the permanent wooden bandstand.

Long summer evenings are perfect for informal folk music.

USER GROUPS

- All Davis residents
- Davis Farmers Market (market vendors and shoppers)
- Families
- Children
- Teens
- Performers
- Artists
- Picnickers
- Park Department staff

DESIGN PROCESS

Once the City had the mandate of the electorate, landscape architect and Davis resident Mark Francis began coordinating a series of workshops with several goals in mind. The design process was diverse and extremely inclusive from the outset, incorporating a number of different techniques for soliciting ideas, generating concepts and building both support and an enthusiastic constituency for the expanded park. The participatory meetings—conducted in the park—helped people to understand what was there and to map out "sacred spaces" that individual residents wanted preserved. This was done through walking tours of the park and design workshops held on site (under a tent on some occasions), which helped give form to the overall park master plan. People used styrofoam model pieces to design their ideal park on base sheets.

Two unique user groups, the Farmers Market and the Third & B Teen Center, wanted to be located in the park and each required a permanent facility. Key to the development of the plan was recognizing the importance of the Farmers Market as an integral component of the life and future of the park. After Phase 1 was built, another series of workshops were held with the

Participatory meetings drew the community deep into the design process.

Community members of all ages offered their thoughts about the park design.

Farmers Market to design the first permanent, covered market pavilion in California. It needed to accommodate the vendor trucks inside the park and still be a space suitable for other events outside of market days.

Similarly, the development of the Third & B Teen Center was also perceived as critical to the future of the park, leading design team members to work with local teen advocates and with the landscape architecture faculty of the

University who, because of their previous work with teens and the community, were well aware of the needs of teens in public space. A Teen Facility Task Force evaluated the need for a teen center and surveyed junior and senior high school students on their interest in having a teen center. Then a committee of teens and interested public developed a program for the type of facility, activities and potential users. Every year a teen activity planning group is organized to help plan activities and programs for the coming year. After 13 years, Third & B is still a success. Attendance in 2003–2004 was over 29,000.

The public design process resulted in a program and plan for the park that was consensus based, and that had such a strong set of roots in the community that all subsequent changes and additions to the park have been evaluated through the lens of how well the element or program matches the intent of the master plan.

Inclusive Design Features and Settings

The park possesses a number of key design features that make for a highly inclusive place.

THE BEACH

One of the primary focal points of the park is the plaza at the south end of the park, labeled The Beach by locals. It has as its centerpiece a large at-grade fountain that offers people of all abilities—children on bikes and in strollers, and parents looking for a place to play and stay cool with their children—an opportunity to participate in the life of the place without the need for special accommodations or separate routes of access. And when the fountain is turned off, the plaza is a stage. The simple design and adaptability inherent in this type of fountain is crucial to the plaza's multiple uses, ranging from dances to skateboard demonstrations to musical performances. This area is very popular on all days, market or non-market, particularly on

Water sprays offer a perfect way to cool off in the hot Central Valley summer.

The Beach provides an inclusive, flexible environment where parents can watch their children play in the at-grade fountain close by the market.

When the fountain is off, the area functions as a stage for small groups.

hot Central Valley summer days when schools are out.

THE PAVILION

The pavilion and the large expanse of colored paving was designed for pickup trucks to back into stalls while leaving the central aisle open for shoppers. The structure is filled with the sights, smells and activities of the market twice a week. When not in use, it offers a visual memory of the market, as well as shade and a place for parties and other activities.

THIRD & B

The Third & B facility addresses the needs of a constituency that communities often forget when developing public spaces. Third & B was created to provide a positive, "cool" and fun place for 7th to 12th graders to hang out and participate in activities designed for them in a manner that is neither condescending nor childish. It is a two-story building with a basement and sunken plaza, located on the most public corner of the park, Third and B Streets. It's easy to get to

and is located in the main entry into the park and in the heart of town. Large windows along Third Street give everyone a view in and out of the center. The entry sits three feet above the street, with lots of steps to sit on and watch the crowd go by. The basement is used for community meetings and dances; the first floor is set up for games, snacks and movies; and the second floor is reserved for quieter activities—reading, tutoring, visiting. Third & B offers over 19 different programs, which continually evolve to meet the changing interests of teens.

Formal organized activities include dances, concerts and field trips to amusement parks. It's also a place where students can come for free tutoring, from the basics to advanced subjects. Volunteer tutors are recruited from UC Davis. The Third & B facility provides an opportunity for youth to get involved in their communities through volunteering. Teens have participated in canned food drives, beach and park cleanups, and graffiti paint outs. The informal activities include shooting pool, watching movies

Located in the most used corner of Central Park, Third & B is a very popular place for teens to hang out.

Third & B offers informal drop-in activities and structured programs.

on a big screen TV, or playing foosball and video games. There's even a party package that allows parents to use the basement for a private party for their teenager, with as many as 350 guests. That it is not officially called a "teen center" helps with its level of acceptance with teens in Davis. They know they are part of the community fabric.

PUBLIC ART

Art was incorporated into the design from the beginning: some of it obvious and some very subtle, some conceptual and some functional.

The foundation wall is so functional that few people realize it's actually public art.

The artist incorporated an abstract representation of the valley into a large public wash basin.

The functional wash basin provides people of different needs and abilities a place to wash their hands, splash their faces on a hot day, or rinse produce just purchased at the market.

Children love to ride on the hand-carved animals.

The retaining wall embedded with stones looks like an uncovered foundation wall. It's just the right height and width for sitting and walking on. Its rustic finish hides its newness; very few know that it is actually a piece of public art. More dramatic is a beautiful, yet functional basin for washing hands before a picnic, or for cleaning produce purchased at the market. Made of colored, rammed concrete, the fountain and basin evoke a geological cross section of the Central Valley—from mountains to river.

Two more pieces sit in the public garden. One is a bronze casting of whimsical dancers, another is a larger than life set of ceramic hands. This part of the park can accommodate more public art installations. It's flat and set off from the major activity areas, yet you can catch glimpses of the sculptures as you ride down the street.

THE CAROUSEL

The Flying Carousel of the Delta Breeze was designed as a fundraiser for the Davis Education Association. Parents and children experience the carousel together, in a uniquely interactive fashion. It's pedal-powered, with hand-carved wooden animals for young ones to ride. This piece was proposed after the park was designed and built, and luckily, a perfect spot was found for it. Each market day, the carousel is opened for rides. As appropriate for a City with over 50,000 bicycles, the carousel runs on human leg power. While youngsters sit on top of the carved wooden animals, a "big kid" sits on a recumbent bike and pedals away, turning the carousel round and round. Because of its wonderful gearing, it is very easy to

Parents get some exercise while they pedal to turn the carousel round and round. The interior column is covered in a colorful tile mosaic.

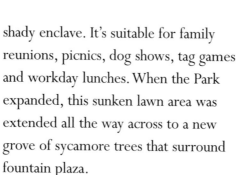

The gardens provide a quiet reprieve from the bustle of the market.

set the carousel in motion. Parents and tots line up to take their turns at riding and pedaling.

SYCAMORE GROVE

The oldest feature in the park is a grove of sycamore trees that dates from the 1930s. It is the sacred place in town, and the community won't allow any changes to the space. The grove was planted in a basin about 3 feet lower than the sidewalk, so it could be flood irrigated. This created a protected and

shady enclave. It's suitable for family reunions, picnics, dog shows, tag games and workday lunches. When the Park expanded, this sunken lawn area was extended all the way across to a new grove of sycamore trees that surround fountain plaza.

STROLLING GARDEN

There is a large garden area that separates the park activities from B Street, a major arterial leading to the University. The original idea for this space was to

create a strolling garden with several "rooms" with different themes, including a rose garden, an herb garden, a grass garden and a peace garden. The City bought the plants and the community gathered to plant over a thousand trees, shrubs and perennials in one weekend. It was a community event with over 100 people participating. The garden is a place where plants and sculptures can support each other. It's a place where all can visit and enjoy a quiet space.

The strolling gardens offer a wide variety of plants and meandering paths.

CHILDREN'S PLAY AREA

A children's play area is adjacent to the market pavilion, allowing parents to shop and visit with friends at the market while their children play nearby. The play lot has two structures—a sand climber where kids have to cooperate to move the sand up and down the structure, and a composite piece where they can climb and slide down poles and run up and down. These are meant to provide some kid-oriented activities while parents shop. The kids feel that they are part of the hustle and bustle of the market place, not segregated from it all.

Management and Operational Issues

The park is so popular that it is almost loved to death. It is a high profile public space that requires regular maintenance. The park's maintenance costs are approximately $50,000 per year out of the City's budget, with some additional costs covered by other organizations such as the Davis Farmers Market

The children's play area incorporates plenty of sand play, and its location right next to the Farmers Market puts kids in the middle of the market day action.

Association. Other areas of the park, such as the garden, can be aided in their upkeep by local residents, although the bulk of the maintenance and capital improvements are the responsibility of the City of Davis.

The fountain is a high maintenance feature. Since the water is recirculated, it has to be chlorinated, and the filter needs to be regularly cleaned. The sprays are controlled by an irrigation controller and are turned off at night, and on windy and rainy days. However, the fountain is now a new sacred place in the park. It's a destination, a place for simple enjoyment for all.

The Farmers Market takes on the responsibility of cleaning the paving where the market is held. The Market Director works closely with the City on facility issues. The Market has been instrumental in finishing the construction of the last corner of the park. The master plan called for a Market café.

Maintaining rose and perennial gardens is labor intensive. As park budgets shrink, maintenance is deferred. A volunteer organization will need to take over the planting and maintenance of the strolling garden for it to continue as originally planned.

User Feedback

The park has been in continuous use for 12 years, long enough for some Davis residents to have grown up in it.

Jake Gilchrist

"The shade structure is one of the best facilities for a farmers market. It makes it feel like Davis has committed to the farmers market. The park itself is pretty iconic. It's really simple but it gets used perfectly. So much of the community uses it—that's testimony to its success."

Brent Hopkins

"The fountain is terrific! What a great place to cool off. I just love watching the kids try to guess which jet is going to shoot up next. [The fountain jets are programmed to turn on in a random pattern.] I was riding my bike down Third Street right after the park was opened. I saw this fountain shooting up out of the paving…I couldn't resist it— I had to ride my bike through it!"

Heather O'Neill

"Coming to the market is like being part of the hustle and bustle of a large city. You get to rub elbows with lots of different folks, everyone's talking, the colors, the people, the amazing choices of food. But it's a small town. I feel comfortable bringing my three-year-old daughter. There are pony rides for her, or a turn on the carousel, and she can play with the kids in the sand box."

Christine O'Neill

"When I was in junior high I went to some dances at Third & B. It's pretty cool that there's a place besides the school cafeteria where we can have dances and hear some music."

DAVIS COMMONS | DAVIS, CALIFORNIA

> *"This is an urban, modern, comfortable space...a new alternative to the large mall or the old strip mall."*
>
> DIRECTOR, DAVIS DOWNTOWN BUSINESS ASSOCIATION

TRANSFORMING RETAIL SPACE INTO COMMUNITY SPACE

CHERYL SULLIVAN

DAVIS COMMONS IS A THREE-ACRE RETAIL SITE WITH TRADITIONAL PARKING AND SHOPS. What sets Davis Commons apart is that it is both a retail shopping center and an urban park. The design turns the concept of a retail area around: it's centered on a one-acre park and the shops are the backdrop to the park. The Commons has become a community meeting place: a place to shop, meet friends, share a meal, take part in community events, hear free music, browse the arboretum garden, read a book—it's a small town square that is its own destination.

Davis is a university town of 60,000 people, about 10 miles southwest of Sacramento, California. It is the home of the third largest University of California (UC Davis) campus. The climate is warm and Mediterranean, with summer lasting five to six months before winter rains begin in November. Davis is flat and a natural "biking" town; virtually every resident owns a bicycle.

Downtown Davis is about five blocks square, rather than a long single street of businesses. Cafés, eateries, bookstores, clothing and shoe stores, house wares, plants and garden supplies, hardware and banking are all within easy walking or biking distance.

Davis Commons is located at an extremely busy intersection at the main entry into Downtown Davis. It's opposite the central business district on one side and the University of California Davis campus on another. The University owned the land adjacent to the Downtown and saw this as an opportunity to incorporate mixed-use, community design principles in the development of the land.

DESIGN GOALS

The goal was to create an open-air plaza and town square that combines the retail experience with a park. Storefronts open onto the plaza, the park and the parking lot, which is at the rear of the site. Parking is in the rear with one entry and exit point and is not visible from any street edge. The buildings form an arc around a central open space which fronts the street and looks very much like a small park.

This design layout creates a space that people can easily see while walking down other streets. Accessible by foot and bike, it creates a welcoming corner into town. It also provides more foot traffic for the shops on E Street. It is a pedestrian-friendly arrangement where people walk or bike to different shops—to buy or window shop.

The Commons adds to the City's pedestrian and bicycle transportation networks and links the Downtown with the University, housing and the arboretum. It provides a comfortable, appealing place where people want to linger. The site design, landscaping, circulation, paving and seating all work together to create a space that's easy to navigate.

PROJECT Davis Commons   **LOCATION** Davis, California   **DATE DESIGNED** 1995–1996   **CONSTRUCTION COMPLETED** June 1998   **CONSTRUCTION COST** $6.5 million (entire site)   **SIZE** 3 acres   **DEVELOPER AND OWNER** The Fulcrum Group, Sacramento, California   **ARCHITECT** DZ Architects   **LANDSCAPE ARCHITECT** CoDesign, Inc. (now part of MIG, Inc.)   **CIVIL ENGINEER** Cunningham Engineering   **ELECTRICAL ENGINEER** Rex Moore   **MECHANICAL ENGINEER** Turley and Associates   **STRUCTURAL ENGINEER** Marr Shaffer Miyamoto   **OTHER DESIGN TEAM MEMBERS** UC Davis Office of Development, City of Davis Planning Department

The shops are a backdrop to the park.

A row of shops forms an arc around the park.

Families can relax with a cup of coffee while children play on the grass.

Three factors make Davis Commons a successful urban park and retail center: the attention to the arrangement of space and features that encourage and enhance social life; the lush and intensive landscaping throughout the site; and the mix of shops that are well-suited to the town and the setting. This retail mix draws many different shoppers and users, creating a critical mass that keeps the businesses prosperous, both in the Commons and in the rest of the Downtown. It's a symbiotic relationship. Davis Commons now generates the most sales tax of any shopping center in town. And it's a space that everyone, from young to old, mobile and not-so-mobile, can enjoy.

Trellises and open spaces provide a comfortable sense of enclosure.

USER GROUPS

- Families
- Singles
- University students
- Teens on their own
- Seniors
- Out of town visitors
- Business owners

DESIGN PROCESS

First and E Streets form the edge of the Downtown core and separate the University campus from the Downtown area. The University owned property along First Street, between E and B

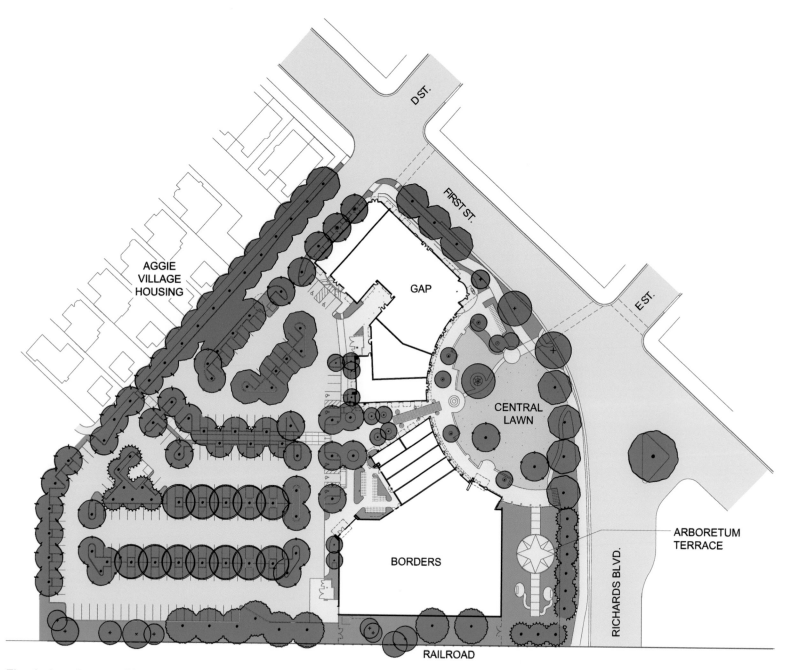

The design places parking at the rear with landscaped open spaces throughout.

Streets, and decided to develop it into a retail center and housing for staff and faculty using New Urbanist design concepts.

The University prepared a master plan for a 12-acre site, including the three-acre retail center and a four-acre residential development now called Aggie Village. (UC Davis students are called "Aggies" because of the school's original emphasis on agriculture.) In addition to generating revenue, the project would be compatible with the architectural style and scale of the existing mixed-use Downtown core.

The design team, UC Davis and City of Davis planners worked together to refine the site plan with input from local business owners.

The University also modified the site plan for Aggie Village, reducing the number of inner streets in the residential zone and locating granny flats along the retail parking lot. This change made

Bicyclists are ubiquitous in Downtown Davis.

for a smoother transition and an animated visual buffer from the shopping center to the single-family residential housing.

The Davis Commons design team saw an opportunity to create a town square by relocating the public plaza space so it would face Downtown businesses, rather than the quieter, residential section of Downtown. This change in orientation linked the new retail to the old Downtown and gave the public plaza its urban life. This is the first thing one sees when entering Downtown and the last place one sees when leaving Downtown. With the plaza space at the corner, the buildings were placed around the park with parking in the rear.

During the planning process, the businesses and community in general expressed concerns that the intensity of vehicle traffic on First Street would impede pedestrian access and discourage people from crossing the street. During this same time, voters defeated a measure that would have widened E Street and First Street.

To address community traffic issues, the City of Davis undertook several actions:

- First Street was striped for three lanes of traffic (one in each direction with a right turn pocket).
- A new bike and pedestrian tunnel was installed underneath the freeway providing an alternate route from south Davis to Downtown and Davis Commons.
- Traffic signals were finely tuned to alleviate congestion.
- The new streetscape was designed to slow traffic and improve bicycle and pedestrian safety.

Plantings soften the edges of the open areas.

Inclusive Design Features and Settings

The open space is divided into a paved plaza and a large, circular lawn. The large open lawn area is wrapped with plantings and seating. The plaza fronts

Colorful, seasonal flowers provide visual interest and wayfinding cues.

the retail shopping and provides spaces for eating, sitting and visiting. There are a variety of seating options—shaded tables, curving seatwalls, the lawn, benches and patio tables. Here, inclusive design is functional without being obvious.

LANDSCAPING

Lush landscaping gives the Commons a special quality, transforming the retail center into a large public garden. Plantings soften edges, create a sense of enclosure and protection, provide visual

Plants are a mix of colors, textures and heights so everyone can touch and smell.

Native grasses are hardy yet visually appealing.

interest, control access and guide people along paths. Plants are located at many levels so everyone has a chance to touch and smell. All spaces are well landscaped, even those utilitarian areas like trash enclosures, delivery bays, the back property line and the bike and car parking lots. Every space looks and feels part of the whole.

Plants were selected for their texture, seasonal color, variety, scent and ability to withstand public activity. Ornamental

grasses and roses direct pedestrians in the desired direction. This planting design illustrates the large selection of plants that can be used in a commercial setting. It adds park-like qualities and makes the space inviting.

OPEN LAWN AND PLAZA

The large, open lawn is the entry to the Commons, creating a green plaza. This space is large enough to host civic events and small summer musical performances. A mixture of ornamental grasses and shrubs encircle the space, leaving just one opening towards the street. The street edge plantings discourage cut-through pedestrian traffic. Parents feel comfortable letting their children run around the lawn area. It's big enough for kids, and small enough for parents to see their children. The success of the space is its use of plants to wrap the space and create a feeling of enclosure. Grasses and shrubs are softer and less formal than ornamental metal fencing.

The large green space is perfect for families to hear music on a summer evening.

At the top of the green lawn is the concrete plaza where bands often perform.

The lawn gently slopes down towards the street. From across the street, this sloped lawn creates a view up and into the Commons. Densely planted perimeter greenery defines the spaces. Trees provide summer shade.

ARBORETUM TERRACE DEMONSTRATION GARDEN

The Arboretum Terrace is a secluded patio space with teak tables, chairs and umbrellas, and a collection of California native and Mediterranean plants suitable for the Central Valley climate. Many plants attract butterflies and insects. This is a sensory garden with plants at different heights so that everyone has an opportunity to see, touch and smell.

PLAZA SEATING

There are two types of seating in the Plaza: concrete seat walls and metal chairs. The Plaza is full of tables with umbrellas and movable chairs and a row of patio trees. Tables and chairs are located opposite the restaurants and cafés so patrons can take their meals

Teak furniture and umbrellas are available in the arboretum patio.

California native and Mediterranean plants attract butterflies.

Visitors can find secluded benches for a quiet urban moment.

Plants are labeled for those who would like to create their own gardens.

Visitors can arrange chairs and use the seat walls in many different ways.

There's plenty of room between tables for strollers and wheelchairs.

outside and arrange seating for their group. The spacing between tables is adequate for people to move in and out, including those in wheelchairs. The colored concrete seat walls, shaped in arcs, separate the Plaza patio from the lawn. People can sit in either direction, lean against them and use them for tables or foot rests. They provide a generous amount of seating space.

ENTRYWAYS

The main entry from First Street is marked with a huge elm tree, as well as signage and a change in paving from plain concrete and asphalt to highly colored and patterned concrete paving.

Shops and restaurants are arranged in two buildings, separated by a triangular shaped space and a long vine-covered trellis. This serves as the gateway between the parking lot and the plaza

The entry from First Street is across from residences, marked with a huge elm tree and whimsical signage.

A long vine-covered trellis between retail buildings invites visitors in from the parking lot.

Pedestrians have plenty of time to cross the very busy intersection.

Pedestrian-only paths are decomposed granite and narrower than multiple-use paved paths.

space. It's cool, the space is comfortable and there's activity along the edges.

PEDESTRIAN CIRCULATION

Even though pedestrians have to cross the busiest street in Downtown Davis, pedestrian traffic flows smoothly and safely. Controlled intersections and marked crosswalks signify the formal entries into the Commons. Traffic light intervals are long enough for safe crossing.

A raised central walk travels through the parking lot, connecting the Commons to the arboretum trail and adjacent residential neighborhoods.

Footpaths through the lawn and along the outside perimeter are decomposed granite, and are narrower than the paved walks.

MULTIPLE PATHS

Davis Commons can be reached by car through one driveway. However, bikes

and pedestrians have four clearly defined routes and several other casual paths to and through the Commons, which join other paths connecting to the University and the City. The paths through the Commons link the University campus to the Downtown. This arrangement continues the pattern of mid-block passages found in other parts of the central business district.

Along First Street, pedestrian and bike routes are separated. Because of limited

Along First Street, a screen of plants separates bikes from pedestrians. (Pedestrians walk on the left, next to the buildings.)

Roses keep these bikes in line.

Other bikes are nestled in the lantana.

space, the potential for conflicts between pedestrians and bikes is significant. Paths are no greater than six feet wide, and are separated by a thickly planted screen, so that neither bicyclists nor pedestrians can inadvertently stray into the other's path.

BIKE PARKING

In Davis, conflicts between bike parking and pedestrian paths are an everyday occurrence. To lessen these conflicts at Davis Commons, large bike parking lots are located on each side of the complex. Bike parking lots are adjacent to the main path. These spaces are surrounded by beautiful landscaping—with a prickly purpose. Daylilies and thorny roses line one parking area, while the other has lantana and spikey pyracantha. They are located near entrances and main walkways with enough bike racks to meet demand.

CAR PARKING

Vehicle parking is located behind buildings and is not visible from the street. The parking lot is heavily landscaped with large shade trees that shade over half of the paving. The parking lot has several short to medium length rows so it is a short walk from even the furthest parking space. A raised pedestrian crossing and shaded pedestrian walkway connects the Commons with the arboretum path and the residential housing adjacent to the parking lot.

Management and Operational Issues

LANDSCAPE MAINTENANCE

The Commons is densely planted with a wide variety of plants not typical at traditional shopping centers. Most plants lie in close proximity to the public. Consequently, landscape maintenance is a daily task. With the exception of the demonstration garden, the landscape is designed for ease of maintenance. The plants are not too large for their space, so little pruning is needed. The landscaping around the building's front entry has to be planted and maintained to a high standard. Everything is "the front yard."

The Arboretum Terrace is a demonstration garden using California native and Mediterranean plants, arranged around a patio and little trails. This is a high-maintenance landscape that is closed off at night.

SITE FURNISHINGS

The outdoor tables and chairs are not just for shop patrons. They encourage people to have coffee, read a book and

Much of the concrete parking area is shaded.

Flowers and trees are highly visible across the parking lots.

linger. They add life to the plaza and outdoor spaces.

The color and quality of materials gives the message that the Davis Commons is a special place. Quality materials maintain their appearance.

MULTIPLE ENTRIES FOR STORES

The arrangement of the buildings in the center of the site, with a park on one side and a parking lot on the other, means that some stores have two front doors. This requires more staff and a higher operating budget.

STORE FRONTAGE

Stores usually want a long store frontage. However, the only portion of the building that has street frontage is not conducive for a shop entry. In place of long store frontage, the bookstore has a tower that marks the corner of the complex. The walkway on the north side of the building is a passageway, not a place to stop and linger. It's a close space opening right on the pedestrian path. It is better suited for window displays. Most people enter the site for shopping from the parking lot side or from E Street.

SECOND STORY RESIDENTIAL UNITS

The design guidelines allowed a maximum building square footage of 50,000, with second floor residential. The developer built a 45,000-square-foot building with no residential units. If they were to do it again, the developers say they would include the second story residences. The residences would animate the public space to an even greater degree. The plaza could then be used for longer hours every day, which would add to the town plaza ambiance.

PARKING

Several spaces in the parking lot are reserved for granny flat residents nearby. In the original development plan, vehicle parking was not included. The loss of these spaces to the general public does not appear to have an impact on the availability of parking.

User Feedback

The first four comments are from visitors to Davis Commons.

Jasmine Lautzenheimer

"I love the rose arbor, walking under it to get to the lawn and Pluto's Restaurant. The combination of flowers is gorgeous. It's kid-friendly; the lawn and seating and restaurants are separated from the parking lot. It has a nice feeling of enclosure. And the people watching is great! The spaces are broken up, with shade and lots of different plants to see. And shaded seating in the garden area. The kids love exploring for bugs and butterflies in the garden. It's like being in a park."

Ron Lautzenheimer

"Having the parking in the back is a great idea. But this parking lot is a nice place, too. There's lots of shade, and the planters are full of grasses and roses. It's not a sea of asphalt."

Mike Navillus

"I love going to the music events, seeing little kids and families and older folks, all talking and enjoying the music and the summer evening, and each other. It's a great way to spend a summer evening."

Laurie Hopkins

"I like the mix of businesses. It's fun to wander through the stores, and then go outside and read the new book, eat an ice cream and watch the people."

Laura Cole Rowe, Director,
Davis Downtown Business Association

"The compactness of the space is good. The mix of stores is excellent for shopping, visiting, wandering. It's an urban, modern, comfortable space. It's a new alternative to a large mall and the old strip mall image.

"This is the easiest space to host events. The setting works so well that I am able to charge more for the space than I can for others. Bands set up in the circle and play out to the crowd. The lawn slopes away. People bring their blankets and small lawn chairs to sit on. Parents don't worry about their little kids dancing and running around. The place is circled with low plantings and seat walls. The space is small enough so that the kids don't get lost in the crowd. People either bring their own food and drinks, or get refreshments from the eateries and cafés at the Commons. There are tables and chairs surrounding the lawn that people can sit at, too. There could be more space for additional tables. It's a very popular place to eat and listen to music in the summer."

R STREET URBAN DESIGN AND DEVELOPMENT PLAN | SACRAMENTO, CALIFORNIA

"I grew up on this street—this was my playground...Now I'd love to purchase a loft and live here myself...walk, ride my bike, and be part of helping this community grow."

BUSINESS OWNER ON R STREET

RECONNECTING WITH THE STREET

DANIEL IACOFANO
MUKUL MALHOTRA

EVER SINCE SIR WALTER RALEIGH LAID HIS CLOAK DOWN TO PROTECT QUEEN ELIZABETH'S shoes from that mud puddle, traffic engineers have attempted to protect urban pedestrians from the "muddy" streets. As cars and trucks turned streets into busy thoroughfares, it became even more important to keep pedestrians safely relegated to the narrow sidewalk space between buildings and the street. Safety became the priority, but in so doing, the community connections that are created when pedestrians stroll, shop and gather in welcoming public spaces were lost. It's time to reclaim neighborhood streets for pedestrians.

R Street is envisioned as a living street, where pedestrians and autos share the public realm, depending on the time and day of the week. Shown here is Portland's Ankeny Burnside District with weekend uses for a weekday parking lot.

PROJECT R Street Corridor   LOCATION Sacramento, California   SIZE approximately 20 square blocks   CONCEPTUAL DESIGN 2004–2005   CONSTRUCTION 2007 (tentative) URBAN DESIGN AND PLANNING MIG, Inc.   INFRASTRUCTURE Kimley-Horn & Associates   ECONOMIC ANALYSIS Bay Area Economics   HISTORIC PRESERVATION Historic Environment Consultants   CLIENT Capitol Area Development Authority

The R Street project in Sacramento, California, will change the relationship between people, their urban environment and cars. The concept goes beyond a discussion of the proper sidewalk width; it obliterates the sidewalk. Yet it is not "anti-car." Rather, it proposes a shared public realm, with pedestrians and bicyclists having equal rights to the streets. Breaking pedestrians and bicyclists out of their narrow confines will allow residents, employees and visitors to experience the dynamic urban environment that a "living street" offers. Currently, as much as 70 percent of our urban land is planned by traffic engineers. But, if any place should reflect our urban values and priorities, our streets should.

By capitalizing on R Street's public transit infrastructure, bringing its historic attributes to the forefront, focusing on catalyst development projects and implementing inclusive design concepts, the project will transform this under-utilized

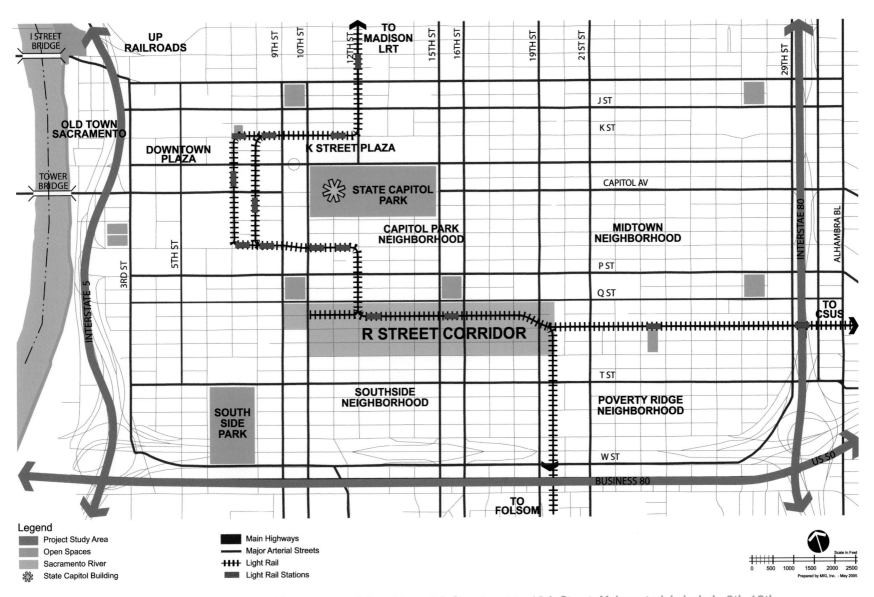

Legend

Project Study Area	
Open Spaces	
Sacramento River	
State Capitol Building	

Main Highways	
Major Arterial Streets	
Light Rail	
Light Rail Stations	

Scale in Feet

0   500   1000   1500   2000   2500

Prepared by MIG, Inc. - May 2005

The R Street Corridor project focuses on a 20-block area on R Street from 9th Street east to 19th Street. Major arterials include 9th-10th Streets and 15th-16th Streets, which connect to nearby residential neighborhoods.

R Street is home to a wide mix of uses, including residential, light industrial and commercial in converted historic buildings. Pedestrians already use the street as a pathway, although it's not designed as such.

Underused surface parking lots, neglected open spaces and a lack of any pedestrian amenities characterize R Street today.

The gritty industrial quality of this landmark signal tower provides inspiration for the R Street detailed design palette.

former rail corridor and transitional warehouse district into a vibrant, mixed-use residential and commercial district that provides new physical, economic and social connections—while celebrating its original industrial spirit.

PROJECT GOALS

R Street is a mixed-used, urban neighborhood street. The project area covers 20 blocks on R Street—running east-west from 9th Street to 19th Street—and two blocks to the north and south of the street. R Street is in the heart of Sacramento near the State Capitol building. It was the site of the first railroad west of the Mississippi and features an eclectic group of industrial land uses that date back to the early days of the City.

The area was home to metal foundries, warehouses and shipping companies—and some of those uses remain today.

In the past, industrial corridors such as R Street functioned as the economic and social backbone of a city. Over time, as manufacturing needs evolved and employment and residential patterns shifted, these industrial areas frequently became underused, blighted and perceived as unsafe. But today their rich cultural and architectural history can be the basis of revitalization. And as the capital of California, Sacramento is one of the most historically significant cities in the State.

In the mid-1980s, Sacramento Regional Transit completed the starter line of a light rail system. As part of the system, a major line serving the central business district runs adjacent to R Street, with two transit stations along the corridor. That stimulated interest in redeveloping the corridor and a multiyear planning effort began.

In 1996, the City Council adopted a land use guide for a 54-block area that envisioned a long-term transformation into a transit-oriented, mixed-use neighborhood. R Street has already seen development based on that land use vision, but there were no specific design guidelines that would create a cohesive neighborhood. The light rail stations lacked seating and shelters, surrounding buildings didn't relate to the stations, and unkempt alleyways created an unfriendly pedestrian environment. Some historic buildings had been converted to modern offices, shops, studios and art galleries, but many of those buildings had "turned their backs on the street," with blank walls or dark glass facing the pedestrian environment. There had been an influx of new restaurants, clubs and a grocery store, but a significant portion of the area was still vacant buildings, underused surface parking lots, neglected public realm and open spaces and brownfield sites, which gave the area a blighted and negative reputation.

The City realized it needed a cohesive design framework to improve the area's

Vacant buildings lead to an impression of blight and lack of safety.

Unfriendly building facades often turn their backs to pedestrians.

Well-established residential neighborhoods, especially to the south, will be reconnected to R Street.

Employees in the nearby Downtown area to the north can easily stroll and shop on R Street.

The State Capitol is also just a few blocks away.

streetscape, weave the project area into the urban fabric of the City, increase accessibility, and meet the needs of residents, employees and visitors.

The "R Street Urban Design and Development Plan" provides an urban design roadmap for future built and open space development. It does not propose a standard new streetscape with sidewalks, trees and benches because that would obliterate the area's unique historic character. It preserves the his-

toric street design and the urban "edginess" lent by its industrial past.

The concept supports diverse uses: high-density housing (mainly above ground floor retail), live-work lofts, neighborhood-serving retail, restaurants, art galleries, offices, commercial and light industrial. The light rail stations at 13th and 16th Streets will become centerpieces of the R Street core. R Street will be a connector between neighborhoods north and

south, rather than a barrier between them. Development on S Street, to the south, will be compatible with the existing residential areas there, and development on Q Street, to the north, will reflect the changing character of that street as it transitions from office commercial of the Capitol area, east to the residential midtown neighborhood.

Improvements focus on both neighborhood- and visitor-serving mixed uses and activities, key infill opportunities,

The community participated in a series of planning and design workshops.

During design charettes, community members offered feedback on different design options.

transit-oriented development, site and building design that is in keeping with the industrial context, public realm and open space amenities, safe pedestrian connections, efficient parking and circulation, and universal access.

The Plan provides a complete set of tools to guide future physical and service changes: a neighborhood urban design concept plan, a comprehensive set of design guidelines, infrastructure standards that complement streetscape design recommendations, infrastructure financing strategies and implementation action steps.

USER GROUPS

- Residents of varied incomes and abilities
- Employees in offices, retail, light industry and warehouses
- Shoppers and visitors of varied abilities
- Tourists

DESIGN PROCESS

The City of Sacramento 1996 R Street Corridor Plan serves as the foundation for the R Street Urban Design and Development Plan.

The Capitol Area Development Authority (CADA) is a joint powers authority of the State of California and

Community workshop participants first took a walking tour of the area.

Charette participants manipulate a land use block model to illustrate future possibilities.

the City of Sacramento. Its primary job is to carry out the residential and commercial portions of the Capitol Area Plan, setting the standard for affordable mixed-income and mixed-use property development. In 2002, the State expanded CADA's redevelopment boundaries to include the R Street corridor and accelerate investment and redevelopment of the area. In January 2004, CADA began working on a plan to design the preferred future for the corridor and develop specific action steps to get there.

CADA and its consultants conducted an extensive analysis of existing conditions, including a site organization study, an assessment of street language and character and an infrastructure assessment. The project team worked closely with the City Planning and Public Works Departments, the Design Review and Preservation Board and ADA groups.

An initial CADA Board workshop in February 2003 included a walking tour to identify which buildings to preserve ("keepers"), the image of the area, community connections, and the type of investment in infrastructure needed to revitalize the street.

CADA held a series of three community workshops and design charettes to build consensus on a shared vision of the corridor, neighborhood assets, planning issues and development opportunities. Workshops in April, May and June 2004 focused on overall vision, assets of the area, issues and opportunities, design concepts and a street language and palette. In March and November 2004, separate workshops addressed the nearby 16th Street and 13th Street Light Rail Stations.

Through this extensive community process, property owners, public officials, developers and the professional design community agreed on a vision and conceptual design for the area.

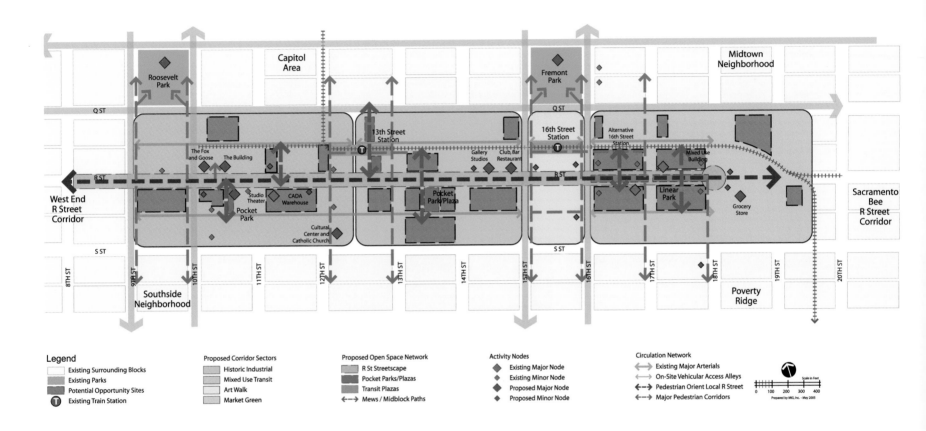

Legend

Existing Surrounding Blocks
Existing Parks
Potential Opportunity Sites
Ⓣ Existing Train Station

Proposed Corridor Sectors

Historic Industrial
Mixed Use Transit
Art Walk
Market Green

Proposed Open Space Network

R St Streetscape
Pocket Parks/Plazas
Transit Plazas
←--→ Mews / Midblock Paths

Activity Nodes

◆ Existing Major Node
◆ Existing Minor Node
◆ Proposed Major Node
◆ Proposed Minor Node

Circulation Network

←→ Existing Major Arterials
←→ On-Site Vehicular Access Alleys
←-→ Pedestrian Orient Local R Street
←-→ Major Pedestrian Corridors

Scale in Feet
0 100 200 300 400

Prepared by MIG, Inc. - May 2005

The Design Strategy Framework emerged after extensive analysis of current conditions and development opportunities, as well as several community workshops to develop a consensus vision for the corridor.

Inclusive Design Features and Settings

DESIGN VISION

The R Street corridor is designed to be a mixed-use transit hub that increases community connections and access, and celebrates its original industrial spirit. The community and the planning team determined that the new plan would be derived from five main design strategies:

1. Maintaining and Enhancing Historic Character

The area's interesting background and rich physical historic fabric provide R Street with a unique character and sense of place that should be maintained and strengthened. The Plan calls for these actions:

- Preserve and integrate buildings that are historically, architecturally and culturally significant, such as the old warehouses and loading docks.
- Preserve and integrate the area's building materials and streetscape elements, such as cobblestone streets, encased railroad tracks, loading docks, wide metal awnings and metal sash windows.
- Respect the utilitarian aesthetic of the corridor by emphasizing an urban, industrial design language.
- Maintain a vibrant mix of uses, including light industry, offices, retail

A neighborhood's industrial character can be maintained and enhanced as in this Berkeley, California, warehouse area, now home to a chocolate factory and restaurant.

and housing, which will also generate tax revenue.

2. Uniting Neighborhoods

The area should unite surrounding residential neighborhoods, providing amenities and acting as a connection or seam of the urban fabric. The Plan calls for these actions:

- Provide pedestrian-oriented design features on streets perpendicular to R Street to link north and south neighborhoods.
- Build on existing neighborhood amenities, such as restaurants, theaters, art galleries and neighborhood-serving retail that support community life.
- Enhance pedestrian and bicycle activities by developing underused or vacant buildings and open spaces with pedestrian-friendly edges, by incorporating innovative traffic calming features and by continuing pedestrian and bicycle paths through streets that had been blocked by railroad tracks.

Historic loading docks, such as this one in Portland, Oregon, can be converted to retail shops and cafés.

In Portland, transit-oriented development has brought new vitality to an older part of the City.

Streets will be the centerpieces of the corridor, with warehouses, industrial operations, art galleries, offices and residences co-existing. The Plan calls for these actions:

- Improve the physical environment and uses at the stations with station plazas, canopy trees, pedestrian-friendly building façades, street cafés, convenience stores and other commuter-oriented retail.
- Develop safe pedestrian connections to the stations by improving visibility, installing signage, and enhancing pathways along major corridors.
- Use vacant buildings and underutilized sites to create high-density residential and commercial uses, especially in the area immediately surrounding the stations.

- Accommodate existing industrial uses that serve the central city, are compatible with residential mixed use and that create jobs.

3. Creating Transit-Oriented Development

The corridor can be transformed into a vital transit hub by promoting high-density transit-oriented development. The light rail stations at 13th and 16th

4. Reclaiming the Public Realm

A reclaimed public realm will be a signature element of the R Street area.

While cities need streets that move traffic quickly and efficiently, they also need pedestrian-friendly streets that create community and encourage gathering. R Street is that kind of street.

The design will draw on successful projects in the Netherlands, Canada, Germany and Denmark that have merged architecture, urban design, landscape architecture and traffic engineering techniques to guide pedestrian, bicycle and vehicle behavior. In some cities planners have done away with conventional traffic measures of control and separation (for example, traffic signals, pedestrian curbs and crossings, bulb outs and bicycle lanes) that provide an illusion of order and safety. Without defined spaces and familiar road markings, motorists in those cities are guided by design and context, instinctively slowing down and interacting with pedestrians. While vehicles move slowly, they do keep moving rather than stopping and starting. The result is that grid-

Universal access in the context of a mixed mode street can mean removing curbed sidewalks where possible, and allowing other streetscape elements to perform the "curb" function.

lock has been reduced, traffic accidents have dropped dramatically while pedestrians and bicyclists freely share the roadway with autos. The advantage is that the entire roadway becomes public space where people safely walk and gather.

The quality of the R Street pedestrian experiences will be enhanced with attractive, well-articulated building façades, welcoming building entries facing the street, shade and shelters, public art, improved pathways, pocket parks and plazas, cafés, and neighborhood-oriented retail. R Street offers excellent opportunities for transforming the public realm into

Santana Row in San Jose, California, employs pedestrian-friendly bollards, benches, trees and planters to separate the street from the sidewalk and improve access.

active pedestrian corridors. The Plan calls for these actions:

■ Improve the pedestrian experience by creating built edges that relate to pedestrians, building massing that provides a sense of enclosure, and uses that activate the corridor.

■ Ensure universal access, while maintaining the area's historic character. This can mean removing curbed sidewalks where possible, and allowing other streetscape elements to perform the "curb" function.

■ Create a series of "activity nodes," major hubs of pedestrian activity, at the light rail stations and between 10th and 11th Streets, 14th and 15th Streets and 16th and 18th Streets. The nodes concentrate activity-generating uses, such as high-density residential, restaurants, theater, art galleries and retail.

■ Create a variety of open space amenities such as pocket parks and plazas for residential and commercial users

The loading dock of this former Berkeley warehouse now serves as a lunchtime oasis for nearby office workers. What was once a parking lot is now a pedestrian plaza.

Every forecourt, mid-block mew and passageway can potentially be pedestrian space.

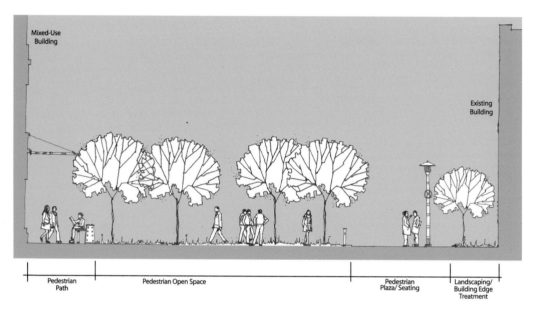

Pocket parks of almost any width between buildings can serve as connectors and gathering spaces.

Alleys can be designed to accommodate people and vehicles—like this one in Vancouver, B.C.

that complement existing parks in nearby neighborhoods. The network of parks and plazas would be linked by pedestrian-friendly pathways. The parks themselves often serve as mews or mid-block connectors, strengthening universal access to the light rail stations.

■ Re-use loading docks of warehouses and factories. Their current form protrudes into the normal sidewalk or pedestrian pathway and creates a

People and cars often coexist, separated by an industrial-style fence.

barrier. The challenge is to increase safe access while maintaining the docks. The solution for R Street was to expand the definition of the pedestrian pathway—without confining pedestrians to a traditional sidewalk between the building edge and the automobile-dominated roadway. Instead, the areas pedestrians can use were expanded to include the roadway around the loading dock. Pedestrians, bicycles, wheelchairs, strollers, autos and trucks will follow new "rules of the road" with clearly designated areas for each.

■ Activate the numbered cross streets (10th, 13th, 16th and 17th Streets) with infill development. Those streets are important connectors between adjacent neighborhoods, recreational resources and other key destinations both north and south of R Street.

5. Encouraging High-Density Mixed Use

The City should develop incentives and streamlined regulations that can encourage high-density mixed use. The Plan calls for these actions:

- Improve infrastructure such as sewers and storm drains so the lack of basic facilities doesn't stop new development.

- Offer financial incentives for brownfield remediation to private property owners to encourage reuse of vacant lots and blighted historic buildings.

- Realign the regulatory framework to speed and modify preservation projects, promote creative adaptive reuse of buildings, integrate universal access improvements that maintain the historic character, and explore creating a private maintenance district to maintain non-standard facilities within the City.

UNIQUE CORRIDOR SECTORS

The urban design concept delineates four separate sections of R Street, each with distinct uses, historic elements, architecture and clusters of vacant buildings or underused space. Future development should reflect the character of each section.

The City of Portland is an urban laboratory of creative, adaptive reuse of industrial buildings.

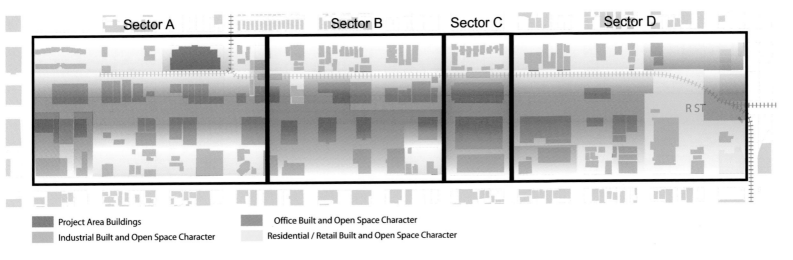

Project Area Buildings

Industrial Built and Open Space Character

Office Built and Open Space Character

Residential / Retail Built and Open Space Character

The final design concept for R Street reflects the predominant character in each of four sectors: Sector A is historically industrial, Sector B is office and mixed use, Sector C is office and Sector D is mixed use and residential.

SECTOR A: *Historic Industrial*

The western section of the corridor features a concentration of historic brick warehouses and industrial uses. Key destinations such as restaurants, theaters and art galleries already make this the most well known section of R Street. Plans for this area include new transit-oriented development based on the 13th Street Station and strengthening the unrefined, industrial character through streetscape improvements and building edge articulation.

- *Public Realm.* The defining feature of this section is a unique, carefully marked 80-foot-wide public right of way shared by pedestrians, bicyclists, autos and trucks. This area never had sidewalks so pedestrians always used the street to get around the many loading docks. The plan calls for five-foot ADA accessible pathways along both sides of the street, at the same level and texture as the rest of the roadway. People in wheelchairs particularly like this aspect of the plan because there are no curbs. People with visual impairments will find detectable warning strips for navigation. Cars park parallel to the road around loading docks. Loading docks of former industrial buildings will be converted to retail and restaurant space, delineated with industrial-style wire railings.

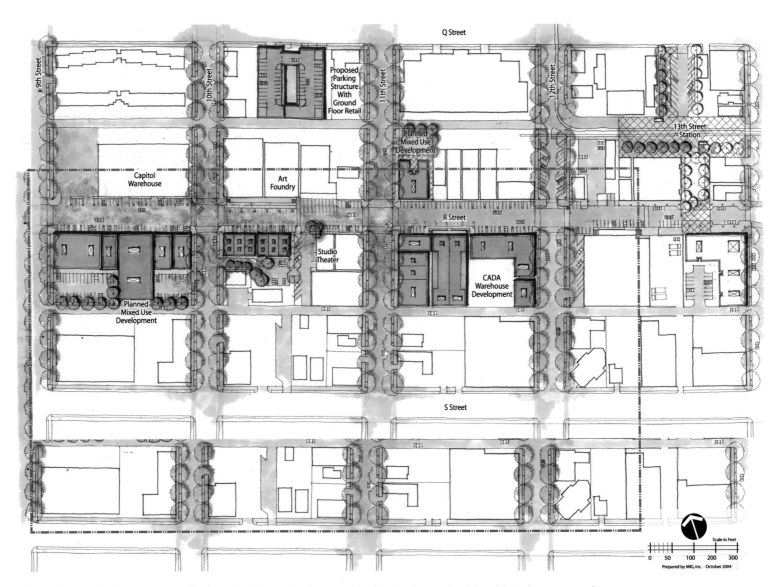

The R Street design concept calls for mixed-use development in Sector A, emphasizing historic preservation.

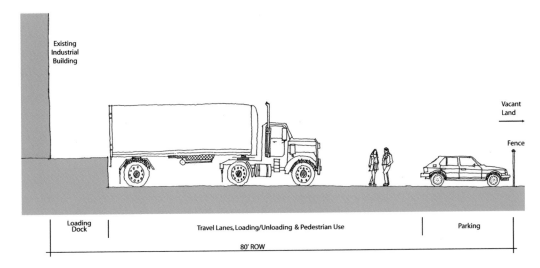

Loading Dock | Travel Lanes, Loading/Unloading & Pedestrian Use | Parking

80' ROW

Currently, Sector A's many loading docks force pedestrians into the street, with no marked path of travel.

Pedestrians currently make do with no clear walkways.

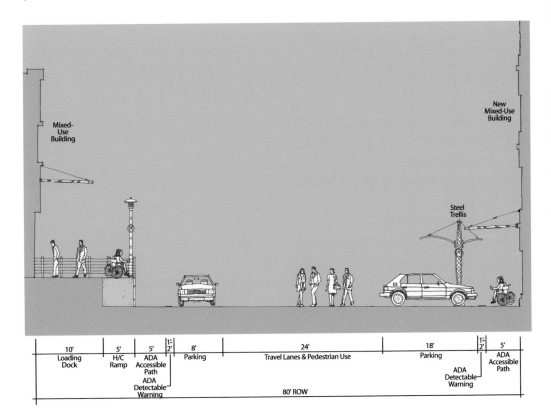

| 10' Loading Dock | 5' H/C Ramp | 5' ADA Accessible Path ADA Detectable Warning | 1½' | 8' Parking | 24' Travel Lanes & Pedestrian Use | 18' Parking ADA Detectable Warning | 1½' | 5' ADA Accessible Path |

80' ROW

With the new design, pedestrians will have clearly marked paths of travel around loading docks.

Detectable warning strips will clearly delineate pedestrian routes.

A historic landmark signal tower will be retained and used as a basis for other design details on R Street.

- *Streetscape*. The gritty industrial quality of the nearby landmark signal tower provides inspiration for the R Street detailed design palette. Elements include steel trellises and shade structures, utilitarian lighting, I-beam bollards that articulate a pedestrian plaza in front of the Studio Theater, wide awnings, trees dispersed asymmetrically, and buildings made of steel, brick and paned glass.

- *Circulation*. Traffic will be restricted to 5 miles per hour. The mid-block alley between R and S streets will become the primary auto access route to parking located in the rear of new developments. Circulation on 12th Street, currently blocked by rail development, will be improved for safe and pleasant pedestrian and bicycle access to the 13th Street Station.

- *New Development*. CADA's 100-unit residential loft and mixed-use development will be a catalyst to generate more activity in this section. New mixed-use development will be oriented toward the 13th Street Station

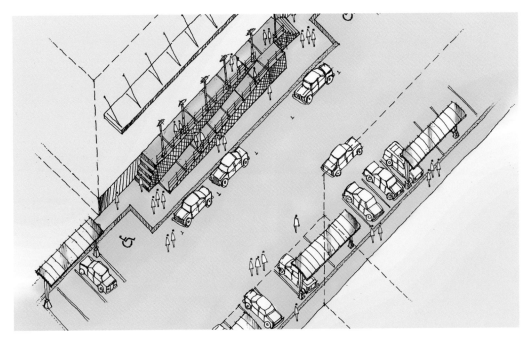

Loading docks will be spillover space and used for retail or cafés.

A former railroad spur in the City of Emeryville, California, has been transformed into a shared roadway, which also serves as parking for businesses. On workdays, parking spaces are filled, and bollards—fashioned from the upturned remains of the train track—serve to delineate the pedestrian pathway.

On the weekends, pedestrians use the entire width of the street.

and should be at least 3 to 4 stories high to maximize transit-oriented development potential. Unused or vacant buildings will be converted to office and retail, and vacant lots and surface parking lots will be developed or become parking structures with ground floor retail facing the street.

This is Sector A as it looks today.

CADA's 100-unit residential loft and mixed use development will be a catalyst for more activity in this section.

PAUL TUTTLE

SECTOR B: *Mixed-Use Transit Hub*

This sector runs from mid-block between 12th and 13th Streets east to 15th Street. It contains a large cluster of single-story office buildings and huge, underused surface parking lots. The current low-density usage doesn't capitalize on the opportunities presented by a prime location near both the 13th Street and 16th Street light rail stations. This section is very auto-oriented, with stark building façades that are typical 1960s style. However, a bustling new restaurant and club has already activated part of the street and can be a catalyst for further development. Plans for the

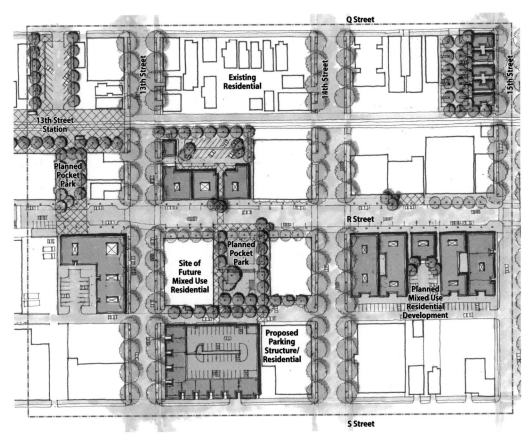

Sector B will become a transit hub centered on the 13th Street Station, with high-density mixed-use infill development.

The existing 13th Street Station design allows shared use by people and transit vehicles.

Several properties surrounding the 13th Street Station present many opportunities for adaptive reuse and intensification.

section include transit-oriented, high-density infill development with a mix of uses, including live-work lofts, artist studios, corner cafés, ground-floor neighborhood-serving retail with commercial space above and light manufacturing and warehouses.

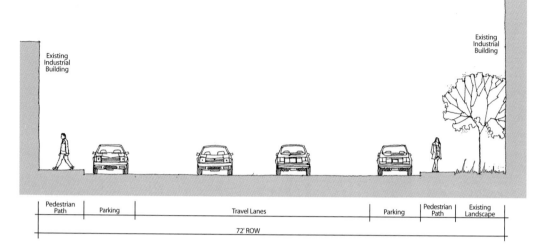

Current building façades are unwelcoming with many surface parking areas and flat building façades.

■ *Public Realm.* The existing 80-foot public right of way will be reconfigured to allow for a more generous accessible pedestrian pathway. In the long term, the sidewalks will be removed so the pathway is at the same level as the roadway. There are few loading docks so the pathway can be nine feet wide plus space for shade trellises and ADA detectable warning strips.

■ *Streetscape.* This area will benefit from pocket parks and plazas for local residents and employees. The 13th Street Station will have a new plaza, with the current north parking area renovated to allow for a landscaped, tree-lined pedestrian connection to Q Street. A pocket park just south of the station and another further west will feature groves of trees, seating and water features, serving as a green oasis and social gathering place for employees and future residents. Streetscape elements are similar to those described in Sector A.

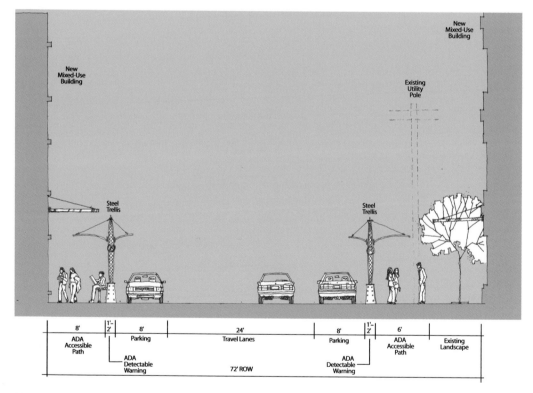

New pedestrian comfort features such as trellises, seating and a wider path of travel will enhance the street for pedestrians.

After removing curbs, a planting strip—no matter how small—can further improve the pedestrian experience.

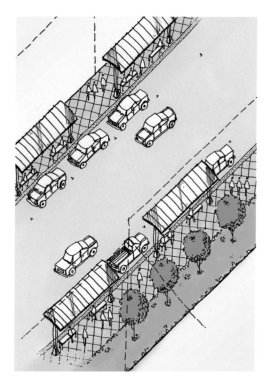

The new R Street design continues the area's use of the "mixed mode" street environment: pedestrians, bicyclists, autos and trucks share the roadway.

Sidewalks in the existing public right of way can be removed so the pathway is at the same level as the roadway.

■ *Circulation.* Traffic will be slowed to 5 miles per hour. Cars will continue to park parallel to the street on both sides, with 24 feet remaining for traffic flow. All new development has adequate off-street parking tucked away in the rear of buildings, which can be accessed through mid-block alleys.

■ *New Development.* Historic buildings should be converted to uses that support transit activity and residential living, such as art galleries, artists' lofts and design studios. The buildings will be used with a greater intensity, with a minimum of three to four stories. Development along

Produce shoppers can enjoy the ease of walking from shops to outdoor stands, all on the same block.

Sector B, with its low density and auto-oriented usage, currently doesn't capitalize on the opportunities presented by a prime location near both the 13th Street and 16th Street light rail stations.

the numbered streets will be high-density townhomes or apartments that respect the adjoining residential character. Because surface parking lots will be re-used, the plan proposes a new mixed-use parking structure that will provide residential uses fronting the street and access to parking from the alley.

Artist's rendering of Sector B Phase 2 illustrates how streetscape elements help to unify all four sectors.
PAUL TUTTLE

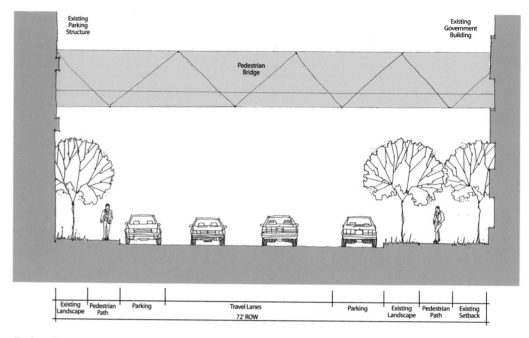

Pedestrians are now wedged between a parking structure and offices.

| Existing Landscape | Pedestrian Path | Parking | Travel Lanes | Parking | Existing Landscape | Pedestrian Path | Existing Setback |

72' ROW

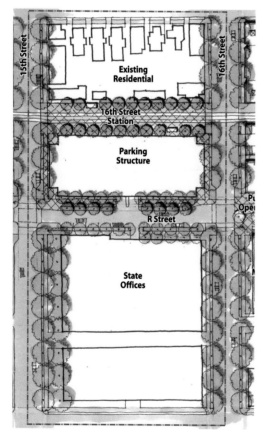

Sector C, a relatively stark area, will benefit from an improved streetscape and public art; no new development is planned.

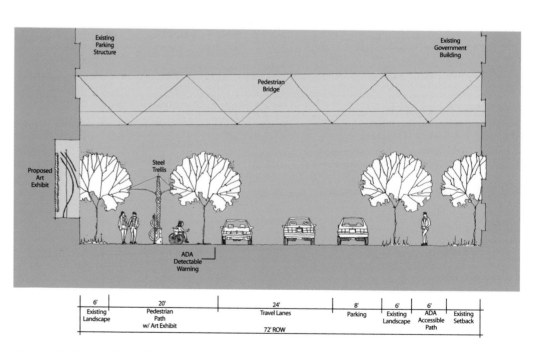

| 6' | 20' | 24' | 8' | 6' | 6' | |
| Existing Landscape | Pedestrian Path w/ Art Exhibit | Travel Lanes | Parking | Existing Landscape | ADA Accessible Path | Existing Setback |

72' ROW

A new 20-foot-wide pathway and art space will break pedestrians out of their current narrow, unattractive confines and encourage public gathering.

SECTOR C: *Art Walk*

This one-block section currently offers very few pedestrian amenities. It is mainly government office buildings, including one five-story office building, and a seven-story parking structure. While these tall buildings provide shade and a sense of enclosure, their imposing façades have no human-scale detail. The residential structures along the north edge of the 16th Street Station face the other direction, with their backs to the street, and reinforce the unappealing nature of the street environment at this point. Plans for this section include improving the interface between the existing buildings, the public realm and the 16th Street Station, and evolving this small sector into an "art walk" that connects activity nodes to the east and west. Both ground floor building façades and the pedestrian right-of-way will be transformed into a pedestrian-friendly space that celebrates the arts.

■ *Public Realm*. An immediate improvement will be widening the northern

edge of the current six-foot sidewalk to 20 feet and reducing the roadway to 24 feet for two lanes of traffic (taking away an on-street parking lane). This will create space for a generous promenade for various art exhibits, such as display boxes, murals, sculptures and space for art-related events and festivals. The current ground floor dark glass of the parking structure will be replaced with transparent glass and the edge of the structure will be reconfigured into a public gallery. The alley between R and Q Street, along with the adjacent 16th Street Station, will become a transit plaza with a row of shade trees. Seating along the tree-lined southern edge will be complemented with uses that serve foot traffic, such as temporary food and hawker stands. Cafés, small convenience stores and other pedestrian-friendly retail will activate the plaza around the clock. Increased numbers of people on the street will increase safety as well.

■ *Circulation*. Traffic will be slowed to 5 miles per hour on R Street. 15th

Parking structures can give life to the street by providing retail space, art displays and other active uses on the ground floor.

and 16th Streets will continue as major one-way arterials across R Street.

- *New Development.* This section is fully developed, so short-term improvements will take advantage of the close proximity to the 16th Street light rail station, creating an aesthetically pleasing station plaza. If any buildings are demolished, high-density, mixed-use would replace them, preferably with ground floor retail.

Temporary events and artisan stands will enliven Sector C on weekends.

A building façade in this Berkeley art and theater district provides a high level of eye-catching detail at the street to entice pedestrians.

Sector C is already fully developed, but lacks connections between building façades and pedestrian activity.

An immediate improvement will be widening the northern (left) side of the current sidewalk. This will create a generous promenade for art exhibits and events (artist's rendering of Sector C, Phase 2).

PAUL TUTTLE

Unique seating creates connections between the sidewalk, the building façade and pedestrians.

SECTOR D: Market Green

This easternmost section has the largest inventory of vacant and underused historic buildings and vacant brownfield sites. The area is now auto-dominated, with perpendicular parking on the north side and an 80-foot-wide travel lane for truck loading and cars. The few pedestrians clamber around loading docks in the street. The new R Street Market will become a key destination point for the surrounding community

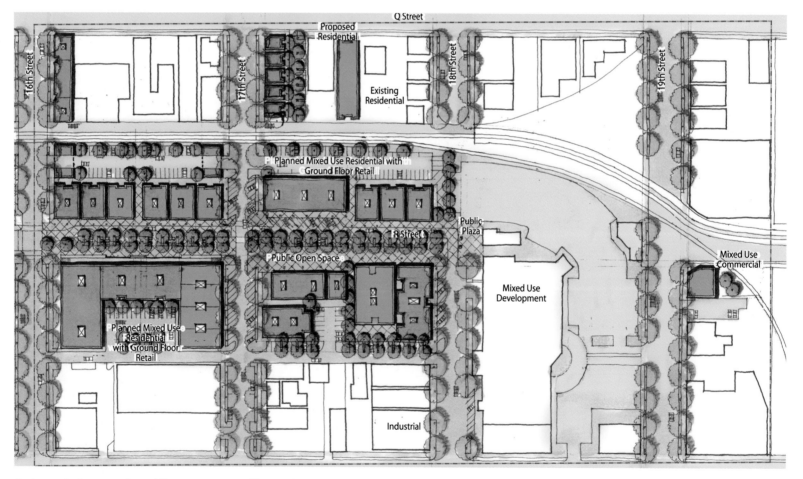

A dramatic increase in public open space will completely change the nature of this sector; new retail shops also will activate the area.

with the new grocery store, restaurant and café on the ground floor with housing above. Plans for this section include building on that anchor development and providing a signature public open space that dramatically reconfigures the current street.

- *Public Realm.* The "Market Green" is a shaded area with a double row of trees, running right down the middle of R Street between 16th and 18th Streets. It will be a vibrant, landscaped, multi-use area that freely mixes all modes of travel and changes character depending on the time of day and day of the week. Trellis shelters, awnings and tall building on the south side of the street will provide shade during the hot summers. Benches and new lighting accentuate pedestrian-friendly spaces. During the week, the Green serves as a pocket park with limited parking. During weekends, it transforms into space for cafés, farmers markets and other community events and festivals. A public plaza at the east end of the corridor (fronting the mixed-use

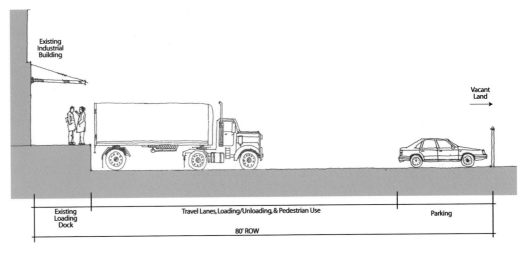

Currently, trucks loading and unloading, traffic and parking dominate the street.

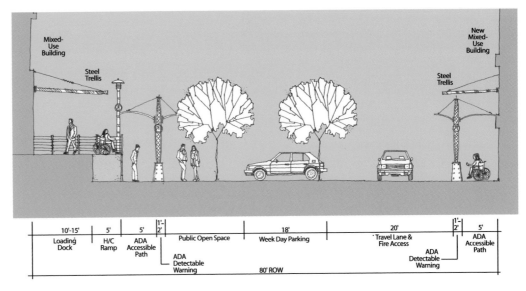

The R Street design concept adds 5 feet of pathways plus about 15 feet of open space and 18 feet of shared space for pedestrians.

On weekends, Sector D will host farmers markets and other community events and festivals. This is Santana Row in San Jose.

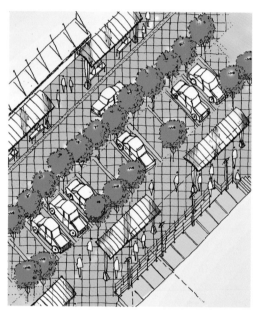

The Market Green area in the center of the street freely mixes all modes of travel and changes character depending on the time of day and day of the week.

anchor development) will have a feature gateway similar to the historic signal towers at the corner of R and 8th Streets.

- *Circulation*. Pedestrians and autos will share the roadway; traffic will be slowed to 5 miles per hour. A one-way, single vehicular lane will accommodate slow-moving service vehicles and fire trucks. On weekdays, on-street parking is restricted to a single row of perpendicular parking in the center of the street. On weekends, there will be no on-street parking. All new development will have off-street parking in the rear that can be accessed by alleys and numbered streets.

- *New Development*. The large parcels of vacant land and the unused historic buildings, such as the Crystal Ice Building, offer prime development opportunities for high-density housing and other transit-oriented, neighborhood-scale uses.

During weekends, Sector D transforms into a space for cafés, farmers markets and other community events and festivals. A public plaza at the east end of the corridor (fronting the mixed-use anchor development) will have a feature gateway similar to the historic signal towers at the corner of R and 8th Streets (artist's rendering).

PAUL TUTTLE

DESIGN PALETTE

All design features will reflect and strengthen the historic industrial character of the area, drawing on the existing building and streetscape elements as a street design language. Metal sashes, multi-paned industrial windows, awnings at entries and over loading docks, and brick (exposed or painted), plastered concrete, glass and corrugated metal façades reflect a utilitarian aesthetic.

The streetscape palette includes metal, steel and cobblestones. Artwork and gateways will also be primarily metal and stone.

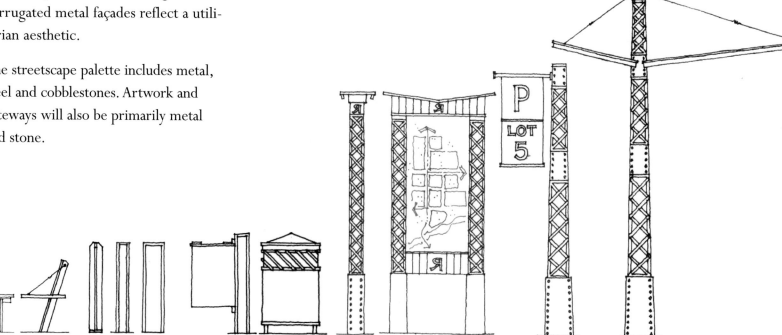

Streetscape elements will be consistent throughout the street; they will be made of metal, concrete and glass to reflect the historic industrial character of the area.

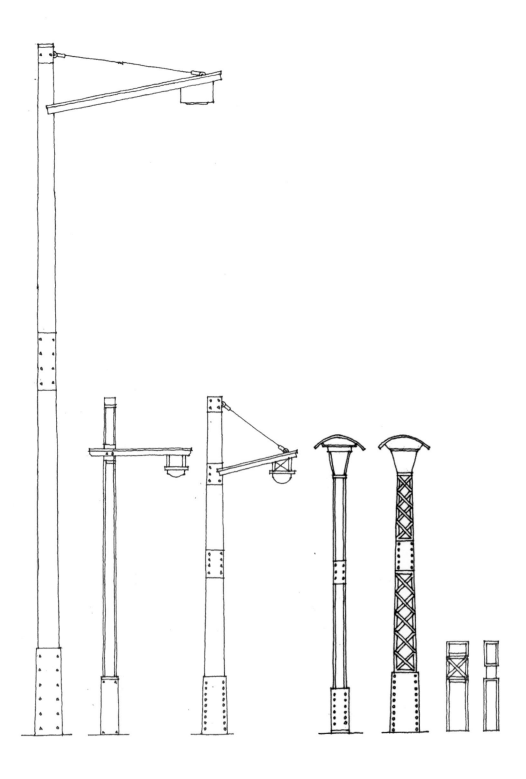

UNIVERSAL DESIGN

Eliminating sidewalks and curbs makes accessibility far easier for people using wheelchairs and other mobility devices. To ensure that those with visual impairments also feel comfortable, design elements other than curbs will be used. The plan recommends a 5-foot-wide ADA accessible path on at least one side of the street with detectable warning strips, trellises, streets lights and bollards to provide tactile clues.

Detectable warning strips can be tactile and brightly colored to provide wayfinding for those with visual impairments.

Management and Operational Issues

The R Street Urban Design and Development Plan outlines the steps for directing future investment in the area, ensuring efficient and economical progress. Because improvements are being completed in stages, it's critically important that everyone involved in the project—for example, City planning staff, developers, businesses, residents, and Public Works staff—share the same vision of R Street and work together to solve anticipated management and operational issues.

STREET MAINTENANCE

Efforts to create an inviting and active streetscape can be undermined if the street isn't well maintained. Maintenance staff needs to understand the vision and goals for the area as they make day-to-day maintenance and repair decisions. All trash, graffiti, broken or burned out streetlights and vandalism need to be addressed immediately to maintain the look and feel of the area. Once the look and feel is undermined, the perceptions of blight and lack of safety quickly return.

The City will likely not have all the resources to maintain the new street surfaces, furniture, landscaping and other aesthetic features, so the solution may be a Business Improvement District (BID) or Property-based Business Improvement District (PBID). Both are self-help organizations created to fund physical and programmatic improvements. A BID is a self-taxing, merchant-based organization created with the help of local government. They're often used for smaller retail-oriented revitalization and economic development programs, including farmers markets. A PBID is a property-based assessment district that supplements local government funds by directly assessing property owners. PBIDs typically help fund security, maintenance, marketing, economic development and special events. It's created and governed by those who pay the assessment.

AGENCY COORDINATION

All of the public agencies and private businesses that play a part in R Street need to maintain good, ongoing communications. A PBID can be the leadership organization for the R Street area, communicating with and coordinating agencies such as Sacramento City Planning, Sacramento Regional Transit, Sacramento Police and Fire Departments, Public Works, CADA, property owners (commercial and residential) and developers.

INFRASTRUCTURE DEVELOPMENT

As new development comes into the area, property owners will be required to contribute resources to complete the infrastructure and ensure that new designs harmonize with the R Street development standards and design guidelines.

PROGRAM MANAGEMENT

A unified management approach will help operate the street as a whole. For example, on weekends the east end of R Street becomes a gathering space for markets and musical events, replacing parking. The community, including residents, will need to participate in decisions about issues like lighting, banners and use of the shared roadway. It's critical that community members feel connected to the street and that they are also stewards of the R Street environment.

User Feedback

Steve Cohn, City Councilmember

"R Street revitalization is key to bringing the south part of mid-town back into the rest of the Central City. The CADA projects and the grocery store are showing people the great development opportunity this area offers. And the housing project at 4th and R is showing us what mixed-use housing, retail and office can offer."

Allyson Dalton, Owner, Fox & Goose Pub and Restaurant

"This is the first cohesive vision for the entire corridor. My parents opened our pub in 1975 and before that they owned an art gallery in the same building. I grew up on this street—this was my playground. My parents were visionaries for what could happen here.

"The potential for developing this corridor is tremendous. It can revitalize all of Sacramento Downtown.

"Long-term, I think the main issues will be ensuring that everyone shares the same vision and knows how to implement and maintain it. They should set the architectural detail all the way down the corridor so the benches, lighting, awnings, furniture, etc., are all the same. It's critical that we all take responsibility for maintaining our areas. For example, plants have to be well maintained and graffiti has to be cleaned immediately or it will attract more graffiti.

"All the business owners are very excited. Of course, many are a little skeptical because we've heard there will be a new vision for so long. But, this is the closest I've ever seen it; I believe it will happen this time. I'd love to purchase a loft and live here myself. I'd love to walk, ride my bike and be part of helping this community grow."

Todd Leon, City of Sacramento, Planning Division

"We can change an entire strip of the City and do something really exciting with it. This old industrial area is full of history and surrounded by so many different types of neighborhoods. Right now, it splits the north and the south. Yet, it has tremendous contextual and relational value. Its transformation can link up the two sides.

"We're moving people away from the idea of separate places for offices and suburbs, toward the idea of what a city was before the car dominated our lives.

Shared roadway and light rail, as in the Ankeny Burnside neighborhood, Portland, can reinvigorate older areas.

The plan was originally started to stop the infill of large office buildings where everyone goes home at night. The neighborhood stepped in and said, 'No, we want a real neighborhood we can embrace.' So the primary goal is infill housing—we're not yet at our goal of 3,000 units—and small shops, mixed-use with housing on top. The market had to catch up with the idea of mixed use, and I think Sacramento has reached the tipping point now. The neighborhood needs time to find the balance between housing, retail and office.

"The shared roadway concept keeps the historical context. There are no sidewalks here now so when people walk, pedestrians and vehicles already mix. When it's built out more, this will maintain the sense of place and enhance it. People are drawn to an area with a sense of place—they want the unique experience of being someplace that doesn't look like everywhere else. And we don't have many unique places in Sacramento.

"The disabled community has played a big role as well. The plan provides linkages and paths to all elements. It's a colorful plan that allows you to easily move up and down the corridor. We're creating a place that everybody will want to go to. And when we say everybody, we mean everybody.

"There will be some infrastructure issues to overcome. The sewer system is old and complicated. Land costs are tricky. If the land costs too much because of speculation, it's difficult to finance a project. There are several key spots that are owned by large landowners. We need to show a developer who might be used to creating tilt-up buildings that you can make money following this vision. Then that project can be an icon, a catalyst for the rest of the developers.

"We also have to be sure the improvements are kept up. And whenever you have a 24-hour city, you'll have issues of noise, congestion, and people on the streets. But we can do it, working as partners: CADA, the City, and the neighborhood."

Paul Schmidt, Executive Director, Capitol Area Development Authority (CADA)

"There aren't a lot of people living here now but we have a large condo project starting up. In fact, a main feature of the street is the potential to build housing. The Capitol Lofts projects between 10th and 13th Streets will show people the new character and life of living on this street, living the loft lifestyle. We actually got a $1.5 million grant for that project.

"Funding is always a challenge. We've been successful in getting some grants to jump-start projects but we'll need a PBID and we'll have to sell everyone on that idea.

"This is the oldest industrial corridor in the country and we think the historic look of bricks and loading docks—features that aren't usually found in Sacramento—will give us a marketing edge. This is an opportunity for us to

create our own identity: it's edgy, gritty and industrial with a great view of Downtown. We think people will want to move here not just from Sacramento but also from the Bay Area and other cities."

Carol Bradley, ADA Coordinator, City of Sacramento

"R Street is being designed to incorporate the idea of universal design from the beginning—it's a benefit of having a slower-paced industrial area.

"I liked the process of developing R Street; its community feedback helped architects and technical folk understand things like why having street furniture is so difficult for people with disabilities. We had a lot of discussions. Take detectable warnings for example. In California, if the state standard is higher than the federal, the state prevails. In California, we have to have yellow truncated domes to mark when you're

entering a street. In other states, it just has to contrast. But yellow is the last color you see when you're losing your sight, so here, yellow it must be. But people hate the yellow; it's not historical and it's not aesthetic. We compromised. It's not an ADA path of travel, it's an accessible path of travel and it doesn't have to be yellow. But we increased the original two feet to three feet of domes.

"Another thing that came out of all the discussion is moving the signage and furniture out of the path of travel entirely. Then people can follow the truncated domes. The curb-less streets were also an issue. For people in chairs, it's great. But if you're blind, you need some delineation. The design solution was a raised crosswalk.

"In the final outcome, we kept the historic character and it will also be truly accessible for everyone."

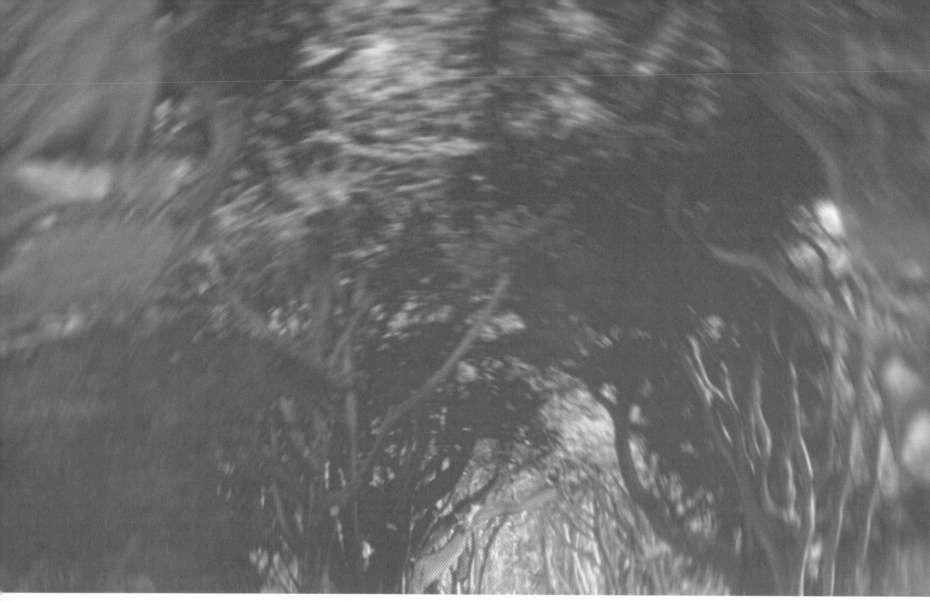

PRESIDIO TRAILS AND BIKEWAYS | SAN FRANCISCO, CALIFORNIA

"One thorny issue we have is how to put an accessible link from the Bay up to the vista point....Is it worth the expense to have that link? The answer is, yes. We have to provide an accessible experience for all our visitors."

LANDSCAPE ARCHITECT, NATIONAL PARK SERVICE

CONNECTING URBAN AND NATURAL SETTINGS

LARRY WIGHT
SALLY McINTYRE

THE NEW PRESIDIO TRAILS AND BIKEWAYS MASTER PLAN PROVIDES AN INTERCONNECTED, safe and enjoyable trail and bikeway system that enhances all park users' experiences—while protecting and preserving the Presidio's natural and cultural resources. It's the first comprehensive trail and bikeway network for the area. The Presidio of San Francisco is a former Army base converted to an urban National Park. It encompasses 1,491 acres at the northwestern tip of San Francisco, touching both the Pacific Ocean and San Francisco Bay and offering spectacular vistas.

The Presidio offers miles of trails, wide beaches and spectacular vistas.

Located at the threshold of the Golden Gate Bridge, the park includes nearly 500 historic buildings and structures (including historic coastal defense bunkers), a national cemetery, a historic airfield, and miles of hiking and biking trails. Its varied natural landscape includes coastal bluffs and beaches, a saltwater marsh, dense forests and native plant habitats that contain endangered species. It is a component of the Golden Gate National Recreation Area (GGNRA) and a National Historic Landmark District.

PROJECT Trails and Bikeways Master Plan   **LOCATION** San Francisco, California   **DATE DESIGNED** 2003   **SIZE** 1,491 acres   **CLIENT** National Park Service/Presidio Trust   **LANDSCAPE ARCHITECT** MIG, Inc.

The Presidio offers views of the world famous Golden Gate Bridge, from the west and east sides.

Previously, there were about 19 miles of designated pedestrian and multi-use trails and bike lanes in the Presidio. But there were also many miles of additional unofficial trails and shortcuts that had been developed through informal use. These user-defined trails criss-crossed much of the Presidio, including natural areas and sensitive habitats. They were of uneven quality, confusing to navigate and didn't connect well to park features. Some trails presented safety and access issues. Others caused environmental degradation, increasing erosion, fragmenting native plant communities and wildlife habitat, disrupting drainage

The City of San Francisco is developed right up to the edge of the Presidio.

patterns and even degrading historic coastal fortifications.

The Plan identifies new trails, upgrades or modifies selected existing trails and service roads, and identifies unofficial trails that should either be closed or incorporated into the official trails network. The Plan improves connections between key features of the Presidio, enhances the public's exploration and experience of the Presidio's open spaces and resources, increases accessibility for people with and without disabilities, enhances visitor safety, and encourages use of alternative modes of transportation.

With this Plan, the Presidio will have 19.2 miles of pedestrian trails, 14.4 miles of bikeways and 20.1 miles of multi-use trails.

DESIGN GOALS

The Trails and Bikeways Master Plan accomplished five major goals:

- Enhance public use of, access to and experience of the Presidio by providing logical, comprehensive and user-friendly connections, and a network of trails that provides a variety of experiences with access and challenge for different ages, skills and physical abilities.

- Help preserve the Presidio's valuable natural and cultural resources.

- Create a system that supports alternative transportation, reducing dependence on cars, and coordinates with regional and national trails and local bicycle routes.

- Design an environmentally responsible trail system that fully incorporates the best in sustainable design and construction practices.

- Begin an ongoing process of public engagement in educational and stewardship programs.

The Presidio encompasses almost 1,500 acres of varied uses, including golf, beaches, miles of trails, historic sites, offices, and access to the Golden Gate Bridge (at top of photo).

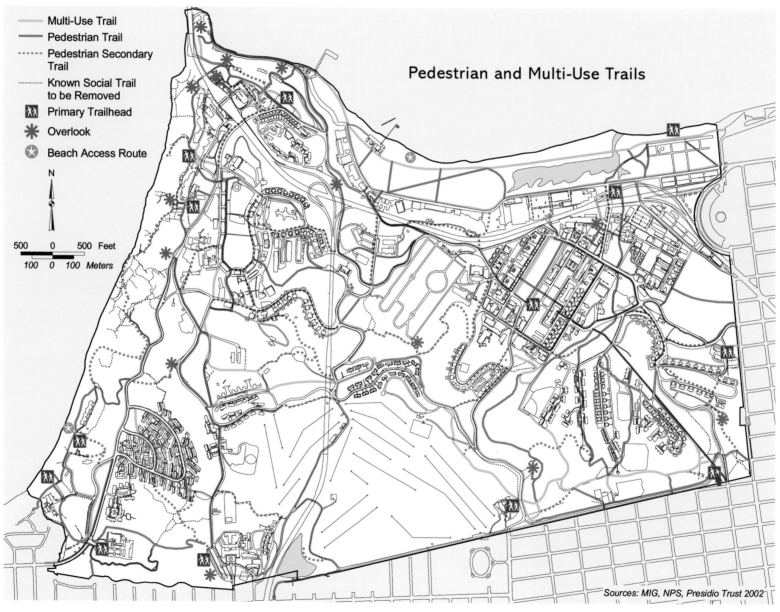

Pedestrian and Multi-Use Trails

Legend:
- Multi-Use Trail
- Pedestrian Trail
- Pedestrian Secondary Trail
- Known Social Trail to be Removed
- Primary Trailhead
- Overlook
- Beach Access Route

N

500　0　500 Feet
100　0　100 Meters

Sources: MIG, NPS, Presidio Trust 2002

Disparate walks, trails and bike paths will be linked to create a unified new cross-Presidio trail, safe access to beaches below the steep bluffs, and become a beautiful segment of the California Coastal Trail.

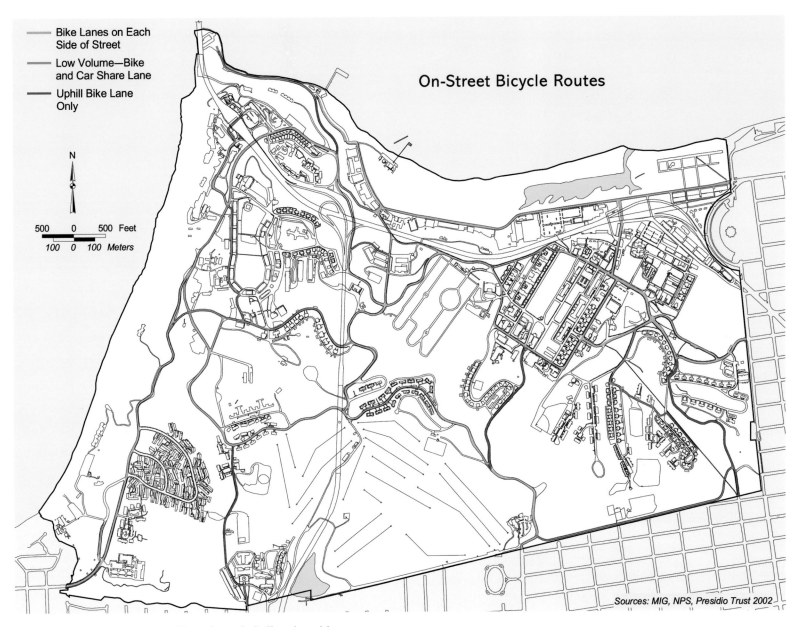

On-Street Bicycle Routes

Bike Lanes on Each
Side of Street

Low Volume—Bike
and Car Share Lane

Uphill Bike Lane
Only

N

500   0   500 Feet

100   0   100 Meters

Sources: MIG, NPS, Presidio Trust 2002

On-street bicycle routes provide safe and challenging rides.

Bicyclists can take advantage of miles of trails and stunning vistas.

Touring bicyclists want to see the sights and the beauty of the Presidio, sharing multi-user paths with pedestrians.

The Trails and Bikeways Master Plan is a joint effort of the National Park Service (NPS) and the Presidio Trust (Trust), the two agencies responsible for managing the area. It will guide management of the Presidio trails and bikeways for the next 20 years.

USER GROUPS

The specific needs of user types directly affected the routing, configuration and design guidelines for trails and bikeways.

■ Pedestrians

Pedestrian users vary greatly, from those seeking physically challenging walks to those who want a convenient connection between two activity centers. Sub-categories of pedestrian users include: recreational walkers, commuters, runners and exercisers of different abilities, and self-mobile wheelchair users.

■ Bicyclists

Bicycle users form three distinct sub-groups.

Bicycle commuters who live or work in the Presidio or pass through the Presidio want a direct, easy-to-use route to their workplace, and would prefer designated bike lanes or low-volume roadways and routes that minimize their travel time.

Serious recreational cyclists who often are out for a long ride and are not intimidated by hills or traffic prefer wide shoulders or bike lanes, but the lack of these facilities does not affect their choice of a route. Unlike bicycle commuters, this group puts more importance on a scenic route where they can ride fast than they do on time savings.

Family or touring bicyclists (with and without children) want to see the sights and the beauty of the Presidio. Their choice of routes is affected by traffic and hills, and just as importantly, the route's access to the Presidio's major attractions.

They prefer to be on multi-use trails or roadways with little or no traffic. Often, these users don't ride unless bikeways meet these specifications.

Off-trail mountain bikers were specifically excluded. They would like to have single-track, off-road dirt trails, but park regulations and the need to protect sensitive habitats and other natural resources made it necessary to exclude this group.

■ Other Wheeled Sports Users

In-line skaters and skateboarders are the primary non-cyclist wheeled sports user group. People pushing children in strollers or wheelchair users are included with pedestrians. In-line skaters and skateboarders who are out for a recreational skate or ride can be accommodated on hardened pedestrian and multi-use trails.

Wide trails can often be shared by pedestrians and those using wheelchairs or pushing strollers.

Access to the water's edge at high tide is possible with floating boardwalks.

Not all trails can be fully accessible, but improvements will increase safety and access, while protecting resources.

DESIGN PROCESS

The core planning team consisted of NPS and Trust staff and consultants with experience in park planning, natural and cultural resources, facilities manage-ment, interpretation, visitor protection and transportation.

The team engaged the public in identifying needs and issues, proposing alternative solutions, and reviewing the Plan.

Since the Trails and Bikeways Master Plan included an Environmental Assessment, the public involvement was formalized to meet requirements of the National Environmental Policy Act

Boardwalks protect resources and provide access to sandy beaches.

Multi-use trails such as the Golden Gate Promenade accommodate cars and bicycles, and often have a soft-surface pedestrian trail alongside.

Raised pavement markings or raised traffic separators can pose hazards to cyclists of all abilities. Except in special circumstances, bike lanes should be separated from motor vehicle traffic by painted lane markings.

On-street bicycle routes link major park sites. This cyclist is using a low-volume road with no bike lane.

(NEPA). The first phase of public involvement included a public meeting, a series of focus group meetings, a design concept workshop, a survey of park users, communications with other agencies, and various opportunities for written comment. As the process continued, other public involvement activities included newsletter articles, public presentations, on-site walks and rides, wide distribution of planning documents, open-house style displays in the park, and website publication of the Plan.

Inclusive Design Features and Settings

In special areas such as the Presidio, where the mandate for resource protection is equal to the mandate for visitor experience, providing trails designed to serve all visitors is extremely challenging. It is especially difficult to provide access to extraordinary visitor experiences that are by their nature not accessible. The desire for restricted access often competes equally with the desire to increase accessibility for all visitors.

The trail system was developed with the following universal design principles in mind:

- Consistency and continuity of trail design benefits all users.
- Trail gradients of 1:20 or less benefit recreational cyclists as well as wheelchair users.
- Safety considerations—such as median islands where trails cross roadways—aid families with small children and other users, as well as people with disabilities.

Wide multi-use trails can accommodate many different types of users.

This overlook also functions as a trailhead, providing wayfinding signage.

Trail alignments take advantage of unique viewpoints.

- Trail signage can clarify a trail user's expectation of a trail's challenge, allowing design for varying levels of accessibility.

- Not all portions of all trails can or should be fully accessible to all users, due to constraints of slope, natural resources, or the desire for a variety of experiences.

- A wide variety of trail types increases accessibility for all users, and provides the opportunity for equivalent experiences.

- Pedestrian trails that are designed to be accessible require park policies that manage bicycle use to ensure safety.

TRAILS

Trails in the Presidio traverse a wide range of settings, from beaches to forests, from historic places to high-density urban development, and from spaces that are dark and enclosing to expansive vista points. Terrain varies from flat to very steep and trails vary from narrow footpaths to wide, multi-use paved promenades.

Although trails and bikeways are designed for consistency and continuity, the design guidelines allow flexibility to respond to each unique setting to enhance the visitor's experience of that setting. Trails providing access to these varied settings are classified in three basic categories: pedestrian trails, multi-use trails and bikeways.

Pedestrian Trails

There are two types of pedestrian trails. Primary trails occur in the major trail and road corridors, and provide connecting routes to important Presidio destinations. Primary trails are generally wide and often hard-surfaced to accommodate a large number of trail users.

Secondary trails provide an opportunity to experience many of the Presidio's less visited environments and the many cultural, historical, natural and scenic resources. Secondary trails are typically soft-surfaced, single-track footpaths.

Some trails have a special character, such as a boardwalk designed to protect resources or provide access to beaches or areas with sandy soils. Other trails are designed with grades ranging from flat to steep to provide trail users with a variety of challenges.

Multi-Use Trails

Multi-use trails provide major connections between important Presidio destinations, entry gates and other local, regional and national trail systems. To reduce impact, they are located in previously developed areas or on former service roadways as much as possible.

Most multi-use trails have easy grades of less than 1:20 (5 percent) to provide greater accessibility for persons with disabilities and recreational bicyclists.

Trails wind through groves of eucalyptus trees.

The trails generally have hardened surfaces, often with adjacent soft-surface pedestrian shoulders that can be used as walking or running paths.

Bikeways

A primary goal of the Trails and Bikeways Master Plan was to improve roadway safety for bicyclists and ensure that there are no gaps in the bicycle circulation network. Bikeways were therefore designed to work in conjunction with traffic calming measures. The Plan addresses on-street bike lanes and signed bike routes where bikes and cars share a traffic lane. Bicycle use occurs on multi-use trails and on nearly all roadways in the Presidio.

TRAILHEADS

Trailheads typically serve as multi-modal transfer points, allowing users to change from public transit or automobile to bicycle or foot, or from bicycle to foot. Trailheads provide trail information and user amenities where appropriate.

Primary trailheads at major trail starting points include automobile parking, wayfinding signage and amenities. Secondary trailheads provide a limited set of standard components such as trail information and perhaps bicycle parking at a footpath, but no automobile parking.

OVERLOOKS

Overlooks allow park visitors to pause and enjoy a spectacular natural feature, observe wildlife, or take in a unique view of a special structure. There will be primary overlooks along Presidio roadways and in some cases an overlook may also function as a trailhead. Secondary overlooks occur on trails without auto access, and are designed to take advantage of unique viewpoints resulting from trail alignment and topography. These "off the beaten track" overlooks are intended as quiet places of solitude.

Boardwalks through sensitive areas are designed to meander around vegetation.

Management and Operational Issues

Providing safe and enjoyable trails requires an understanding of user requirements at the design stage, and appropriate management of trail use after construction. Management and operational issues fall into three categories: trail use policies, natural resource management and trail construction and maintenance.

One measure of success will be a low level of user conflicts. Conflict between bikers and pedestrians is one of the most common trail issues. The Trails and Bikeways Master Plan reduces conflicts by providing adequate width of multi-use trails, a greater choice of a variety of pedestrian and multi-use trail routes, and by designing some trails for pedestrian use only.

Trail markers inform users which trails are appropriate for the experience they want...

...through promenades...

Natural resource management policies greatly affected trail planning, requiring compromises to visitor access and experience of the Presidio, and in a few instances, extraordinary design

measures to protect sensitive habitat. For example, on one heavily used major multi-use trail, width is reduced from a standard 14 feet to only 6 feet, to protect habitat. Some areas require

...to historic buildings and...

...to steep trails down to the Pacific Ocean.

Andrea Lucas
Landscape Architect and
Project Manager, National Park Service

"Significant issues at the Presidio are balancing historical, cultural and visual impacts. From an accessibility point of view, there are issues of finding your way from one point to another, when historical issues are also important. For example, one of the things we wanted to do with the Presidio Promenade was to make it recognizable as a trail going through various sites. We talked about making it a consistent trail surface all the way through, but the Presidio Trust decided to make it an urban concrete walk through the main post area. Outside of the main post area it would then be a consistent look so it would be identifiable to all users as the trail.... We're trying to make a sensible trail system because it's so confusing

fences or other barriers adjacent to trails to keep users from straying into sensitive habitats.

To address on-going trail design, management, construction and maintenance

issues, NPS and Presidio Trust trail managers will follow the Park Design Guidelines, which are also included in the Trails and Bikeways Master Plan.

Overlooks provide stunning views of the Pacific Ocean and coastline.

now, with all the different walks and trails and routes that are possible here.

"With the historic roads, we have a lot of issues. They have steep crowns from being paved over and over, and there is a historic drainage ditch to meet, so we are looking to see if it's worth the expense to grind the paving off to deal with our allowable cross slopes.

"One thorny issue we have is how to put an accessible link from the Bay way up to the vista point near the toll plaza—it's a couple of hundred feet up. We looked at various routes and chose

narrowest area. So we looked at having a single uphill bike lane....two lanes of cars, and then a retaining wall dropping down about three feet to a four foot wide accessible pathway that has landings for rest stops per the trails guidelines.

"We've gone back and forth between cultural resources and natural resources on that road because it is in a serpentine area and serpentine is a special rock here at the Presidio. It is a Civil War-era road, so its original width is of interest. And evidently there are still some of the old granite cobbles, which many San Francisco streets were paved with, under the existing asphalt. So that is a very expensive trail. The question is, is it worth it (grinding down the asphalt, adding the retaining wall and additional trail) to have that accessible link? The answer is, yes. We have to provide an accessible experience for all our visitors."

Richard De La O
Accessibility Coordinator, Golden Gate
National Recreation Area

"One of the big issues is that even though a project is designed for universal access, it needs continual supervision during construction or it will not comply. It may look good on paper and meet code, but it's not always constructed correctly. The contractor often doesn't follow the guidelines carefully, because they still have the mindset of how it's always been done."

Long Avenue, which is a linking street that varies about 8 to 10 percent in existing slope and was the only one that was close to accessible trail standards. But the road is only 20 feet wide in the

ALFRED ZAMPA (CARQUINEZ) BRIDGE | SAN FRANCISCO BAY, CALIFORNIA

"The bridge is now a meeting point....It's a pleasure to stop and meet friends halfway."

CROCKETT RESIDENT

SPANNING THE COMMUNITY

BART NEY
DANIEL IACOFANO

WHEN THE CALIFORNIA DEPARTMENT OF TRANSPORTATION (CALTRANS) ANNOUNCED AN elegant suspension bridge as the design solution for retrofitting one of the State's oldest steel cantilever bridges, engineers thought that the local community would be pleased to have a new architectural icon in their backyards. They were not.

This is the story of how a large state agency and a small community worked together to build that new bridge—and how their partnership changed the dynamic of future transportation projects in California. Because the community was involved in the

The Town of Crockett (top) watched as the new bridge (the suspension span on the right) joined the two earlier bridges. C&H Sugar is at the upper left.
BILL HALL/CALTRANS

project from the beginning, the bridge became the means to physically and psychologically reconnect the Town of Crockett with the region. Caltrans made a dramatic change in the overall public perception of the project. Townspeople came to embrace the new bridge as their own because they were allowed to become a part of the process that created it.

The new Alfred Zampa (Carquinez) Bridge (named for an ironworker who worked on many San Francisco Bay Area bridges) is 3,400 feet long, carrying westbound traffic on Interstate 80 over the Carquinez Strait between the City of Vallejo and the Town of Crockett, just northeast of San Francisco. It has four automobile lanes and a fully accessible

bicycle and pedestrian lane with stunning views of the Bay—the ultimate streetscape.

Crockett is a small, unincorporated Town of about 3,500. It was founded in 1867 and became known as the hometown of C&H Sugar. It overlooks the Carquinez Strait in the San Francisco Bay, bordered by rolling hills and parklands. It still retains its small-town feel, home to many families that have lived there for generations.

In 1927, two businessmen built the Carquinez Bridge—the first of the eight San Francisco Bay bridges—and operated it as a private toll bridge. After previously operating a ferry service, they were looking for a faster way to

PROJECT Carquinez Bridge Retrofit and Replacement **LOCATION** California Interstate 80 between the Town of Crockett and the City of Vallejo **DATE DESIGNED** 1995–1998 **CONSTRUCTION COMPLETED** November 2003 **CONSTRUCTION COST** $500 million **SIZE** 3400 ft. length; 2400 ft. main span (world's 27th longest suspension span) **CLIENT** California Department of Transportation (Caltrans) **DESIGN AND ENGINEERING** DeLeuw Cather & Company; OPAC Consulting Engineers, Inc.; D.B. Steinman; Caltrans **CONSTRUCTION** FCI Cleveland Bridge, a Joint Venture, and C.C. Myers, Inc. **PUBLIC INVOLVEMENT/PUBLIC INFORMATION** MIG, Inc.

transport vehicles across the strait's swift waters. This steel cantilever bridge was seen as a modern miracle. Governors from four different states attended its opening. President Calvin Coolidge officially opened the bridge from Washington, D.C., by pressing a button that set off fireworks. But all of this fanfare was overlooked by the news media, which instead flocked to cover Charles Lindberg's record shattering transatlantic flight completed on the

same day. Locals were heartbroken that their bridge did not get the national and worldwide attention they felt the longest bridge span west of the Mississippi deserved. But they were very happy with their new bridge.

In 1958, a second Carquinez Bridge was built parallel to the first to accommodate increased automobile traffic in the region. Each bridge carried traffic in one direction. The new bridge mirrored the original in type, although made from stronger steel and welded together instead of bolted. But this bridge did not receive the same support from the community as the first bridge—and for good reason. The new highway alignment now cut right through the middle of the Town of Crockett, forever dividing it and creating a "no man's land" that would harbor undesirable activity for decades to come—a not uncommon result of transportation projects. Pedestrians on one side of town had to brave heavy traffic to get to the other

side. There was no public involvement with this project; there was only eminent domain. Homes were taken by the block—150 in total. The construction team also left behind remnant materials too large to easily clean up. This unsightly mess remained in place for future generations to correct. Families with deep roots in the area lost their homes, but most did not leave town. They remained—only to see a third bridge rise to potentially threaten their homes again.

DESIGN GOALS

In 1988, Caltrans was considering replacing the original 1927 span because it was nearing the end of its useful life. Then, in 1989, the Loma Prieta Earthquake killed over 60 people in the Bay Area when a freeway structure collapsed. One person was killed on the Bay Bridge when a section of steel cantilever failed and sent that motorist into the bay. Following this disaster, Caltrans created a seismic retrofit program and

In 1927 this steel cantilever bridge was seen as a modern miracle, the longest bridge span west of the Mississippi.
CALTRANS

began evaluating all its bridges. At this point, a green light was given to begin environmental evaluation for building a new Carquinez Bridge.

Caltrans' design solution was a daring and quite striking suspension bridge. This type of bridge had not been built in the United States in over 30 years. In the Bay Area, known for the famous Golden Gate Bridge, it had been over 60 years since the birth of one of these elegant structures.

But Crockett residents were not impressed. They complained that bridge construction would impair access to their homes and disrupt their daily lives incalculably. They remembered the unhappy experience of the previous bridge and how it had severed pedestrian connections. Many felt that Caltrans was unceremoniously condemning a piece of history to the scrap heap by demolishing the original bridge. They also felt that a suspension bridge would not look good architecturally with the remaining steel cantilever bridge; they wanted to match the original bridge. Simply put, they didn't trust Caltrans and they demanded a say. Caltrans decided to work directly with the community to find solutions.

A group takes a tour down the footbridge, while workers continue their efforts on the main cable. Mixing tour groups of community members with engineering and design consultants created a better overall understanding of the project. Various groups could exchange their experiences and expertise directly onsite.

BILL HALL/CALTRANS

USER GROUPS

- Motorists and truck drivers on Interstate 80
- Bicyclists
- Pedestrians
- Residents of Crockett
- Residents of Vallejo

DESIGN PROCESS

Because of the scale of the project and its proximity to homes in Crockett, Caltrans placed a Public Information Office (PIO) in an office in town. The PIO's initial objective was to inform the public on the progress of construction and help mitigate as many construction difficulties as possible. From this office the public would be informed on any local road or freeway

Engineers from other countries were guided over a temporary footbridge to witness "cable spinning."
BILL HALL/CALTRANS

closures during the construction. They would also be kept up-to-date on construction operations that produced noise, dust or vibrations that could potentially affect them.

It quickly became apparent that a secondary public information objective would become even more important and demand a new approach: educating and involving the community in the project.

So during the three years of construction, the Carquinez Bridge Public Information Office became a nexus of communication for the public, commuters, a wide variety of community groups, project staff, politicians, other government agencies, contractors, consultants, trade organizations, professional associations, and media worldwide. The PIO office was the place to go for joint planning.

Caltrans began extensive community outreach through the PIO during the preliminary engineering design and environmental clearance phase, holding community workshops in nearby towns. Scale models, display boards with graphics and information sheets were used to inform the local communities on the project. The PIO and Caltrans Construction developed a series of community and media presentations. Caltrans videographers captured construction operations and produced video presentations, updated at milestones and placed on the Caltrans website so the community could learn about the bridge at its convenience.

The public commented on local access options, the on- and off-ramps alignments and "leftover" spaces, and potential effects of large-scale construction within a small town. Caltrans sent some of its best experts in noise abatement, hazardous materials, landscape architecture and architectural design, aesthetics, engineering, and construction to educate the community on key design issues.

The community involvement worked both ways. Caltrans worked with Contra Costa County Supervisor Gayle Uilkema to form the Carquinez Bridge Community Advisory Committee (CBCAC), a group of seven residents who represented the Town of Crockett. They met monthly with the PIO and Caltrans officials to work through issues. The CBCAC formed subcommittees that looked specifically at site development for the entry to Crockett, bridge aesthetics and preserving the 1927 bridge. Caltrans listened closely to community concerns and implemented many of their suggestions. The CBCAC members then became ambassadors for the project. They took what they learned back to their own local civic groups and as people began to understand the reasoning behind the project and realized Caltrans was listening to them, public opinion began to change. Caltrans transformed community members from project "victims" to project participants.

The Carquinez Bridge Community Advisory Committee stops for a group picture after a boat tour of the site.
BILL HALL/CALTRANS

Engineers from Caltrans and Japanese steel manufacturer IHI worked with the public information officer to talk with local school children about the bridge. This class participated in an art exchange with Japanese school children who live near the steel plant that constructed the deck of the bridge.
BILL HALL/CALTRANS

neath the bridge during some operations to allow pedestrians safe access through the area.

The site quickly became a favorite for educators because of the engineering and historic significance of this project. Students from the second grade through college visited the Public Information Office to learn about the building of this bridge. One group of girls, from Benjamin Franklin Middle School in Vallejo, followed all three years of bridge construction. They visited the site every month, took photos and met with Caltrans project leaders. They created a website that became one of the best sources of information about construction, visited by other students and engineers across the country.

The best example of how the community's attitude changed to one of pride and cooperation is the name of the bridge. The new bridge was named for a local resident and former ironworker

The CBCAC then helped Caltrans work with other state and local agencies. CBCAC members went with Caltrans to make presentations for review and approvals, offering visible proof that Caltrans was working with the community and had their full support for crucial and sometimes controversial decisions.

Because the Crockett on and off ramps would be closed for two years, Caltrans extended a nearby exit to flow into the Town of Crockett. Two routes were always maintained for motorists to move through the area under the bridges during construction. Caltrans also provided a shuttle service under-

Hogan High School library media teacher Gail Allison and then-freshmen students Breyana Scales, Kayla Woodfork and Lanaudia Woodfork took a tour of the Vallejo side of the Carquinez Bridge construction to update their website that tracked the work on the westbound span.
DAVID PACHECO/TIMES-HERALD, VALLEJO

named Alfred Zampa, who passed away at the age of 95, shortly after performing the ceremonial groundbreaking for the bridge. Al is a legend among Bay Area bridge workers. He worked on the original Carquinez Bridge—and every major bridge in the Bay Area. A fall from the Golden Gate Bridge put him on extended disability, but he returned to the work he loved and worked on the second bridge crossing the Carquinez Strait with his sons. His sons and grandsons are still ironworkers today. A grassroots movement began among local residents to name the bridge for him. The bridge, once considered by many to be a disruption to their community, was now a source of great civic pride; the community wanted the name of one of their own attached to it. The State of California

granted their request—the first time a California bridge has ever been named for a "regular guy."

By the time the bridge was ready to open, the local Chambers of Commerce had banded together to form a Bridge Celebration Committee to help publicize and celebrate the opening of the bridge. They raised almost $100,000 to sponsor a fireworks show and a street fair to complement the opening celebration planned by Caltrans. In a show of community pride, the Crockett Chamber of Commerce recently incorporated an image of the new suspension bridge into its logo. Crockett residents believe the new bridge and the pedestrian and bike lane will put their Town back on the map as a place to visit, shop and enjoy.

The new Carquinez Bridge was named for iron worker Al Zampa.
CALTRANS

Inclusive Design Features and Settings

NEW ON/OFF RAMP ALIGNMENTS

The old off ramps dumped traffic right onto Pomona Street, Crockett's small main street. Large trucks barreled up and down the street to get to the C&H Sugar refinery. The trucks completely changed the small-town pedestrian circulation patterns. A possible alternative route, Wanda Street, had such an extreme grade that trucks would not use it.

Caltrans initially gave Crockett a choice: remove the on/off ramps in Crockett and extend a local road to the freeway, or replace the on/off ramps in a new alignment (leaving no easy town access for two years). The community felt that both choices were inadequate. Caltrans felt the community was being unreasonable.

The solution came through an inclusive community workshop that joined Caltrans representatives with community members in small groups. All of the groups came up with the same answer independently: they needed both options. Caltrans then partnered with Contra Costa County and a local oil refinery that owned land needed to extend the local road to the freeway when the old access ramps were closed during construction. That became the access road during construction.

Caltrans engineers found a way to realign and regrade Wanda Street, so heavy trucks can exit the freeway on Pomona and use Wanda as a bypass, heading back under the bridge instead of driving through town. This solution helps reconnect the portion of the community that was severed by the second bridge. With trucks now off the main street, pedestrians and bicyclists can reach both sides of town in safety.

REVIVING NO-MAN'S LAND

Land underneath bridges and overpasses often causes problems for communities because they attract transients and undesirable activities. The second bridge in particular created a "no-man's land" in the middle of town. Caltrans landscape architects and right-of-way agents worked with CBCAC, local county supervisors and assemblypersons to find ways to reconnect Crockett. They developed a plan for a walking and bike path under the bridge that features low-maintenance native plantings, well-marked trailheads and parking. The paths link up with the pedestrian and bike lane over the bridge.

PEDESTRIAN AND BIKE PATH

Bicycle coalitions from around the Bay Area lobbied Caltrans to include an accessible pedestrian and bike lane on the bridge. The well-lit lane, separated from the travel lanes, provides users with unique vistas of the Bay. It's now a vital link in the Bay Trail (an effort to build a continuous recreational path entirely around the Bay) and connects the communities of Crockett and Vallejo in a way that hasn't existed for decades.

COLOR AND LIGHTING SCHEMES

CBCAC's aesthetics subcommittee didn't want the color of the new bridge to be overbearing; yet they wanted it to be distinctive. Caltrans created simulations of the bridge and identified a color palette that worked well with the green and yellow surrounding hillsides. Three potential colors were painted on sections of the old bridge so the community could see it in context. The final choice was a steel deck gray to match the concrete interchange towers, and a red cable system (darker than the international orange of the Golden Gate Bridge, yet reminiscent of it), with a complementary green used on the railing and light standards, which also provides a human scale to the bike and pedestrian lane.

Children at Tsutsujigaoka Elementary School in Japan were fascinated by the large steel decks they saw being constructed next door at the IHI steel plant. When they discovered it was for a new bridge in California, they wanted to correspond with American schoolchildren near the bridge. Art proved to be the universal language—they created a mural on the protective covering for a deck, which then crossed the Pacific.
BILL HALL/CALTRANS

Students at Hillcrest Elementary School in Crockett and Glen Cove Elementary School in Vallejo received blank deck covers to create their own mural, in response, for Japanese schoolchildren.
BILL HALL/CALTRANS

Children from Glen Cove Elementary School and their principal Greg Allison admire the "mural" sent as a friendship message to them from children in Japan.

BILL HALL/CALTRANS

Pedestrians and bicyclists take their first stroll across the Carquinez Strait on the bike and pedestrian lane's opening day.
BILL HALL/CALTRANS

Lighting on the bridge towers is reminiscent of the Golden Gate Bridge. The necklace lighting of the cables echoes the Oakland-San Francisco Bay Bridge.
BILL HALL/CALTRANS

The aesthetics committee also worked with Caltrans to develop an architectural lighting scheme for the bridge. Caltrans explained all the options and fixture types, and their effect on color. The final scheme lights up the towers like the Golden Gate and adds the necklace lighting of the cables like the Oakland-San Francisco Bay Bridge.

CBCAC and Caltrans jointly presented the color and lighting schemes to the San Francisco Bay Conservation and Development Commission (BCDC), which has jurisdiction over architectural aesthetics on the Bay. It was the first time Caltrans had ever gone before the BCDC with such strong community support. Although BCDC strongly disagreed with the color scheme, the community stood firmly behind Caltrans and their plan was implemented.

VALLEJO ART WALL

Caltrans had planned a traditional gray concrete retaining wall along the hilly approach to the bridge past Vallejo. Because this was considered a motorist gateway to the Bay, Caltrans was inspired to create a more decorative wall. It's a striking wall sculpture, depicting sailboats along the strait. One sail soars above the top of the wall, lending a three-dimensional look. This was the first time Caltrans had ever made a structural element into an artistic element. Caltrans says this project opened the door for creative solutions to retaining walls in other locations as well.

Caltrans had first created a test art wall, about a foot thick and 15 feet long. Workers had planned to destroy the test wall, but Caltrans decided to leave it to the surrounding community. That wall is now installed on the City of Vallejo waterfront.

CROCKETT ART WALL

On the other side of the bridge, because of community involvement, Caltrans decided to create an architectural treatment on a highly visible retaining wall that covers an entire hillside in a residential community. Designers gave it a rocky texture with plantings to make it look more natural. Retaining walls closer to the freeway have the standard Caltrans wall treatments.

HISTORIC 1927 BRIDGE

Since the 1927 Carquinez Bridge held such a place of pride in the Crockett community—and because it was the very first bridge over the Bay—the CBCAC wanted to preserve it. Although it soon became clear to the community that the bridge would have to be demolished, they identified key sections to preserve in a museum. In addition, two large sections will be incorporated into vista points that Caltrans created, one on each side of the Strait. In Crockett, a 400-meter section will become the railing of the vista, maintaining a link to the past for the community.

USER FEEDBACK

Howard Adams, Chairman, Carquinez Bridge Community Advisory Committee

"The pedestrian lane has been much more widely used than most people had ever expected. I think there is a special feel for connecting two landmasses—you get more of a sense of a geographical connection on foot than by car. It's really been very useful. One Crockett resident has walked it over 130 times since it opened!

"We hope our communication (with Caltrans) has been a two-way street. We certainly have learned a lot about bridge construction and now appreciate the nuances and the magnitude of it. At the same time, we hope that Caltrans has learned more about the impact of transportation projects on residential areas located close to projects of this size. OSHA standards don't really cover impacts on residents."

Caltrans was inspired to go beyond the traditional retaining wall with this depiction of sailboats in the strait.
BILL HALL/CALTRANS

*Kent Petersen, Previous Chairman,
Carquinez Bridge Community
Advisory Committee*

"Crockett is a small town that once again found itself in the way of a new bridge. This time, Caltrans has been responsive. They've listened. They've worked well with us.

"People still remember, angrily, the extension of I-80 that took out some 150 homes. It cut Crockett in two. People weren't given fair compensation, they weren't given much time to leave and they had nowhere to go. You had highway departments all over the country running roughshod over cities.

"Facing construction this time, we demanded a say and we worked with Caltrans on everything from design and traffic to compensation issues. Some 14 homeowners were displaced, but they got fair value for their homes."

*John LaViolette, Secretary,
Carquinez Bridge Community
Advisory Committee*

"Caltrans has been exceptionally responsive to the concerns and impacts of construction on our small town. The project has been a model for partnering between Caltrans, the bridge contractors, the County and the community. Participation in the CBCAC has truly been the most rewarding experience in my entire career. I have now entered the graduate engineering program at U.C. Berkeley to conduct an investigation of the 1927 Bridge, in order to better understand corrosion and fatigue of steel structures in a marine environment."

With flashlights to lead the way, hundreds of area residents sang Happy Birthday and celebrated the Alfred Zampa (Carquinez) Bridge's first year.
MIKE JORY/TIMES-HERALD, VALLEJO

The grand opening of the Alfred Zampa (Carquinez) Bridge became a major community celebration.
BILL HALL/CALTRANS

Gene Pedrotti, Chairman,
Crockett Bridge Celebration Committee

"This represents the heart and soul of Crockett. (We're) really proud of this bridge. The walkway is as graceful as it is sweeping! From the center span, standing perhaps 100 feet above the Strait, you can nearly cast a fishing line or step onto the deck of a passing ship.

And from the vista promontory on the north, you can feel the strength and power of all three Bay bridges, but especially the towering Zampa. The views are breathtaking. I think in a lot of ways this will help put Crockett back on the map. This span connection is as vital to the Bay Trail as the first span was in 1927 to motor traffic."

Dennis Trujillo, Crockett Resident

"I like that I can walk across the bridge. The bridge is now a meeting point, providing beautiful views and a great place to get exercise. It's a pleasure to stop and meet friends halfway."

DOWNTOWN AREA | SPOKANE, WASHINGTON

"What happened completely reversed a fast-moving tide of despair and neglect to one of community engagement, hope, action and results."

FORMER CHAIR, DAVENPORT DISTRICT

REMAKING AN AMERICAN DOWNTOWN

DANIEL IACOFANO
MUKUL MALHOTRA
ROSEMARY DUDLEY

WHETHER WE LIVE IN A SMALL TOWN OR A METRO AREA, HOW WE FEEL ABOUT WHERE WE LIVE is largely based on how we feel about our city's central downtown. As the focal point of a city, great downtowns provide us with a sense of identity and remind us of what we have in common as a community. Great downtowns draw people, jobs and resources.

In 1995, Downtown Spokane was bleak. Stores were closing, jobs were disappearing and people no longer chose to live there. Residents described a Downtown in "freefall." But after ten years of planning, hard work and active community participation, new investment exceeding $1.6 billion is revitalizing the Downtown with jobs, retail, entertainment, arts and housing. In 2004, Spokane earned the All-America City Award from the National Urban League. This is the story of remaking an American downtown.

The Spokane River is the central identity for Downtown Spokane (left). The Clock Tower in Riverfront Park is a City icon (right).
DON HORTON

It is the inherently unique character of a city's downtown that distinguishes one urban center from another. The downtown is a city's visual repository of centuries of dreams, ambitions and hard work. It is a living record of its society, culture, business, architectural styles and artistic innovations.

Great downtowns must be more than just a retail core or a skyscraper-filled financial center and their success must be measured by more than growth statistics and tax receipts. Successful downtowns like the one Spokane has created are complex, multifaceted, diverse, colorful mixes of interconnected commercial, entertainment, cultural and residential districts.

This isn't the first time that Downtown Spokane has remade itself.

PROJECT Spokane Plan for a New Downtown, Downtown Spokane Zoning Ordinance and Design Guidelines, North Bank Development Plan, Davenport District Strategic Action Plan, Riverfront Park Master Plan, The Great Spokane River Gorge Strategic Master Plan **LOCATION** Spokane, Washington **DATE DESIGNED** 1998–2005 **CONSTRUCTION** Ongoing **NEW INVESTMENT** currently $1.6 billion **CLIENT** City of Spokane Planning Department, City of Spokane Parks and Recreation Department, Spokane Business Improvement District, Spokane Arts Commission, Downtown Spokane Partnership **CONSULTANTS** MIG, Inc. (project lead, land use, planning and urban design, design concepts, community participation, implementation strategies), Keyser Marston Associates, Inc. (economic analysis), Fehr & Peers Associates, Inc. (transportation analysis), Jim Kolva Associates (land use planning), Robert Odland Consulting (plan implementation strategy), Integrus Architecture (institutional architectural consulting), RAMM Associates (landscape architecture), David Evans and Associates, Inc. (planning and urban design, design concepts, community participation, implementation strategies)

Native Americans first inhabited the area on the banks of the Spokane River, located at the intersection of four mountain ranges in the high desert of southeastern Washington. In 1810, members of John Jacob Astor's Pacific Fur Company established a trading center on the river. Missionaries, miners and farmers settled the region in the 1860s, harnessing the river's power to run their flour mills and, later, to generate electricity. The Northern Pacific Railroad reached Spokane in 1881, the year the City incorporated. The area bustled with mining, lumber and farming. The burgeoning metropolis suffered its first great setback in 1889, when "The Great Fire" ravaged Downtown and destroyed 32 city blocks. Spokanites rebuilt Downtown as an industrial and railroad center for the Inland Northwest: seven transcontinental railroads and 14 branch lines ran through the City, crisscrossing the river. And by 1909, Spokane was thriving with a population of 14,000. But the Downtown river area had become a sprawling, ugly railroad yard—the City had turned its back on the river.

In 1913, the City recognized the importance of its river and its Downtown by adopting a remarkably forward-looking master plan developed by renowned landscape architects, the Olmsted Brothers. The plan once again centered the City on the Spokane River, creating "green" streets and trails to connect a series of community parks. Much of the plan was implemented, as Spokane became a modern, growing city.

But by the 1960s, Spokane fell victim to the same plight as many American cities: an aging infrastructure and increasingly suburbanized landscape led to a decline in the downtown area as residents and businesses left.

As host of the World's Fair Expo '74, Spokane undertook another monumental revitalization. The City ripped out

In 1925 an Indian Congress was held at Glover Field on the banks of the Spokane River.

NORTHWEST MUSEUM OF ARTS & CULTURE/EASTERN WASHINGTON STATE HISTORICAL SOCIETY, SPOKANE, WASHINGTON, L87-1.29943-25, LIBBY STUDIO COLLECTION

Rail bridges, such as the 1914 Union Pacific High Bridge, crisscrossed the river and the City.

NORTHWEST MUSEUM OF ARTS & CULTURE/EASTERN WASHINGTON STATE HISTORICAL SOCIETY, SPOKANE, WASHINGTON, L84-197.18

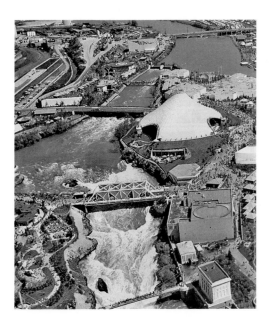

Old rail yards were reclaimed as a new Riverfront Park for Expo '74.

After the World's Fair, the graceful Expo Pavilion and Clock Tower remained as Spokane landmarks.
STEVE DAWSON III

the rusty railroads along the river and turned the jumble of tracks and outdated buildings into the beautiful Riverfront Park. A new downtown mall north of the river, called River Park Square, was anchored by the first Nordstrom store outside of Seattle and included a movie theater and a mix of large and local retailers.

The Expo showed the community what the City and Downtown could be. But the economic base continued moving to the suburbs, profiting from low-cost development opportunities. When two of four major retailers left, nearly two entire blocks were vacant. The Downtown was dotted with empty storefronts. The graceful Expo Pavilion and the Romanesque-style Great Northern Depot Tower with its four clocks remained as tributes to the past—and waited for a new downtown.

Twenty years later, in the mid-1990s, Downtown Spokane was in real economic trouble. The City had invested in a new Downtown transit center, a public library and a sports arena—it was time to look at the Downtown in light of a modern economy and changing needs of its residents. Building on a spirit of innovation, its inherent natural beauty and its cultural and economic strengths, Spokane embarked on a plan to transform its Downtown into a thriving and truly modern Northwest city center.

In 1994, the owners of the River Park Square mall proposed a key first step: a $115-million two-block redevelopment to stimulate the City's economy by increasing jobs, revenues and tourism. The new mall would include a renovated Nordstrom store, a 20-screen theater and specialty retail stores and restaurants—many of them locally owned. The City joined the developer in a public/private partnership to secure funding. That partnership sparked a joint effort by the City and business and community leaders to develop a coordinated, long-term revitalization plan for the entire Downtown. It was co-led by the City of Spokane and the Downtown Spokane Partnership, a nonprofit organization that worked to build economic vitality through a healthy downtown. Its priorities were developing the convention and visitors industry, retail and office offerings, arts and entertainment venues, emerging industries and technologies, and parks and recreation.

Beginning in 1998, Spokane, now a City of 200,000, engaged the community in creating a new vision and master plan for the City that addressed the business environment, housing, education, public space and greenbelts, transportation and sports, entertainment and arts venues. The aim was to take advantage of the huge investment that had already been

Spokane is the largest economic center in the Inland Northwest trade area.

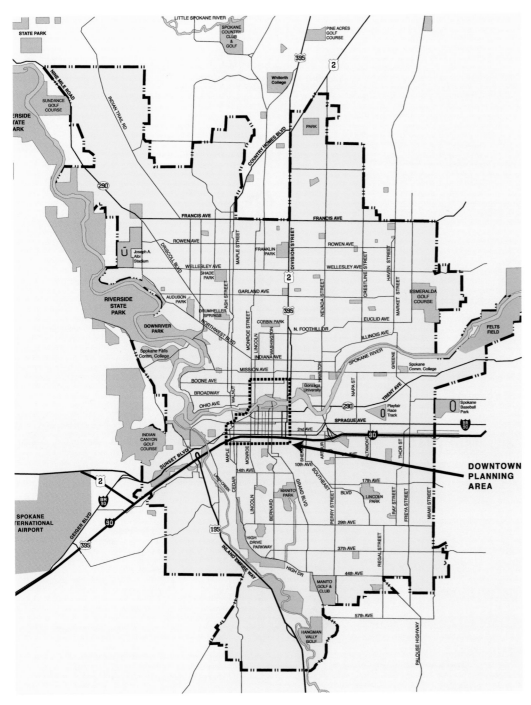

The Downtown area serves the larger City of Spokane.

made in the City infrastructure by refocusing investment into the Downtown core.

For Downtown Spokane, remaking itself has resulted in a renewed relationship with the river, a new convention center, a vibrant arts and entertainment district, new housing, preserved historic buildings, and thriving restaurant and retail areas.

Over 500 new development projects have already redefined the Downtown experience. The amount of retail space available increased by four times between 1999 and 2005—today there is more total leased retail space in the central business district than at any time in the past 20 years. The office market has increased by 400,000 square feet, with a 3 percent increase in overall occupancy rate. Revitalization has also sparked a surge in market rate housing, introducing lofts, apartments and condominiums. Long-time and new residents will find a mix of affordable and market rate housing, pedestrian walkways and green streets as the City grows. And Downtown Spokane has many more projects on the drawing boards.

Project Goals

The Downtown concept focuses on key activity nodes, supporting uses and connectivity.

As the main economic symbol for the entire Inland Northwest region, the success and vitality of Downtown Spokane directly influences public and private growth opportunities throughout the region. Spokane needed to look beyond the Downtown alone and connect Downtown with its supporting neighborhoods and the region.

The City aimed to create an engine for Downtown Spokane's economic growth—to generate new investment, create new jobs, and improve everyone's quality of life with enhanced services and

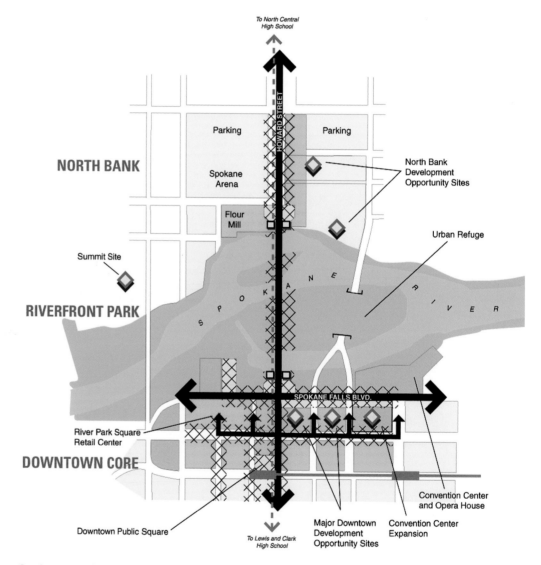

Spokane needed to link the Downtown with surrounding neighborhoods.

facilities. Running this economic engine would require coordinating and supporting both public and private investments. The City hoped to attract private investors by demonstrating its commitment to a vibrant Downtown marketplace. Private development needed to be organized so that it would support public investment in key design projects: street activation, intensity of activity and the concentration of development in and around key City resources.

To create the engine, the City focused on five overall goals:

■ *Catalytic Sites:* Catalytic development sites would spur additional investment as developers gained confidence in the viability of projects in the area. By directing new projects toward existing Downtown infrastructure, the City would provide a solid foundation for public support of the plan. The City's Riverfront Park, the "Jewel" of Spokane, served as the nexus for project initiatives, as development efforts focused on a Convention Center, the International Airport, historic buildings, and nearby Gonzaga University.

■ *Downtown / Neighborhood Connectivity:* The City hoped to invigorate interest in the Olmsted Brothers' original "green street" vision, connecting high-density development and surrounding neighborhoods with Spokane's natural beauty and the river, while providing a safe network of scenic streets shared by pedestrians, cyclists and automobiles. Howard Street will be the "string" that connects the pearls of the Riverfront Park, the Downtown retail core, a new public square, the North Bank and the South Side.

■ *Unique District Identities:* By crafting complementary strategies for individual Districts within the Downtown, the City aimed to create Districts that could individually stand on their own, while creating a cohesive marketing and planning strategy for the whole City center.

■ *Reconnections with the River:* The City aimed to enhance Riverfront Park as an urban refuge in the center of Downtown, opening new vistas and planning new activity centers.

■ *Preservation of Spokane's Historic Past:* Organizing catalytic sites around existing City landmarks would promote a renewed interest in Spokane's signature buildings—strengthening Spokane's identity as a distinctive Downtown.

To achieve these goals, the City developed a series of strategic action, master and development plans to revitalize Downtown Spokane and its interdependent neighborhoods. Five of these Plans are discussed in this chapter:

1. Spokane Plan for a New Downtown
Ultimately, the City aimed to create a Downtown Spokane that was "every-

body's neighborhood"—a place that would generate excitement and comfort for residents and visitors, night and day. With the primary five goals in mind, a series of projects included improving housing, retail, economic development, transit, accessibility, community connections and usable open space.

Along with the Plan, design guidelines and a new Downtown Spokane zoning ordinance would enable new developments to better respond to site-specific conditions and surrounding conditions and character. (More information about these types of guidelines can be found in Cityscapes Design Guidelines, page 454.)

2. Riverfront Park Master Plan

Riverfront Park is a 100-acre open space area in and adjacent to the Spokane River. The City envisioned it as a peaceful urban refuge in the heart of Downtown, operated and maintained by the Spokane Parks and Recreation Department. It's closely linked with the North Bank Development Plan (below).

3. North Bank Development Plan

A focused development plan for this region would reconnect and revitalize the entertainment district with the City core and guide major public and private investment entertainment projects.

4. Davenport District Strategic Action Plan

Working with the nonprofit "Friends of Davenport," the City hoped to establish this historic area as a dynamic arts, entertainment and creative district.

5. The Great Spokane River Gorge Strategic Master Plan

The Spokane River Gorge is the area's key natural treasure. Primary goals were to enhance public use and protect its natural beauty, reflecting local history and culture.

User Groups

- Businesses (local, regional, national)
- Current Downtown residents
- Nearby neighborhood residents
- Regional residents who might relocate Downtown
- Outdoor recreation users (walkers, bikers, boaters, kayakers, etc.)
- City agencies
- Higher education institutions
- Medical/healthcare institutions
- Visitors and tourists

Design Process

Each of the five Plans included extensive community and business involvement, including large public meetings, small group discussions, and design charettes.

SPOKANE PLAN FOR A NEW DOWNTOWN

Spokane's Plan for a New Downtown was developed by a joint public-private partnership between the City of Spokane and the Downtown Spokane

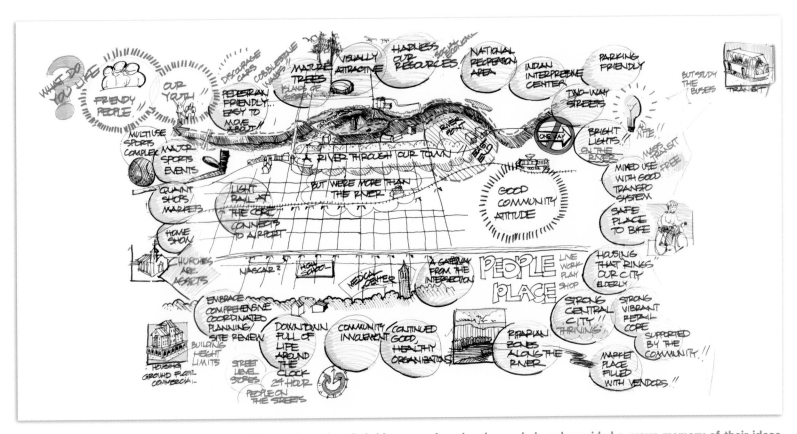

Large wall graphics visually assured community members that their ideas were heard and recorded, and provided a group memory of their ideas.

Partnership (DSP), a not-for-profit coalition of business, government and community leaders. The City and DSP established a 26-member Steering Committee, composed of business owners, property owners, residents and community leaders. The Committee helped formulate initial plan recommendations and guide the plan through an extensive community outreach program. To guide community participation and ensure feasibility of Plan recommendations, three technical focus groups were convened on transportation, economic development and urban design issues.

Community participation played a critical role and presented the greatest

Participants used modular maps to help visualize the effects of land use planning on the City.

tive interchange confirmed the importance of Downtown's future and identified key issues that later comprised the Vision for Downtown Spokane.

A second workshop, the Planning and Design Charette, transformed the priorities identified in the first meeting into a series of "planning stations." At each station, participants engaged in interactive

activities unique to specific design and topic areas—allowing City staff and steering committee members to directly record community feedback on emerging concepts for the plan.

Three more community meetings followed, allowing community members to review major plan policy elements and, finally, to celebrate and review the

challenge in the planning process. "Envision Spokane," a community newsletter designed to update citizens on new planning information, helped attract 1,500 attendees to five community meetings. The first meeting, The Downtown Vision Workshop, took place at the Spokane Convention Center on February 5, 1998. Broadcast on local television, the workshop's posi-

Community members participated in an outdoor festival to help plan the future of Riverfront Park.

Individual booths highlighted different alternatives and proposals.

draft plan. Almost all of those in attendance agreed with the Plan for a New Downtown and its action items.

The breadth and success of the community outreach process and Downtown Plan earned Spokane the 1998 Washington American Planning Association award.

RIVERFRONT PARK MASTER PLAN AND NORTH BANK DEVELOPMENT PLAN

Stakeholder interviews played a key role in the gathering of public input for the Riverfront Park and North Bank Plans. Community members representing a diverse range of interests were asked a series of open-ended questions intended to gather opinions and solicit ideas for specific redevelopment concepts. Questions focused on key areas within the Park and North Bank, directing the resulting Plan on specific development areas. Four community workshops and a telephone survey helped develop the types of attractions and recreation the Park should offer.

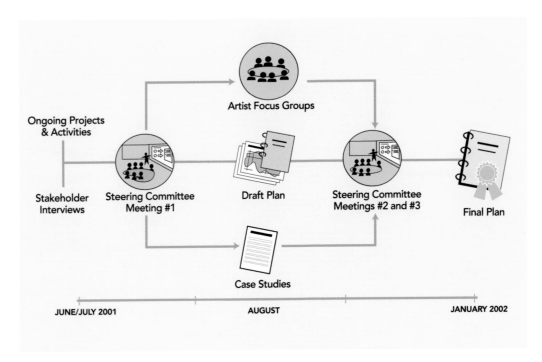

The strategic planning process for the Davenport District included artists, business owners and residents.

DAVENPORT DISTRICT STRATEGIC ACTION PLAN

The first planning document for the area was drafted in 1990 by Friends of the Davenport, a nonprofit group promoting redevelopment. A group of volunteers began organizing and holding community meetings in 1997. They formed the Riverside Neighborhood Council and provided input to the City. In 1998, the City then involved those community members in the Plan for a New Downtown process—including

local artists, business owners, the Davenport District Arts Board, the Downtown Spokane Partnership, the Spokane Arts Commission and the Business Improvement District. The Spokane Arts Commission and the Downtown Spokane Partnership gathered additional community feedback through an artist's focus group and by distributing over 500 questionnaires to arts and cultural organizations and individual artists. During three planning workshops, district stakeholders developed a vision for continued revitalization and established priority strategies and actions necessary to implement the Davenport Plan.

THE GREAT SPOKANE RIVER GORGE STRATEGIC MASTER PLAN

In May 2004, a 25-member steering committee worked to identify projects and programs in the Spokane River Gorge to reacquaint local residents and visitors with this dramatic and unique natural resource.

Led by Friends of the Falls, the Spokane River Gorge planning process included Indian tribes, residents and government agencies.

Led by Friends of the Falls (FOF), a nonprofit organization dedicated to preserving the historic waterfalls and river gorge in Downtown Spokane, the planning process included months of interviews with government and park agencies, residents' boards, representatives from local American Indian tribes, business organizations and outdoor recreation groups. To better understand the river from varied perspectives, stakeholders visited river trails and overlooks, and even rafted through the river gorge.

The City hosted an initial community workshop in June 2004 to gauge community response to a Plan for the gorge area; about 100 people provided feedback on the Plan's principles, vision and proposed projects. FOF hosted a final public workshop, generating feedback on the Great Spokane River Gorge Strategic Master Plan and its priority projects. The Plan was revised to incorporate public comments and it was subsequently approved by the Park Board.

Inclusive Design Features

SPOKANE PLAN FOR A NEW DOWNTOWN

"Our Downtown is a mixed-use regional center for shopping, living, recreation and entertainment. Riverfront Park is the center of the City and Downtown. It is the 'Jewel' of the City. Riverfront Park is a great public open space in the center of a growing, vital and urban City."
—*Vision of Downtown Spokane*

To reinvent and revitalize Downtown Spokane, the City developed action strategies for nine elements the community considered crucial:

1. *Land Use*
2. *Downtown Districts*
3. *Special Districts*
4. *Economic Development*
5. *Housing*
6. *Transportation and Circulation*
7. *Community Design*
8. *Historic Preservation*
9. *Neighborhood Economic Development*

For each strategy area, the City determined key actions, a time frame to complete these actions, agencies responsible for implementation, and potential funding sources. In some instances, the City far exceeded the Plan's goals. In others, Plan initiatives are still in process.

1. Land Use

Using a detailed Land Use map (see next page), the City arranged office, commercial, residential, cultural, institutional, and light industrial uses to create "mixed-use urban villages" and core retail, entertainment and office centers, based on current uses and potential for new investment. The City also updated the zoning ordinance to reflect the Plan objectives.

A "mixed-use urban village" is a return to the traditional town—encouraging high-density development with a mix of housing and offices located above retail spaces. Housing would be 18 to 110 dwelling units per acre (gross) with building heights ranging from 3 to 13 stories.

By integrating ground level services with residential and office spaces, retail shops and restaurants are encouraged to stay open on evenings and weekends to serve a lively, active community. The 24-hour vitality of these villages ensures a safe environment and attracts visitors, new residents and businesses—and investors.

To facilitate the growth of mixed-use urban villages, the City:

■ Classified office developments according to floor plate size and directed large office developments outside of the City center, into new Office Campus Park areas; and

Downtown combines high rise offices with pedestrian level amenities.

■ Distributed four types of commercial land uses (auto-oriented, visitor-serving, specialty entertainment and general commercial) to strategic locations throughout Downtown.

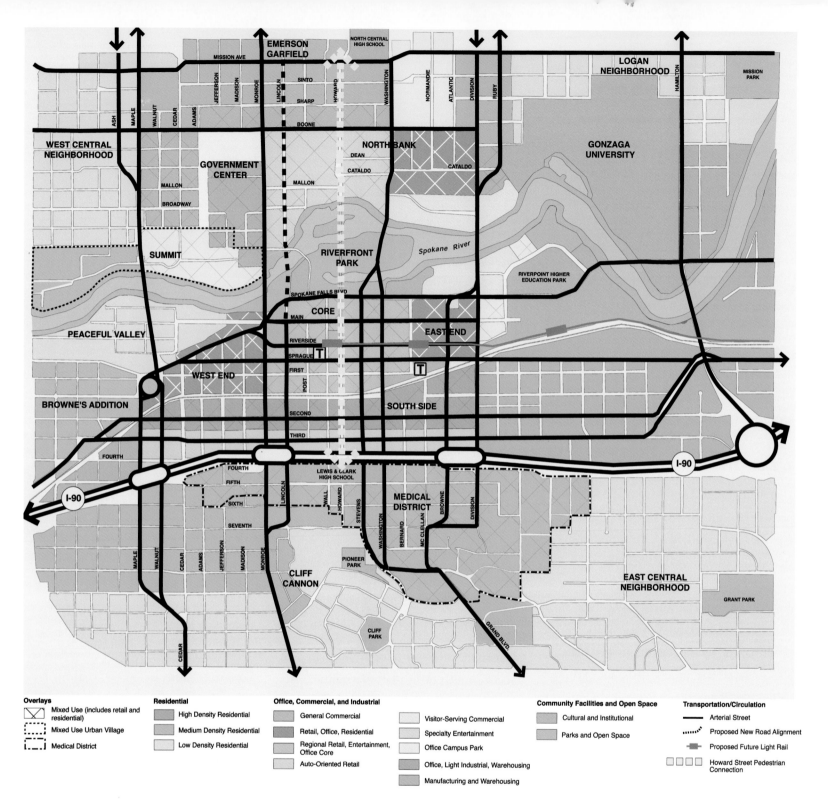

Overlays

- ⊠ Mixed Use (includes retail and residential)
- ⬚ Mixed Use Urban Village
- ⬚ Medical District

Residential

- High Density Residential
- Medium Density Residential
- Low Density Residential

Office, Commercial, and Industrial

- General Commercial
- Retail, Office, Residential
- Regional Retail, Entertainment, Office Core
- Auto-Oriented Retail
- Visitor-Serving Commercial
- Specialty Entertainment
- Office Campus Park
- Office, Light Industrial, Warehousing
- Manufacturing and Warehousing

Community Facilities and Open Space

- Cultural and Institutional
- Parks and Open Space

Transportation/Circulation

- ▬▬ Arterial Street
- ⋯⋯ Proposed New Road Alignment
- ▬■▬ Proposed Future Light Rail
- ⬚⬚⬚⬚ Howard Street Pedestrian Connection

The City aimed to develop a fine-grained mix of uses throughout the Downtown.

2. Downtown Districts

The Downtown Plan identified six distinct Districts, each with unique development goals, historic elements, architectural considerations and populations. For each corridor, the plan suggested land use goals and key opportunity sites to stimulate growth and define the area's character, and successive action plans detailed inclusive design features.

Downtown Core

The Downtown Core is the center of Downtown, with high-density office and commercial uses, as well as housing. Successful completion of the Spokane Convention Center, is one of the plan's primary catalytic Downtown projects. The 100,000-square-foot expansion places the Spokane region at the forefront for attracting major national conventions, expositions and

A new AMC theater at River Park Square has boosted the local economy by stimulating adjacent retail activity.

STEVE DAWSON III

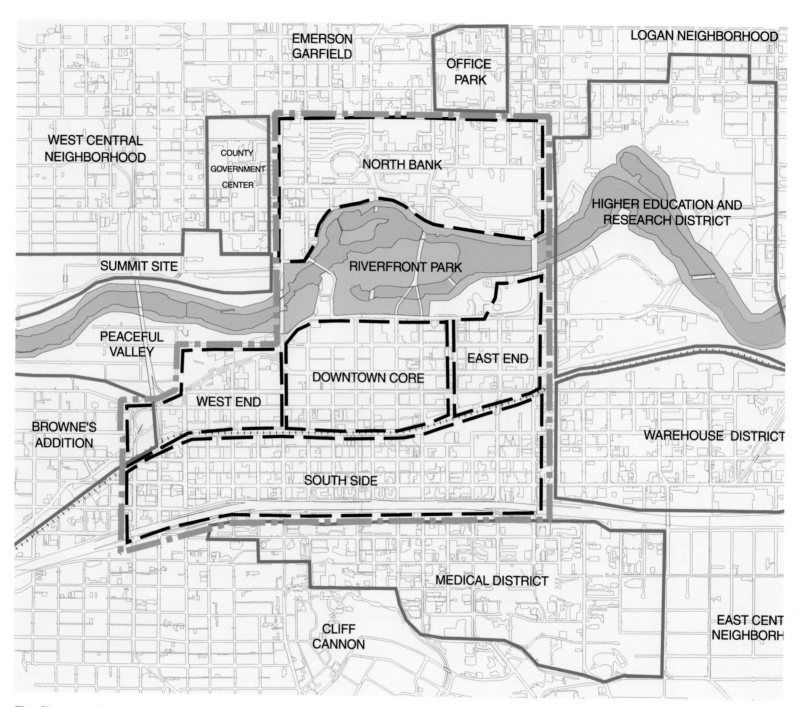

The City created six distinct Districts in the Downtown planning area (within the orange line).

trade shows. The convention center also hosts meetings for local organizations, graduations and other area events. The City plans to secure a location for a public plaza to focus potential residential and retail investments.

River Park Square, the project that started the current Spokane revival, was renovated in 1999. The basement now houses the Mobius Children's Museum. The Square features a five-story glass atrium housing a 20-plex movie theater, retail stores and bistro. Adhering to the City's design guidelines, the development includes its own parking structure and pedestrian-friendly window displays and entrances. The Square has generated more than 1,100 new hospitality jobs and provided $13.6 million in tax revenues to the City by 2005.

The Spokane Convention Center—being expanded to 100,000 square feet—and the Opera House were catalytic sites for Downtown development adjacent to Riverfront Park.
DON HORTON

The Downtown's former J.C. Penney Building, across from River Park Square, is reopening as "809 West Main" and incorporates ground floor retail with 21 loft condominiums.

ALSC ARCHITECTS

The historic Gallagher Building on Jefferson Street, in the west end of Downtown, was an abandoned warehouse for two decades. The building has been renamed the Jefferson Street Auto Lofts for the historic auto corridor along the Downtown railroad tracks. It is now office, retail and residential condominiums.

RENCORP

West End

Planning activity focused on the development of high-density, mixed-use buildings with a concentration of retail activity along First Avenue. Key devel-

Riverview Condominiums, a new housing project, may spur infill housing in the west side of Downtown. It follows the new design guidelines by incorporating low-rise brick façades at the street.

STEVEN MEEK ARCHITECTS

opment sites on First Avenue would be developed with wider sidewalks and plazas, creating a linear pedestrian link from the area to the Downtown Core and the Davenport Arts District.

East End

East End development also promoted high-density, mixed-use office and residential developments with ground floor

retail, while encouraging the preservation and active use of the area's historic structures. The Plan identified vacant and underutilized sites along Bernard Street for development, suggesting wider sidewalks and plazas to create a pedestrian link between the Convention Center and Riverfront Park.

In accord with the Downtown Plan, the Community Building opened in 2001 on West Main Street. It features an open

The renovated Community Building, on West Main Street, is now home to nonprofit organizations involved in social justice issues.

ROBERT ZELLER

The vacant 97-year-old Saranac Hotel at 25 West Main Street will be renovated as a green building, providing 32,000 square feet of floor space for a potential ground floor movie theater and offices for social justice or environmental justice missions.
ZECK BUTLER ARCHITECTS PS

North Bank

The City owns a large portion of the North Bank, and planning efforts for this area are detailed in the Riverfront Park Master Plan and North Bank Development Plan. The Downtown Plan called for mixed uses in this area, including new sports, entertainment and recreation activities, support for commercial and entertainment retail close to the Arena and Riverfront Park, and medium- and high-density residential developments around Washington Street, with supporting service retail.

South Side

Located south of Interstate 90, Downtown's South Side became the focus for large office spaces, light industrial and residential uses. The Plan recommended retaining the area's signature warehouse and light industrial uses,

floor plan, solar panels that provide 12 percent of the building's power, and a vegetable garden. It's now home to non-profits involved in social justice. Tenants don't pay rent, but split the cost of operations, maintenance and taxes. The adjacent Saranac Hotel is now being redeveloped and expanded, and could include a smaller movie theater for independent films, a café and more office space.

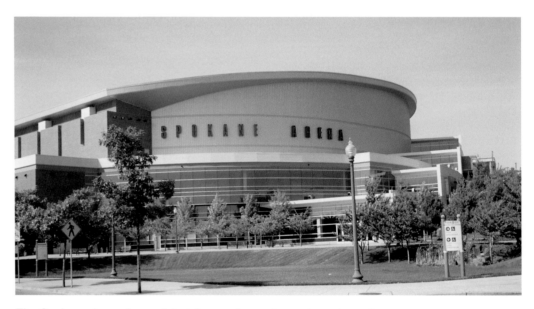

The Spokane Arena is a catalyst for nearby restaurants and sports venues.

while encouraging commercial development near Interstate 90 directed at commuters and other motorists.

Riverfront Park

Ambitious efforts to improve the park focused on a center pedestrian spine with increased street activity—relocat-

The larger-than-life "Radio Flyer" sculpture and slide is a park favorite.

Jogging, walking and biking are popular park activities.

The park offers an urban respite.

The river even has fish!

Warm weather encourages a variety of activities in Riverfront Park.

ing passive recreational uses to the east and west sides of the park. Plans for Riverfront Park are presented in detail in the Riverfront Park Master Plan.

3. Special Districts

The City also created an overlay of Special Districts, each demarcated in a general area of the City, to encourage flexible implementation strategies.

Intended to cluster similar visitor-attracting and employment activities, Spokane focused efforts on streetscape projects, connecting the Downtown Core with the City's entertainment district via improvements to Post Street. These special districts are designed to create an exciting atmosphere for residents and visitors, and allow Downtown establishments to coordinate marketing and promotional activities.

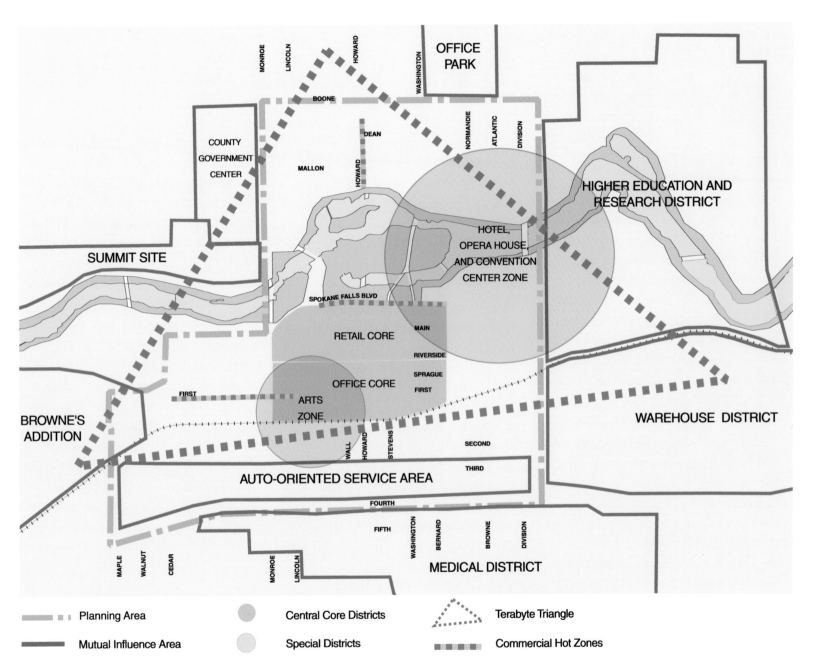

MONROE
LINCOLN
HOWARD
WASHINGTON

OFFICE PARK

BOONE

NORMANDIE
ATLANTIC
DIVISION

COUNTY GOVERNMENT CENTER

DEAN

HOWARD

MALLON

HIGHER EDUCATION AND RESEARCH DISTRICT

SUMMIT SITE

HOTEL, OPERA HOUSE, AND CONVENTION CENTER ZONE

SPOKANE FALLS BLVD

RETAIL CORE

MAIN

RIVERSIDE

OFFICE CORE

SPRAGUE

FIRST

FIRST

ARTS ZONE

WAREHOUSE DISTRICT

BROWNE'S ADDITION

WALL
HOWARD
STEVENS

SECOND

THIRD

AUTO-ORIENTED SERVICE AREA

FOURTH

FIFTH

MAPLE
WALNUT
CEDAR

MONROE
LINCOLN

WASHINGTON
BERNARD
BROWNE
DIVISION

MEDICAL DISTRICT

▪▪ ▪ Planning Area

⬤ Central Core Districts

△ Terabyte Triangle

— Mutual Influence Area

⬤ Special Districts

▬▬ Commercial Hot Zones

An overlay of Special Districts helps focus planning and promotional efforts. The Terabyte Triangle—a free high-speed wireless zone—has been a tremendous success, attracting over 150 new businesses.

- *Terabyte Triangle:* This is Spokane's successful high-speed connectivity hot zone. Spokane laid over 500 miles of fiber-optic cable and created a free 100-block wireless (wi-fi) zone to foster high-tech businesses and attract supporting professional services (accountants, lawyers, video and music producers). The network also provides secure police, fire, parking enforcement, and other safety and management communications.

Hoping to attract ten new "triangle" businesses a year, the City far surpassed expectations—adding over 150 businesses in five years and causing *Time* magazine in October 2004 to label Spokane "the wireless hotspot of the future." A June 2004 article in *SkyWest* magazine dubbed the City "a 21st-century power player in an entrepreneurial world fueled by technology and innovation." And The Intelligent Community Forum, a New York–based technology think tank, recently identified Spokane as one of seven of the world's brightest cities for investment in communica-

tions technologies—it was the only U.S. city chosen.

- *Arts and Entertainment:* This area later evolved into the Davenport District Strategic Action Plan, detailed later in this chapter.
- *The Hot Zones:* This area includes three restaurant and entertainment "hot zones" where new restaurants and entertainment are encouraged to locate to increase pedestrian density and business vitality. The zones are located along Spokane Falls Boulevard at the edge of Riverfront Park to strengthen the connection between the Convention Center and the Downtown retail core, along First Avenue in the West End to serve theatergoers and the neighborhood, and along Howard Street north of the river to support the sports and entertainment uses of the North Bank.
- *Opera and Convention Center:* This district includes hotels, the opera house and the Convention Center. The City improved pedestrian connections and devised marketing and promotional strategies to attract both supporting services and visitors.

- *Downtown Influence Areas:* These areas both influence and are influenced by activities in the Downtown. The City is in the process of developing better physical (pedestrian and transit) and policy connections to the County Government Area, Medical District, Summit Area and Higher Education and Research District.
- *Medical, Higher Education, and Warehouse Districts:* These districts don't have rigid boundaries, but are designed to encourage agglomeration of similar institutions and supporting businesses. In the university area, campus population is expected to top 11,000 students by 2010 and the master plan calls for a mixed-use environment with student housing, shopping, dining and gathering spaces.

4. Economic Development

In one of the most successful strategies, Spokane paved the way for future investment by streamlining development-related issues. The City added a new cabinet-level division—the Economic

This project at Howard and West Main Street is characteristic of the revitalization encouraged by the Economic Development Council's initiatives.

STEVE DAWSON III

Development Council (EDC)—merging Spokane's planning and building services departments into a single agency to manage all development initiatives. The EDC:

- Created the Downtown Spokane Ventures Association, and used the

Association's tax-exempt status to secure and leverage public, foundation and private funding to implement new projects. Ventures played a key role in fundraising strategies, funding streetscape and preservation projects and renovations of the historic buildings.

- Reduced processing time for a new commercial building permit to just over one month by simplifying permit and development processes and produced new educational materials, applications, economic incentives and a comprehensive website.

- Strengthened ties with regional agencies, collaborating on a Strategic Action Plan for Spokane and the Inland Northwest, a framework for delivering measurable results to both Downtown and regional economies.

- Collaborated with the Chamber of Commerce to change State of Washington constitutional provisions to allow the creation of tax increment financing (TIF) districts. TIF districts encourage redevelopment in depressed areas by allowing many project development costs (such as infrastructure, parking, streetscape, etc.) to be paid for by the *new* property taxes generated by redevelopment.

5. Housing

In 1995, Downtown Spokane's housing stock was mostly multi-family units, many targeted for low-income or elderly occupants. The City hoped to accommodate young professionals and "empty-nesters" with 200 new housing units per year, while continuing to provide for low-income and elderly residents. The Plan objective was to create a wide range of housing, from affordable below-market-rate to luxury units. The City developed a set of strategies which were designed to:

- Create incentive programs to encourage rehabs and infill projects (loan or grant programs in target areas);
- Support market-rate and high-end housing;
- Work with public, private, nonprofit housing developers to create affordable housing options;
- Leverage public and private funds to renovate deteriorated buildings;
- Change State law to allow City Redevelopment powers, such as

eminent domain, to acquire vacant or underused structures that can be sold to housing developers;

- Use federal and local housing district designations to create opportunity for federal housing tax credits; and
- Establish a consortium of local lenders to finance Downtown housing.

The City also held "Quadrant Open Houses" to involve the community in updating residential development codes to include more housing options such as cottage housing, zero lot lines, accessory dwelling units ("granny flats"), provisions for building on smaller lots, and transition areas between existing and new developments.

Market rate housing has increased and more is coming. A recent DSP study

Vacant for the past twenty years, the Borning Building is now slated to be transformed into 50 units of workforce housing.

STEVE DAWSON III

The historic Parsons Building on First and Jefferson was renovated as a five-story community for the elderly and disabled. The community room has a full kitchen and there's a rooftop garden area. Free social services are available on site.

STEVE DAWSON III

documented that a range of people—students, young professionals and empty nesters—*want* to move to the Downtown area. The study concluded that

Downtown could support 1,500 new market-rate dwelling units over the next five years. Small, vacant historic buildings are being renovated and entirely new construction is underway. A new ordinance allows use of woodframe construction in buildings up to 65 feet tall (50 feet was the previous limit). The change—worked out by the Spokane Fire Department, the City and the DSP—allows developers to add height to an existing building without major reconstruction. That directly led to the $18 million Havermale Park project, which will restore the historic Cadillac, Hale, Mearow, National, and Browne Buildings, providing 130 apartments and 37,000 square feet of retail space (including grocery store, unique restaurants and boutique shops).

Plans have also been approved for hundreds of residential units in a mixed-use development on the Summit site in the West Central area (just outside the plan area) and planning began in 2005 for a

17- to 20-story hotel and residential tower in the Downtown Core.

The historic Parsons Building was converted from a hotel and card room into a community of 50 apartments for elderly and disabled residents. On the books is a potential rehabilitation of the Borning Building, which has been vacant for 20 years. It would provide 50 units of workforce housing—one- to three-bedroom units with various rent structures for people who earn from 30 to 60 percent of the median income for the area.

6. *Transportation and Circulation*

As Downtown Spokane becomes an increasingly popular destination, transportation and circulation issues will become critical. The City will bring back the green streets plan to create pedestrian-friendly streets while efficiently moving people into and around Downtown via all modes of travel. One

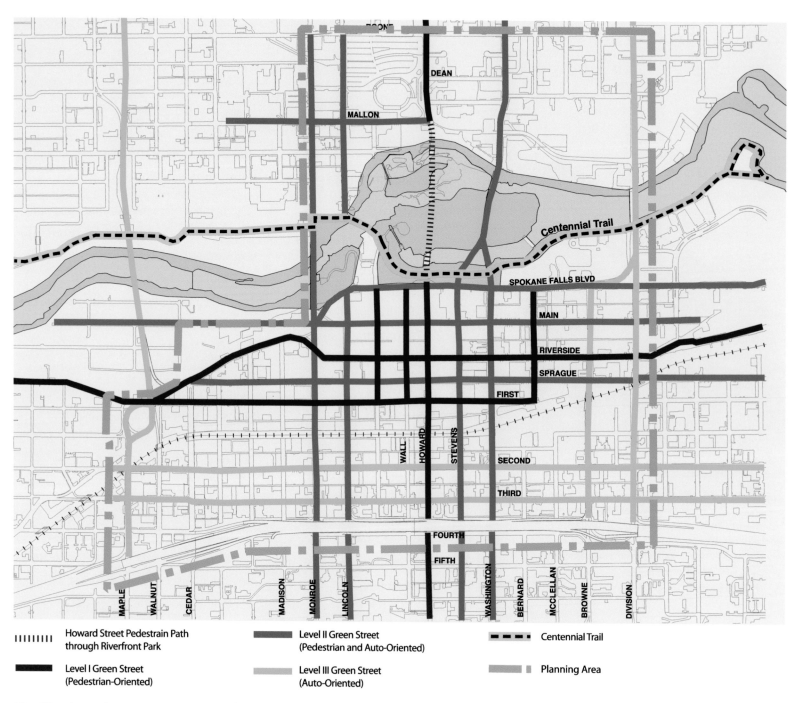

Howard Street Pedestrain Path through Riverfront Park

Level I Green Street (Pedestrian-Oriented)

Level II Green Street (Pedestrian and Auto-Oriented)

Level III Green Street (Auto-Oriented)

Centennial Trail

Planning Area

The City planned a green streets network: connected landscaped, tree-lined corridors that range from pedestrian only to auto only. (See "Cityscapes" in the Inclusive Design Guidelines for more information on types of streets.)

of the more substantial strategies in the plan, transportation and circulation initiatives showed private investors that the City supported increased density in specific areas and provided a long-term set of initiatives that would progress according to economic and population growth.

Pedestrian Circulation

Good pedestrian circulation and connections are essential to creating mixed-use urban villages. Spokane initially concentrated pedestrian improvements on single locations; the success of individual areas would then promote public investment in streetscape improvements elsewhere.

The City reconsidered the purpose of specific one-way and two-way streets. Two-way streets can slow traffic down and improve pedestrian accessibility, which is appropriate for pedestrian-oriented streets. (See "Reconnecting with the Street: R Street" for more discussion about pedestrian-oriented and auto-oriented streets.)

Post Street, a major artery connecting the Downtown Core with the new arts district, changed from a one-way to a two-way street. This, along with various streetscape improvements, including plant boxes and trees, helped fulfill the City's vision of "green streets" with pedestrian activity. By strengthening the enforcement of pedestrian right-of-way laws, the City helped redefine its image as a pedestrian-friendly Downtown. In 2004, residents approved a $117 million, 10-year street improvement project to renovate 110 miles of arterial and residential streets.

River Crossings

The City completed reconstructing the Monroe Street Bridge in September 2005, once the largest concrete arch bridge in the United States. A 1998 engineering investigation determined the bridge had as few as five years

When it was built in 1911, the Monroe Street Bridge was the largest concrete bridge in the country. The $20 million reconstruction preserved a City landmark. The original intricate details, such as this buffalo skull, were painstakingly recreated.
STEVE DAWSON III

The Monroe Street Bridge is an important connection between Downtown south of the river and the Centennial Trail north of the river.
STEVE DAWSON III

before deteriorating conditions might close it entirely. By essentially reconstructing the original bridge, the City retained its effect on Spokane's historic character, provided a direct connection to recreational opportunities in the Spokane River Gorge, and extended the bridge's life by at least 75 years.

Bicycle Accommodations

The City plans new bike paths and has added key connectivity features to the Spokane River Gorge. As the City adheres to design guidelines for new streets and sidewalks, improvements to bicycle accommodations will continue.

Monroe Street Bridge re-opening festivities included a community street fair with entertainment and a nighttime gala with fireworks.
STEVE DAWSON III

Parking

The City added new parking structures to support major visitor attractions at River Park Square and the Davenport Arts District, as well as a $1.25 million Park and Ride station in the South Hill area. All new parking structures conform to design specifications outlined in the City's "Downtown Design Guidelines" and accompanying zoning ordinance. The Downtown Spokane Business Improvement District (managed by the Downtown Spokane Partnership) completed a Downtown Comprehensive Parking Management Plan in 2005. The Plan calls for the creation of a new nonprofit organization and parking manager, guided by the efforts of public and private stakeholders, and for a physical inventory, use study, and future demand projection for all Downtown parking.

7. Community Design

Community design enhances the quality of private and public spaces by integrating features such as pedestrian friendliness, accessibility, view corridors, historic preservation, public art, landscape, parks and plazas. The City plans new plazas for public events and informal gatherings in the Downtown Core and at City Hall.

To ensure pedestrian-sensitive development and cooperation between public and private developments, the City drafted the "Downtown Design Guidelines" and zoning ordinance detailing specific design elements to enhance the livability of the Downtown area. (Design guidelines from this document are featured in this book's Cityscapes Design Guidelines.)

8. Historic Preservation

Historic preservation stimulates private investment. One by one, local businesses and property owners have been investing in renovating buildings and creating new housing and retail space. Lewis and Clark High School, built in

The American Legion Building sat completely vacant during the 1980s and 1990s. It was built in 1900 for the Spokane Club, by the same architects that built the Empire State Building. Renovations included restoring the original mansard roof, destroyed by a fire in 1910.

1912, completed a major renovation in 2001 that triggered renewal of deteriorated buildings and streetscapes in a three-block surrounding area.

The new Economic Development Division incorporates a Historic Preservation Department, dedicated to retaining historic buildings as valuable

The strikingly renovated Courthouse features Gothic Revival architecture.

STEVE DAWSON III

Lewis and Clark High School's renovation preserved its craftsman-style woodwork interior and terra cotta and brick façade.

LEWIS AND CLARK HIGH SCHOOL

assets that strengthen the City's unique character and sense of place. The City streamlined a set of preservation forms and applications for property owners. In 2002 alone, this simplicity resulted in historic rehabilitation investments totaling $27.3 million—almost as much as the rest of Washington State *combined*. A local historic tax credit, implemented to encourage investment in historic structures, currently benefits 100 downtown

The Paulsen Building on the right was completed in 1911 using the all-steel construction for highrises typical of the Chicago School. The adjacent renovated Paulsen Medical/Dental Building (left), designed in Art Deco style, was completed in 1929; its stepped crown rises to a set-back penthouse, a Spokane landmark.

SPOKANE CITY-COUNTY HISTORIC PRESERVATION DEPARTMENT

Built in 1905, the Beaux Arts/Neoclassical Holley-Mason Hardware Building was one of the first reinforced concrete buildings in Washington state. Located in the Davenport District, it was renovated as an emerging technology center—now home to bio-tech and software firms—and received the 2000 Washington State Historical Preservation award.

SPOKANE CITY-COUNTY HISTORIC PRESERVATION DEPARTMENT

The renovated 1923 Chronicle Building in the Davenport District is a prime example of Age of Elegance architecture.

SPOKANE CITY-COUNTY HISTORIC PRESERVATION DEPARTMENT

buildings. In 2005, the momentum of historic preservation projects encouraged Spokane to enact an ordinance restricting the demolition of all historic structures.

Other major properties renovated since the plan's development include the Davenport Hotel, Montvale Hotel and Fox Theater (described in the Davenport District Strategic Plan), the Steam Plant, the American Legion Building, and the Spokane Flour Mill (described in the North Bank Development Plan).

9. *Neighborhood Economic Development*

Recognizing the interdependence of Downtown and neighborhood economic growth, Spokane made the economic development of surrounding neighborhoods a specific component of the City's

The 1916 Central Steam Plant (above and at left) provided Downtown's steam heat for 70 years, but closed down in 1986 and remained vacant for more than a decade. An enormous restoration project turned four massive steam boilers into a coffee shop, restaurant, shop and wishing well. The coalbunker is now high-tech office space suspended from the ceiling. The restoration grew to include the adjacent 1890 Seehorn Building and the Courtyard Building, for a total of 80,000 square feet, including parking. The project won a 2001 National Preservation Honor Award.

STEVE DAWSON III

A new gondola replaced the original structure and links Riverfront Park with the North Bank.
STEVE DAWSON III

Spokane Falls Skyride

A state-of-the-art gondola opened in September 2005 on the western edge of the park, along the Monroe Street Bridge. The new gondola, with 15 fully-accessible six-passenger cabins, is an update of the City's original gondola, designed for the 1974 Exposition. The closed gondolas allow the ride to operate over a much longer season.

master plan. The City and the Downtown Spokane Partnership provided leadership in the creation of neighborhood-specific economic plans—strengthening growth potential downtown and, more importantly, encouraging neighborhood residents and community leaders to invest in the planning process.

The Spokane Community Empowerment Zones now cover most of the West Central, East Central and Hillyard neighborhoods. They are intended to stimulate economic development by offering sales and use tax deferrals, new job tax credits, and business training credits to companies in research and development and manufacturing.

RIVERFRONT PARK MASTER PLAN

The Downtown Core contains high-intensity employment centers, as well as regional retail and entertainment centers. Riverfront Park provides a great open space amenity as an urban refuge, as well as connections between Downtown and the North Bank. The park accommodates recreational, civic and cultural activities that have a broad community appeal.

The Riverfront Park Master Plan addressed specific needs and projects for the park.

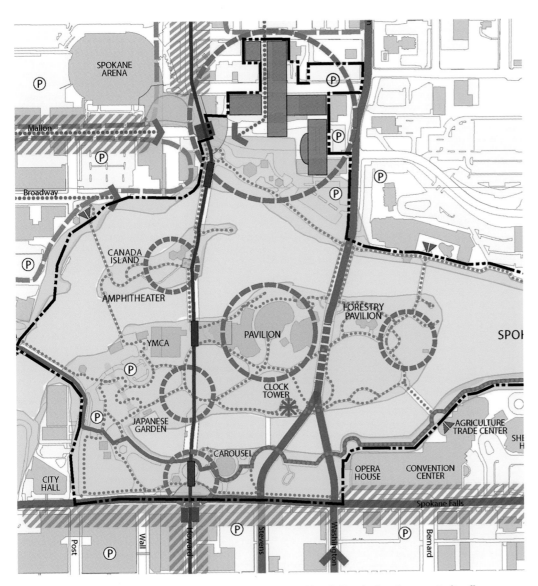

The Riverfront Park Master Plan also addresses the North Bank development site (large dotted circle at top) and the relationship to the Spokane Arena area.

Fall foliage lines the riverside paths.

Howard Street Corridor

Howard Street is the main north-south pedestrian link, running through the park and linking the south and north banks. High-intensity activities clustered along the corridor will help make it a destination rather than just a pathway. Kiosks will provide interpretive information about the City and the park. Food and gift vendors will create destination points. Design elements such as patterned brick pavers, landscaping,

The south entry to Riverfront Park includes a carousel and grassy areas.
DON HORTON

The Rotary Riverfront Fountain, at the south entrance, was designed by well-known Spokane sculptor Harold Balazs. It features 150 jets that pump water in changing patterns and is lit at night. It is fully accessible to wheelchairs, walkers and strollers.

STEVE DAWSON III

The entry on the North Bank will be enhanced with a plaza and seating.
PAUL TUTTLE

lighting, street furniture and signage will create a distinctive pathway and enhance safety.

A potential future project is an electric trolley connection on Howard Street that would provide both transportation and a fun experience—with minimal pollution.

Entries

Major entries will be welcoming and distinctive and help create community connections. The main south entrance feature is the carousel, which was expanded and enhanced, with a new, interactive water feature. The North

Entry is a critical link between the park and North Bank activities, including the Spokane Arena and the new North Bank development. Landmark elements that identify the entry, shaded seating areas, and a plaza will increase community and group experiences.

Pavilion Area

The pavilion is a central element of the park, immediately adjacent to the river. However, it blocks views of the river.

Since it was built for the 1974 Expo, it must be updated. One of the main improvements will be removing pieces of the structure to open views, while

retaining the tent covering that makes the facility distinctive. The structure can be adapted to create a theater in the round with amphitheater and lawn

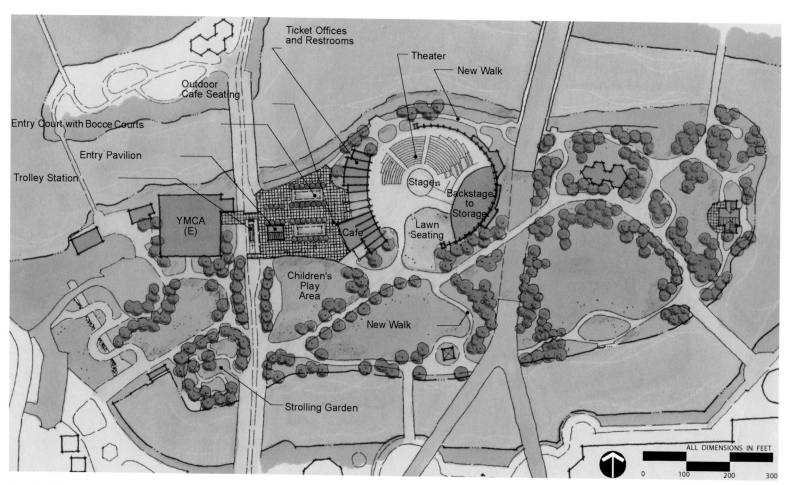

The Pavilion area is one of the renovation projects identified in the Riverfront Park North Bank Master Plan.

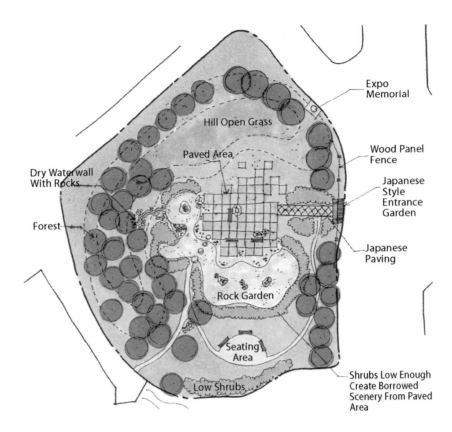

The existing tent structure of the park pavilion...

STEVE DAWSON III

...and the Japanese Garden area will also be renovated.

seating. Improved landscaping, lighting, sculpture and public art will enhance physical appearance and safety. A café with outdoor seating will also contribute to a more welcoming environment.

A major renovation in the area will be removing the existing IMAX building (replaced with a new IMAX on the North Bank), which is underutilized. Instead, an entry plaza (with an attraction such as bocce ball courts or ice rink) and children's play area or lawn will open up the views and provide gathering space.

East Havermale Island

East of the pavilion area, the forestry pavilion and small amphitheater benefit from beautiful views of the river and the dramatic buildings on the South Bank, such as the opera house. The amphitheater will be enhanced to provide a small venue for concerts and performances, benches, picnic tables and landscaped garden spaces will be added and pedestrian access improved. A picnic shelter and additional restrooms on the eastern edge of the island

will enhance the area for parties and family reunions.

Japanese Garden

The garden is a quiet, contemplative area that will be restored as a traditional Japanese garden. Traditional elements include a wood panel fence, new entrance, rock garden, dry water wall with rocks and possibly a native plant interpretive center.

Canada Island

Canada Island is underutilized and could provide many more recreational opportunities. The existing storage structure will be renovated as a small log-frame picnic shelter, with rock walls and totem pole. Native vegetation will be restored and interpretive signage will create an educational and interactive environment for park visitors. The entire island could be rented for private functions such as weddings and parties.

NORTH BANK DEVELOPMENT PLAN

Plans for the North Bank area proposed specific catalytic sites in the City's main entertainment and recreation hub. The primary element was a new Science Technology Center, supported by parking and transportation improvements and, eventually, a new IMAX theater. The Plan also called for major improvements to existing park access—improving the park entrances on the North Bank and connections to the Spokane Arena. By successfully reorganizing the area's public activities and developments, the City created greater potential for private investment along the North Bank while addressing the community's need for an urban refuge in a peaceful, accessible Riverfront Park.

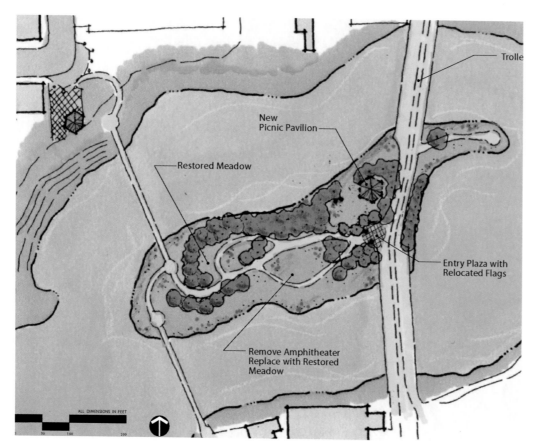

The Riverfront Park Master Plan proposes to revitalize Canada Island.

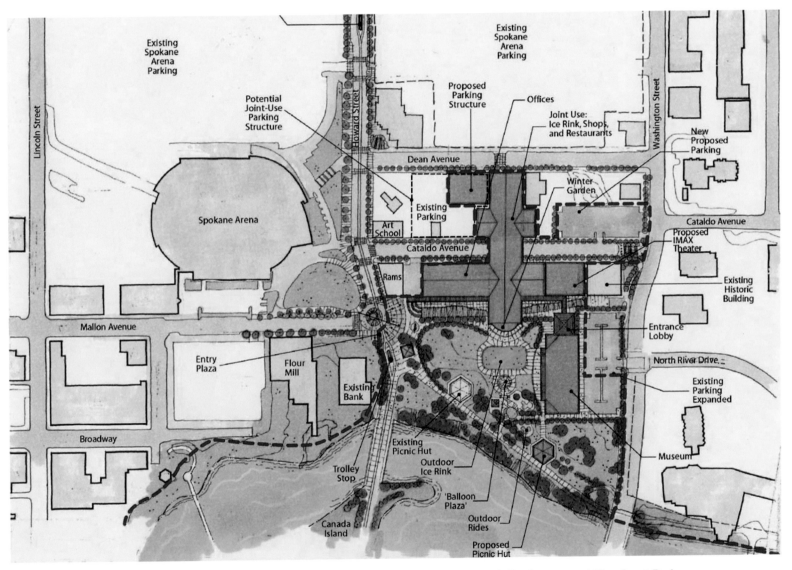

Existing
Spokane
Arena
Parking

Potential
Joint-Use
Parking
Structure

Proposed
Parking
Structure

Offices

Existing
Spokane
Arena
Parking

Joint Use:
Ice Rink, Shops,
and Restaurants

New
Proposed
Parking

Lincoln Street

Howard Street

Dean Avenue

Washington Street

Winter
Garden

Spokane Arena

Art
School

Existing
Parking

Cataldo Avenue

Cataldo Avenue

Rams

Proposed
IMAX
Theater

Existing
Historic
Building

Mallon Avenue

Entry
Plaza

Flour
Mill

Existing
Bank

North River Drive

Entrance
Lobby

Existing
Parking
Expanded

Broadway

Trolley
Stop

Existing
Picnic Hut

Outdoor
Ice Rink

'Balloon
Plaza'

Outdoor
Rides

Museum

Canada
Island

Proposed
Picnic Hut

The North Bank site design aims to create better links between the Spokane Arena, North Bank area, and Riverfront Park.

The concept diagram from the North Bank Development Plan shows locations for outdoor elements, park offices, a new science technology center and an IMAX theater.

PAUL TUTTLE

Science Technology Center

Construction of Mobius, the region's first science center, is scheduled to start in late 2007 on the location specified in the development plan. The 75,000-square-foot building will be called Mobius at Michael Anderson Plaza, after the fallen astronaut who grew up nearby, and will incorporate sustainable design and a strong tie to the river and the local geography. The aim is to attract children and ignite their interest in science. With sheltered views from beneath the eaves of its porch and public access to a waterfront beach, the building will also serve as a dynamic civic gathering area. (Mobius at River Park Square, a Children's Museum, was completely renovated and re-opened in 2005 with 16,000 square feet of exhibits focusing on arts, culture, literacy, math and science.)

Other Attractions

To pull visitors north of the river, the plan calls for picnic areas and huts, outdoor rides, a plaza, park offices, winter garden atrium, indoor ice rink, and outdoor ice rink or roller rink.

The Flour Mill, now home to boutiques, designer shops, galleries and restaurants, overlooks the Spokane River and stands as a symbol of the City's close ties to the agricultural countryside and Spokane River. A new $16 million Flour Mill office building is planned for the area, with architecture

Mobius at Michael Anderson Plaza is scheduled to begin construction in 2007.
WILLIAM MCDONOUGH + PARTNERS

The old Spokane Flour Mill has been entirely renovated.
SPOKANE CITY-COUNTY HISTORIC PRESERVATION DEPARTMENT

in keeping with the mill. The planned five-story building will also include retail shops and restaurants.

DAVENPORT DISTRICT STRATEGIC ACTION PLAN

Spokane's Davenport District has seen perhaps the most dramatic revitalization in the City. It's home to vibrant performance venues, an emerging arts community, and businesses and community organizations that actively support the District's development and culture.

Previously, the Davenport area was not widely perceived as a cohesive district. It had many single resident occupancy hotels, but lacked family and professional residential housing and resident-serving businesses such as grocery stores. The City needed to increase public safety, access and event coordination to draw public and private support. The community wanted the area to provide entertainment, arts and cultural venues, creative businesses, affordable housing and live/work opportunities for artists, and resident-serving businesses.

The 2002 Davenport Strategic Action Plan is based on three principles:

- *Concentration.* Concentrate resources and development in the District's center, which will lead to further interest and investment in larger areas.

- *Synergy.* Create uses and activities that mutually support each other, such as entertainment, restaurants, galleries and locally owned shops.

- *Coordination.* Build on existing businesses, create a District identity and coordinate operating hours, marketing programs and events.

The Plan identified six primary strategies for the District—each with specific action steps, as well as a timeframe and a lead agency to see each action through, providing quantifiable goals by which to measure progress.

1. Private Investment and Development
A key to success is drawing private investment with strategic public investment. The City set a target of 25,000

With over 300 performances a year, the Met Theater helped drive the Davenport District's revitalization.

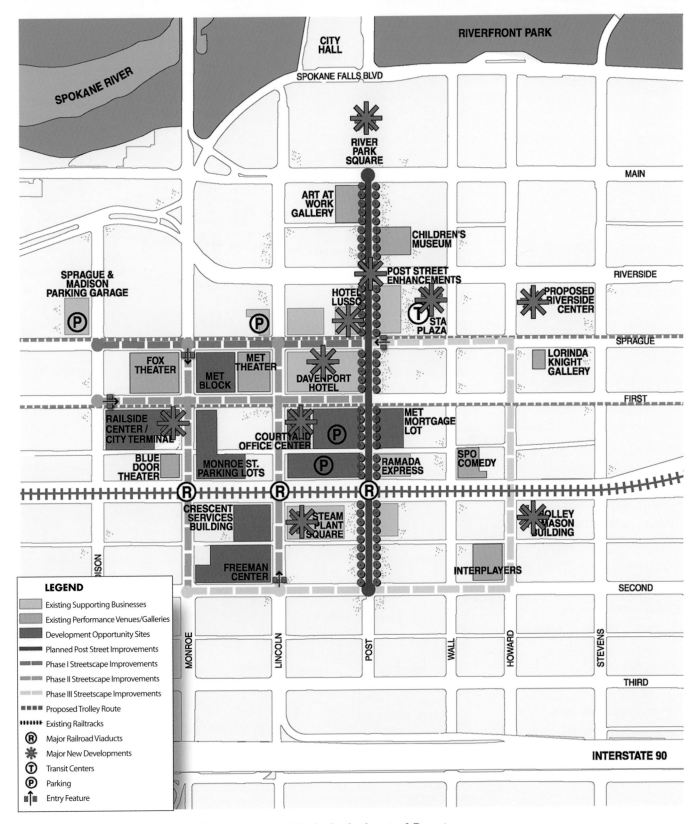

LEGEND

	Existing Supporting Businesses
	Existing Performance Venues/Galleries
	Development Opportunity Sites
	Planned Post Street Improvements
	Phase I Streetscape Improvements
	Phase II Streetscape Improvements
	Phase III Streetscape Improvements
	Proposed Trolley Route
	Existing Railtracks
(R)	Major Railroad Viaducts
✳	Major New Developments
(T)	Transit Centers
(P)	Parking
⬆	Entry Feature

The Davenport District includes about 18 square blocks in the heart of Downtown.

square feet of artist studio space and 50,000 square feet of preferred business investment each year to measure the Plan's success. The Plan identified potential catalytic sites, such as the Met Theater block, surface parking lots, vacant buildings and underutilized commercial and industrial buildings. Preferred businesses included four categories that would mutually complement and energize each other:

- *Cultural/Arts:* Movie and live theater, dance studios, performance space, museums, galleries, art supplies, artist studios, live music clubs, art schools.
- *High Tech/Professional:* Software, multi-media, communications, marketing/advertising, interior design, architecture/landscape architecture, nonprofit organizations, graphic design, legal services.
- *Home Improvement:* Antiques, lighting, custom millwork, imports, custom manufacturing, specialty hardware, textiles/fabrics, designer clothing.

A $38 million renovation of the historic Davenport Hotel spurred tremendous investment in the area.
STEVE DAWSON III

After sitting vacant for almost two decades, the Davenport Hotel now offers 280 hotel rooms and 25,000 square feet of meeting space. An 18-story addition will provide 300 more rooms.
STEVE DAWSON III

■ *Food and Beverage:* Farmers market, culinary school, delicatessens/cafés, coffee bars, unique restaurants, microbrewery, wine tasting, bakeries, butcher/seafood shops, green grocers, natural foods, bed and breakfasts/hotels.

Guided by the plan's investment strategy, major restoration projects added new life to the District's historic buildings. After sitting vacant for more than 18 years, the Davenport Hotel's 2002 grand reopening added 280 rooms and 25,000 square feet of meeting space to the District. The success of its $38 million renovation removed a major psychological hurdle to investing in Downtown and was the catalyst for a torrent of new investment. Between 2002 and 2004, the number of retail operations in the area jumped 52 percent.

Community leaders saved the Fox Theater from demolition with a "Save the Fox" effort—drawing contributions of over $1 million from more than

The 1930 Art Deco Fox Theater is now being renovated, after the community donated $1 million to save it. It is home to the Spokane Symphony.
FOX THEATER

1,300 citizens. New nightclubs, sports bars, jazz clubs, a casino, a dinner theater, restaurants, art galleries and shops have appeared. Renovation of Spokane's historic Odd Fellows Hall includes a new community theater, with multiple stages for dinner and cabaret performances, musical events, poetry readings, and rehearsal space for small and medium-size arts organizations.

The renovated Odd Fellows Hall is home to CenterStage, a new community theater. Distinctive signage has become a hallmark of the Davenport District.
JEREMY BOLTON

The Big Easy is a new concert venue, dance club and Cajun-style restaurant.

STEVE DAWSON III

Art gallery openings attract collectors and artists to the Davenport District.

LORINDA KNIGHT GALLERY

The urbane Montvale Hotel is actually the oldest hotel in the City, built in 1899 and abandoned since 1974. After a $3 million renovation, the hotel reopened in February 2005.
STEVE DAWSON III

2. Public Improvements and Infrastructure
Proposed public infrastructure improvements were designed to attract private development, creative businesses, artists and patrons. The Plan set street improvements on First Avenue (between Post and Madison) as a benchmark for this strategy, though extensive improvements were made throughout the District. Many of the streets in the area are identified as "green streets," emphasizing pedestrian-friendly streetscapes and circulation. The railroad tracks became a unique District experience with improved lighting and art elements.

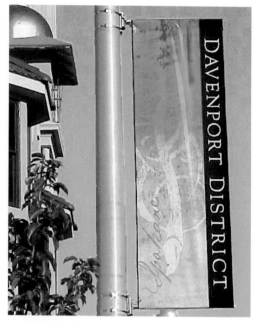

STA plaza is the main City transit hub, with shops, events and concerts throughout the year.
STEVE DAWSON III

Davenport District banners help create a sense of identity.

The Plan also calls for significant transportation improvements, and better utilization of the Spokane Transit Authority (STA) Transit Plaza, a hub for Downtown transit as well as an event and performance venue.

The Davenport District Arts Board (DDAB) used local artists and designers to create banners that emphasize the District's identity, street art, and way-finding kiosks to help residents and visitors explore the galleries, shops, hotels, restaurants, theaters and clubs.

3. *Organizational Capacity* To build the organizational and financial capacity of District partners, the DDAB embarked on a number of strategic initiatives, including increasing DDAB's annual budget to more than $85,000 and adding one full-time staff member. DDAB and the Arts Commission collaborated on developing artist resource packages to help with grants, housing, workspace, business planning and patronage development.

Brochures and a website promote Davenport District businesses and events.

4. *Marketing and Communications* In fulfilling Plan action steps, DDAB and the Arts Commission established a visual identity for the District and developed cross-promotional activities, such as discounts for restaurants and performance venues. The District initiated a new website, davenportdistrict.com, providing a central location for information on events, galleries, performance venues, accommodations, clubs and restaurants.

The DDAB endeavored to increase venue attendance by 75 percent in 2006 through a District-wide marketing program that included advertising and flyers.

5. *Arts Events and Programs* To animate the District and encourage community participation, the DDAB strengthened and promoted a number of events and programs for various age groups. The first Beaux Arts Ball in 2004 raised funds and promoted awareness for District developments. In August 2005, families from the entire Spokane region visited Davenport to enjoy the first-ever Chalk Art Festival, bringing the arts to the streets of Spokane.

6. *Regulations and Incentives* The District developed a coordinated set of regulatory reforms aimed at making it easier to develop retail and entertainment, as well as live/work spaces and performance venues in underutilized buildings. Building codes were revised to make developments less costly without compromising safety

The market-rate Metropole Apartments are within easy walking distance of the river and employment areas.

The new American West Bank, located on the edge of the Davenport District, won Second Place in the 2005 International Masonry Competition as a commercial building with intricate brickwork not commonly seen in modern buildings. The building faithfully followed the new Downtown Design Guidelines.

MICK MCDOWELL PROJECTS

(such as the new ordinance that allows use of woodframe construction in buildings up to 65 feet tall), and tax incentives and adaptive reuse bonuses were provided (such as an increase in allowable floor area ratios if property owners work with local arts organizations to include performance space).

Performance Measures

The Plan set seven priorities with specific performance measures. The targets and measures were designed to be revisited and revised, based on changing economic conditions and further research.

THE GREAT SPOKANE RIVER GORGE STRATEGIC MASTER PLAN

The Spokane River Gorge area is visible from Downtown and adjacent neighborhoods, accessible by public trails and bridge overlooks and adjacent to hundreds of acres of open space. The gorge area has the potential to increase a wide range of compelling recreational opportunities, stimulate adjacent land development, promote tourism and visitation, enhance business development opportunities and restore sensitive habitat areas.

The Olmsted Brothers had proposed a "Great Gorge Park" as early as 1908—an 11-mile area that would be an accessible greenbelt, connecting various parks on its banks. Over the years, the Spokane Park Board purchased and set aside riverbank land. Today, about 80 percent of the land identified by the Olmsteds for parks is maintained as open space and parks.

Existing Neighborhoods

The Plan is designed to coexist with current private land ownership and focuses on five areas:

■ Peaceful Valley, a historic district along the river that has seen significant new investment and development.

The Peaceful Valley neighborhood lies alongside the riverbank.

In recent years new housing, such as these townhomes, has been constructed in Peaceful Valley.

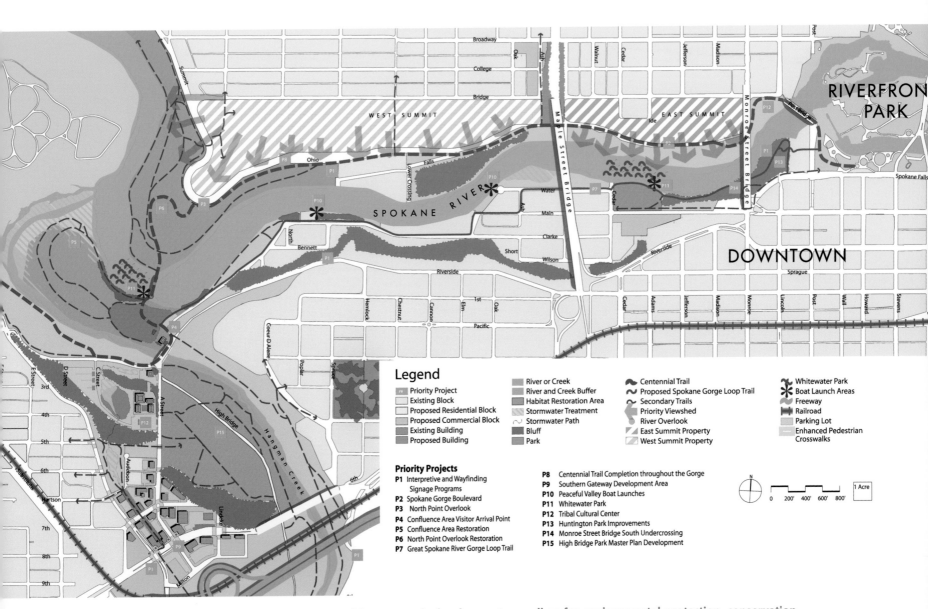

Legend

- **P8** Priority Project
- Existing Block
- Proposed Residential Block
- Proposed Commercial Block
- Existing Building
- Proposed Building
- River or Creek
- River and Creek Buffer
- Habitat Restoration Area
- Stormwater Treatment
- Stormwater Path
- Bluff
- Park
- Centennial Trail
- Proposed Spokane Gorge Loop Trail
- Secondary Trails
- Priority Viewshed
- River Overlook
- East Summit Property
- West Summit Property
- Whitewater Park
- Boat Launch Areas
- Freeway
- Railroad
- Parking Lot
- Enhanced Pedestrian Crosswalks

Priority Projects

P1 Interpretive and Wayfinding Signage Programs
P2 Spokane Gorge Boulevard
P3 North Point Overlook
P4 Confluence Area Visitor Arrival Point
P5 Confluence Area Restoration
P6 North Point Overlook Restoration
P7 Great Spokane River Gorge Loop Trail
P8 Centennial Trail Completion throughout the Gorge
P9 Southern Gateway Development Area
P10 Peaceful Valley Boat Launches
P11 Whitewater Park
P12 Tribal Cultural Center
P13 Huntington Park Improvements
P14 Monroe Street Bridge South Undercrossing
P15 High Bridge Park Master Plan Development

The Spokane River Gorge Master Plan is seen as a tool for economic development as well as for environmental protection, conservation and recreation.

Historic buildings along Broadway characterize the West Central Neighborhood.

- West Central, one of Spokane's treasures, with many historic buildings and 63 acres of conservation land. A 77-acre area (the Summit site) is scheduled for residential development.
- High Bridge Park, a currently under-used 200-acre City park on both sides of the river.

The Spokane River flows through the entire City of Spokane.
STEVE DAWSON III

- Monroe Street Bridge, which was recently renovated. The Plan calls for pedestrian links under the bridge.
- Lower Falls, the center piece of the gorge area and sacred to many Native Americans, marking the transition between Downtown and the river.

Friends of the Falls (FOF) and the City proposed improvements to the Spokane River Gorge that would unite the area with adjacent neighborhoods, concentrate new developments outside the gorge on the periphery, increase use of existing parks, and protect existing neighborhoods and natural areas. Similar to the Downtown Plan, this Plan suggests that all projects value the gorge area's diverse history—strengthening a sense of place while encouraging uniquely related private investment, including recreational outfitters and outdoor retailers.

The Plan integrates seven major elements (with 15 priority projects) to create a comprehensive approach to the entire gorge area.

1. Interpretive Facilities and Program

An extensive new signage and wayfinding program will include new overlooks and visitor arrival points. By coordinating information from local tourism, education, tribal, cultural, historic and

Priority Project 1: More interpretive signage, such as this signage at the hydroelectric development, will help explain the gorge area's diverse natural and cultural resources.

Priority Project 3: A North Point overlook would offer interpretation and panoramic views of the gorge and Downtown.
PAUL TUTTLE

business interests, the Plan envisions a set of wayfinding and interpretive signs to reinforce the cohesive identity of the gorge area. The Plan calls for creating new interpretive sites, including a North Point Overlook and Confluence Area Visitor Arrival Point. A new Tribal Cultural Center located near Downtown would provide a space for cultural activities and exhibits pertaining to Spokane's American Indian history.

The Confluence area's (top) natural beauty and central location make it ideal for an arrival and interpretive point. It is currently underused (above).

Priority Project 4: The new Confluence area arrival point will offer directional and interpretive signage at the south end of the new Sandifir Memorial Bridge.
PAUL TUTTLE

Priority Project 12: A new Tribal Cultural Center could replace this temporary facility, on a bluff overlooking the Confluence area.

Priority Project 13: A pedestrian interpretive plaza could open a grand vista of the river, and connect Huntington Park, the river and the falls.

FRANK SANFORD

2. Transportation, Circulation and Parking Improvement

To develop accessible, ecologically sensitive entries to the gorge area, the Plan recommends creating a panoramic Spokane Gorge Boulevard along the north shore of the river. The Boulevard would include connectivity features to the Summit area, Spokane's West Central Neighborhood and Downtown. To accommodate varied land use and building densities, the Plan outlines an array of road configurations for pull-in parking at overlook sites, integrated bike lanes and access to hiking trails.

Priority Project 2: A new Spokane Gorge Boulevard will be incorporated with the Centennial trail, offering overlook points, pedestrian amenities, multi-use roadway treatments and urban stormwater runoff treatments.

PAUL TUTTLE

At the southwest end of the boulevard, a gateway development would offer a dramatic and easily identifiable entry just north of the I-90 and Highway 95 interchange. The gateway would divert heavy traffic away from southern neighborhoods and invite investment opportunities for visitor-serving amenities, while serving as the central parking hub. Shuttles would connect gateway parking to key sites along the river to reduce the impact of vehicular traffic.

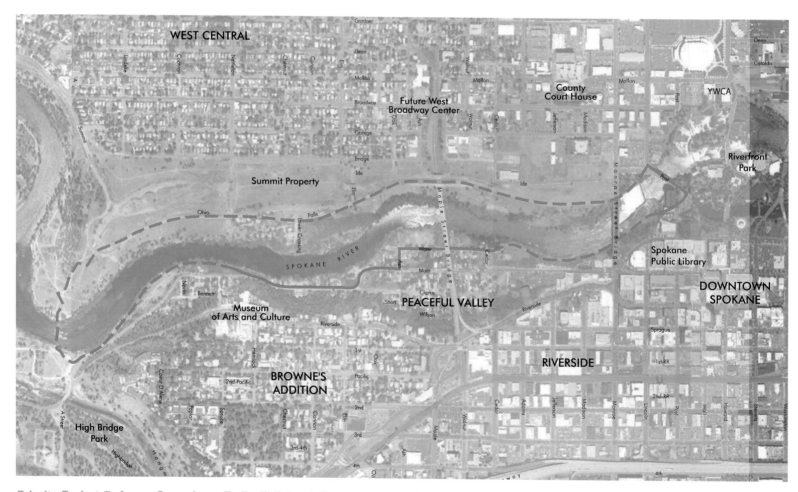

Priority Project 7: A new Gorge Loop Trail will link existing and new neighborhoods with Downtown and the river.

3. Pedestrian and Bike Ways

The Plan calls for a Great Spokane River Gorge Loop Trail, making a complete loop around the gorge area and providing a smaller loop around the Monroe Street Bridge to Downtown. The planned loop, running along the bi-state Centennial Trail, incorporated existing roads and smaller trails including informal pathways to provide direct access to the river's edge. A variety of proposed trail features will adjust the trail according to unique neighborhoods and areas with roadside amenities. Bridge renovations will allow for safe crossings and leveled access on steep grades.

Priority Project 8: The Centennial Trail will link Riverfront Park with Spokane Gorge Drive on the north side of the river; the trail actually begins in Coeur D'Alene, Idaho, and will be fully accessible to people of all ages and physical abilities.
PAUL TUTTLE

Priority Project 14: A new Monroe Street Bridge undercrossing will provide a safe pedestrian connection across the street and will connect with the Centennial Trail.

4. Recreation

To integrate new recreational opportunities, the Plan balances the goals of recreation enthusiasts, private investors, ecologists and community members. Three key recreation sites—Water Avenue, Clarke Avenue and boat launches and a whitewater park—were strategically located to provide easy, low-impact access at active-use entry points.

With 15 time-limited parking spaces, the boat launch minimizes on-street parking by non-residents, provides evening parking for area residents and encourages a turnaround drop-off point for recreational shuttles. Basic facilities, including restrooms, trash receptacles and wayfinding signage, were designed to minimize impacts on nearby neighborhoods.

The Plan also proposes a new whitewater park, adding various waterscape elements to a designated area of the river for use by rafters, kayakers and other recreational enthusiasts. The whitewater park's varied water feature heights ensure an extended kayaking and rafting season despite seasonal changes in the river levels, and provide a manageable focal point for recreational impact in the gorge. Park water features will also create deep pools that provide resting places for trout, and waterfalls that increase oxygen supplies to support river food sources. With the support of the City, the Chamber of Commerce and area legislators, FOF secured a $400,000 appropriation from the Washington State Legislature to begin construction of the whitewater park.

Priority Project 10: The Plan concentrates boat entries with parking at three locations to minimize impacts on nearby neighborhoods.

Priority Project 11: The character of the river lends itself to a whitewater park, which will also enhance fish habitat.

Priority Project 15: The high-quality resources that High Bridge Park offers would be improved with a new master plan, including programming, increased trail access, amenities and protection for sensitive species in areas like Hangman Creek.

5. *Habitat Preservation and Restoration*

Preservation and restoration efforts will be directed at the two most damaged sites in the gorge: the Confluence area and North Point Overlook. The Plan calls for gradual replanting of a native plant palette to provide wildlife cover and support for the river's ecosystem with shade and nutrients. Planned interpretive elements at these sites will highlight cultural, archeological and natural history information. Short loop trails off the main trail are designed to offer interpretation of the native ecosystem, the significance of plants and water to native peoples and historic uses of the landscape.

6. *Economic Development*

By encouraging access and sustainable recreational opportunities, the Plan opens the gorge to a variety of outdoor- and recreation-related private investment. Economic development efforts are focused on the Southern Gateway—both for its convenient access to regional highways and the river's key recreational sites.

Priority Project 5: The Confluence area is a very sensitive ecological and cultural site that is constantly reforming through the river's natural processes of erosion and deposition.

Priority Project 6: The slopes below the North Point Overlook were disturbed during construction and would be improved by restoring the hillsides with native species re-vegetation.

The existing south entrance should signify a connection to the river while providing recreation-related retail development.

Priority Project 9: A new Southern Gateway will become an energized recreation hub that announces the river and provides visitor-serving amenities, revitalizing an area in need of reinvestment.

PAUL TUTTLE

7. *Green Infrastructure*

To ensure a protected natural environment well into the future, the Plan established Green Infrastructure Zones—limiting new developments to strategic locations around the gorge, and setting guidelines to reduce their environmental impact. For example, new structures within a specified region are now required to effectively manage all storm water runoff onsite—reducing potential impact on the gorge.

Design Palette

The Downtown Spokane Zoning Ordinance and Design Guidelines provide direction to developers and innovative design solutions. The guidelines are a collection of ideas for making great places, focusing on improving the social fabric of Spokane's urban environment and how people use spaces.

Management and Operational Issues

SPOKANE PLAN FOR A NEW DOWNTOWN

The Downtown Spokane Partnership (DSP), a private nonprofit organization composed of Downtown business, government and community leaders, initiated the planning process and remains the primary marketing and organizational force behind Downtown projects, coordinating efforts between various agencies. The creation of the Economic Development Council, and the subsequent nonprofit Downtown Spokane Ventures Association, enabled the City to organize key administrative and economic initiatives to streamline and coordinate all development-related issues and to provide support for public and private developments.

The Plan assigns all action strategies to a key responsible agency for implementation and a specific timeframe for each action. The DSP, assigned partial responsibility in nearly all projects, ensures consistency and monitors progress. Streetscape and infrastructure improvements were assigned to the City, and remaining tasks were distributed among private property owners, developers, neighborhood associations, the Spokane Transit Authority, Chamber of Commerce and others.

RIVERFRONT PARK MASTER PLAN AND NORTH BANK DEVELOPMENT PLAN

The Spokane Park Board controls a large portion of the North Bank and Riverfront Park. While private investments have increased public interest in Riverfront Park and the North Bank, many of this Plan's initiatives depended exclusively on investment from the Park Board and major private investments (coordinated by the Downtown Spokane Partnership).

DAVENPORT DISTRICT STRATEGIC ACTION PLAN

The Plan includes eight case studies of successful arts and cultural districts in the United States and Canada. The Davenport District followed the lead of successful arts districts across the country by creating a nonprofit authority to coordinate development efforts and provide marketing services.

The detailed action steps outlined in the Plan include prioritization, a timeframe (ranging between two and ten years), performance targets and the designation

Street maintenance and grafitti removal are high priorities in the Downtown area.

of a lead agency for each action. The lead agencies include:

- *Davenport District Arts Board*—a nonprofit created to lead the District's redevelopment, the board took on the majority of responsibilities delegated in the Plan. The District channeled nearly all organizational development, communications, and programming strategies through the board—as well as various private investment and public improvements projects. As the

Local artists created unique street benches using metal salvaged from the old steam plant.

central organizing agency for the District, the board organized a "Metal to Magic Auction" to kick-start infrastructure improvements. District artists sculpted cast-off metal components from the nearby Steam Plant, and the Arts Board directed revenues from the auction to commission unique benches for placement throughout the District. The Board operates an informational District website and manages all marketing efforts.

- *Downtown Spokane Partnership*—the DSP maintains District statistics and monitors plan implementation against performance targets. The DSP managed all regulation and incentive-related Plan actions, as well as various streetscape and transportation improvements.

- *Spokane Arts Commission*—an all-volunteer organization that maintains a local arts directory calendar and coordinates an annual awards program. The Plan drew on the Arts Commission's strengths in outreach to artists, including commissioned projects and the First Friday Art Walk program.

- *The City of Spokane*—serves as the lead responsibility for all transit- and streetscape-related projects and the secondary responsibility for regulatory reforms and other economic incentives to facilitate private development in the District.

THE GREAT SPOKANE RIVER GORGE STRATEGIC MASTER PLAN

Friends of the Falls (FOF), responsible for initiating the Master Plan for the gorge area, emerged as the convener and coordinator for future developments. Following the success of the similar Three Rivers Community Roundtable project (in the nearby Tri-Cities area), FOF recognized the need to establish an independent nonprofit, tax-exempt agency to facilitate communication and collaboration among organizations, agencies and businesses for implementing the Master Plan. The resulting Spokane River Gorge Coalition (SRGC), supported and administered by FOF, will monitor Plan implementation.

To accomplish this task, the SRGC brings together key stakeholders in voluntary meetings and builds strategic partnerships with community organizations, neighborhood associations and related businesses. To maintain and encourage interest in the gorge area, the SRGC promotes annually programmed events and activities, including competitions and educational outings.

As the landowner of an estimated 400 acres of open space in the gorge area, the Spokane Parks and Recreation Department serves as the primary authority for new developments. By providing a full and complete board approval for all initiatives on their properties, the department ensures continuity between new projects and decades of gorge area stewardship.

User Feedback

Kim Pearman-Gillman, Itron;
former chair, Davenport District

"The transformation of the Downtown area, full of one-of-a-kind historical treasures, has been nothing short of phenomenal! As a result of the planning…almost every historic property within the Davenport District has undergone an amazing redevelopment.

"What happened completely reversed a fast-moving tide of despair and neglect to one of community engagement, hope, action and results. People from all walks of life, as well as artists, business owners, neighborhood groups and civic leaders, banded together to create a vision and, more importantly, a realistic action plan to aggressively attack the issues. This area of former blight is now a thriving center of activity. You can see how treasuring our unique heritage can actually make a community marketable.… We have redefined

ourselves as 'urban chic' and done it by being authentically ourselves.

"The process itself has become a model for our community and an example of what can be accomplished by dedicated people, when given the right tools and thoughtful attention to details of community building."

Mike Edwards, Downtown Spokane
Partnership (former president)

"The biggest idea was to identify projects and put them in a sequence in which they become catalytic, one leading to the next. The first project was River Park Square, which established the area as a regional center. That triggered interest in a new convention center, the largest single new development. That in turn led to more interest in office, retail and hotels, like the Davenport renovation.

"Because we involved all stakeholders, neighborhoods were able to clearly see the advantage to them of helping the areas surrounding Downtown. A whole section on neighborhood economic development went into the Plan. That was a big missing piece that brought everyone on board. When the Plan was done, everyone wanted it, because everyone had ownership of it.

"Spokanites have always loved their Downtown. Now it's become much more vital. It's a great place to be."

Jim Kolva, Kolva Associates

"The Downtown Plan was very inclusive and had a real sense of optimism. It had strong buy-in from Downtown interests, as well as the City as a whole. It's been very successful.

"With the design guidelines, the Downtown Plan has set a pattern for development of new buildings. The Plan recognized the importance of streetscape to the Downtown and the renovation of historic buildings as an asset for Downtown. People recognize the need and see that as positive. So we've had several major historic building renovations, including the Davenport Hotel. Also we've had some buildings redeveloped for lofts and apartments, including the [ConoverBond] Havermale project, which is a historic rehab project. We have a really lively residential market. The City recently adopted an anti-demolition ordinance for historic buildings and the roots of that were in the Downtown planning process as well.

"An example of a new building is the American West Building, which really followed the design guidelines and everyone agrees it is a successful building.

"We still have things to do. We need to focus on office retention and major new office space. But as a user of the Downtown, there's a positive attitude that the Downtown is quite improved... it's become much more vital. It's a really great place to be."

Rob Brewster, ConoverBond Developers

"After I graduated from Lewis and Clark High School, Spokane wasn't very exciting. It was just a spot between Seattle and Minneapolis. From my graduating class, there are very few people who actually still live in Spokane. That was a big educational brain drain. I went to Washington, D.C., to enjoy being someplace that is something. I redeveloped townhouses there and in Seattle. I came back here when I was 30 and found a Spokane that had failed to take care of itself. We hadn't invested in creating environments that are unique to Spokane, fun, energetic and creative. As recently as five years ago, the area around the Davenport Hotel was a blight. Redeveloping it removed a psychological hurdle.

"Redeveloping the Montvale Hotel was a kind of a metaphor for the entire City. It was built by a judge in 1899 as a single room occupancy hotel. But later it became sort of a flophouse and during

Expo, a youth hostel. And then it was empty for 20 years. It was old and decrepit, but it was irreplaceable and had so much potential to be a fun, cool place. It's about creating more of a community and helping the City develop into something that's more interesting.

"The Downtown Spokane Partnership study that showed a range of people want to live Downtown was an important factor in building housing too. Having data to demonstrate demand makes a big difference with lenders.

"There have been so many great things happening Downtown. Market-rate housing is making Spokane a 24-hour city. It will bring needed vibrancy and energy and diversity of living options. Downtown has changed so much over the past few years. This is such an exciting time for Spokane."

Susan Matteson, Peters and Son; chair, Davenport Arts Board

"Taking a run-down, negative area of Downtown Spokane and turning it into the Davenport District has made an immense change in the area. Customers are filling the sidewalks in the District during the day and evenings. Foot traffic is everything to a small business like ours (flowers and gifts) and we would not have stayed in the Downtown area if the District had not been revitalized.

"The Arts Board had been working on this revitalization for many years. When the DSP began the strategic plan, they incorporated our group and our previous work and visions.

"The future of the Davenport District looks very bright!"

Paul Delaney, River City Runners

"I've been involved in the river gorge area for almost 20 years in a whitewater club, but never in the planning of this type of project. The process was remarkable…people saw that from the outset. The presentations, organization of meetings, focus group–type situations…we went from segment to segment and gave our input. I think about how all of the different facets of the community were brought together in one room and I tell you, I was impressed. I felt my input was heard.

"There were areas of real concern—the residents of Peaceful Valley having their part of the world left as it has been for the last 100 years. So we're now working on a whitewater rafting launching area that won't have an impact on them. The Native American population was concerned about protecting traditional gathering and fishing areas, and they said they've been satisfied.

"A lot has been done to open the eyes of politicians and business owners—this has been a huge success. Over the course of the last three years, we've taken trips down the river with political and business leaders. I took (one businessman) under the footbridge in the Riverfront Park area and he said, 'I've been in town for 25 years, and I'm embarrassed to say this is the first time I've seen this bridge!' It's just 10 minutes from Downtown. Hoteliers went on a trip this year, and they just went gaga over the idea of being able to have conventioneers take a trip—they could get out of a meeting at 2 pm and by 3 pm they would be on a raft. This is a huge selling point for us.

"We opened their eyes to what is within a stone's throw of Downtown. There's no river anywhere in the world that rivals the Spokane for proximity to Downtown. We're finally looking at the river for what it offers us."

inclusive design
guidelines

DEPENDENCY COURTS

SCHOOLS (K-12)

MUSEUMS

CHILDREN'S ZOOS

PLAY AREAS

PLAZAS

TRAIL SYSTEMS

OPEN SPACE PERFORMANCE STANDARDS

CITYSCAPES

"City design is the art of creating possibilities….It manipulates patterns in time and space and has as its justification the everyday human experience of those patterns."

KEVIN LYNCH
A THEORY OF GOOD CITY FORM

LESSONS FROM THE PROJECTS

INCLUSIVE DESIGN GUIDELINES

This set of inclusive design guidelines is based on lessons learned from selected project examples. Regardless of the type of public building or space you are designing, reading through all of these guidelines can provide an intuitive sense of how your own projects can incorporate inclusive design. For example, if you're designing a school, you'll find helpful information in the guidelines for an institutional building and for parks, as well as in the guidelines for schools. It is our hope that this information will help you expand your own creative solutions for inclusive environments.

DEPENDENCY COURTS

These guidelines were developed for the Edelman Children's Courthouse. Only the inclusive design guidelines that can be extended to other settings are included here (ADA guidelines must also be followed).

ENTRANCE AND LOBBY

The Court's entrance and lobby provide a reference or orientation point for the building. They create an initial image for visitors so it's critical that these spaces make a bold statement about the character of the building.

The initial entry into a site, either by foot or by car, should have a clear view to the building's main entrance (Figure 2). Easy and safe access and understandable signage are key. The architecture, landscaping and site elements must clearly communicate that this place is about children and families.

The entrance should be one or two story, with maximum natural light. The perceived scale of the building is essential to creating a friendly entrance. Provide a transition from the drop-off zone into the building with outdoor rooms, gateways and trellises that create

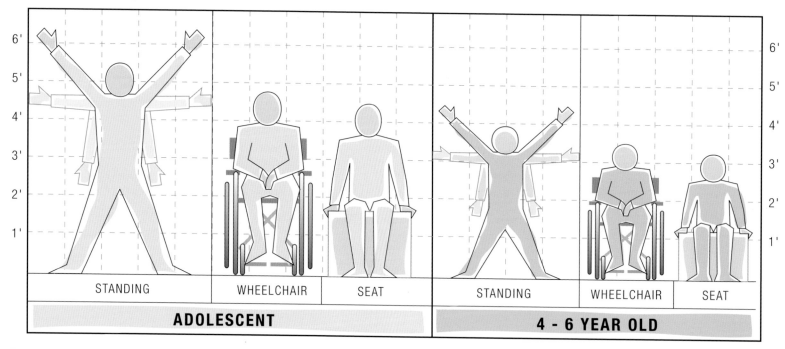

Figure 1. The anthropometric scale for children brings buildings and furniture down to appropriate heights.

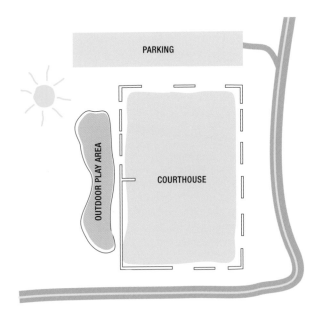

Figure 2. The building orientation places the play area in the sun and ensures that the parking structure is not so visible from the highway.

Figure 3. Children feel less intimidated by an entrance with more natural and familiar forms and plants.

an intimate setting. Use window details, color, vegetation and artwork to enhance the intimacy (Figure 3). Provide numerous places to sit.

The lobby should have a feature that causes people to stop and look around them. The feature should be symbolic or spiritual, providing an interpretation of family and the spirit of childhood.

BUILDING APPEARANCE

Dependency court buildings should reflect a friendly yet dignified appearance. A *friendly* building possesses the following attributes:

- Human-scaled dimensions and proportions, especially in windows, doors, stairways, roofs, columns, canopies and ceiling heights (Figure 1)
- Continuity between elements such as between the building façade, approaches and entrance
- Plants and vegetation to soften building lines and edges
- Warm materials such as brick, wood and canvas
- Views out of the building
- Daylight entering through skylights and windows

A *dignified* building appearance can be achieved with:

- Clean, simple geometric lines
- Geometric, symmetrical spaces
- Well-defined gateway entrances
- Subdued colors
- Durable, contrasting materials such as marble, stone, brick and steel
- Proper use of symbols of authority

CIRCULATION

Create clear orientations through the lobby with a brightly lit reception desk about 50 feet into the lobby, and information boards behind. Create an easy transition to elevators (Figure 4). If security is required, orient the security to one corner. It should be clearly visible so people know someone is watching, but should not make people feel locked in. Provide direct, clearly marked circulation routes between the reception area, waiting areas and other rooms (Figure 5).

CORRIDORS

Avoid creating long, cave-like corridors. Break them up with windows in walls and doors that offer views outside or into other activities. Differentiate corridor segments by varying colors and widths (Figures 6 and 7).

PUBLIC WAITING AREAS

Public waiting areas should be more than a space for passing time; through proper design and management, the setting should help reduce the child's and family member's anxiety as they prepare for the hearing process. It should be a comfortable setting near the family mediation and interview rooms.

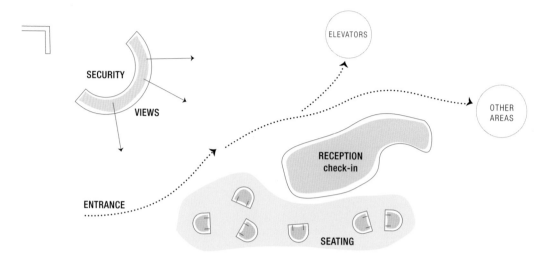

Figure 4. The lobby area sets the tone and ambience for the entire building.

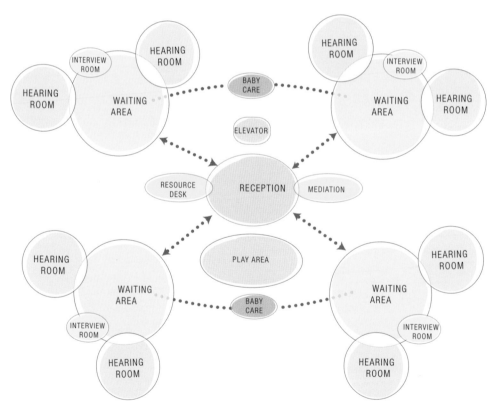

Figure 5. Hearing rooms require support facilities including areas for waiting, interview rooms, reception and information materials, and play.

Set up the area with movable furniture to accommodate adults and children in mixed and segregated groups of between one and five people. A group of semi-permanent seats in an "L" configuration can anchor seating clusters (Figure 8). Provide small, low tables and end stands that can hold plants, magazines and pamphlets. Seats with backs create spaces for quiet reading or study, while "bean bag" seats are ideal for children to relax in.

Locate a Resource and Referral Desk on each floor adjacent to the waiting and children's play area. While parents are at the desk, children can play. Partial walls provide some privacy while allowing views into the play

Figure 6. Interesting alcoves and interior windows break up long corridors.

Figure 7. Doors with windows break up corridors and provide additional security.

Figure 8. An "L" configuration anchors seating clusters. Movable furniture lets groups and individuals arrange their own space.

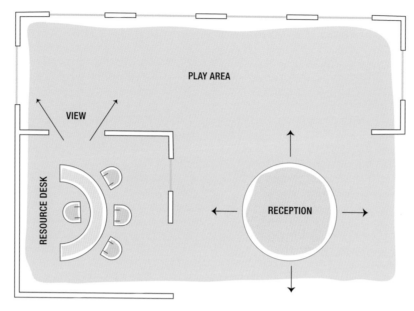

Figure 9. Parents and staff can consult at the Resource Desk while children play.

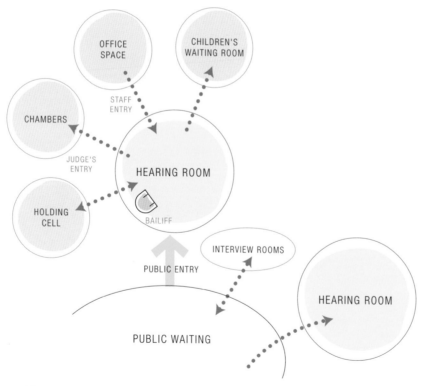

Figure 10. Each hearing room requires its own support facilities with separate entries.

area (Figure 9). Provide a special "trouble area" near the hearing rooms and the security desk to separate contentious adults from each other and from children and their caregivers.

HEARING ROOMS

The hearing room must be designed to serve its function as effectively as possible, while protecting and respecting the child's special interests and needs.

Provide a central entry to the hearing room to create a greater sense of formality. The Judge should enter directly out of the Judge's Chambers. Staff should have separate entries that can also double as the entry for children in dependent care (Figure 10). Consider providing separate entrances and exits so that families do not exit directly into the waiting area and instead can transition into another area to calm down after a hearing. Provide a small anteroom as part of the entry to create a transition from the informal waiting area to the dignified hearing room.

The furniture should be modular so each Judge can rearrange as needed, and regular office size, not monumental in scale. Place clear signage on each desk so children know the role each person is

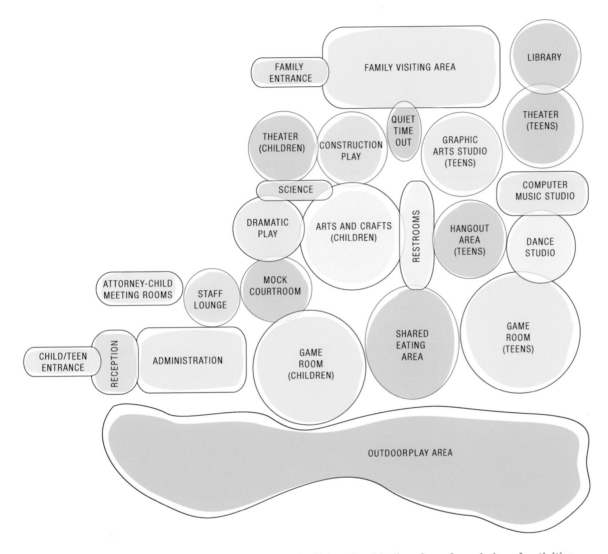

Figure 11. The design and layout of Shelter Care facilities should allow for a free choice of activities.

playing. Provide natural light if possible, or at least indirect light and natural color. Carpet the rooms and provide a thick pad for sound absorption. State flags can be effective decorative elements. A state seal can be displayed as a piece of art.

Create a dignified, yet friendly appearance in each room. Basic functional criteria include clear sight lines, flexibility to allow the child a choice of where to sit and where to testify, and clear visual and physical access for the Bailiff (see Configurations 1 through 4, pages 40–41 in "Helping Children Heal: Edelman Children's Court" for sample room configurations).

SHELTER CARE

Shelter Care sets the tone of the entire court experience for detained children and youth. As with any physical setting, it is influenced by the program of activities within it, the management policies that govern its use and the attitude of the people who staff the facility. The physical environment must respond to the needs of the children it serves by providing a range of experiences. But strong, positive experiences can only be created by a well-structured program of activities and quality staff-child interaction. All three aspects of the facility—physical setting, programs and management—must work together to create a truly child-sensitive environment.

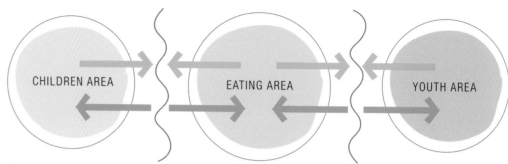

Figure 12. The eating area separates age groups, yet is also a common place to meet.

Structure the environment so that rules of behavior are clearly communicated in the spatial layout and through provision of "props" (play and recreation items, reading materials, etc.) rather than through heavy-handed adult instructions. A carefully structured environment will allow a good measure of personal responsibility and control, reducing feelings of powerlessness and expressions of frustration. Design spaces to accommodate fluctuations in the number of children (70–120) and age distribution. Provide separate primary areas for children (5–12) and youth (13–17), subdividing each area into a variety of activity zones (Figure 11).

■ Children and youth entrance. Provide a separate, smaller children's entry that is distinct from the main entry so children do not have to interact with the public or their family if they don't wish to. The approach and entry should emphasize inviting views of child- and youth-related activities that create a friendly feeling rather than intensifying a fear of walking into the "unknown." Window details, color, vegetation and artwork also add warmth. The reception area should provide a space for children and youth to check in and become oriented to the space. There should be easy physical and visual access to outdoors.

■ Primary areas. Subdivide the primary care area into different activity zones so children and youth can choose the area in which they feel most comfortable (Figure 11). Children's zones can include small gathering areas, manipulative play and building, wall areas with felt or magnetic boards, games, resting, movie corner, art center, dramatic play (with props and costumes), science area and animal care (with small animals such as hamsters, guinea pigs, fish and turtles).

The youth area should look different, with different management policies so youth don't feel that they're being treated as children. Youth who come to court are fighting for independence, yet may be scared, confused and angry. The physical environment must support their basic needs for comfort, privacy and interaction, and offer high-quality programs and plenty of adult support. Zones can include music and dance, games, study and resting, telephone, conversation "pit," multimedia studio, and personal care and make-up areas.

■ Eating areas. Arrange the area as a flexible, multiple-use space adjacent to "home bases" for children and youth so siblings can choose to meet and eat with each other (Figure 12). An outdoor eating area can double as a gathering spot and a transition between indoor and outdoor areas.

- Outdoor play areas and nature areas. (See "Trail Settings" and "Play Areas" for more details on outdoor areas.)

- Family visiting rooms. Visiting rooms can be located near the Shelter Care facility so "detained" children can have a monitored visit with their families. The rooms can also become interview rooms for attorneys to meet privately with children before hearings. Rooms should be set up like a family living room with a variety of movable furniture (Figure 13). The room should be large enough to accommodate six people. Interior windows and angled corridors seem less formal and provide good sight lines for security. The security desk should be positioned to provided unobstructed visual and physical access to both the rooms and the private entrance to Shelter Care (Figure 14).

- Time-out areas. Create special quiet areas for children who are anxious, tense and unable to handle their emotions outside main rooms and out of sight of other children (Figure 15). Provide visual access, and if possible, direct access from the quiet area to natural elements. Filtered, natural light, views of greenery and the sound of running water can help calm emotions. A rocking chair and hammock offer seating with relaxing movements.

- Restrooms. Provide appropriately scaled toilets for children that are separate, single toilet rooms, opening directly into the activities area. Each

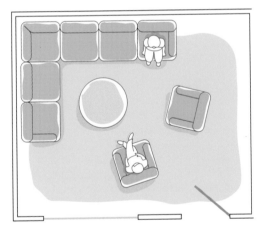

Figure 13. An informal "family room" with table and movable chairs provides a homey feeling.

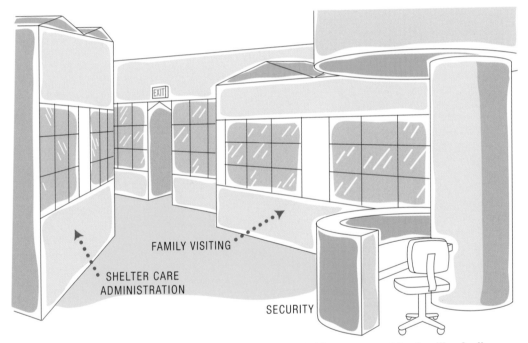

Figure 14. The home-style windows of the family visiting rooms add a familiar feeling and provide clear sight lines for security.

room should have a door with a window starting at three feet off the ground (head height when seated). This provides privacy and visual access. Door levers should be six inches lower than standing height. Doors should be slow closing with locks that can be opened from the outside with a key.

For youth, provide toilets in individual rooms with a sink and mirror. Locate the rooms so they open into the main activity room. All doors should have locks with a key on the outside, not latch locks. Do not put windows in the doors.

FAMILY INTERVIEW ROOMS

Interview rooms, located near the hearing rooms, are for attorneys to meet privately with parents before hearings. They should be large enough for a round table and four chairs—80 square feet minimum (Figure 16). Furnish with wood furniture and paint walls in warm tones. Provide a carpet with a deep, warm color. Each room should have a window looking into the waiting area, with thick enough glass to serve as a sound barrier (Figure 17). This makes the room seem larger and friendlier and provides visual access for security. Provide enough interview rooms to meet demand (six to eight per waiting area).

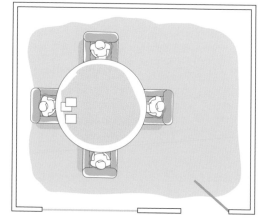

Figure 16. Interview rooms should be large enough to accommodate all parties that need to meet.

Figure 15. Time-out areas should be very informal to induce calmness.

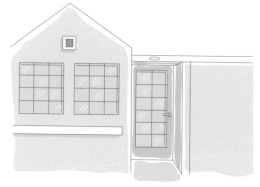

Figure 17. Windows help create a human scale.

Figure 18. Round tables are conducive to socializing while plant dividers provide a sense of privacy.

Figure 19. Outdoor vegetation visible from indoors adds a human touch to rooms.

PUBLIC EATING AREAS

Design the eating area with individual tables and chairs that can be moved to accommodate different size groups and opened up to create a larger room for large groups. Create intimate indoor eating areas by providing task lighting over tables, warm colors, vegetation (with large plants as dividers), children-created artwork and movable tables (Figure 18). Outdoor eating areas should be located adjacent to the indoor areas and visible from the inside (Figure 19).

Provide large doors that can be opened in warm weather to increase the connection to the outside and provide an open, sunny feeling inside. Provide picnic tables with shade outdoors.

OTHER AMENITIES

Several design amenities can make a building a friendlier place for staff and other professionals who use the building every day.

- Ad hoc work space. Provide a hierarchy of spaces (ideally on every floor) that are flexible and usable by different professions: rooms separate from the interview rooms where attorneys, social workers and police can meet or work; a number of small workspaces next to waiting areas and hearing rooms; and rooms equipped with desks, storage, book cases and privacy phones.

- Employee childcare center. Provide for children of employees: a quality childcare center can increase morale and peace of mind, and decrease absenteeism.

- Staff gym. Provide an exercise facility with shower for staff. Exercise before work, at lunchtime or after work reduces staff stress levels.

COMMUNICATIONS LINKS

Effective communications links between the hearing room and the other areas of the courthouse keep operations flowing smoothly. Communications can be audio or visual.

- Chambers to hearing room. Children testifying in chambers should be seen and heard in the hearing room so testimony doesn't need to be reread.
- Hearing room to waiting room. The bailiff needs to easily inform people in the waiting room of the next case so people can be prepared when it is their turn.
- Hearing room to attorney's offices. Direct phone links and quick transit routes reduce the amount of time needed for attorneys to reach the hearing room.
- Court office to DCS field staff. A direct phone link between the court officer's desk in the hearing room and relevant field staff offices can help contact staff quickly.

- Court Clerk to other court staff. The Court Clerk needs to quickly communicate with staff elsewhere to access files and documents needed in the hearing room.
- Bailiff to Shelter Care and jail. The bailiff needs to quickly communicate with Shelter Care and jail facilities to request individuals needed in the hearing room.

LIGHTING

Lighting reinforces the social character and importance of space. Light contributes to the spirit of an activity and affects people's feelings of spaciousness or enclosure. It can also affect people's attention and behavior in an environment. In a courthouse:

- Maximize natural light through use of windows and skylights.
- Provide electric lighting that emulates the qualities of natural light (warm, soft, diffused).

- Allow user control of lighting to the extent feasible.

VENTILATION

Whenever possible, provide windows that can be opened.

ACOUSTICS

Create a calm ambience in each space by providing good acoustic control. Use sound playfully or as an orientation tool. Wind chimes, bells or flapping banners can create pleasant and calming effects. Minimize any traffic noise through special treatments of windows that face highways. Pay particular attention to noise levels if a play area is located outdoors; install a sound wall if needed.

SCHOOLS (K-12)

Both interior and exterior areas can be wonderful learning environments. These guidelines emphasize basic planning and design, assuming that designers will meet building codes, ADA requirements and safety laws.

Most of the current accessibility guidelines and regulations are based on the anthropometrics of adult wheelchair users. When designing spaces for children one must consider an additional set of dimensions because children have smaller, shorter bodies and less strength and coordination than adults. They may have more trouble maneuvering with wheelchairs or mobility aids and more difficulty seeing or reaching for certain objects (see Dependency Courts Design Guidelines, page 388, for an anthropometric chart for children).

EXTERIOR ENVIRONMENT

The outdoor settings of the school should be considered as extensions of the classroom—places where children can exercise their bodies and minds. Outdoor school settings should be designed for four purposes:

- To allow movement and gatherings of large groups.
- To be used by teachers as outdoor classrooms.
- To provide quiet, green "respite" areas.
- To provide areas for recreation and sports activities.

SITE ACCESS

Schools should have an organized, welcoming entry that appears secure and friendly. Entries serve as gathering areas where parents and community members become oriented to the school. Both parents and children often wait there during drop-off and pick-up times. Entry areas should be large enough to accommodate a small group of people and provide some seating (a minimum of 625 sq. ft.). Seating can be sculptural with tiles or murals to add an artistic element. Other aspects of the entry include:

- Signage with school name (on or near the building), orientation sign, regulatory signs
- Information kiosk and school bulletin board
- Seating for parents and students using benches or a seat wall
- Perimeter fencing that is 6' to 8' high (often depending on size of schoolyard—a higher fence will keep in bouncing balls). If funding is an issue, an ornamental metal fence can be selected for the entry and chain link for the perimeter. A see-through fence is desirable.

Attractive, colorful and fragrant planting announces the entry and adds a warm, homey touch. Planting should also be provided along the perimeters of the site. Planting should be low enough so that the playground is visible from a car driving by on the street.

CIRCULATION

From the main entry, the route to classrooms and offices should be clearly stated in multiple languages and/or graphic symbols. Pedestrian walkways can be opportunities for artwork, such as impressions in the pavement or painted patterns on pavement for games. People regularly move through walkways and corridors so they are good places to locate core messages, school philosophies or themes to inspire people.

Roads around and within a school site need to take into account a relationship with pedestrians at heights that are lower to the ground because small children walking or persons using wheelchairs can be difficult to see from a driver's point of view. Ideally, circulation should allow vehicles to drive through the loading zone by means of a circular route, so they can enter and exit without having to back up. Additional design elements to consider:

- Keep plantings low (2'–3' maximum) at median islands, corners and pedestrian crossings to provide clear views (see Figure 20).
- Locate crosswalks convenient to areas where children congregate such as loading zones or entries.

- Crosswalks should be clearly visible to both pedestrians and vehicles with identifying marks such as striping and signage. Add flashing lights and chirping sounds at signals to aid individuals with hearing and visual impairments.
- Crosswalk surfaces should be stable and non-slippery when wet.
- If additional speed enforcement is needed, post signs or install traffic calming measures such as speed bumps, textured pavement or road narrowing to serve as visual cues to drivers.
- Bulb-outs at corners or protected median islands assist those with limited mobility who may need additional protection when crossing the street.

Figure 20. Keep plantings low at pedestrian crossings to provide clear views.

- Install bicycle paths next to the sidewalks adjacent to schools. These paths should have a level surface, be well lit, and have signs and clearly identifying pavement markers.

PARKING

Parking is typically on the street or at a nearby parking lot. Parking should be convenient to school entries but should not have a dominating visual presence. It should be safely separated from pedestrian walkways and from drop-off and pick-up zones. Bike parking should be separated from vehicle traffic and convenient to school entries. Permeable durable surfaces are friendlier to the environment than paving and asphalt. Shade trees can mitigate unsightly expanses of paving and parked cars. Ground cover and low shrubs should be planted below the trees in islands and in perimeter areas.

Schoolyard Settings

CLASSROOM PATIOS

The classroom patio is a paved, outdoor multi-purpose area adjacent to or attached to each ground floor classroom. The patio is an extension to the classroom area and offers a transition zone between the playground and the classroom, as well as a place to do messy projects. Where possible, provide one per classroom, about 300 square feet in size.

Provide movable work tables and seating: one picnic table per patio with two benches (or seat wall) per patio. For this area, concrete paving works best. Outdoor elements can be playful and educational, while softening the pavement. For example, bright windsocks, weather vanes or tile work on seat walls can be made by children as class projects. Surrounding each patio with shade trees and plantings, even in containers, provides privacy between classrooms and a more natural setting.

MULTI-PURPOSE OUTDOOR CLASSROOMS

The multi-purpose outdoor classroom is a laboratory space to practice project-based learning that expands the classroom curriculum. This area is designed to be flexible, supporting a variety of curriculum activities including those related to science, environmental education, art and social studies. They can be large enough to accommodate several

classes at the same time. For example, to accommodate 50–75 students, about 900–1,200 square feet should be provided. They should be located in areas where they are accessible from more than one classroom.

Where possible, include a platform or stage area, power outlets, water and storage.

As with the small patio areas, provide movable worktables and seating to accommodate different size groups. Concrete paving for the main areas can be softened with soft surface pathways, shade trees and plantings (that also help divide up the area). Include playful art elements created by children.

GARDEN OUTDOOR CLASSROOMS

The garden outdoor classroom expands the classroom and provides an area for outdoor curriculum projects related to science and art. The area should have a central, prominent location to encourage visibility and use. It should be near the kitchen if possible to encourage food preparation activities. An area about 50' x 50' would be ideal with additional room for expansion. Students can create playful and educational

Figure 21. Multi-purpose outdoor classrooms can also serve as a stage or group project area.

elements such as birdhouses and sundials, and decorated fences. Some site elements to include are:

- Secure storage for tools and project materials
- Compost boxes and soil bins
- Raised planter boxes for accessible gardening
- Shade
- Site drainage as required
- Ornamental plants at the community edge of the site
- Movable worktables and seating
- Potting table
- Fencing (4'–6' high woven wire fences to allow views to planting)
- Trash receptacles

Figure 22. Outdoor gardens are multi-sensory learning environments.

Gardens must have a steward. This can be a classroom teacher, specialized teacher or community member. Basic infrastructure should be provided with the expectation that the garden stewards will further develop the garden.

NATURAL AREA OUTDOOR CLASSROOMS

The natural area outdoor classroom serves as a teaching station for science and ecology studies as well as an area for student projects and outdoor instruction. It is a protected area of primarily native vegetation that supports habitat, controls stormwater run-off, and stimulates play and learning. This area is optimally located near a natural area adjacent to the school such as a creek, hillside, park, rock outcropping or grove of trees (Figure 22). It can also be integrated with a natural play opportunity. Areas for observation and an outdoor classroom support science studies. Ideally, provide a water element such as a simulated stream segment or natural drainage of sufficient size to foster a habitat attractive to insects and other wildlife. Provide plants that support occasional harvesting such as reeds, willow, grasses and bamboo.

Informal seating such as boulders, logs and tree stumps work well with wood tables. Provide accessible pathways made of wood fiber or decomposed granite (bare soil is not accessible to all users).

Natural areas need to be about 50' x 50' to provide enough area for habitat. The area does not require fencing, though some separation from the schoolyard at large is desirable. Low fencing and/or shrub plantings can serve this purpose. Views into the area allow for supervision.

Natural areas must have a steward. This can be a classroom teacher, specialized teacher or community member. Basic infrastructure should be provided with the expectation that the natural area stewards will further develop the environment over time.

OUTDOOR EATING AREA

The outdoor eating area is a shaded outdoor eating facility for use during lunch, group picnics and other activities during non-school hours. The area may also be used as an outdoor classroom or gathering area. The surface should be concrete paving, with shade trees. This area also provides an excellent opportunity for art projects, poetry reading and games. Design should take noise, circulation, light and air circulation into account.

Site elements include:

- Tables and seats for 120–150 students
- Shade (steel or wood arbor shade structure—not an impervious cover—for locations away from the building)
- Trash receptacles
- Trees

LARGE GATHERING AREA

The large gathering area is a 2,000–3,000 square foot assembly area for the staging and viewing of outdoor programs and events that can accommodate approximately 100–150 children, parents and staff. It can also be used after school hours. The area should have a central, prominent location to encourage visibility and use, but should be located away from the most active play areas. It needs accessible pathways and seating, in addition to lawn seating. Noise, circulation, light and air circulation should be given careful consideration.

Site elements include:

- Stage or raised platform
- Provisions for simple stage sets
- Shade for viewers
- Formal seating with benches, movable chairs or seat walls and informal seating such as a lawn area
- Trash receptacles

SMALL GATHERING AREA

The small gathering area is a 300–700 square foot shaded area for small group instruction, reading and storytelling, or quiet space for students during recess. It is separated from other activity areas by planting with seating for 5–12 students.

Site elements include:

- Small stage presentation area
- Seating (benches without backs or seat walls)

- Work table or game table
- Shade
- Planting

HARD COURT AREAS

The hard courts are large paved areas that support the physical education curriculum during school; they could also be used by the community during non-school hours. They also serve as gathering and waiting spaces before and after school. The courts are secured with high perimeter fencing (8' at street edge) and gates to accommodate maintenance and emergency vehicle access. A pedestrian gate will provide access during non-school hours. Perimeter planting and shade trees create a more inviting court area. Each school community should determine the appropriate mix and configuration of courts.

Site elements include:

- Basketball half-court
- Basketball full court
- Basketball standards
- Ball wall
- Running track and lanes
- Compass rose (painted)
- Circles, 30" diameter each (painted)

- Foursquare and other school games (painted)
- Mazes (painted)
- Benches
- Tetherball
- Hopscotch
- Trash receptacles
- Drinking fountain
- Lighting
- Lockable storage

TURF FIELDS

The turf field is a multi-purpose play field with well-drained and easily maintained turf. Fields are usually located next to the hard courts and should be sized so that they meet the requirements for children's community and local sports field user groups. They could also be used by the community during non-school hours. The courts are a secured space with 6' high perimeter fencing and gates to accommodate maintenance and emergency vehicle access. A pedestrian gate will provide access during non-school hours. Turf fields require a structured management program that includes field maintenance and management of field use. A heavily used field will require a shutdown period for renovation at least once a year.

Site elements include:

- Benches and/or bleachers
- Equipment storage
- Portable goals and back stops
- Trash receptacles

PLAY EQUIPMENT AREA

Play equipment areas include age-appropriate play structures and equipment settings for social play and exploratory learning and physical development. Play equipment should also provide upper body strengthening activities.

The area should be a minimum of 40' x 40' in a central location that is easily supervised. It should offer community access during non-school hours. The ground surface can be wood fiber or synthetic rubber safety surfacing. Adult yard supervisors should be present to ensure safe behavior and to ensure that the proper age group is using the play equipment.

Site elements include:

- Manufactured play equipment with a variety of components for climbing, swinging, crawling, socializing, sliding, etc.
- Safety surfacing such as modular tiles, wood fiber safety surfacing with

drainage blanket or poured-in-place synthetic safety surfacing
- Sub-surface drainage inlet (connecting to the site storm drain system)
- Concrete curb to contain safety surfacing
- Access ramp

KINDERGARTEN AND PRE-SCHOOL AREA

The play area is a multi-purpose, outdoor play and outdoor classroom area for children between the ages of 3 years and 5 years. The area must be fully enclosed and secure; a waiting area for parents should be located directly outside. The area should be sized to allow a minimum of 75 square feet per child. There should be a minimum 3'6" fence or wall around the yard, with gates to the main schoolyard and to the community. The ground surface should be asphalt or concrete paving, turf and sand, with synthetic safety surfacing at play equipment areas and decomposed granite paths. Staff supervision and daily site inspection and maintenance should be provided.

Features and activities should support a learning-through-play approach. Site elements include:

- Play equipment (linked play structure)
- Ball play area (paved)
- Painted wheeled toy path
- Sand and water play with sand cover
- Gardening area with planter boxes
- Display area
- Shade
- Tricycle storage
- General storage
- Seating
- Small stage
- Movable picnic and work tables and benches
- Trash receptacles

Interior Settings

STANDARD CLASSROOM

The classroom plays an essential role in providing accessible education. The classroom environment influences personal attitudes, levels of participation and quality of work. People are more attentive and productive when they are physically comfortable and can clearly see, hear and be directly engaged with the instructor.

Classrooms should be arranged so that students have an unobstructed view of the instructor, audiovisual screens and demonstration areas. To make exhibits and demonstrations clearly visible, consider using movable desks and tables with an adjustable mirror over the demonstration table.

Desks should be arranged so that there is clear, adequate aisle space for children with mobility aids to circulate freely about the classroom without having to ask others to move their chairs, desks or personal belongings.

Work areas should be comfortable and adjustable to meet individual needs and preferences. Tables with adjustable heights allow users to modify the height to meet their physical needs and the activity at hand. For example, activities requiring fine motor skills (such as writing or drawing) should be performed with the desk or tabletop at elbow level. Activities that are more physical and require some degree of force (such as molding clay) should be performed approximately 10 inches lower than the elbow to ease the effort required.

Movable furniture allows instructors flexibility to rearrange the classroom to meet the changing needs of a particular curriculum or the students. Furniture should be stable and firmly situated on the ground so that when people lean on the table for assistance in getting up, it resists firmly without wobbling. Tables with raised leaves will help accommodate people who use wheelchairs with high armrests. All furniture in the classroom should respect knee and toe clearances for wheelchair users.

Work surfaces should be smooth with a matte finish to minimize glare. Items that are used frequently, such as writing materials and art supplies should be placed within a child's range. This will enable the child to work more independently.

FLOORING AND SURFACES

Floor coverings and surfaces should be selected to promote wheelchair mobility and minimize tripping hazards. Walking and wheelchair surfaces should be slip-resistant and firm, level and easy to maintain. Carpets should be low profile, tightly woven and secured firmly to the floor. Carpet pads that add sponginess and height to the carpet profile should be avoided if possible; they can hinder wheelchair users and create problems for people with weak lower extremities.

In general, floor patterns should be muted. Complicated or high-contrasting patterns can decrease the functionality for those with vision impairments or diminished depth perception.

VISUAL CUES

In some cases color can serve as a visual cue for demarking hazards, such as stairs, or offer orientation and directional guidance, such as marking entries or different parts of a room.

LIGHTING

Provide general light and enough electrical outlets around the room (or at desks) so that individual "task lights" can be provided at desks or tables to assist in individual work if supplemental light is needed. Those outlets will also be useful for personal readers, recorders or listening devices.

WINDOWS

Exposure to natural light is necessary for physical and emotional health. However, the amount of light entering the room should be controlled (through curtains, blinds or other window treatment) because direct sunlight can cause glare and visual distractions. Windows that open with a twist, slide or push motion are easier to open than traditional double-hung windows that open and close by a push-up and pull-down motion.

COMPUTERS

Provide adjustable elements so that individuals can modify the workstation to meet their physical needs (the type of chair, monitor height, knee space and other assistive devices).

ART ROOMS

The art room should be designed so that all students can participate actively in all art processes to the fullest extent of their skills and abilities. All art rooms should have ample lighting (and task lighting), good ventilation and storage, sinks and display areas.

Storage should be provided at a variety of heights. Peg boards for hanging tools and shelves and cupboards for general storage should be accessible to persons in a wheelchair or with limited reach. Provide adjustable height wheelchairs and printing presses or tables that can be raised or lowered.

Provide extra-wide drawing implements or holders for chalk and pencils that offer gripping assistance. Lightweight, easy to maneuver rolling carts can help students with mobility difficulties transport art supplies from storage areas to art tables, drying areas or display cases.

MUSIC ROOMS

Music classes are an opportunity to develop both individual skills and to be with others in a group setting. Students who have limited verbal abilities can participate in classes that engage multiple senses.

Access to performance areas and tiered seating must be provided. Additional lighting at music stands may assist those with visual impairments. Provide secure, accessible lockers near the music room for storage of instruments and equipment so that students do not have to carry them throughout the day.

HOME ECONOMICS

Home economics classes teach life skills such as cooking and sewing that will help students lead more independent lives. These classrooms generally contain work tables or counters, storage areas and various appliances.

Work tables should have clearance as required by code. Pedestal-type tables eliminate the obstruction caused by table legs and allow many users to sit next to each other in either standard chairs or wheelchairs. Portable raised table leaves also enable a person with a larger wheelchair to sit as part of a group at the same table (Figure 23).

The room environment should have good ambient light and task lights available for handwork such as sewing and other detailed work.

The activities associated with home economics, such as students working in groups and operating appliances, can generate noise that may be distracting or disturbing to some students. To mitigate, provide acoustic treatment such as fabric wall hangings, acoustic panels and window treatment to help absorb noise.

If there is a living room or lounge associated with the home economics room, armchairs should be provided for students with weak muscle tone or for those who need leverage assistance to stand up from a sitting position.

COOKING AREAS

Stovetops should be mounted on a low-height counter so that seated individuals can participate fully in the activity. This range should be flush with the adjoining counter so students can slide pots and pans safely from the range to the adjacent surface. The stove appliance should be selected for safety considerations of those who may be seated. An appropriate appliance would have staggered burners so a person can use the back burners without reaching over the front ones, and front or side controls so a person can reach them without reaching over the front burners.

Ovens should have side hinges and a pull-out board beneath the oven to rest hot or heavy dishes. Exhaust fans should be located on the counter apron so that seated individuals can access them.

Serving and eating utensils should be selected for ease of use by students with limited motor control or weak grasp; they should be symmetrically designed for use by right- or left-handed people. Consider providing large-diameter handles on silverware, textured glassware, large and easy-to-grasp handles,

Figure 23. Work tables with pedestal-type bases allow students to sit next to each other in either standard chairs or wheelchairs.

and small, but lightweight containers (such as pitchers or serving dishes).

Fire extinguishers should be centrally located. Portable, lightweight extinguishers can be provided in more than one location including near workstations for easy access.

SCIENCE LABS

Science lessons and demonstrations are significantly enhanced by hands-on activity and experiments. However, much of the equipment in a lab poses safety risks such as fragile glassware, open flames

and hazardous chemicals. Design workspaces to allow students to work as independently as possible with the lowest potential for accidents.

Equipment and supplies should be stored within a variety of reach ranges and all equipment should have large on-off indicator lights so people with visual or hearing impairments can easily determine when equipment is on.

LAB STATIONS

Accessible lab stations should be located as close as possible to the accessible path of egress so that individuals with disabilities may be assisted in case of emergency evacuation. Placement of accessible lab stations should allow easy access to shared equipment and should minimize conflicts with circulation patterns in the room to facilitate wheelchair maneuvering and pedestrian activity.

A drop-leaf in a section of the accessible workstation will allow wheelchair users to access the workstation (see Home Economics Room for additional ideas about work tables).

Sinks and storage areas should be accessible.

SAFETY EQUIPMENT

All users should have access to safety equipment such as first aid kits and fire extinguishers. Emergency procedures and instructions are mandated by federal standards. Provide instructions in multiple languages using graphic and accessible formats.

Provide protective eyewear for all students. Heavy rubber aprons for protection from spilled chemicals should be made available for seated individuals and those with sensory limitations.

Provide an eyewash station, and additional eyewash solution at the lab areas of students who cannot easily reach or access the station. Flexible hoses can also be used to dispense solution.

Accessible lab stations should be located near emergency showers or near another means of "hosing down" in case of spills. A pull-chain for operation should be provided within easy reach.

Building and fire codes regulate the location and placement of fire extinguishers in a room. In addition, lightweight portable extinguishers should be provided at lab stations or worktables.

Gas jets often have a "hissing" sound when turned on. Consider adding an odorant to the gas supply so people with hearing impairments can detect the presence of gas.

In case of power outages, emergency lighting is helpful for people with hearing impairments who rely on visual cues.

ASSEMBLY AREAS

School auditoriums and other assembly areas are places for people to come together for special gatherings and performances. Assembly areas, dressing rooms, backstage and ticket booths must be accessible to accommodate audience members, speakers and performers. Audience members need adequate seating and aisle circulation, views of the stage and assistive listening systems when necessary.

Ideally, wheelchair seating should be integrated into areas of fixed seating in a variety of locations with equivalent viewing. Wheelchair seating should be located along an accessible route and in close proximity to a means of egress.

Adequate stage lighting assists persons with hearing and sight limitations to read lips, facial expressions and body language. Special attention should be paid to avoiding shadows on hands, faces and torsos. Provide proper, non-glare lighting on the sign language interpreter. The sign language interpreter should be located to the side of or directly behind the person speaking.

GYMNASIUMS

The gymnasium often serves a double purpose as an assembly and performance area. All areas should be fully accessible to performers and audience members. Special consideration may be needed to ensure that the sound system is of good quality (to obtain a static-free sound). Provide bleachers with gradual, accessible slopes and handrails, and slip-resistant floor coverings.

The height of athletic equipment such as basketball hoops should be adjustable if possible to allow persons in wheelchairs to participate in games.

CAFETERIAS

Cafeterias are multi-purpose spaces, serving as dining rooms, gymnasiums, study halls and assembly and meeting areas.

Aisles, food service lines and circulation, countertops, tables and vending machines should all be accessible. Every opportunity should be made to achieve equivalent experiences. The accessible entry should provide the same decor and services as the rest of the area and be usable by the general public.

To promote interaction with the entire school community, accessible seating should be provided throughout with a mix of seating options. This may include tables of a variety of shapes, sizes and configurations with fixed and removable seats or no seats for wheelchair access.

LIBRARY/MEDIA CENTERS

Libraries offer a variety of books, computer programs and audio-visual materials that allow people to engage fully in learning. The design of these spaces must accommodate a variety of users.

Many of the required elements have been discussed previously. Although library collections are mostly catalogued now on computer, for facilities that have a card-catalogue system, a lateral filing system is preferred because the backs of card catalogues are easier to reach by

those seated. For catalogues on computer, auditory and large-print directions should be available on request.

Other Site Elements

LANDSCAPE AREAS

Landscape can be functional as well as aesthetic. Lawns, shrub borders and trees can be designed to promote play, socialization, relaxation or other learning experiences. These elements can also be used to define areas, provide shelter and shade, and reduce background or traffic noise levels.

Landscape areas can serve as buffers that separate pedestrian traffic from vehicular traffic, creating a safe zone for pedestrians. Additionally, they provide locations for signage with a natural buffer around the pole, so persons with limited vision or attention span are less likely to bump or walk into the pole (Figure 24).

Select, locate and maintain plants and trees to minimize protruding objects and maximize lines of sight. For example, trees should be located 3'–4' from a walkway. Branches should be pruned so

they do not hang lower than 80" above a walkway as they pose a danger to people with limited or no vision. Walkways should be swept regularly to remove fallen debris such as leaves, seedpods, twigs and small branches.

Earth berms should not be more than 3 feet high so a seated person (such as in a wheelchair) can see over them.

EDGED WALKWAYS

Raised edging along walkways, especially between the walkway and a soft surface such as grass or landscaping, can help keep wheelchairs from slipping off the walk.

BARRIERS

Ensure that barriers are clearly visible. Chains should not be used adjacent to landscape areas because they are difficult for those with limited vision to see (due to the lack of contrast), and are not easily detected by a cane.

SITE FURNITURE

Place site furniture next to walkways. Turnouts with a space adjacent to a bench allow for wheelchairs to move subtly off the path and transfer onto the

Figure 24. Landscaping serves as a protective buffer around a sign pole or tall tree.

bench or sit next to a friend who is on the bench.

Seating (benches or chairs) should be located so there is clear space in front of the bench to accommodate people's feet without impeding the adjacent walkway and path of travel.

Pavement that surrounds site furniture should be accessible: smooth, yet slip-resistant. The pavement could be designed with a different color to alert people with limited vision that furniture or other elements are located in this area.

EXTERIOR LIGHTING

Lighting helps increase safety and security on school sites and provides illumination for evening events. Along pedestrian walkways, light fixtures should be located to provide even illumination rather than pools of light with dark stretches between. Lighting is especially critical in these areas:

- Entrances
- Locations where there are abrupt changes in grade or levels
- Areas where there are automobiles such as driveway entrances, parking lots, transit stops and loading zones
- Circulation routes such as pathways, ramps, walkways, crosswalks and curb ramps

MUSEUMS

Autonomous visits to museums are made possible by the simplicity and precision of the directional information systems.

SPATIAL ORGANIZATION

Simplicity is the key to a successful tactile visit through a museum as is the case for any large facility. Reduce the number of navigational decisions to a minimum. For example, a straight line is easy for visitors to follow, but an itinerary with sculptures placed in a "treelike" pattern, especially involving more than one room, is difficult.

If the museography can be redone, arrange the art pieces in straight rows. If the art cannot be moved, select pieces for the tactile itinerary that will allow visitors to follow a simplified route if desired. Use a tactile map, as shown in the Valenciennes case study, (see "Rediscovering the Touch of Art: Musées des Beaux Arts," page 105) and Braille instructions, as well as audio information that all visitors can use.

NAVIGATIONAL AIDS

Three navigational elements should be used at the entrance to each gallery: tactile maps, Braille signs and audio programs.

Be precise about how to move through the room by describing the number of paces and angles. Explain angle orientation with the times on a clock face (e.g., 2 o'clock, 3 o'clock, etc.). Present distances in paces. For example: "The elevators are straight ahead, ten paces." If possible, use a continuous handrail and send visitors from the rail to the art pieces, stating exactly how many paces to take and whether they should turn. If a continuous rail is not feasible, simplify the tactile itinerary route as much as possible.

FLOOR MARKINGS

Tactile floor markings are an excellent method for directing people with visual impairments. They can be made of different materials than the floor, such as fiberglass or granite, with a rugged surface or a raised edge, and when possible, they can be in bright or contrasting colors. Marks should be about six inches apart so people can follow them or tap them with their canes.

SIGNAGE

ADA regulations in the United States include signs that identify permanent spaces such as stairways and room numbers. To achieve a truly unified system, every sign in the facility must be considered, including the means by which people are directed to reach the signs. Children, the elderly and people in wheelchairs need to be able to move up next to the sign to touch or read it, without being in the way of traffic or doors.

PEDESTALS

Pedestals with signage not only enhance the sculpture, but also facilitate their discovery. The pedestal height must be adapted to the scale of the artwork, but ideally, the height should be no lower than 32" and no higher than 48". To eliminate the challenge of searching for information on an adjacent wall, the Braille and text should be incorporated into the pedestal design. The information should be presented on a slanted or horizontal surface, as reading Braille on a vertical surface is uncomfortable for the wrist. The text color should contrast with the background, which must be a non-glaring surface. Tactile signs take longer to read than Braille, so the words must be short so readers don't lose their place. Typeface size should be at least 24 point.

CHILDREN'S ZOOS

Three overall design parameters relate to children's zoos in general, as well as to other types of non-formal educational institutions that also target children and families (such as botanical gardens and children's museums, if they have a central focus on nature and learning).

A children's zoo is about immersion in nature. This means literally being surrounded and engulfed by touchable, smellable, visible, audible nature. This is the crucial motivational dimension for children. To be active and rewarding, a zoo must be a place for hands-on experiences with nature.

A children's zoo is a non-formal educational facility. Its environment must express and reinforce the zoo's educational mission and means of delivery. The Hamill Family Play Zoo (see "Growing Caring Children: Explore! A Child's Nature," page 111) has an extensively researched and well-articulated

educational mission, which is to foster a love for animals and nature in children early in life. The chosen strategy is manifested through play in a nature-rich, playful environment facilitated by trained play staff. Other children's zoos may choose different strategies; however, given the wealth of research about nature and children, it is difficult to imagine any strategy being effective in an environment where live nature is not dominant.

A children's zoo contains a mix of indoor and outdoor spaces. These can take many forms according to the size and shape of the site, whether the facility is new construction or a renovation (or both), budgetary constraints, and other factors. The normal distinction between indoors and outdoors is whether or not the space is air-conditioned. This leaves out a realm of intermediate space that is neither fully outdoors nor indoors. Examples include pavilions, gazebos, covered decks and porches, open

corridors, walkways, pergolas—spaces that accommodate activity settings, provide gathering areas, make transition zones between indoors and outdoors, and increase the feeling of being immersed in nature. To design effective environments in these terms, close collaboration between architects, landscape architects and other design disciplines is required. This is fundamental to success.

INDOORS AND OUTDOORS

A children's zoo should contain a variety of relationships between indoors and outdoors to:

- Increase climatic adaptability and usability year-round
- Increase activity options for a broader range of user groups, particularly those who must rest frequently in the shade, cool or warmth because they have a low tolerance for extreme weather conditions and/or a low threshold for fatigue

- Increase program flexibility by providing ad hoc activity stations
- Increase closeness to nature by providing a "fine grain" mix of indoor, outdoor and intermediate spaces

FACILITY APPROACH

A children's zoo is likely to be part of a larger facility, typically developed as a low-density site with relatively large spaces between indoor facilities. Visitors will approach the children's zoo facility from a distance. As they approach:

- The feel of living nature must be dominant, ideally achieved by a variety of plantings or trees, perennials and possibly annual plantings.
- Messages about the mission and/or themes of the children's zoo should be presented in a friendly style using a variety of means (banners, boards, flags, paving inscriptions, archways, etc.).

FACILITY ENTRY

A children's zoo entry should feel friendly, inviting and fun.

- Design elements such as gates, arches, pergolas and ticket counters should be child-scale.

- Clearly detailed wayfinding should be provided to ensure that visitors of all ages are made aware of the choices that lie ahead.
- Motorized vehicles and vehicle spaces (except visitor shuttles) should not be present in the facility entry zone.

BUILDING ENTRY

Similar to the facility entry, the building entry should be inviting, friendly and easily accessible.

- If ADA ramps are required, they should be designed as an integral part of the entry landscape and not perceived as a separate element.
- If possible, providepower doors for ease of ingress and egress for caregivers with hands full and for young children unable to open heavy doors.
- In cold climates, provide an airlock with a double set of power doors.
- Provide stroller parking, preferably just before the building entry in a covered area or just after the building entry.
- Lockers and/or clothes hooks should be provided to leave unwanted personal possessions such as clothing during the visit.

WAYFINDING

Wayfinding should be considered an integral part of the design.

- It should be executed via a primary circulation system (accessible route) with a simple form (e.g., circular or linear), limited branching (not more than 4-way at any primary node), and cul-de-sac settings (entry and exit at the same point).
- Use a system of landmarks (e.g., totems, signage, repeated design feature such as seating, etc.) to mark major and minor nodal points and setting points of entry and exit.
- Wayfinding signage should follow a graphic standard and consistent location within the facility—inside and outside.
- Place names indicating different settings within the zoo may use customized type faces. Titles should function as visual landmarks: type should be bold, with strong figure/ground contrast, and contain no more than three words per title.
- Create aural, tactile and olfactory cues, for example, by using chimes, bells, gongs, etc., and variations in paving textures and patterns, hanging textiles, fragrant plants, etc.
- Locate windows to exhibit particular views and outdoor view frames to direct attention.

CIRCULATION/PATHWAYS

The structure of the circulation system and pathway hierarchy mirror and support clear wayfinding.

■ *Indoors,* the primary circulation should follow a clearly and consistently identified spine (accessible route). In the Hamill Family Play Zoo and Play Gardens (see "Growing Caring Children: Explore! A Child's Nature"), the circulation system was extremely simple—a loop around the central mountain, with individual settings immediately off it—like stores on an airport concourse. In another facility, the next level of complexity could be several such "loops," always returning to a central meeting point. The most important principle for user comfort is that the geometry should have a cognitively memorable form.

■ *Outdoors,* the same principle applies, that is, a primary circulation (accessible) route should connect directly to all activity settings, ensuring that the whole site is accessible. Primary pathways should have a strong identity through consistent visual treatment such as tinted concrete, inlaid animal footprints or other appropriate decorative motifs.

As primary pathways are designed to take the highest traffic, especially on the busiest days, they should be the widest. They should have shady seating opportunities such as benches, sitting walls and tree stumps at frequent intervals. Lighting levels should be the highest. Drinking fountains should be located on primary pathways. They can be associated with sitting areas as landmarks.

Outdoors is a more extensive environment than indoors and therefore provides opportunities for secondary and even tertiary pathways. Often, secondary pathways are necessary to connect subsettings or to provide access within the subsetting (e.g., the walkway though the Play Zoo Bug Walk). Secondary pathways should be wheelchair accessible if possible.

The tertiary pathways in the Play Gardens are designed as "secret pathways"—small loops connected to a primary or secondary pathway. The narrow, woodchip-surfaced pathway through the forest maze is an example of a natural path that can still be accessible to a manual wheelchair user with help, although it does not meet the ADA requirements.

INDOOR ACTIVITY SETTINGS

Ensuring that there is sufficient space, but not too much, for visitors within settings is a challenging issue. There is a tendency in the design of children's environments to oversize them by overestimating the space required for children's activities or by assuming children need lots of space because they are going to be running around. But this does not happen if children are engaged, i.e., if the exhibits are designed to respond to their interest. Play does not need to be boisterous to be effective.

A key issue is to ensure sufficient space for periodic wheelchair users or a permanent staff wheelchair user. The most effective strategy is to ensure flexibility by designing as many elements as possible to be movable. Spaces can be reconfigured or adjusted to accommodate wheelchair space. Reach range is not such an issue since the reach of young children and wheelchair users is similar.

OUTDOOR ACTIVITY SETTINGS

Depending on the setting, universal design considerations may be major or minor issues. Topographic change in level can be challenging. Sometimes an asphalted path up a hill would be too expensive and result in erosion and drainage issues. Try a decomposed granite, woodchip or dirt trail. This type of trail is not ADA compliant, but with help, manual chair users can get to the top of a hill, while power chair users can make the trip independently.

Water features designed at ground level can be problematic for wheelchair users. Parts of a stream can be elevated to enable wheelchair users to make contact with the water and possibly to transfer to get their feet into it. Elevated or partially elevated water features are more universal as they allow young children to play in the water with their hands, even when the weather is not warm enough to get wet. Elevation also makes it much easier for caregivers to join in the play.

BALANCING SUN AND SHADE

In the context of a facility such as a play zoo, shade is a subtle universal design variable. Visitor comfort and protection from the sun must be balanced with full sun requirements of many of the most vigorous, showy perennials that are there to attract visitors. Large shade trees usually cast shade over too wide an area, which reduces the diversity of understory plantings.

Small pockets of shade or semi-shade work best, so full exposure to the sun is not long enough to raise visitor body temperatures to uncomfortable levels.

Shade relief is always just a few steps away. This is especially important for individuals who must walk slowly (elderly, sight impaired, walker users) or manual wheelchair users. Shade pockets can be provided by small trees, large shrubs, trellises, pergolas, arbors, and bowers or manufactured shade structures. A wide variety of attractive textile shade structures are available. They can be installed as a temporary measure until natural shade is established or designed as permanent features.

Install water misters in several locations for use during the hottest time of the year. Kids love to stand under them, and even adults find relief from the sun. And for the landscape, they can supplement irrigation quite nicely.

PLAY AREAS

A quality play area is more than just a collection of play equipment. It is a place for play and learning—a place where children develop essential physical, social and cognitive skills, where different generations share common experiences, and where community members gather and build relationships.

Play areas should support a range of both mental and physical challenges. Well-designed play areas provide access for a person to physically arrive at a play element, interact socially and choose whether to do an activity on or at the play element.

Play areas are heavily regulated by safety and accessibility codes. The guidelines described here emphasize inclusive planning and design principles based on the assumption that compliance with all applicable codes and regulations will be achieved.

PUBLIC PARTICIPATION

Public park design must consider the needs of children with and without disabilities, adults with disabilities and the elderly. Site analysis and planning should include surveys to identify any physical and perceptual barriers to accessibility.

- Community workshops that bring together a park's various constituent groups can help assess needs and involve people in the design process. First, ask the group to define the term "people with special needs" so that everyone understands the variety of abilities and disabilities, and the level to which people's needs are being met.
- Second, ask the group to walk the park site, using maps to identify opportunities and constraints for accessibility. Individuals should observe and note physical accessibility (i.e., slope, path width, drop-off area, proximity to restrooms, access to equipment, activity and natural areas,

etc.), program accessibility (for use by people with a range of abilities) and communication accessibility (i.e., maps and signs, telecommunication devices for the hearing impaired and wayfinding).

Discussion at community meetings may also lead to the identification of place-based themes when held in the early stages of the planning and design process. Designers should ask about the historical, cultural and natural elements that are meaningful to people and that invoke pride of place. The theme can be developed using these aspects of a community, helping to make the park distinctive and, at the same time, providing an ongoing education about the place in which people live. For example, at Ibach Park in Tualatin, Oregon, the play environment draws on the natural and cultural history of the area by including a Mastodon rib cage climber, a climbing meteor, Native American Indian petroglyphs carved into the sand play area, and a stylized river that runs through the park—historical elements that have been adapted and interpreted for this contemporary setting.

CHILDREN'S INVOLVEMENT

A children's design workshop is an excellent way to gather information directly from one of the primary users of the park, especially regarding the imaginative play opportunities that provide the context for manufactured play equipment. Children's ideas can be drawn out creatively by asking kids to build models or draw pictures of an ideal park (Figure 25), selecting their favorite idea using photos of different environments or telling a story to a "park reporter."

To recruit children who use or may use the park, post flyers or set up a booth at

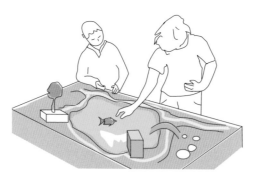

Figure 25. Children can construct simple models using preconstructed elements to convey their ideas for a park's design.

the park itself, make announcements at nearby schools or local youth groups, and authorize youth to invite or speak to their friends. If an event is not possible, questionnaires or surveys can be a good, quick way to get input on what children would like or dislike in a park.

SOCIAL ACCESSIBILITY

Play areas must make the social experience accessible to all. Children, including those with disabilities, can interact in many ways. Placing less challenging activities next to those that are more physically challenging encourages interaction across all ability levels. Providing access to a featured play structure by using synthetic or rubberized safety surfacing allows a wheelchair to roll right up to, through and underneath the structure so that a child can be in the center of action.

ACCESSIBLE ROUTES

An accessible route should connect every activity and accessible play component in the play area. The route provides children with an opportunity and allows choice and integration with others. It can be designed to be a play

experience in itself, such as a pathway that supports wheeled toys, running games and exploration.

SETTINGS

Provide a variety of settings and diverse play opportunities within the settings. Inclusive design addresses a variety of interests, senses and skills. Settings should incorporate a diversity of elements so children have choices. Provide a range of settings that address functional needs as well as play opportunities as described throughout this section.

ENTRANCES

Entrances help orient and inform play area users, introducing them to the site. Entrances are transition zones, places for congregating and areas for posting local information.

The entrance should convey the message: "All users are welcome."

PATHWAYS

Pathways can be designed to create different play behaviors and experiences. Consider pathways as play elements, supporting wheeled toy activity and running games, as well as opportunities for exploration. Pathway patterns set the tone: they can be wide with small branches, long and straight, or circuitous and meandering. They can wind through trees or lead directly to a primary destination. A pathway can be enhanced for play if it has unique items embedded into it such as colorful mosaic tiles, stamped animal tracks, leaf impressions, letters or numbers. Access throughout the area must be provided for all children without creating hazards (for example, don't design access ramps that double as skateboard ramps). Synthetic surfacing will allow wheelchair access alongside, under and through equipment and different areas.

FENCES AND ENCLOSURES

Boundaries are not only safety devices; they differentiate the children's play area from other areas within a park or urban area. They help children orient themselves to the places designed for them. Fences and enclosures can be used to define spaces, protect planted areas or fragile environments and define pathways. Fences and enclosures can also enhance social settings (Figure 26): a

Figure 26. Fences can define areas for social interaction.

nook in a fence creates a small gathering space; a hole in a fence creates a passageway.

SIGNAGE

A combination of text, color, form, pictures, graphics and tactile qualities make signs—and the park—more accessible (Figure 27). Graphics and tactile information, such as Braille, should be placed at a child's level. For young children, tilted signs should be approximately 24–30" above the ground, or if vertical, about 36–42" high. Consider anthropometric data for the primary user. For example, average eye level for a stand-

Figure 27. Informational and identification signs should be placed at a child's level.

ing six year old in the U.S. is about 41", and about 38" for a five year old in a wheelchair.

PLAY EQUIPMENT

Play equipment offers unique experiences such as swinging and sliding, and activities that require large-muscle coordination. Equipment also supports nonphysical aspects of child development. It allows children to experience height and can serve as wayfinding and landmarks for orientation. Equipment also becomes a gathering place for social interaction—a place to display skills, hide, chase and practice sharing. The small, semi-private places on or under equipment and themed elements such as steering wheels, windows and counter tops encourage a quieter social and dramatic play. Allowing children with disabilities to get into the middle of the action is as important as being able to reach the highest point.

MULTIPURPOSE GAME AREAS

Flat open spaces, either a hard court or soft groundcover such as turf, are valuable spaces for large group games, ball games and team sports. Hard surfaces also accommodate wheelchair access very well.

LAND FORMS AND TOPOGRAPHY

Topographic variety stimulates imaginative and creative play. Children use hills to create hide and seek games, develop orientation skills, roll, climb and jump. High points or summits should be made accessible to wheelchairs and provide support to children with other disabilities.

TREES AND VEGETATION

Vegetation and trees provide sensory stimulation that cannot be replicated by manufactured materials. Children use natural materials as backdrops and props in fantasy play (for example, trees become a magic forest and sticks become horses), and in cognitive activities (for example, counting and comparing, etc.). If trees and vegetation are used as a specific play feature, provide a means of access to and around the natural elements (Figure 28). Tree grates and other site furniture can support and enhance use by persons in wheelchairs and those using other mobility devices.

GARDENS

Gardens enhance the multi-sensory experience in a play area through the visual, scented, sound, taste and tactile qualities of the plantings. Gardens should be made accessible by providing at least one garden bed in an area that is raised above the ground surface with adequate circulation around it. This not only makes it so that persons in wheelchairs can garden, it's good for teachers and adults who have trouble bending over and reaching down.

Figure 28. A small grove of trees becomes a "forest" for children's play.

ANIMAL HABITATS

Children develop responsibility by caring for other living things. Often, children in urban areas haven't had much contact with natural animal habitats. Plantings, feeders and birdhouses can attract insect and bird life. Contact with or observation of wildlife and domestic animals produces a therapeutic effect and offers learning opportunities. Animal habitats should offer adequate protection for the animals and all users.

WATER PLAY

Water is a universal play material because it can be manipulated in so many ways. Children can splash and pour it, float objects in it, and use it to mold dirt or sand. At least a portion of water play areas must be wheelchair

accessible. Water sources and courses can be raised to allow children to roll up to and access the water (Figure 29).

SAND PLAY

Children will play in dirt wherever they can find it; a sandbox, essentially a structural version of plain old dirt, works best if it retains some natural dirt

play qualities including small rocks and twigs. Sand play areas can be made accessible through raised areas so that wheelchairs can roll up to the sand and children can place their hands in the sand's surface (Figure 30). If children are allowed to get into the sand with their whole bodies in a digging area, a

Figure 29. Water tables provide access for children using wheelchairs; there are many design alternatives.

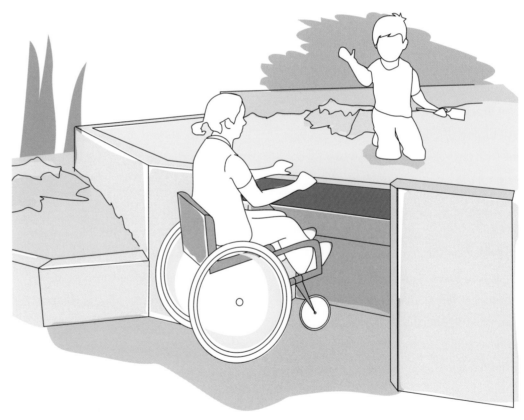

Figure 30. Elevated sand areas allow children in wheelchairs to play. Natural elements such as logs and boulders add interest and aid in transfer into sand play area.

Figure 31. A defined space with a wall and seating can become a stage for dramatic play.

transfer system should be provided so that children can get down into the sand for play. A place within the sand area should be provided so a person can rest or lean against a firm, stationary back support in close proximity to the main activity area.

LOOSE PARTS

Children love to manipulate their environment. Being able to do so builds fine-motor, social and cognitive skills, and provides opportunities to practice independence, self-control and management. Found objects such as stones, sticks, bottle caps and popsicle sticks and plant parts, and larger manufactured items such as blocks, dress-up clothing and wheeled toys can enhance play and social interaction. These items are relatively accessible.

GATHERING PLACES

Gathering places should be designed to promote social interaction and accommodate various size groups. A portion of gathering places within a play area should be located adjacent to an accessible route with an accessible ground surface. Elements within the gathering space should offer variety (in type and arrangement) and support for play, eating, watching, talking or congregating for an activity. Some of the seating should be without backs, and tables or game tables should include an accessible space on one side.

PERFORMANCE PLACE

An informal stage can provide a place for storytelling, impromptu performances or group productions, adding another dimension to play, and often serving as a focus for community gatherings (Figure 31). Provide a well-defined stage, which may be slightly elevated, and if possible an adjacent "prep" space. An accessible route to the stage area and the elevated stage itself, as well as accessible audience seating is required. Designing the space for

multiple uses extends its value and integrates activities in the overall setting.

STORAGE

Storage facilities for play equipment, loose parts and maintenance tools should be provided. Users, including employees and children, should have easy access to these facilities.

GROUND COVERING AND SAFETY SURFACING

Soft and hard play surfaces support different types of activities. Consider how the ground covering and safety surfacing can support the play area's theme. Turf and natural ground covers support running games, provide contact with nature and may encourage some amount of wildlife. Safety surfacing comes in many color variations, which could be used to interpret thematic elements such as water, lily pads or planets. Rather than simply providing access up to a piece of equipment, the surfacing could expand to create forms that inspire dramatic play. Engineered wood fiber, an accessible, shock-absorbing safety surface with a natural appearance, could be used to support settings with outdoor themes.

PLAZAS

Inclusive design seeks to make quality space for everyone. The following guidelines can be applied to retail plazas and urban parks. The goal is to create public spaces that speak to a wide constituency.

LANDSCAPE

- Use landscape to soften the edges of buildings and street; landscaping provides a friendly feeling.
- Provide lawn areas for sitting with adequate drainage.
- Use plants that have seasonal color and interest.
- Use deciduous shade trees in the public areas (to allow for winter sunlight).
- Use a variety of plants.
- Place plantings at different levels so all can touch, smell and experience the landscape.
- Install quality plant materials to give a subtle message that the space is important.
- Locate planters so they create space and enclose or direct movement.
- Use tree grates in paving to reduce soil compaction and increase the usable walking surface without com-

promising tree health and longevity (grates must be accessible).

- Provide a landscape maintenance manual to ensure that the intent of the design is maintained over time.

SEATING

- Provide a combination of movable and permanent seating.
- Provide seating with and without backs and arms to increase choices and accessibility.
- Use durable and well-finished surfaces for seating (e.g., colored concrete seatwalls, metal or teak chairs, etc.) and ensure that wheelchair users can congregate as part of a group.
- Locate seating so that there is always some in the shade.
- Arrange some seating at right angles to facilitate conversation.
- Locate seating along the edges of activity areas and settings.
- Allow lawn areas to be used as impromptu seating.

ENTRYWAYS AND CIRCULATION

- Use artificial or natural elements to mark entries into the space.

- Locate signage at entryways.
- Use an entry or gateway feature to direct people from one space to another.
- Use changes in paving color and texture to mark change from street edge to interior walks.
- Use a change in paving material and color to mark major entries.
- Make wide pedestrian passageways for people to safely pass each other, including strollers, toddlers, the elderly, and people using mobility devices.
- Locate paths in a route that helps to organize the space.
- Denote the hierarchy of path systems by changes in material and width.
- Provide space at pathway intersections for people to gather without blocking circulation.

BIKE PARKING

- Locate sufficient bike parking adjacent to main entries.
- Connect bike lot to main pedestrian path system.
- Provide enough bike racks for bike security and to control illegal bike parking.

- Use landscaping to partially screen bike lots from main activity areas.
- Provide lighting and shade at bike parking areas.
- Provide two entries into bike parking lots.

VEHICLE PARKING

- Provide sufficient on-street parking, in addition to any parking structures to accommodate people with limited mobility so they can park close and travel with relative ease.
- Shade the parking lot; about 50 percent shade is ideal.
- Design the parking lot so that it does not hinder safe pedestrian travel.
- Use raised pedestrian crossings to slow traffic in the parking lot and driveway traffic and to connect pedestrian corridors, without creating barriers to access.
- Use barrier plantings to deter pedestrians from walking through parking medians and between cars.

VARIETY OF SPACES

- Provide positive outdoor spaces (positive spaces are partly enclosed—they seem bounded even when sides are open). People tend to feel safer when they are partly surrounded and their backs are protected.

- Surround each space with wings of buildings, trees, hedges, fences, arcades and trellised walks.
- Provide a space large enough for community events, rallies, musical performances, etc.
- Provide spaces where parents can let their children run around and play without disturbing shoppers.
- Incorporate a "stage" area into the plaza paving.
- Provide quieter, smaller spaces.
- Create positive spaces around the buildings, using trees, seat walls and hedges to create a sense of enclosure and safety.

INTANGIBLE FEATURES

The intangible qualities of spaces are often what makes an open space unique. "Proximity of uses" addresses the physical arrangement of inside and outside spaces; "sacred spaces" recognize the importance of the community's memory and tradition.

PROXIMITY OF USES

Urban parks are often bounded by major traffic spines that link one major land use, such as a city hall or retail area, with another. Successful downtowns locate retail, restaurants, copy shops, banks, offices, churches, daycare and housing in close proximity. This same concept can be applied to the layout of activities in a park or plaza. A central lawn can be the spine, with different "rooms" and paths located on its edges. This proximity of uses, both on the exterior and the interior, makes a place for everyone. It creates excitement, encourages social interaction, and makes the place a community destination.

SACRED SPACES

A sacred space lives in the hearts and minds of the community. It's a place where people go for renewal, community, connection and memory. It's important to recognize the significance of that space, even if it is not unique in design: it may be as simple as a grove of trees or a fountain. The challenge is to recognize the qualities that make the space sacred and incorporate these into expanded designs without altering their fundamental nature. The community itself will often provide the essential direction. Keep spaces simple and flexible; be careful not to overbuild, and keep the sacred space intact.

TRAIL SYSTEMS

For the most part, trails designed for the Presidio of San Francisco are similar to back country settings and were designed to comply with Federal Access Board (Regulatory Negotiation Committee 1999) guidelines for accessible trail construction and trail rehabilitation, rather than the ADA Accessibility Guidelines (ADAAG) that are applicable to buildings and facilities (see "Connecting Urban and Natural Settings: Presidio Trails and Bikeways"). A major difference is that steeper slopes are allowed because of the constraints posed by the natural environment and different expectations of trail users. Since natural settings often have a dual mission of enhancing access to natural, cultural or historic resources and at the same time protecting those resources, special techniques are often required.

These design guidelines supplement local design standards, such as those published by transportation agencies for bikeways and the Access Board guide-lines. They are intended for back country, informal, park-like settings where the natural environment predominates in rural, suburban or urban areas. The guidelines provide trail design and construction techniques that promote resource conservation, enhance trail sustainability and maintainability, increase trail safety, and minimize user conflicts. They are not only sound construction practice, they also enhance trail access for people of all abilities.

ACCESSIBLE TRAILS

It is not realistic, or desirable from a visitor experience point of view, to make all trails accessible to all users. Increasing accessibility would not be appropriate if doing so would:

- Cause substantial harm to cultural, historic or significant natural features or characteristics
- Substantially alter the nature of the setting or the purpose of the trail
- Utilize construction methods or materials that are prohibited by law
- Require technically infeasible solutions due to terrain or prevailing construction practices

If a trail cannot meet the guidelines because of any of the above exceptions, efforts should be made to ensure that as much of the trail is as accessible as possible. In locations where trails are not accessible, ensure equivalent accessible trail experiences.

PEDESTRIAN TRAILS

Providing variety and choice increases access for people of all abilities. A system that provides both primary and secondary trails, for example, allows a non-athletic wheelchair user or a pedestrian who wants an easy stroll to enjoy an excursion on a moderately wide, gentle path, while a more adventuresome person would try a narrower, steeper trail.

Accessible portions of pedestrian trails should comply with Access Board guidelines for outdoor developed areas. One of the chief distinctions between recreational trails and a path of travel governed by ADAAG criteria for buildings and facilities is slope. No more than 30 percent of the total length of a designated accessible trail should exceed a running slope of 1:12 (8.3 percent) or have a cross slope greater than 1:20 (5 percent). In general, the running slope of an accessible trail should be less than 1:20 (5 percent). However, steeper trails could be considered accessible in the following conditions:

- Maximum "running slope" (in the direction of travel) of 1:12 (8.3 percent) for 200' with resting intervals
- Maximum running slope of 1:10 (10 percent) for 30' with resting intervals
- Maximum running slope of 1:8 (12.5 percent) for 10' with resting intervals (Figure 32)

MULTI-USE TRAILS

Multi-use trails should meet all the special requirements of pedestrian trails. Although steeper grades are per-

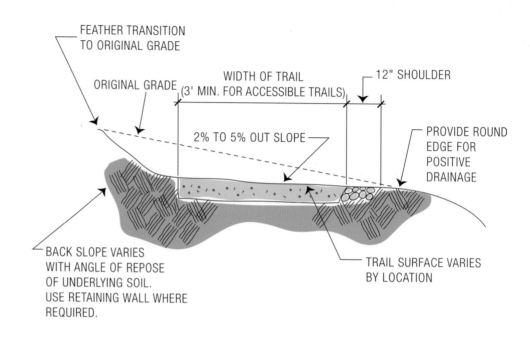

Figure 32. Cross slopes can reach a maximum of 5 percent in areas to increase drainage.

mitted, easy grades of less than 1:20 (5 percent) are recommended to provide greater accessibility for persons with disabilities and recreational bicyclists.

Typically, multi-use trails are a minimum of 8' wide. This allows bike lanes with a minimum of 4' in each direction. Depending on the number of people using the trail, the width could be much greater (Figure 33).

To increase accessibility for runners or the elderly who desire softer surfaces

that minimize impacts on bone structure, provide soft surface pedestrian shoulders on one or both sides that can be used as walking or running paths.

A typical multi-use trail corridor might then be a minimum of 12' wide, assuming a minimum width hard surface and 2'-wide soft surface shoulders in each direction. If the multi-use trail is to be used by maintenance vehicles, a minimum 10'-wide hard surface is recommended.

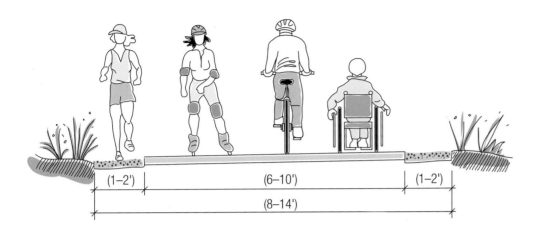

(1–2') (6–10') (1–2')

(8–14')

Figure 33. Multi-use trails can range from 6 to 10' wide, plus shoulder width for runners and other users.

Hardened surfaces are usually asphalt or granular aggregate material stabilized with a binder. Soft surface portions can be fine granular stone (crushed rock or decomposed granite). Trails for skaters should have a smooth, paved surface.

Tread obstacles such as steps or water-bars should be avoided on multi-use trails. Drainage grates generally should be located outside the trail, or designed with small openings perpendicular to the path of travel for wheelchair and bicycle safety.

Figure 34. If width is a constraint, give preference to uphill bicycle lanes, while downhill bikers share the road with cars.

BIKEWAYS

Road width constraints and volume of traffic are the primary determinants for the type of on-road bikeway provided. Where possible, provide striped bike lanes on both sides of major roads. Where road width is a constraint, priority is given to uphill bike lanes (Figure 34).

Although the American Association of State Highway and Transportation Officials (AASHTO) minimum width for bikeways is 4', the recommended minimum width for marked bike lanes on each side of the roadway should be 5' to accommodate a wider spectrum of cycling skill. Even wider lanes of 6' or more should be considered in those areas where recreational cyclists predominate to allow two cyclists to ride side by side.

Some roadways and service roads have low traffic volumes with low speeds. If the roads are appropriately signed, bicyclists and autos can share them safely without marked bicycle lanes.

Most bikeway grades are the same as existing roadway grades, which vary from nearly flat to very steep.

Therefore, when designating bikeways, roadway topography should be reviewed and routes chosen with gentle grades, preferably 1:20 (5 percent) or less where possible. Where roadway grades are steep, off-road bikeways should be considered that permit gentle slopes. In areas such as large parks where a range of visitor experience is important, bikeway routing should offer a range of difficulty, from easy to challenging.

Bicycle Lane Markings

Bikeways should be signed to indicate appropriate usage for cyclists and motorists. For example, where autos and bicycles share the road, it is important that both drivers and cyclists be alerted to the conditions.

Raised pavement markings or raised traffic separators can pose hazards to cyclists of all abilities. Except in special circumstances, bike lanes should be separated from motor vehicle traffic by painted lane markings.

Conflicts and safety concerns often occur at intersections or where trails or bikeways cross roadways. A number of improvements or traffic calming tech-

niques can increase safety and accessibility for all users.

- *Crossing islands or medians* decrease the distance across a wide or heavily trafficked roadway. To maximize accessibility, crosswalks should cut through crossing islands or medians at the same elevation as the roadway.

- *Curb extensions or bulb-outs* can narrow the roadway and increase safety at points where trails cross streets. Curb extensions should not extend into travel or bicycle lanes. This may require that traffic and bike lanes be narrowed at the intersection.

- *Curb radius reduction* is particularly effective in improving pedestrian safety at crossings by slowing right-turning vehicles, reducing crossing distances, and improving visibility between drivers and pedestrians.

- *Raising an entire intersection or crosswalk* is an effective means of encouraging motorists to yield the right-of-way to pedestrians. Tactile warning strips at edges enable people with visual disabilities to detect the crossings, and also alert sighted people that they are entering a roadway. Since raised crossings are effectively speed bumps that also slow down emergency vehicles, their placement should be limited and their location should have adequate sight distances. Depending on traffic

volume, textured warning strips for approaching vehicles or other devices such as flashing lights should be considered.

- *Textured crosswalks* can be visual and tactile markers for pedestrian traffic, and also can provide aesthetic enhancement. However, crosswalks should not be constructed of materials that create unsafe or inaccessible conditions for bicyclists or people with disabilities. Since textured paving is uncomfortable for some wheelchair users, use a pattern that includes a smooth crossing path.

TRAILHEADS

Trailheads, at a minimum, should provide orientation, a place to meet or wait for others, and a place to rest. These are the required elements:

- Standard trail signs with information regarding trail conditions and degrees of difficulty

- Places to sit, including space for wheelchairs and companion seating

Trailheads also function as links to other modes of transportation. Therefore, where appropriate, include:

- Convenient access to shuttle and/or transit stops

- Automobile parking, including parking spaces reserved for persons with disabilities
- Secure bicycle parking (racks or lockers)

To create "full service" trailheads, also include as many as possible of the following elements:

- Wayfinding kiosks, with orientation and interpretive information (see Wayfinding below)
- Drinking water
- Trash receptacles
- Restrooms or directions to restrooms
- Scenic viewpoints or overlooks
- Staging or gathering spaces

OVERLOOKS

Most overlooks can be accessible to all visitors. Minimum considerations include:

- Interpretive signage, accessible to people in wheelchairs, including Braille and possibly other languages
- Places to sit, including space for wheelchairs and companion seating
- Places outside the circulation path for viewing

If viewing places are provided, each area should have at least one wheelchair maneuvering space with a firm and stable surface a minimum of 5' in diameter, and typically 1:50 (2 percent) slope in any direction. Although the Access Board guidelines permit slopes of 1:33 (3 percent) as an exception to ensure proper drainage, it is not recommended.

Overlooks should provide at least one unrestricted viewing opportunity for each distinct point of interest at a height between 32" and 51". Railings or safety barriers should not intrude on the viewing "window."

Successful primary overlooks will also include such facilities as:

- Automobile parking, if the overlook is also adjacent to a roadway, including parking spaces reserved for persons with disabilities
- An accessible route to site features associated with the overlook
- Other amenities, such as trash receptacles and bike parking

Secondary overlooks, intended as places of rest or quiet sanctuary, should only include accessible places to sit, since other features might distract from the purpose of the overlook.

WAYFINDING

Signs that provide visitors with information about directions, trail conditions and trail locations, as well as specific accessibility information serve trail users and visitors of all abilities. Multiple languages, including Braille, may also enhance accessibility for a wide range of users. Signage will need to comply with the standards of the agency having jurisdiction.

Trailhead Signs

Signage at trailheads should provide information about trail conditions for all visitors, so they can judge any difficulties the trail might cause. Locate trailhead signs at the starting points of trails and at key intersections of major trail corridors. Designated accessible trails should display the international symbol of accessibility. If the trail is not accessible, it should be signed "Not Accessible" at the trailhead. Trailhead signs should provide as much as possible of the following information:

- Name of the trail
- Direction and distance to points of interest
- Trail elevation change
- Trail surface characteristics
- Running and cross slope
- Clear tread width

Trail Markers

Trail markers identify each trail along its entire route, providing signage that helps trail users navigate the entire length of trail. Trail markers provide an opportunity to create a distinct visual identity for each trail, contributing to wayfinding and a sense of place. Each marker should include the trail logo, a symbol indicating permitted trail use and a directional indicator.

Trail Guides

Although not a part of trail construction, trail guides may be developed to supplement park signage, and contribute to greater accessibility for all. Possible topics include a general trail guide, children's guides, guides for historic loops and ecology guides.

OTHER ACCESS ROUTES

Outdoor Recreation Access Routes and Beach Access Routes are two special categories of an accessible trail system. The first is a continuous, unobstructed path designed for pedestrian use, connecting accessible elements at picnic areas, campgrounds, designated trailheads and designated overlooks.

Beach Access Routes link nearby main trail routes to the water's edge. Since access to water is so important to human enjoyment, make every effort to exceed the Access Board's minimum requirements. For example, while recognizing the maintenance issues, providing a means to safely reach (and retreat from) points of low water levels vastly increases enjoyment of tidal areas or rivers and reservoirs with fluctuating water levels.

In general, guidelines for outdoor access routes and beach access routes are very similar to, but slightly more restrictive than accessible trail requirements. The Access Board guidelines should be consulted for exceptions.

TRAIL EDGE PROTECTION

Edge protection has two purposes: to protect the trail and adjacent resources, and to protect the user. Conditions must be examined on a case-by-case basis to determine whether edge protection provided for one purpose does not in fact create a hazard for another user.

Clearly defined edges help keep users of all types on the established trail surface and help protect natural resources. Properly constructed edges also protect trails from water damage and erosion. Edge protection such as a 3" or higher curb can increase trail safety by helping a person using a wheelchair keep on track. A lower edge might not be obvious or detectable to people with limited vision who use canes. Natural objects such as logs also work well.

Since vertical objects constitute a potential hazard for cyclists, curbs or railings should not be used within 2' of a bikeway or paved portion of a multi-use trail.

DRAINAGE CONTROL

Drainage control measures on trails, such as waterbars and drain channels, often create obstacles to accessibility. However, two methods can both control drainage and aid accessibility: outsloping and rolling grade dips.

Outsloping is slightly elevating the uphill edge of a trail. This encourages water to flow evenly across the trail surface and reduces the potential for erosion.

Rolling grade dips are short sections of trail that channel water off the trail surface (Figure 35). Grade dips work best on trails with slow, steady grades and are best placed at naturally occurring drainage-ways. Increasing the trail cross-slope at the point of the grade dip provides better drainage. Approaches to grade dips should be about 4 to 6' long to eliminate abrupt grade changes that may be barriers to access.

TRAILS IN WET AREAS

Trail users of all abilities generally try to avoid wet patches on trails by walking to the sides, causing destruction of adjacent vegetation. However, relocating these trails to higher or drier ground may not be the answer if the existing trail location provides special benefits to users or if rerouting the trail would disturb sensitive habitat areas. Providing a hardened trail surface in the current trail alignment, designed to accommodate the water, may be the best choice for resource protection, maintenance and visitor enjoyment.

Surface Reinforcing

Placing flat stones or cobbles on the trail surface, especially in combination with geotextile fabric, is an aesthetically pleasing way to provide a more stable trail surface in wet areas. If carefully installed with narrow joints and maintained, this technique can improve accessibility while retaining a natural appearance. A short section paved with

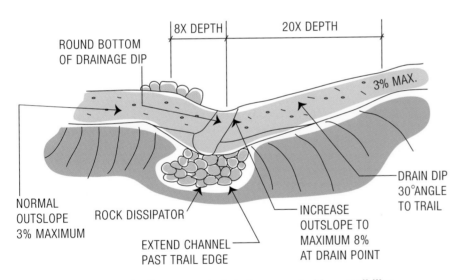

ROUND BOTTOM OF DRAINAGE DIP

8X DEPTH

20X DEPTH

3% MAX.

NORMAL OUTSLOPE 3% MAXIMUM

ROCK DISSIPATOR

EXTEND CHANNEL PAST TRAIL EDGE

INCREASE OUTSLOPE TO MAXIMUM 8% AT DRAIN POINT

DRAIN DIP 30°ANGLE TO TRAIL

Figure 35. A rolling grade dip can control drainage and aid accessibility.

permeable concrete, or paving with deep grooves to allow passage of water, would be even more accessible for people using wheelchairs.

Boardwalk Bridge

Trail structures such as bridges help maintain drainage patterns. To remain accessible, approaches to trail structures need to be at grade, and raised edges will likely be required (Figure 36).

Drainage Lens

A drainage lens can help manage low-volume water flow on trails caused by ephemeral springs or seeps (Figure 37). Fill the area beneath the trailbed with progressively smaller quarry rock, then cap it with fine aggregate or suitable native fill. Sandwiching the rock lens between two layers of geotextile material provides a more stable base, and prevents rock from mixing with surrounding soils.

TRAILS ON FLAT GRADES

Since trails exist in dynamic environments, it is not always possible to keep them clean and dry, especially on

primarily level terrain. Without proper drainage, trails on level ground tend to pond and collect debris, creating obstacles for all users and eventually degrading the trail. Elevating the trailbed or providing a boardwalk can provide a firm, stable, slip-resistant surface that is free of ponding.

Above-Grade Trail

A trail that is raised 3"–6" above surrounding grade, with drainage swales on each side, will improve access for all users (Figure 38, page 434). To provide additional subsurface drainage, use a coarse gravel bed to elevate the trail or

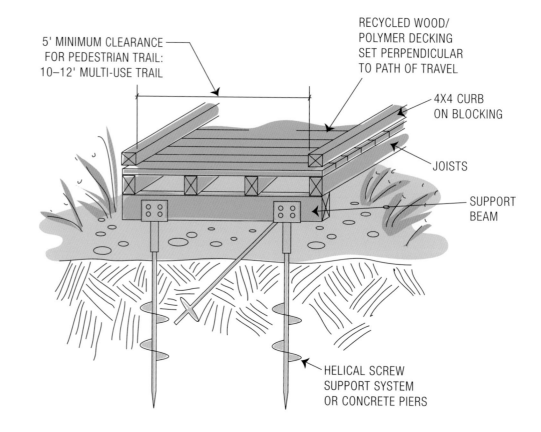

5' MINIMUM CLEARANCE FOR PEDESTRIAN TRAIL: 10–12' MULTI-USE TRAIL

RECYCLED WOOD/ POLYMER DECKING SET PERPENDICULAR TO PATH OF TRAVEL

4X4 CURB ON BLOCKING

JOISTS

SUPPORT BEAM

HELICAL SCREW SUPPORT SYSTEM OR CONCRETE PIERS

Figure 36. Boardwalk bridges improve accessibility in sensitive or sandy areas and encourage people to stay on the trail.

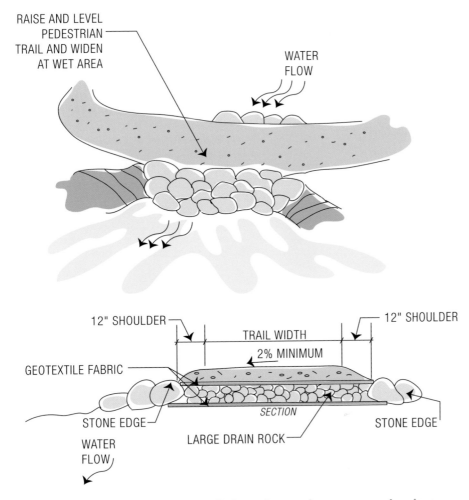

RAISE AND LEVEL PEDESTRIAN TRAIL AND WIDEN AT WET AREA

WATER FLOW

12" SHOULDER

TRAIL WIDTH

2% MINIMUM

12" SHOULDER

GEOTEXTILE FABRIC

STONE EDGE

SECTION

LARGE DRAIN ROCK

STONE EDGE

WATER FLOW

Figure 37. A drainage lens helps keep trails free of water from seeps and springs.

provide a drainage lens to facilitate water movement. An elevated trail offers a more convenient pathway for users during wet periods, provides the greatest degree of accessibility, and may require less maintenance. Variations of

this technique are sometimes called "turnpikes" in trail construction jargon.

Boardwalks

Boardwalks provide an accessible trail surface and are often the most appropri-

ate solution on erosion-prone soils, such as sand or other loose, uncompacted soil, or across wetland areas (Figure 36). They also protect natural or historic resources by encouraging people to stay on the designated trail.

An important consideration in board-walk design is to ensure that two people using wheelchairs can pass each other. Providing pullouts or overlook alcoves increases accessibility by allowing rest-ing or observation without impeding the movement of other trail users. Boardwalk decking installed perpendi-cular to the direction of travel is best for visitors in wheelchairs or pushing strollers. In most cases, a raised curb at the edge will be required.

TRAILS ON SANDY SOILS

It is difficult to maintain a stable trail surface in areas with sandy soils. Reinforcing the trail base or providing trail structures can improve usability for many different park visitors.

Subsurface Geogrids

Geogrids or geocells, when used in combination with geotextiles, provide a

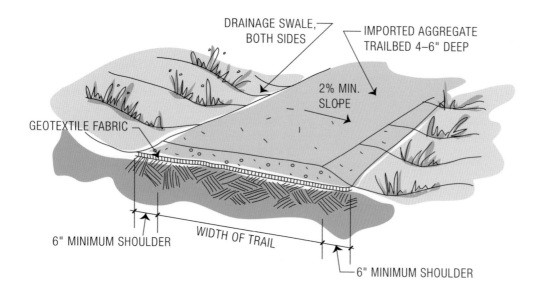

Figure 38. Above-grade trails, often in combination with drainage lenses, are designed to be firm, stable and slip-resistant.

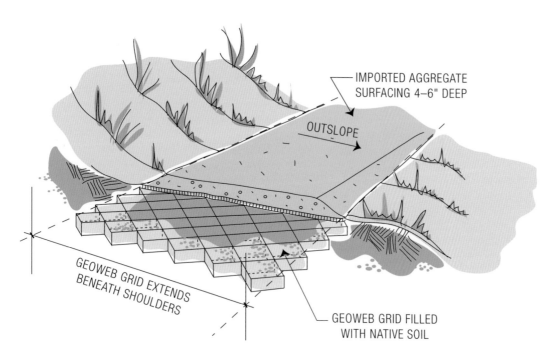

Figure 39. Subsurface geogrids can stabilize sandy soil.

relatively unobtrusive means of stabilizing sandy trails (Figure 39). The geogrid confinement chambers prevent lateral displacement of sandy soils, distribute trail tread loads over a greater area, and reduce settling—all of which help keep trail surfaces intact, in place and dry. The geotextile material can provide separation between saturated soil and the tread fill or increase containment over a sand base. Permeable tread fill can improve drainage; however, in areas of sensitive natural habitat, imported soils may be restricted.

Above-Grade Trail Structures

Boardwalks are often used for access across sandy soils. Another option is textured panels with drain holes, which are installed directly on the leveled surface without substantial subgrade excavation. These panels meet current accessibility guidelines and can be relocated. They may require additional maintenance, such as sweeping and readjustment of linked panels to provide a uniform surface.

OPEN SPACE PERFORMANCE STANDARDS

These guidelines apply to open space elements that taken together create an overall system within a city: parks, connecting green corridors, staging areas, activity nodes and small neighborhood greens. The aim is to enhance a community's use of trails, greenways and outdoor spaces, improve how those areas complement or supplement a city's park system and natural areas, and make a city more walkable. See Trail Systems Design Guidelines for more specific details, including ADA requirements.

Open space systems must meet the needs of individual people in their daily lives; guidelines can ensure that the open space system actually provides the expected benefits. The guidelines will assist in designing open space systems that meet individual human, biological, social and cultural requirements.

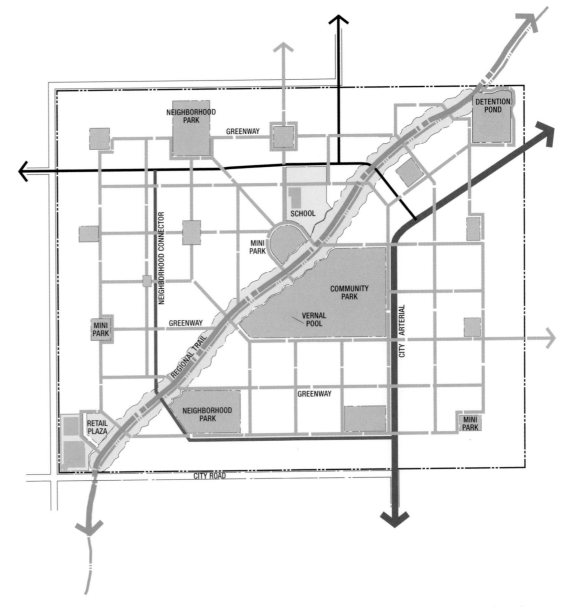

Figure 40. An open space system connects green corridors, gathering areas, trails and parks, as well as amenities such as commercial areas and schools.

Open space elements include:

- *Parks.* Parks provide space for people to come together across cultural and socio-economic lines to enjoy recreational activities, appreciate nature, relieve stress, learn about the natural environment and feel a sense of identity and connectedness to nature and their community. Park design should provide activity settings that take into account the site's physical, social and cultural conditions. (Also see the Play Areas Design Guidelines, page 417, for more detailed information about designing areas for children.)

- *Regional Trails.* These multi-use facilities are the backbone of open space connections throughout a community. New developments should be required to extend or connect to a regional trail system. The goal is to allow a person to travel or commute safely from one side of the community to the other, without leaving a city's open space network. (Also see Trail Systems Design Guidelines, page 425, for more detailed information about trails.)

- *Green Infrastructure.* Development sites often have public facilities that should be incorporated into the site design, such as drainage channels and utility corridors. Public infrastructure should be developed for multi-use, thus adding neighborhood and community connectivity.

- *Greenways.* These smaller-scale linear corridors are pathways within or between developments. They are generally linear in nature and connect different site locations, encouraging walking or biking between them. Greenways should terminate at a regional trail, a park or a major activity node such as a town center.

Figure 41. Utility corridors can provide multi-use open space, strengthening community connectivity.

■ *Neighborhood Greens.* These small open space areas (sometimes called pocket parks) should be dispersed throughout neighborhoods and within close proximity to residential units. They should provide opportunities for passive or small-scale active recreation (for example, play equipment) and staging for activities within the greenway system. (Also see the sections on Plazas and Gathering Spaces in the Cityscapes Design Guidelines, pages 463–464, for more urban-style open space.)

Open Space Framework

These general site design guidelines are for open space amenities within greenfield and infill developments.

1. *Variety:* Provide a wide variety of usable open spaces that connect major community destinations (such as community parks, neighborhood parks, pocket parks and commercial plazas) through open space connectors (such as greenways, trails, etc.).

2. *Location:* Every residential unit in a planned new development should be within 1/4 mile (or 5 minutes or less walking distance) of a park or neighborhood gathering place.

3. *Accessibility and Connectivity:* Access to parks, open space areas, different land use types and community amenities (schools, playgrounds, community buildings, transit stops, etc.) should be enhanced with a network of open space connectors, thereby enhancing the desirability of using alternative methods of transportation (e.g., walking and bicycling). These connectors should link residential units, parks, commercial areas, schools and other areas to provide a comprehensive open space network.

4. *Relationships:* The location and configuration of regional trails, greenways and neighborhood gathering places should complement existing and proposed schools, libraries, city parks and commercial developments.

5. *Block Size:* Provide walkable and bikeable neighborhoods by limiting the size of residential blocks and creating a network of multi-use non-vehicular pathways in the new development. For blocks longer than 600', intersperse mid-block pedestrian pathways to create smaller blocks. Uninterrupted blocks or portions of blocks generally should be no longer than 400'.

6. *Multi-Use Utility Corridors:* Use major utility corridors (e.g., storm water drainage, underground and overhead utilities, etc.) to also provide usable open spaces consistent with their utilitarian function.

7. *Sustainability:* Where feasible, maintain and respect all natural features of the site, including the natural drainage of the land, natural preserves and habitat areas.

8. *Safety:* Enhance safety by minimizing at-grade crossings of arterial roads that interrupt major pedestrian-friendly pathways connecting to parks and schools. When open space trails intersect with roadways at grade, street widths and pedestrian crossing distances should be kept to a minimum. Arrange buildings to provide for visibility and surveillance opportunities. Locate and design buildings to allow open space areas to be viewed from inside residences and other buildings. This allows open space areas to be watched over by neighborhood residents and discourages anti-social and illegal activities.

OPEN SPACE PATTERNS FOR NEW DEVELOPMENTS

The diagrams at right illustrate a systematic process for creating an open space framework for new developments.

Figure 42.

a. Identify existing natural features on development sites, preserve significant features and create new naturalistic features to enhance projects. Provide connections for regional trail routes. Connect the open space network on individual developments to the citywide network.

b. Locate at least one major non-vehicular, multi-use corridor. The pedestrian spine may be located along a natural feature such as a natural drainage corridor. Landscape the pedestrian corridor to provide summer shade and create a sense of identity and cohesion to the entire development.

c. Locate major built amenities (neighborhood commercial areas, schools and community parks) along the regional trail or greenway system. The trail system should also connect residential areas to employment or commercial areas.

d. Locate parks such that all individual residential units are within 1/4-mile walking distance of a city park or neighborhood gathering place.

e. Create a network of pedestrian and bike connectors, such as trails and greenways, to connect all the built and open space amenities. All residential units and commercial areas should be within 1/8-mile walking distance of a connector.

f. Organize street networks, neighborhood blocks and lots in combination with open space elements to tie into surrounding developments and link with natural amenities of the site (access to nature, views, sun, wind, etc.)

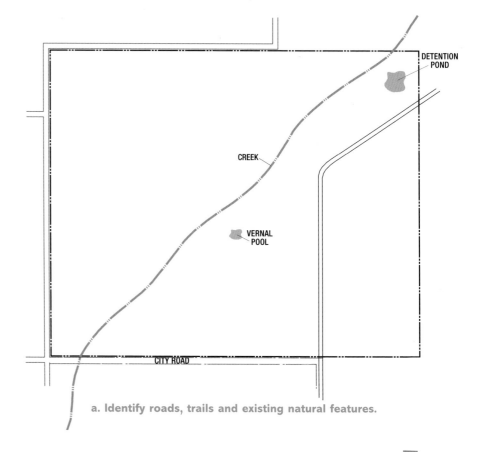

a. Identify roads, trails and existing natural features.

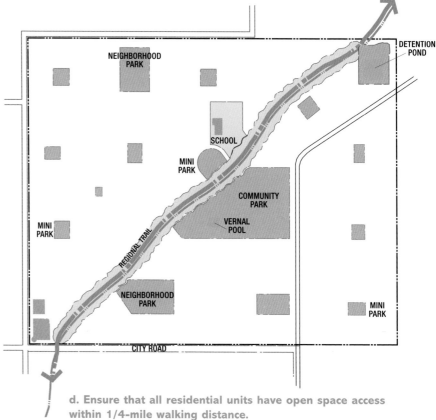

d. Ensure that all residential units have open space access within 1/4-mile walking distance.

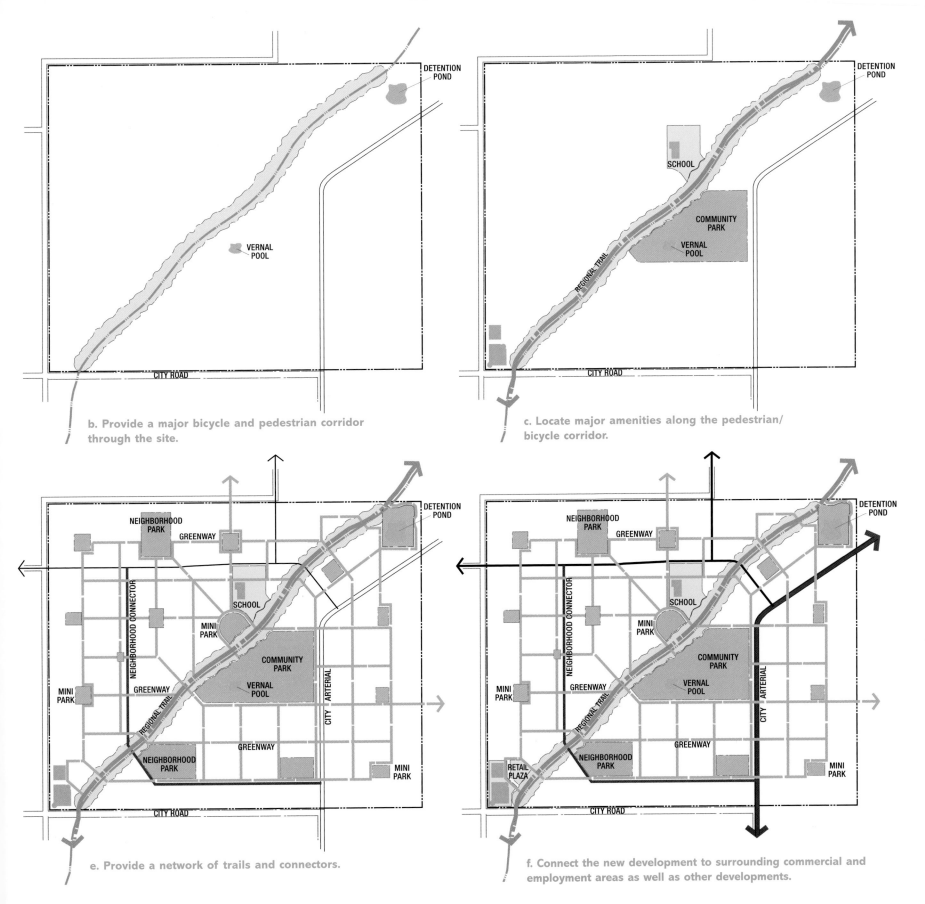

b. Provide a major bicycle and pedestrian corridor through the site.

c. Locate major amenities along the pedestrian/ bicycle corridor.

e. Provide a network of trails and connectors.

f. Connect the new development to surrounding commercial and employment areas as well as other developments.

Diagram labels (b): DETENTION POND, VERNAL POOL, CITY ROAD

Diagram labels (c): DETENTION POND, SCHOOL, COMMUNITY PARK, VERNAL POOL, REGIONAL TRAIL, CITY ROAD

Diagram labels (e): NEIGHBORHOOD PARK, GREENWAY, DETENTION POND, NEIGHBORHOOD CONNECTOR, SCHOOL, MINI PARK, COMMUNITY PARK, VERNAL POOL, CITY ARTERIAL, MINI PARK, REGIONAL TRAIL, GREENWAY, NEIGHBORHOOD PARK, GREENWAY, MINI PARK, CITY ROAD

Diagram labels (f): NEIGHBORHOOD PARK, GREENWAY, DETENTION POND, NEIGHBORHOOD CONNECTOR, SCHOOL, MINI PARK, COMMUNITY PARK, VERNAL POOL, CITY ARTERIAL, MINI PARK, REGIONAL TRAIL, GREENWAY, RETAIL PLAZA, NEIGHBORHOOD PARK, GREENWAY, MINI PARK, CITY ROAD

Parks

"Placemaking" is an approach to creating public spaces that are intentionally designed for social interaction and community identity, and results in parks that are not just public places but *community places*. Community parks should not all look alike. High-quality, distinctive parks can be designed with different features, activities and identities to reflect unique cultural, historic or environmental qualities of an area or community. Facilities that support the activities should be grouped or combined to create activity settings for a wide range of experiences. In other words, a ball field must be more than a ball field. For example, any large patch of grass can be used to play ball, but to be a complete activity setting—a place for the entire community—the field should be designed in combination with a shade structure, picnic area, young children's play area, a gathering and game-watching area, a small café or coffee bar, as well as supporting restroom, drinking fountains, storage and parking. To make the area distinctive, one or more of these elements can be designed to reflect something about the community.

Place-based park design provides activity settings where people of all ages and abilities share experiences with each other and their environment. To provide users with meaningful or special experiences, each setting should be context-specific: it should take into consideration the site's physical, social, and cultural conditions. For example, the ball field can be combined with other settings such as a library, farmer's market, or water play area to create multiple reasons for the community to gather. This type of design has a higher probability of resulting in "community" places that are equitable and usable by a wide variety of people.

GENERAL PARK SYSTEM GUIDELINES

1. Park types should be geographically dispersed throughout the community.

2. Every residence should be within a 1/4 mile (or 5 minutes walking distance) of a park.

3. Every park should be connected to every other park by a "green" circulation system of trails, streets and bikeways.

4. No park should be located in isolation from other community-serving facilities or residences. Locating parks near adjacent gathering places will help activate the park, support

neighboring facilities and generate customers for nearby businesses.

5. Facilities or activities in and around the park should provide a reason for the community to gather and interact. The facilities selected for a particular park should reflect a set of activities specific to that park and should be grouped into settings that help define the park and create an identity. Each park should have unique features that are appropriate to the park function and neighborhood context.

GENERAL PARK DESIGN CRITERIA

The following design criteria will help ensure that each park fits its context and functions effectively in connecting community members to one another and their environment.

1. Every park should be designed to fit a specific site, with its own character, and have features that make it a destination.

2. Parks should be designed around activity settings. The number and type of settings will be determined by park location, park size, park function, adjacencies and community need.

3. Parks should be designed with community involvement. In the case of new parks in new neighborhoods, some parks will be designed based

Figure 43. Placemaking features in parks should reflect the culture, values, history and social needs of the local community through landmarks, water features, art, special facilities and layout. For example, a play structure made to look like large mastodon bones is designed for an area where these prehistoric animals once lived.

10. Take into account that neighborhood needs change over time; build flexible space into every project to allow for adaptation as the community grows and changes.

PARK TYPE STANDARDS AND GUIDELINES

Well-designed park systems incorporate different types of parks: small, medium and large neighborhood parks; community parks; central parks; regional parks; sports parks; and destination parks. (Neighborhood greens can also function as parks—see Neighborhood Parks sections below for more details.)

Small Neighborhood Parks

Small neighborhood parks range from 2 to 5 acres in size and emphasize small group settings, with a minimal number of sports activity settings (primarily informal). Balance these high-intensity activity areas (large groups, lots of noise and energy) with low-intensity settings (small groups and quieter activity). Locate the high-activity areas to minimize impacts on low-activity areas and adjacent residences. Include a minimum of four activity settings that can be used by all age groups. Elements should

on overall community need as determined by a parks and recreation master plan. Some neighborhood parks or mini-parks will be designed after the neighborhood is occupied, so the community can participate in their development.

4. Placemaking features in parks should reflect the culture, values, history and social needs of the local community through landmarks, water features, art, special facilities and layout. These features can be layered throughout the design to create meaning and community connection.

5. Design should also build on existing environmental conditions or re-create previous environmental features that define the area. The result will be a park design that will also function as a teaching tool for learning about the local or regional environment and

may offer opportunities for environmental restoration as well.

6. Parks should use high-quality, diverse and long-lasting building materials, and have a variety of well-considered landscape details.

7. Art can be integral and functional to the setting and not just a stand-alone element. Benches, bridges, lights, signs, water, walls, planters, and shade structures can all be works of art.

8. Incorporate materials and facility maintenance standards and requirements as part of the design review process.

9. Incorporate both capital and operations and maintenance costs in the design process so that a complete financial understanding of each design evolves as design decisions are made.

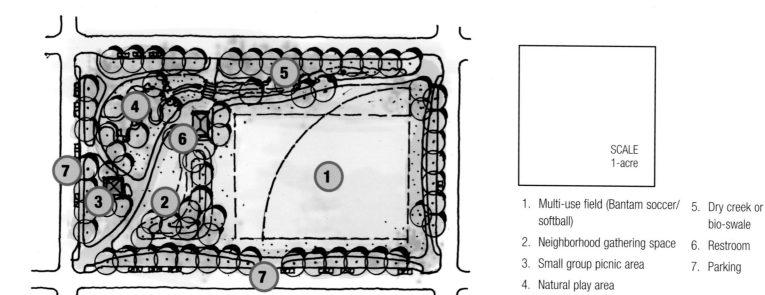

1. Multi-use field (Bantam soccer/ softball)
2. Neighborhood gathering space
3. Small group picnic area
4. Natural play area
5. Dry creek or bio-swale
6. Restroom
7. Parking

SCALE
1-acre

Figure 44. A sample layout for a 2- to 5-acre small size neighborhood park includes an informal active play area.

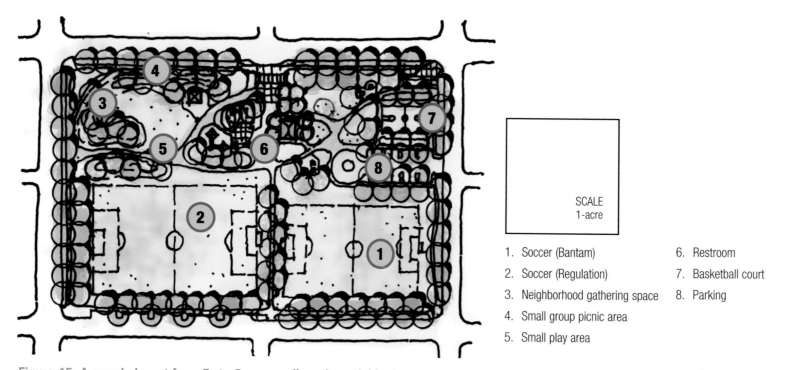

1. Soccer (Bantam)
2. Soccer (Regulation)
3. Neighborhood gathering space
4. Small group picnic area
5. Small play area
6. Restroom
7. Basketball court
8. Parking

SCALE
1-acre

Figure 45. A sample layout for a 5- to 8-acre medium size neighborhood park includes formal as well as informal play areas.

include open space and gardens, small gathering and seating areas, picnic tables (1 per park acre), paths and walkways (connected to the local greenway system), and play areas (built and natural). They can also include areas for informal sport activities such as half-court basketball or multi-use turf areas. Shade structures should be provided if there are no mature trees, and restrooms may also be included.

Medium Size Neighborhood Parks

Medium size neighborhood parks are 5 to 8 acres with an emphasis on settings for small groups, with space for limited sports activities. They should follow the same general guidelines as for small parks, but include a minimum of six activity settings that can be used by all age groups. They should provide everything contained in a small park plus multiple small group picnic areas and sports options such as baseball and softball practice fields, full-size outdoor basketball courts, bantam and regulation soccer fields, multi-use turf areas, horseshoe/bocce courts, skate/BMX features, and water play areas. Supporting facilities such as restrooms and parking should also be provided.

Large Size Neighborhood Parks

Large neighborhood parks are usually 8 to 20 acres. Again, follow the same general guidelines as for small parks, but include a minimum of eight activity settings. They should include everything in a medium park plus options that the community can determine, such as sand volleyball courts, dog parks, water features, and large group picnic and large multi-use turf areas. They should also provide restrooms, concessions and parking.

Community Parks

Community parks are about 20 to 100 acres and designed to accommodate a wider variety and higher intensity of recreational uses than neighborhood parks. They should be adjacent to schools, nature preserves, or other community-serving institutions, such as libraries, service centers or commercial areas, especially areas with coffee shops, cafés, or other food service. They may have amenities such as unique natural features or special use facilities (for example, a community center or aquatic center, café and major food concessions) or publicly accessible natural preserves. Because of its greater size, the community park should have more expansive open space areas. Each park should also be accessible via both the greenway system and a major road. Community parks include a minimum of ten activity settings. In addition to all of the activities at neighborhood parks, community parks can include lighted baseball and softball practice and playing fields for youth and adults, soccer practice and playing fields of all sizes, amphitheater, community marketplace, disc-golf courses, handball courts, tennis courts, ponds and reflecting pools, community center, aquatic center and destination play areas. They should also provide larger restrooms, concessions, storage, and parking.

Sports Park

These parks should be a minimum of 40 acres, with facilities for sports leagues that are integrated with areas attractive for the whole family, such as picnic and play areas. These high-activity areas should be located to minimize impacts on adjacent residences. The sports park may be adjacent to a community park, with a road separating the two, and it should also be adjacent to other community-serving institutions, such as service centers or commercial areas. Because the park could include

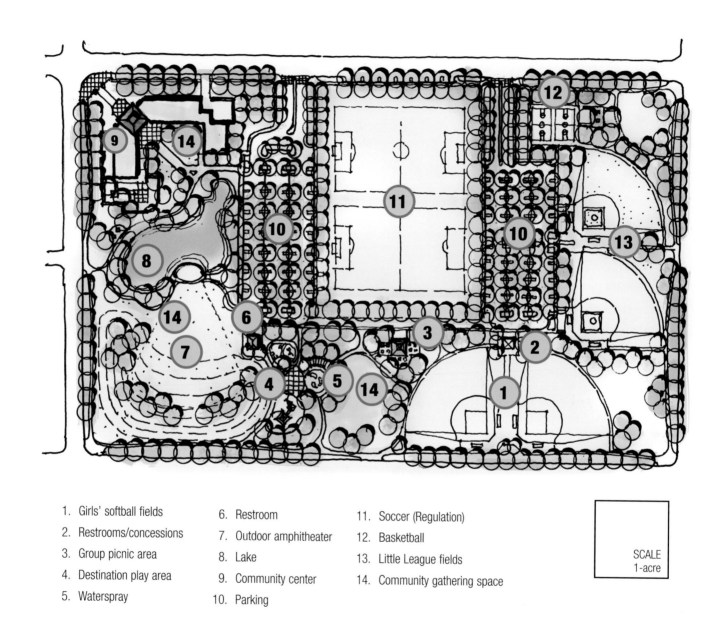

1. Girls' softball fields
2. Restrooms/concessions
3. Group picnic area
4. Destination play area
5. Waterspray
6. Restroom
7. Outdoor amphitheater
8. Lake
9. Community center
10. Parking
11. Soccer (Regulation)
12. Basketball
13. Little League fields
14. Community gathering space

SCALE
1-acre

Figure 46. A sample layout for an 8- to 20-acre large neighborhood park includes a minimum of eight activity settings.

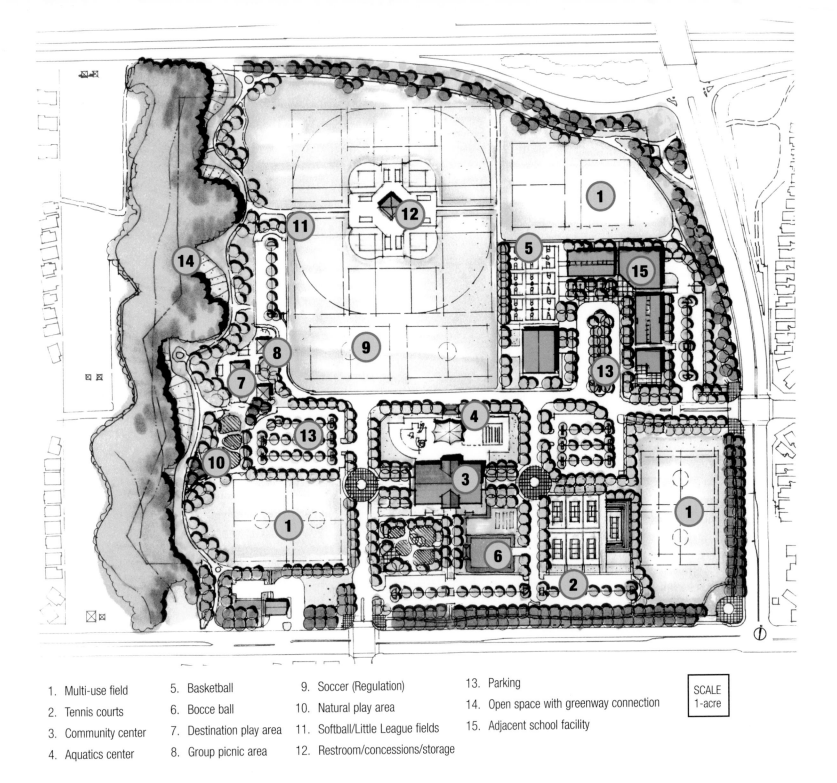

1. Multi-use field
2. Tennis courts
3. Community center
4. Aquatics center
5. Basketball
6. Bocce ball
7. Destination play area
8. Group picnic area
9. Soccer (Regulation)
10. Natural play area
11. Softball/Little League fields
12. Restroom/concessions/storage
13. Parking
14. Open space with greenway connection
15. Adjacent school facility

SCALE
1-acre

Figure 47. A sample layout for a 20- to 100-acre large community park includes settings for major sports activities as well as non-sport activities.

adult beverage service, it should be located away from incompatible uses, such as schools or other child-focused environments.

Regional Parks

Regional parks support multiple jurisdictions. They are usually developed around a highly desirable natural amenity such as a mountain, forest, lake, river or ocean shore. The activities at the park should also reflect the character of that natural resource. Regional trails should also connect to the regional park.

Central Parks

A central park is the place where the community celebrates, honors and commemorates its city. It is centrally located, ideally adjacent to government and commercial centers, sized to accommodate civic gatherings and events.

Regional Trails

Regional trails are major corridors with few interruptions. They should span an entire city and connect major open space amenities and locations (e.g., rivers and creeks, preserved open spaces, city parks, commercial centers and other cities). They provide non-car, multi-use environments for people to walk, hike, jog, bike, roller blade and ride horses, while also creating opportunities for people to relax and picnic. While not all uses can be accommodated on every regional trail, the emphasis is to serve a variety of user groups while minimizing user conflicts.

■ While the preferred alignment for regional trails is along the perimeter of parks and nature preserves, some

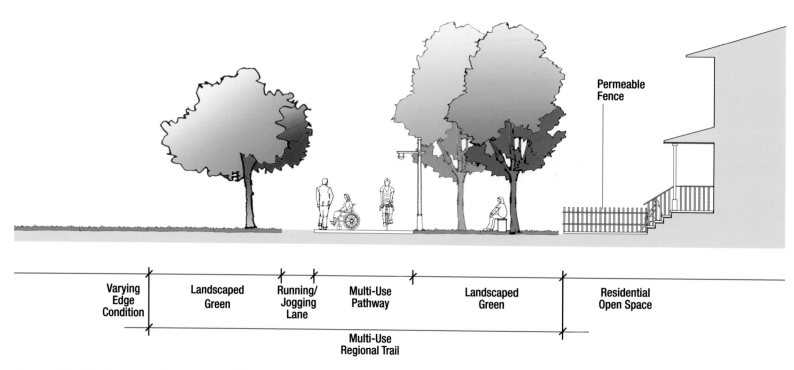

Figure 48. A trail can provide opportunities for social interaction for nearby residents.

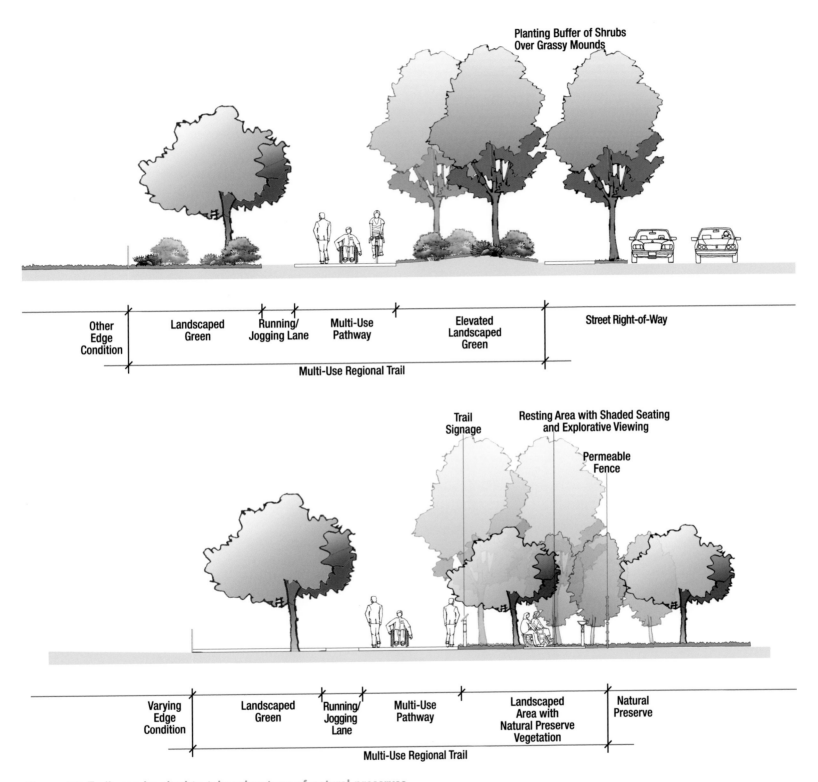

Planting Buffer of Shrubs Over Grassy Mounds

Other Edge Condition	Landscaped Green	Running/ Jogging Lane	Multi-Use Pathway	Elevated Landscaped Green	Street Right-of-Way

Multi-Use Regional Trail

Trail Signage

Resting Area with Shaded Seating and Explorative Viewing

Permeable Fence

Varying Edge Condition	Landscaped Green	Running/ Jogging Lane	Multi-Use Pathway	Landscaped Area with Natural Preserve Vegetation	Natural Preserve

Multi-Use Regional Trail

Figure 49. Trails can be sited to take advantage of natural preserves.

portions of regional trails may be sited adjacent to streets and/or regional facilities such as utility corridors.

- Trails should relate to natural features and lands set aside as preserves. They should vary in width and follow natural topography to reinforce their relationship to parkland and wildlife habitat.

- Trail settings should be comfortable, inviting and safe. Shade trees should be planted generously and amenities such as benches and occasional drinking fountains should be incorporated along the corridor. Signage, lighting and other features should be incorporated into the design.

- Trails should be visible and easily accessible from adjacent land uses for security and to create activity.

- Frequent connections should be provided to the trails, either through activity nodes and neighborhood gathering areas along the trail, or through connecting neighborhood greenbelts. Connections should include staging areas.

- Trails can be programmed with annual walking, running and biking races that increase usage and visibility.

Basic Guidelines

1. Create unencumbered hard-surface multi-use pathways for movement of pedestrians, recreational bicycles, people in wheel chairs, etc., and a soft-surface pathway for runners and joggers. Provide shade for the trail with deciduous trees, generally on both sides of the pathway.

2. Provide a wide "green" buffer consisting of trees, shrubs, groundcover, etc., between the multi-use pathway and edge of trail. This buffer may also accommodate an equestrian trail.

3. Consider use of bio-swales if appropriate.

4. Maintain safety and security of the trail by providing adequate lighting and allowing visual and physical connections between the trail and adjacent built and open space uses.

5. Celebrate key entrances to trails and trailheads with appropriate signage, parking, restrooms, etc.

6. Provide rest areas along trails every half-mile. All nodes should have a seating area and drinking fountain. Rest areas should have other amenities, including restrooms, bike racks, picnic tables and trail information.

7. Provide separation from adjacent roadways using a green buffer, change in grade or landform.

8. Regional trails should have easy grades. Minimum running slopes for multi-use trails (no more than 1:20 or 5 percent) provide greater accessibility for persons with disabilities and bicyclists. Where feasible, cross slopes should be kept to a minimum (1:50 or 2 percent), unless a curve requires super elevations for safety or to ensure proper drainage.

Green Infrastructure

Drainage corridors, detention and retention basins, and regional utility corridors can function as multipurpose "green infrastructure."

- Ensure that infrastructure and utilities within project sites are integrated into site design in an aesthetically pleasing manner (e.g., chain-link fences without landscaping should be avoided).

- Use required infrastructure facilities for multiple purposes (e.g., a power line corridor can double as a linear trail).

- Create comfortable, inviting and safe settings.

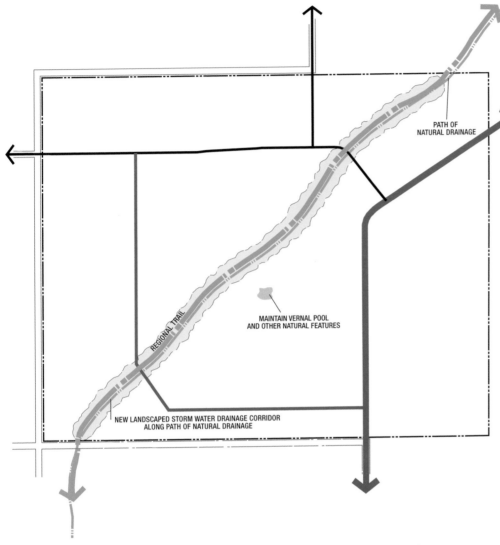

PATH OF
NATURAL DRAINAGE

REGIONAL TRAIL

MAINTAIN VERNAL POOL
AND OTHER NATURAL FEATURES

NEW LANDSCAPED STORM WATER DRAINAGE CORRIDOR
ALONG PATH OF NATURAL DRAINAGE

Figure 50. Utility corridors and drainage channels can become elements of a green infrastructure network.

Basic Guidelines

1. Provide a green corridor along or within utility infrastructure areas.

2. Create unencumbered pathways within drainage corridors for movement of pedestrians, people who use wheel chairs and bicyclists.

3. Provide a green buffer consisting of trees, shrubs, perennials and groundcover between the multi-use pathway and edges of the green corridor. Provide shade trees along the entire length and on both sides of the pathway.

4. Maintain safety and security of the trail by providing adequate lighting and allowing visual and physical connection between the trail and adjacent built and open space uses.

5. Ensure that all retention and drainage basins are designed by an experienced and qualified multi-disciplinary team of biologists, hydrologists, storm water engineers and landscape architects to ensure that the requirements for wildlife, plant life, hydrology and human interaction are effectively addressed.

6. Ensure that newly created storm water drainage corridors follow the natural drainage slope of the land. Avoid drainage corridors at the edge of new developments along arterial roads.

7. Incorporate existing natural features, such as vernal pools, woodlands, hillsides and other natural site features in new developments. Where possible, new trails and other connectors should enhance existing natural habitats.

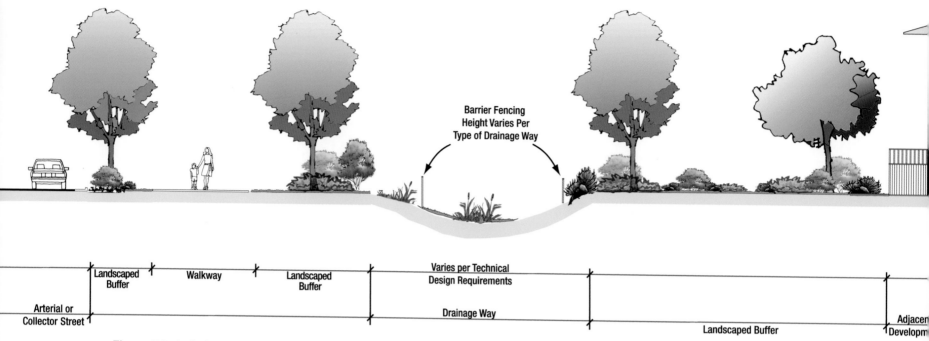

Barrier Fencing Height Varies Per Type of Drainage Way

Arterial or Collector Street | Landscaped Buffer | Walkway | Landscaped Buffer | Varies per Technical Design Requirements — Drainage Way | Landscaped Buffer | Adjacent Development

Figure 51. A drainage corridor becomes an element of green infrastructure in a built area.

8. Use maintenance practices that effectively support the corridors as habitat for local wildlife.

9. Provide interpretive opportunities throughout the corridors in order to provide the community with a greater understanding of the natural systems, flood management, and technological infrastructure that support their daily lives.

10. Encourage creation of homeowner associations or volunteer organizations to help with maintenance.

Greenways

Neighborhood greenways are linear systems that connect residences to the regional trail and park system and to community-serving facilities such as schools, parks and village greens. They provide car-free, pedestrian-friendly environments for people to walk, bike or otherwise travel without a vehicle from one place to another, as well as places to pause, sit and relax.

■ Provide a continuous connection to a regional trail, park or other destination to tie into the overall community open space system. A person should be able to walk out a front door and easily find a greenway within close proximity.

■ Create comfortable, inviting and safe settings. Trees and landscaping should be planted generously to provide shade and a pleasant environment. Provide amenities such as benches, lighting and signage.

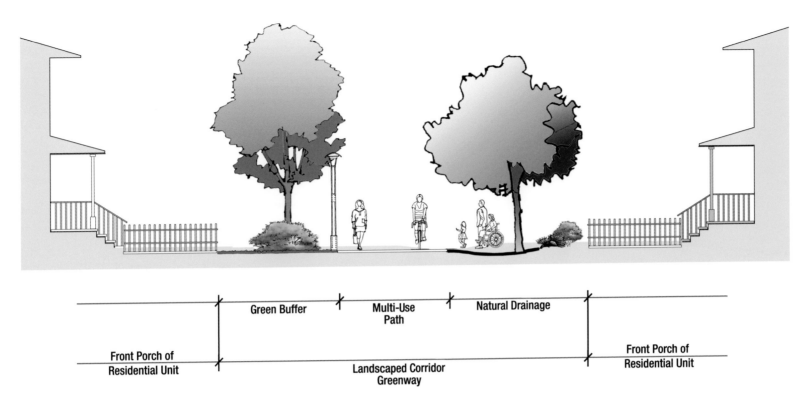

Green Buffer   Multi-Use   Natural Drainage
                Path

Front Porch of   Front Porch of
Residential Unit   Landscaped Corridor   Residential Unit
                        Greenway

Figure 52. A greenway can link the front porches of residential units.

■ Greenways should be visible and easily accessible from the front doors, windows and porches of adjacent buildings for security and to create activity.

Basic Guidelines

1. Provide generous landscaped buffers. Greater widths allow greenways to be used as spaces for social interaction.

2. Create unencumbered multi-use pathways for movement of pedestrians, bicyclists, etc.

3. Provide a green buffer consisting of trees, shrubs, groundcover, etc., between the multi-use pathway and greenway edge. Provide shade trees on both sides of the pathway, if possible.

4. Maintain safety and security of the greenway by providing adequate lighting and allowing a visual and physical connection between the greenway and adjacent built and open space uses.

5. Where yards face greenways, provide fencing that is semi-transparent to allow visual access.

6. Encourage creation of homeowner associations or volunteer organizations to regularly manage and maintain the greenway.

7. Depending on the location of the greenway, program the open space with community gardens, art and other creative uses.

8. Encourage celebrations, block parties and other festivities to take place on greenways.

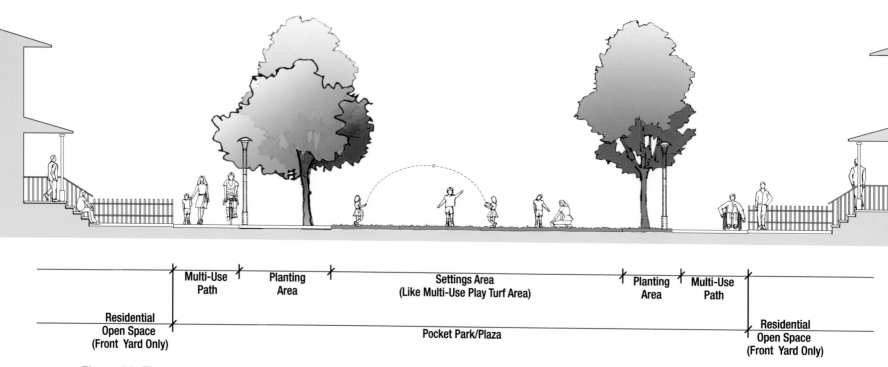

Figure 53. The open spaces in front of alley-loaded residential units become potential outdoor gathering places.

Neighborhood Greens

Neighborhood greens (also called pocket parks) are intimate neighborhood-scale spaces, about 1/4-acre to 2 acres in size, that supplement the traditional city park system. Bounded by public and private built spaces and streets, they provide a place for relaxation and play areas for children. These gathering spaces enhance community life and create a unique sense of place by providing small park-like spaces close to residential units.

■ Allow for multiple activities such as playing, relaxing, etc.

■ Provide comfortable spaces through the use of trees, landscaping and hardscape elements.

■ Ensure that spaces are visible and easily accessible from the front doors, windows and porches of adjacent buildings and from adjacent streets to create activity and enhance security.

■ Ensure that the size of neighborhood gathering places in individual developments reflects the character of housing (a larger or more complex gathering place may be more appropriate where there is a higher ratio of people or homes per acre).

Basic Guidelines

1. Provide a minimum of three settings: a young children's play equipment area (for children 2 to 5 years old), a gathering place for parents and children to meet, picnic, etc., and a multi-use play area, preferably turf, which could include paved areas, grassy mounds, water features, etc. Other settings could include a sand play area with a water source and themed gardens.

2. Profide generous widths so the gathering place can provide multi-use paths, natural drainage corridors and landscaped planting strips along the setting area.

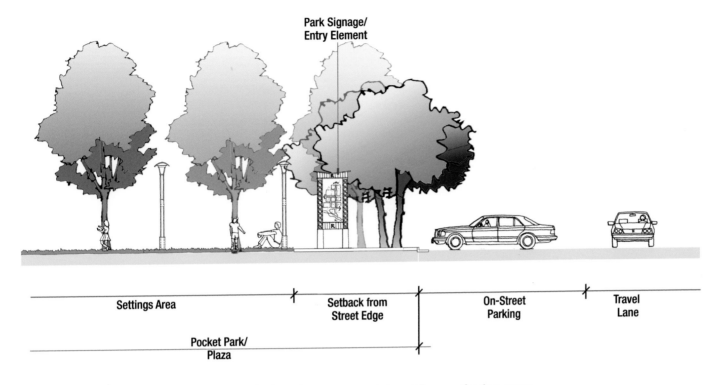

Park Signage/
Entry Element

Settings Area

Setback from
Street Edge

On-Street
Parking

Travel
Lane

Pocket Park/
Plaza

Figure 54. A neighborhood street can be designed to accommodate outdoor gathering areas.

3. Provide multi-use paths that create unencumbered movement of pedestrians, bicyclists, etc.

4. Provide a landscaped area between settings and the multi-use path on at least one side of the pocket park.

5. Provide a setback from the edge of the street right-of-way to provide adequate space for a landscaped buffer.

6. Encourage a sense of arrival for the park at its key entry locations through signage, groves of trees, etc. Provide each park with a unique sense of identity by creative use of materials, plantings, art and water features.

7. Provide shade on the multi-use paths and other parts of the park by providing deciduous trees.

8. Create a sense of enclosure for the park through the use of trees, vertical entry features and the mass of adjacent building elements fronting the park.

9. Maintain safety and security of the park by providing adequate lighting and allowing visual and physical connections between the greenway and adjacent built and open space uses.

10. Where private residential open spaces face the pocket park, provide fencing that is semi-transparent to allow visual access.

11. Discourage locating the backyards of public and private developments at park edges.

12. Provide on-street parking along at least one side of the park.

13. Encourage creation of homeowner associations or volunteer organizations to regularly manage and maintain the pocket park.

14. Encourage celebrations, block parties and other festivities at pocket parks.

CITYSCAPES

Design guidelines for urban areas address the physical aspects of buildings, sites, landscaping and circulation. They are essential for improving quality of life, economic vitality and a positive image for a city. Guidelines should encourage variety and creativity and suggest design solutions for making great places and great spaces, taking into consideration the social, cultural and economic fabric of the community and how people actually use spaces. Master plans, specific plans and zoning ordinances spell out permissible land uses and the quantitative development measures that must be met. Design guidelines are used to maintain the integrity of areas that have special character or significance, protect public and private investment, provide design direction to designers and decision makers, conserve existing properties by showing how they can be altered, and describe how new developments can be designed and constructed to be compatible with the existing urban character.

Each city has its own unique character, so no single set of guidelines will be appropriate. The following guidelines have proven successful in urban environments and can lead to more inclusive downtowns and cities.

SITE DESIGN AND LAYOUT

Building Edges

Building edges help define street and sidewalk areas as active public spaces. Historically, downtown buildings cover the entire lot with no front, side or rear setbacks.

- Parking should be provided within the building, below grade, or at a separate parking structure so as to minimize disruption to pedestrian circulation areas.
- Locating building entrances so they open onto the street helps maintain visual surveillance of the street and sidewalk areas and activates the pedestrian zone.
- When feasible, new construction should provide appropriate side set-

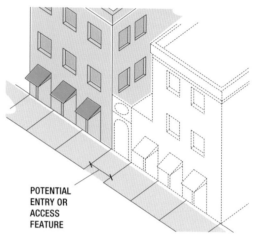

POTENTIAL ENTRY OR ACCESS FEATURE

Figure 55. Side setbacks can provide opportunities for entry features, patios and service access, and help preserve natural light.

backs to adjacent existing buildings that have windows facing rear and side yards, allowing for light, air and usable space between the buildings.

Outdoor Areas

All site spaces should be improved for uses and activities to provide more attractive and functional spaces that help reduce vandalism and increase safety. Sites should be designed with attention

Figure 56. Cut-away corners create "defensible space" because they increase visual access for pedestrians.

to visual surveillance, lighting and safe circulation. The rear portions of many commercial buildings often face alleyways that are dark, underused and uninviting—and attract trash.

- Use controlled access points, good lighting and cut-away corners to provide "defensible space."
- Use well-lighted rear-yard areas and alleyways for service access, which

will preserve pedestrian-friendly public street fronts and increase safety in those areas.

- Where appropriate, provide small outdoor dining areas, patios and gardens on the public sidewalk immediately adjacent to buildings or in rear-yard areas.

Building Heights

Building heights often vary in different downtown districts. Tall buildings shape the skyline and create strong visual landmarks. Tall buildings on corner sites can serve as anchors for the block.

- The tallest buildings should be concentrated in the downtown core, with decreasing size and intensity as one moves away from the downtown core.

Figure 57. Small, outdoor dining areas add life and energy to pedestrian areas.

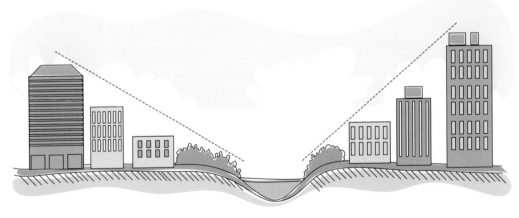

Figure 58. Building heights should decrease as one moves closer to a natural landmark, such as a river, or away from the downtown core.

- Buildings should decrease in size as one moves closer to a natural landmark such as a river.

- Maintaining the alignment of cornices, rooflines and building lines of new buildings with existing buildings preserves architectural continuity. Match cornice lines and step back upper floors of tall buildings that are above average building heights in the area.

- Matching heights at the ends of blocks on adjoining corners creates a unified architectural character.

- In the odd-shaped and "leftover" areas near freeways, all types of building heights can be appropriate. Those areas can be appropriate for a wide variety of freeway-oriented businesses.

Parking Lot Placement and Design

While parking is an obvious need in a downtown environment, surface parking lots destroy the pedestrian character of a downtown and preclude retail activity and public gathering spaces on the street. Too often, they create the appearance of a vacant, underused and unsafe downtown that deters visitors and shoppers. Lots in front of buildings increase the walking distance to the establishment and discourage foot traffic.

Figure 59. Designing seating and other amenities near parking lot screening walls contributes to a comfortable pedestrian environment.

- Parking lots should not intrude on the urban character and pedestrian quality of downtown.

- Large expanses of paved parking lots should be sited to the rear of buildings away from major pedestrian commercial streets with access from side streets and alleyways.

- Use perimeter landscaping to screen cars from public view along sidewalks and soften the edges of expansive, paved areas. Decorative fences with narrow landscape buffers and trellis-type structures also provide an attractive barrier. Use semi-transparent screening materials with appropriate planting heights to maintain visual access for safety.

- Design parking in parking garages below or above street level or commercial uses.

- Seating, lighting, trash receptacles, telephones and other pedestrian amenities can be designed into screening walls and landscape areas to make a more comfortable human-scale pedestrian environment.

BUILDING DESIGN

Building guidelines usually address only the exterior of buildings and the relationship of buildings to the surrounding setting and the street. Building design decisions need to balance many factors, including economic constraints, programmatic needs, functional requirements and aesthetics. For most downtowns, two major design principles should be considered: contextual fit and pedestrian-friendly streets.

Contextual Fit

Contextual fit is how well the proposed building fits into the urban setting. That requires building designers to evaluate the existing buildings on the block and determine the major reoccurring design elements that contribute to the character and image of the downtown. These elements can include: setbacks, heights, form, rhythm of openings and horizontal building lines, color, materials, texture, and building styles and design elements. A new building does not need to match every other building in order to "fit." Elements of the new building should be *related* in some way to achieve a harmonious result.

In some cases, the opposite may be appropriate: for example, the creation of a landmark or signature building. These buildings stand out because of their unusual and innovative design. However, too many signature buildings within one district creates visual confusion. Landmark buildings may be created for civic uses, such as museums, churches, schools and major recreation facilities, or in areas where there are relatively fewer older buildings that form a historical context.

Pedestrian-Friendly Streets

Building design can contribute to creating an active, urban pedestrian street life. The primary concern is the street level that is visible to pedestrians—and those in cars who may be tempted to get out of their cars. The types of design elements that contribute to this include: street-level activities, building to the edge of sidewalks, windows and openings at the ground floor level, awnings and canopies over window displays and entries, pedestrian amenities along the street and extensions of building activities into the sidewalks (such as outdoor seating, dining and sales displays).

Proportion of Openings

Building openings, windows, doorways and entries contribute to consistent urban character. Often, older buildings have narrower, vertical window openings with regular spacing, while newer buildings have continuous horizontal ribbons of windows that wrap the building with no spacing between them.

- Building widths and historic proportions, as well as the spacing of building openings should be maintained at least at the lower levels of buildings.
- Building openings at the pedestrian level may vary and incorporate modern styles and materials.

Horizontal Rhythms

Older buildings often have a distinct horizontal rhythm of openings along the street using common building materials. Repetition of these elements creates a continuous band along a block. Usually, the common band is the division between the storefronts on the street level and upper façades of buildings. Maintaining a strong horizontal band within the range of human visual perception creates a sense of enclosure, reinforcing pedestrian activity at the street level and unifying each block. Individual landmarks, such as churches or a public institution can gracefully interrupt the rhythm. But too many interruptions disrupt the overall unity of the urban streetscape.

- The horizontal rhythm in new buildings can be reinforced by using a similar alignment of windowsills, building lines, floor lines, cornices, rooflines and floor-to-floor spacing.
- Cornice lines, floor canopies and awnings, overhangs and windowsills help maintain a clear visual division between street level (ground floor retail uses) and upper floors (office or residential uses).

Building Form

In many downtowns, buildings in the urban center are rectangular forms over two stories covering entire lots. This building shape creates a regular rhythm of building mass and edge along commercial streets. The mass is articulated with building details, commercial window displays and entries at street level. In recent years, buildings have increased in size and scale, with taller buildings covering larger areas, including entire blocks.

- Newer buildings can maintain a pedestrian scale through window openings, ornamentation, cornice lines, signage, awnings and canopies, and articulated wall surfaces that are sized to be proportional to the human body.
- Avoid uninviting and unattractive blank walls on the ground floor of street frontages. Commercial and office building frontages should feature display windows and entries.
- High-quality materials and architectural ornamentation at the street level of buildings accent buildings and provide visual interest.
- If the form and mass of existing buildings are rectangular, avoid adding curving, undulating or diagonal building forms.

Building Styles

Downtowns usually have buildings representing several historical periods and many different architectural styles. New buildings don't need to replicate one specific architectural style, if the overall design objective of creating an urban,

pedestrian-friendly setting is met. Buildings should draw on the materials and details reminiscent of the styles that are already present in order to support continuity in downtown architecture. Evaluating site context, architectural styles and the character of adjacent buildings can help determine the appropriate style for a new building. The architectural styles described in the table on the following page are represented in many downtowns across America.

Roof Forms

Roof shapes should reflect the urban character of a downtown. Taller buildings also contribute to an attractive and interesting skyline. While flat roofs with parapets are typical of urban commercial buildings, some buildings have unique elements such as towers, spires and special cornice designs.

- Special roof shapes on corner locations can help accent corners of blocks.
- Articulated and varied roof shapes on taller office and residential towers add interest and serve as reference points. Stepped building setbacks, unique rooftops and varying building materials also contribute to light penetration and interest.
- Pitched roofs, especially on one-story buildings are more typically suburban

styles and not appropriate for downtowns. Other inappropriate roofs may include slope shapes on one-story buildings, gable-end, single pitch (shed), false mansard and curving roofs.

TRANSPORTATION AND CIRCULATION

Streets

A major difference between urban and suburban streets is the quality of the pedestrian environment. Downtown streets should accommodate the movement of people and goods by all modes of travel (foot, car, bus, bicycle and light rail); provide orientation, safety and comfort; encourage a sense of community and place; foster a sense of neighborly ownership and responsibility; avoid disturbing nuisances; and enhance the economic value of adjacent properties. Urban streets should also be designed to support social interaction and enhance the pedestrian experience between buildings and travel lanes. They should be well-landscaped corridors for both vehicles and pedestrians.

Pedestrian-Oriented Streets

These streets encourage walking and shopping at the street level and provide pedestrian connections within the

BUILDING STYLES: Commercial Buildings & Warehouses

Revival

From the early 1800s to the early 1900s, buildings are typically of brick, stucco or stone in a style recalling the past. Among the major styles are: Greek Revival (bold, simple moldings, symmetrical windows, low-pitched roofs, heavy cornices, columns and wide friezes); Gothic Revival (arched windows, steep rooftops and decorative ornamentation reminiscent of medieval times); Second Empire (simple, symmetrical blocks, heavy window molds, bays); and Italianate (flat roofs, corniced eaves, Corinthian columns and pilasters). By the late 1800s and early 1900s, styles include Queen Anne (balconies, projecting bays, terra cotta patterned brickwork, stone, corner turrets, towers, dormers); Richardsonian Romanesque (monochromatic, red brick and terra cotta, rusticated stone, horizontal lines, classical decorative features); and Neoclassicism (Beaux Arts styles) which again revives Greek, Roman and classical styles.

Kansas City Union Station, Missouri

Chicago School

The development of steel-frame construction heralds the first skyscrapers. Louis Sullivan's Carson, Pirie, Scott and Company Building in Chicago exemplifies the principles of combining form with function. Modular construction is openly expressed in the upper stories while intricate ornament, in terra cotta, animates the lower exterior.

Carson, Pirie, Scott and Company Building, Chicago, Illinois

Art Deco/Art Moderne

The 1925 *Exposition Internationale des Arts Decoratifs and Industriels Modernes* in Paris marks the onset of Art Deco/Art Moderne. These twin, progressive movements anticipate the future but also revive the past: Art Deco is notable for its revivals of Egyptian and Mayan motifs; Art Moderne incorporates Bauhaus and other modern styles and anticipates the International Style. Both the Machine Age and the Jazz Age show their influences in such building details as rounded corners and zigzags. Building decoration consists mainly of low-relief geometric designs, often in vivid colors in the form of straight lines, zigzags, chevrons and stylized floral motifs. Materials include tiles, terra cotta and glass.

Department store, Pasadena, California

International Style

Modern structural principles and materials such as concrete, glass and steel drive the International Style. Nonessential decoration is eliminated and the skeleton frame of construction is revealed. Ribbon windows are a hallmark, as are corner windows. Highrise buildings are designed as one large office placed on top of another. By the late 1960s the International Style evolves into a style of economic efficiency and functionality. Built almost strictly of glass and steel, buildings are devoid of all ornamentation, usually in the form of a simple box with ribbon windows.

Office building, Los Angeles, California

Postmodern

From the late 1970s through the present, Postmodernism emerged in American architecture as a reaction to International Style's lack of ornamentation. Postmodernist buildings use an eclectic array of details from historical architectural periods. Oversize design elements from the past are quoted, and columns, cornices and oversized parapets become common features. While the façades are often ornate, the interiors remain simply large floor plates.

Tourist-oriented businesses along International Drive, Orlando, Florida

ALL PHOTOS THIS PAGE:
THOMAS W. PARADIS

| 1800 | 1900 | 1925 | 1950 | 1975 |

Figure 60. Bulb-outs at corners slow traffic and help pedestrians cross streets safely. Decorative crosswalks extend the sidewalk experience into the street.

downtown and surrounding neighborhoods. They are typically two-way streets with wide, well-maintained sidewalks and pedestrian amenities. Traffic should flow slowly.

■ Bulb-outs at corners slow traffic and encourage safe pedestrian street crossing.

■ Enhance street activity by creating "active street edges" with windows and entrances opening onto the street, outdoor retail activity, street cafés and restaurants.

■ Invite pedestrians to pause by providing street furniture such as fountains, benches and art.

■ Use decorative crosswalks to extend the sidewalk experience into the street.

■ Streets can be made into "places" through strong spatial definition and distinctive design. To maintain a human scale, street width should be sized in proportion to the height of buildings—wider streets with taller buildings and narrower streets with smaller buildings.

■ Improve interface between buildings and sidewalks with awnings and outdoor displays.

Pedestrian and Vehicle Streets

These streets are boulevards and avenues that move both pedestrians and vehicles into and around downtown. They can also provide major pedestrian connections to surrounding neighborhoods, districts, parks and open space.

■ Create an appropriate width of sidewalk and buffering from traffic. A continuous row of trees close to the edge of the sidewalk offers a sense of safety and comfort to pedestrians.

■ Provide convenient connections to public transit.

■ Orient land uses to the street to increase pedestrian activities and create visually interesting sites for car users.

Vehicle-Oriented Boulevards

Designed to move vehicles through the downtown, these streets should nevertheless project a distinctive urban character. They provide vehicle connections to parking and adjoining uses. They can also be improved with street trees and landscaping.

■ Simplify street circulation and access and improve traffic flow by consolidating driveways and parking entries whenever possible and by using shared entry and exit points.

■ Reduce the number of signs on buildings and the site, creating a more attractive and consistent image along the boulevard; reduce clutter.

■ Install landscaping and trees along side-walks—between the on-street parking and moving lanes and the building edge—to help define the pedestrian zone and create a safer pedestrian walkway along the boulevard.

■ Use attractive street lighting and pedestrian amenities along the street (such as benches, trash cans, news-paper boxes, etc.) with a similar design to create a coherent and consistent character.

Pedestrian Circulation

Pedestrians need the same type of continuous travel corridors linking major destinations as do vehicles. Good pedestrian circulation serves local land uses by providing access to commercial and residential buildings, transit and transit facilities, open space and public outdoor activity space. The system requires attention to safety, as well as comfort and ease of access. Adjacent buildings also form the pedestrian environment, so providing strong spatial definition through building fronts and tree canopies adds to a distinct urban character and helps create a "sense of place" that also enhances property values.

■ Divide sidewalks into functional zones. The minimum sidewalk width should

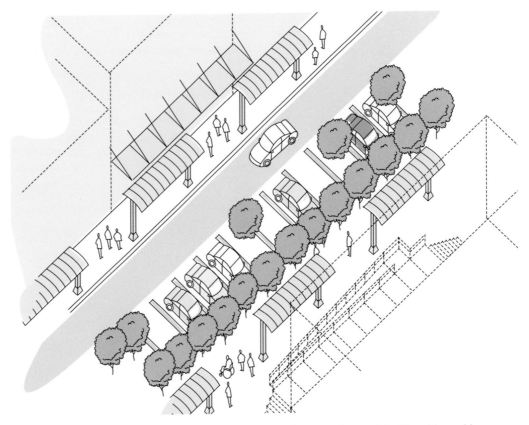

Figure 61. Pedestrian-oriented streets can accomodate one lane of traffic with parking areas that can be used for outdoor events on the weekends and evenings, such as farmers markets and community festivals.

be 12'. Widths of 15'–20' along major commercial streets are preferred so two people walking together can pass others without making abrupt changes in direction. Wider sidewalks can accommodate intensive pedestrian traffic along with retail uses. For example, areas of the sidewalk should accommodate persons walking, win-dow shopping, bicycle parking and street furniture, as well as outdoor eat-ing and displays.

■ Mid-block pedestrian crosswalks can be added where blocks are too long to reasonably expect pedestrians to use corner sidewalks. They should only be added where traffic speed and sight lines allow for safe crossings.

■ Decorative paving treatments can help separate the pedestrian zone from the street travelways at inter-section crossings.

- Wherever possible, new projects and renovations of existing sites should close the gaps between pedestrian connections by providing sidewalk improvements along major arterial streets.

- Bulb-outs at street corners help reduce pedestrian travel time and increase safety. They also provide additional space for street furniture, landscaping and signage.

- Street furniture, utility poles, trees and signage should be positioned to not obstruct movement from a street parking space to a building entry or prevent car doors from opening at the sidewalk edge.

- In general, sidewalks and bikeways should be separate unless they are designed as a multi-use path separated from the street.

- Create universal access pathways on both sides of the street, at least 5' wide. Provide a 2'3" wide detectable warning strip of yellow truncated domes between the ADA pathway and the rest of the roadway and before all street crosswalks and mid-block crossings.

In some historic districts, there may be no sidewalks. The pedestrian pathway then needs to be clearly marked so bicyclists and vehicles remain separated. Pathways should be a minimum of 15' to 20' wide.

On-Street Parking

On-street parking helps create an active street life, offering additional parking and access to commercial and residential uses and a buffer zone between the pedestrian sidewalk and travel lanes in the street. It also decreases the capacity of adjacent travel lanes by up to 30 percent, depending on the number and width of travel lanes and the frequency of parking.

- Through traffic and local access requirements should be balanced when deciding where to provide on-street parking.

- On slower, pedestrian-oriented streets, angled on-street parking can increase the number of parking spaces while maintaining a functional level of vehicle circulation. On major arterials, parallel parking will likely work better.

- On-street parking areas on pedestrian-oriented streets can also serve as outdoor eating and retail display areas during special events or special evening hours.

- Entire pedestrian-oriented streets can be blocked off to vehicles for special events, such as farmers markets or street fairs.

Bicycles

Bicyclists also need continuous travel corridors providing connections to major commercial and residential destinations, transit, open space and parks. Bicycle circulation can be provided through bike lanes and bike paths. A lane is a portion of a roadway designated for exclusive or preferential bicycle use. A path is generally separated from the roadway and may be shared with pedestrians.

- Provide secure bicycle parking on development sites and at transit stops. Bicycle parking can also be on sidewalks or on the street instead of auto parking.

- Bike lanes should be well-signed and well-maintained. Pavement conditions should ensure a smooth, clean travelway by eliminating height differences between gutter pans and asphalt and between driveway curb cuts and the travel lane.

- Bike lanes should be one-way in the same direction of travel as vehicles. One-way streets can allow for opposite direction lanes separated from vehicle traffic by a barrier or other separation.

- Bike lanes should avoid streets with diagonal parking.

Gateways

Gateways tell visitors they have entered the downtown. They serve as landmarks and should be visible to vehicular, bicycle and pedestrian traffic. They should be designed to create a high-quality visual experience; they can provide an opportunity for architectural features, monuments, public art, signage and landscaping.

- Gateways should be located at major access routes.
- Signage should be civic; no commercial or tenant names should be printed.
- Illuminate gateways at night and ensure that they are visible to passing vehicles.

LANDSCAPING

Street Trees

Street trees are one of the least expensive ways to create a more pedestrian-oriented street. Trees also improve air quality, reduce water runoff and improve property values. A continuous canopy of trees defines the pedestrian space along sidewalks, provides shade and generally improves a street's appearance.

- Select urban street trees carefully according to geography and climate.
- Provide large, wide canopy trees about 10'–25' apart along the street.
- Provide adequate growing conditions.
- Select trees that are easy to maintain, with roots that minimize sidewalk damage.
- Consider using structural soil. Designed to be load-bearing for use under pavements, structural soil allows deep root penetration.
- Prune trees to maintain a clear space between the lower branches and the sidewalk to provide clear views of building signage, maintain street-level displays and activities and provide accessible routes.
- Use special treatments such as a double row of trees to differentiate areas of emphasis.

Landscape Elements

Planters, shrubs, ground cover and water elements create soft, colorful pedestrian settings that contrast with the hard physical elements of an urban environment.

- Select plant materials with low water consumption to lower costs.
- Use relatively high-maintenance annuals and perennials selectively and only as landscape accents.

Hardscape Elements

Well-designed and lighted pedestrian kiosks, benches, bus shelters, newspaper racks, trash cans and café tables increase opportunities for people to socialize and spend time outdoors along public streets. However, large front lawns and landscaped front setbacks are not in keeping with a high-intensity urban character.

- Consider adding small entry plazas, seating alcove areas and other pedestrian amenities in the design of buildings.
- Fit the pattern and texture of ground paving materials into the existing context.
- Ensure that hardscape materials are high-quality, functional and able to endure weather conditions and vandals.
- Provide public art such as wall murals and sculptures where appropriate. These elements can also serve as interpretive elements that describe the history of the area.

GATHERING SPACES

Public gathering spaces add to the social quality of the downtown. Parks, plazas and promenades can preserve historic character and increase the amount of usable open space.

Pocket Parks / Plazas

Pocket parks and plazas provide a valuable gathering and relaxing area for residents and visitors, and some respite to the continuous built environment. Each park should have a distinct identity, compatible with the character of the surrounding neighborhoods.

- Replace asphalt or concrete with decorative paving.
- Add shrubs and flowering plants to enhance visual appeal.
- Add trees along edges for shade and a sense of enclosure.
- Provide a grove of trees along one edge that will serve as an identifying vertical marker.
- Provide seating and recreational amenities.
- Maintain existing entries to buildings from the park.
- Consider the use of water features to enhance serenity.

Figure 62. Pocket parks between buildings provide valuable gathering areas and respite from the continuous built environment.

Public Promenades

Promenades provide a unique, flexible open space that can be used for multiple purposes. They can provide a spillover space for adjacent cafés and restaurants, on-street parking during office hours, an exhibition area for public art, open space for farmers markets and other neighborhood events.

- Replace asphalt with decorative paving.
- Provide a 15'–20' wide single, slow moving auto travel lane.
- Provide an 8' ADA accessible pathway along one edge of the street and create angled parking (30–90 degrees) on the other side.
- Provide a double row of trees in the middle of the right of way for shade.
- Include shade trellis canopies, seating and complementary directional signage.

Transit Plazas

Light rail stations and key bus transfer points can be important neighborhood activity areas. A well-articulated transit plaza around the station can enhance civic character and sense of place.

- Provide additional amenities to transit users, including shade structures that provide weather protection, better seating and rows of trees. The hardscape elements should continue the character of the streetscape elements in the area.
- Plant double rows of trees to provide a sense of enclosure.
- Integrate an open space plaza with any adjacent alleys by using the same paving material and pattern.
- Ensure that all building edges fronting the plaza help activate the plaza.
- Improve wayfinding strategies with maps that highlight key activity nodes around the station and tell the story of the area.
- Activate plazas with temporary food facilities or stalls.
- Activate plazas with cafés, convenience stores, small retail stores and commercial space with well-articulated, pedestrian-friendly storefronts and display windows.

SIGNAGE

Building Identification Signs

Signs should be designed as an integral part of the project site and building architecture. Merchants can create their own unique signs that represent their businesses. Attractive, artistic and well-coordinated signage creates an identity and a positive shopping experience.

- Place signs in relation to building elements and avoid obscuring windows, cornices or decorative details.
- Ensure that sign materials complement building façades and relate to other shop signs in a single storefront in design, size, color, lettering style and placement. Chain stores may need to adapt their graphics to meet local guidelines.
- Maintain a minimum clearance above the public right-of-way for signs that project from a building.
- Firmly anchor signs that project from the building to the building façade with attractive, non-corrosive hardware.
- Use darker letters against a lighter background.
- Avoid signs that protrude above rooflines, eaves or parapets—they can detract from the architectural quality of the building.

Flush-Mounted Signs

Flush-mounted signs are signboards or individual die-cut letters placed on the face of a building, usually in a recess or horizontal molded band on the building.

- Size signs to fit within the proportions of the building façade so they do not crown the top of a building wall or parapet.
- On a historic storefront, locate signs along a first floor cornice line, above the awning or transom windows.
- Center signs within storefront bays; avoid extending them beyond the limits of the storefront or over elements such as columns, pilasters or transoms.
- Encourage die-cut letter signs made from materials consistent with the downtown and mounted directly on the building.

Hanging or "Blade" Signs

Hanging signs mounted on the building, perpendicular to the sidewalk are effective because they are near pedestrian eye level.

- Maintain a minimum clearance above the sidewalk.

Window Signs

- Ensure that window signs do not exceed 20 percent of the total window area.
- Use high-quality materials such as paint or gold leaf, or etch into glass.

Icon or Graphic Signs

- Use icons to illustrate the nature of the business. They are creative, easy to read and well suited to pedestrian and vehicular traffic.
- Provide graphic imagery with attractive and informative text.

Lighted Signs

- For internally lit signs, use black or dark colored backgrounds with light lettering to make distant reading easier.
- Contain light within the frame of externally lit signs to accentuate the message and reduce glare and light pollution.
- Orient and shield spotlights so the light source is not visible, focusing attention on the sign and thus preventing light pollution.

Neon and Bare Bulb Signs

- Consider use of neon and bare bulb signs in entertainment areas such as restaurants, dance clubs and bars.

- Use pictorial images related to the business.

Awning Signs

Painting signs on the valence of an awning is an inexpensive and simple signage method that can be distinctive.

- Limit text on awnings to no more than 10 square feet to maintain legibility.
- Limit signage on a sloping surface to small graphic symbols or logos to prevent the information from becoming too cluttered.

Directional Signage for Parking Lots

- Limit directional signs marking entries and exits to no more than one commercial image, logo or message. These signs should be subservient to text identifying "customer parking."
- Limit each driveway to no more than one directional sign near sidewalks.

Banner Signs

Temporary banner signs for special events add color and create a festive atmosphere.

- Attach signs to light standards or project them from building façades.

- Locate banners at least 8' from grade or within 1' of the edge of the curb when projected vertically.
- Remove signs after the event, or when they show signs of fading or wear.

Inappropriate Signs

While every downtown will be different, there are some types of signs that are generally not appropriate for a pedestrian-friendly urban environment.

- Building signs that advertise products and vendors rather than businesses and services
- Flashing, animated, blinking, fluorescent, rotating, reflecting and revolving signs
- Changeable copy signs, other than on a movie marquee
- Chalkboards or blackboards, other than for a restaurant or café
- Portable signs, such as A-frame types.
- Freestanding commercial signs, such as for parking
- Off-site and general advertising signs and billboards
- Advertising on the sloping surface of an awning, other than graphic symbols or logos
- Signs on vacant or closed buildings, other than real estate notices

- Temporary signs and promotional decorations, other than seasonal (which should be removed promptly)
- Signs on privately owned benches
- Private signs on public property

DESIGN DETAILS

Awnings and Canopies

Canopies, arcades, awnings and overhangs provide shade and weather protection and enhance the street level pedestrian environment. They also help articulate building façades, creating variety and interest. They come in many shapes, styles and colors. In general, they should fit in with the historic character of the building and be well maintained.

- Locate these elements over window displays and entries to fit within individual bays rather than extending beyond a single bay to enhance architectural styles. Poorly placed awnings can cover historical ornaments and transoms.
- Use retractable awnings in darker areas or north-facing façades of historical storefronts.
- While a variety of brightly colored and striped awnings are available, remember that canvas will fade over time. Uncolored or light canvas in darker areas allows daylight to filter through.

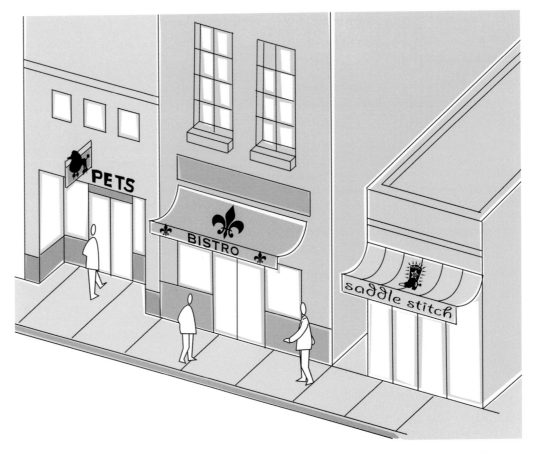

Figure 63. Awnings should be of high-quality material with short identifying text and logos.

- Second-floor and upper-floor awnings that complement the ground floor create a consistent design image for the building.
- Use glass canopies, especially in darker areas.
- Limit use of vinyl, plastic and aluminum. These materials look flimsy and out of place. Fixed awnings or canopies that simulate mansard roof shapes often detract from the urban design vocabulary.

Use of Color

Color is a sensitive subject in guidelines. Using only pre-approved colors can lead to a dull streetscape that lacks distinction and interest. In general, the principle is to be a good neighbor; coordinate with other buildings on the block.

- Ensure that color selection takes the orientation of buildings into account. Colors on south- and west-facing façades often appear warmer than colors on north and east sides due to sun exposure.

- Use subtle colors on large building surfaces to create a more pleasant street environment.

- Avoid a multitude of strong, vivid colors.

- Choose paint colors in relation to the materials used in the building design, such as brick, stone, tiles and terra cotta.

- Use contrasting accent colors for architectural details, awnings and entrances.

Building Materials

Building materials add to the overall character of the downtown, especially on the ground floor where most people come into contact with the building's edge. While structural construction materials vary, the public face and finish materials of buildings should be consistent. For example, some downtowns traditionally use brick, others use stone. Materials such as terra cotta, glass, ceramic tiles, masonry, corrugated metal and steel are also used.

- Avoid use of materials such as artificial stone, mirrored or opaque glass, untreated wood, diagonal wood, rough-sawn wood and horizontal wood siding on large building surfaces.

- Use wood and other nontraditional materials to identify special uses and activities within a building. For example, Japanese restaurants traditionally use wood and stucco materials.

- Use high-quality facing materials to add to the richness of the pedestrian experience.

- Avoid mirrored glass on the ground level (especially on pedestrian-oriented streets). It creates an unfriendly environment and limits visual access. Translucent surfaces at the street level (windows, doors and entry features) create a welcoming and safe environment.

Areas for Service, Loading and Mechanical Equipment

While service areas, loading docks, delivery areas and mechanical equipment are all necessary functional elements of a downtown, they often detract from the pedestrian experience and the visual urban environment.

- Give functional areas the same design attention as more public spaces. The materials and finishes do not need to be the highest quality, but elements should be carefully placed and screened to reduce visual blight.

- Whenever possible, locate loading areas to be accessible from alleyways, side streets, back parking lots and interior parking garages rather than from the front of buildings.

- Erect substantial and attractive fences or walls to screen dumpsters and mechanical equipment such as HVAC, meters, transformers, pipes and ducts.

In some downtowns, historic loading docks are no longer used as loading docks and can instead become public areas such as outdoor cafés, entry porches and small plazas.

- Use permeable railings such as metal and wire, rather than solid boundary walls, and avoid use of cyclone fences.

- Adapt loading docks with ramps, railings and markings to provide accessibility.

LIGHTING

The color, amount, intensity and types of lighting have a dramatic effect on the mood and urban character of a site, as well as on pedestrian safety.

Building Lighting

- Integrate lighting into the design of wall features and façade design. Relate building lighting to the style and character of lighting in the area.

- Match lighting with the history of the area.
- Use modern or historic styles to fit the urban character and image of the downtown.
- Maintain the same type, color and family of fixture styles for all lamps used in both building and parking areas.
- Use special lighting for building features, entries, building towers and architectural ornaments or pilasters.
- Light pedestrian areas with pole or bollard type fixtures (typically not more than 16' high or 3' for bollards) in scale with pedestrians.
- Ensure lighting fixtures do not produce excessive glare or trespass into residential areas. On-site lighting should be designed, installed and maintained to direct light onto the property.
- Attach appropriate shields on street lighting fixtures to minimize glare and night sky pollution.
- Use a minimum of different types of lamps and fixtures to reduce maintenance costs and provide a consistent character to a site. Double-head fixtures can illuminate both sidewalks and travel lanes.
- Use building-mounted downlights to illuminate building service areas without causing glare and spillover.

- Illuminate building entries and other areas with high levels of pedestrian activity. Allow interior light to illuminate through glass entry façades and display windows.
- Use neon and other specialized lighting to enhance downtown commercial streets, restaurants and entertainment venues.
- Use decorative up-lighting to enhance landscape features and building architecture as long as it does not compete with street lighting.
- Use specialty lighting in trees particularly in outdoor patio areas to create a lively and festive setting.

Street Lighting

- Maintain a consistent appearance of all decorative street lighting fixtures, street poles and bases.
- Use modern or historic styles to fit the urban character and image of the downtown.
- Design special styles of fixtures and poles to mark special streets.
- Ensure that fixtures provide light for both pedestrians and vehicles.
- Place light standards symmetrically along opposite sides of a street to produce a pleasing, well-lit street.
- Add midblock lighting to enhance illumination on long streets.

ALTERATIONS AND NEW ADDITIONS

Changes to existing buildings are part of the evolution of a downtown. New additions and alterations should respect the original period and style of the building. But creating a false original can lessen the impact of true historical buildings. All additions do not need to replicate the historic original, especially if the original building is of marginal historic value.

- Encourage restoration of original building façades.
- Preserve historic materials and features.
- Avoid additions to historic building façades.
- Use building finishes on new additions that are similar in material, quality, color and dimension to those used on existing structures.
- Make the scale of additions compatible with the original building.

REFERENCES

The Americans with Disabilities Act Accessibility Guidelines Tech Sheet Series (1994–95), by Ron Mace (Raleigh, NC: Barrier Free Environments).

A Case Study Method for Landscape Architecture, by Mark Francis (*Landscape Journal 19,* 2: 15–29), 2001.

Childhood's Domain: Play and Place in Child Development, by Robin C. Moore (Berkeley: MIG Communications), 1990.

The City in History: Its Origins, Its Transformations, and Its Prospects, by Lewis Mumford, (New York: Harcourt, Brace & World) 1961.

The Death and Life of Great American Cities, by Jane Jacobs (New York: Modern Library), 1993.

Great Streets, by Alan Jacobs (Cambridge, MA: MIT Press), 2003.

Housing As If People Mattered: Site Design Guidelines for Medium-Density Family Housing, by Clare Cooper Marcus with Wendy Sarkissian (Berkeley: University of California Press, Reprint Edition), 1988.

Livable Streets, by Donald Appleyard, (Berkeley: University of California Press), 1981.

Natural Learning: The Life History of an Environmental Schoolyard, by Robin C. Moore and Herb H. Wong (Berkeley: MIG Communications), 1997.

People Places: Design Guidelines for Urban Open Space, by Clare Cooper Marcus with Carolyn Francis (eds.) (Hoboken, NJ: John Wiley & Sons, Second Revised Edition), 1998.

Play for All Guidelines: Planning, Design and Management of Outdoor Play Settings for All Children, edited by Robin C. Moore, Susan M. Goltsman and Daniel S. Iacofano (Berkeley: MIG Communications, Second Edition), 1992.

The Social Life of Small Urban Spaces, by William H. Whyte (Washington, D.C.: The Conservation Foundation), 1980.

A Theory of Good City Form, by Kevin Lynch (Cambridge, MA: MIT Press), 1981.

Universal Access to Outdoor Recreation: A Design Guide, by PLAE, Inc., in conjunction with other public and private partners (Berkeley: MIG Communications), 1993.

Urban Open Space, by Mark Francis (Washington, D.C.: Island Press), 2003.

CONTRIBUTORS

SUSAN M. GOLTSMAN, FASLA

Susan is a founding principal of Moore, Iacofano, Goltsman (MIG), Inc., who specializes in planning and designing environments for children, youth and families, as well as community outreach and education. Her projects range from schools and community parks to zoos and museums. She applies social science to design, creating environments that respond to the community organization, user needs, the functions of the facility and the context. Susan has served on regulatory committees of the U.S. Architectural and Transportation Barriers Compliance Board (ATBCB), developing accessibility guidelines for recreation and outdoor environments. She also served on national committees to adapt the Uniform Federal Accessibility Standards to children's environments and create guidelines for play areas. She has taught at Stanford University and served as an advisor to UC Davis, UC Berkeley Extension, San Francisco State University, the San Francisco Exploratorium and the Adaptive Environments Center. Susan is the author of several books, including *Play for All Guidelines,* a groundbreaking presentation of universal design and accessibility in children's play environments. Her projects have won awards from the American Zoo and Aquarium Association, the Center for Universal Design, the American Institute of Architects, the American Planning Association, the American Society of Landscape Architects, The National Endowment for the Arts and the California Park and Recreation Society. Susan holds a Bachelor of Fine Arts from Parson's School of Design and the New School of Social Research in New York, a Master of Science in Environmental Psychology from the University of Surrey, England, and a Master of Landscape Architecture from North Carolina State University.

DANIEL IACOFANO, PhD, FAICP, ASLA

Daniel is a founding principal of MIG, and internationally recognized as an innovator in strategic planning, urban planning, transportation planning, watershed and river planning, and public participation and outreach. He has consulted with over 100 cities, agencies, educational institutions and private companies to develop strategic plans and has led hundreds of successful urban planning and design programs with communities, business leaders and staff to support land use, urban design, economic revitalization and transportation projects. Daniel is a highly skilled facilitator and consensus builder and is often asked to lead difficult and complex negotiations involving major planning and development projects. His publications include *Play For All Guidelines, Public Involvement as an Organizational Development Process* and *Meeting of the Minds,* which shares his innovative approach to meeting facilitation. His projects have won many awards from professional associations and organizations, including the National League of Cities, the International Downtown Association, the American Planning Association, the American Society of Landscape Architects and the Association of Environmental Professionals. Daniel received a Bachelor of Urban Planning from the University of Cincinnati, a Master of Science in Environmental Psychology from the University of Surrey, England, and a PhD in Environmental Planning from the University of California, Berkeley.

ANDREW ALTMAN

Andy is the former Chief Executive Officer of the Anacostia Waterfront Corporation, a public/private partnership to help plan the future of this Washington, D.C., area. Previously, he was the Director of the Washington, D.C., Office of Planning, which based a complete revision of the city's comprehensive plan on a new vision, called "A Vision for Growing an Inclusive City." Andy served as the Director of City Planning for the City of Oakland, California, and the plan he developed there received the California Chapter American Planning Association Award for Best Comprehensive Plan. He was previously the special assistant to the administrator of the Community Redevelopment Agency in Los Angeles and a special assistant to Los Angeles Mayor Tom Bradley. He has been awarded various fellowships, including the Loeb Fellowship of the Harvard University Graduate School of Design, and has served at the Massachusetts Institute of Technology as a visiting lecturer on city planning. He is currently with Lubert-Adler in New York City. Andy holds a Master Degree in City Planning from MIT and a Bachelor of Arts in Geography from Temple University.

ROSEMARY DUDLEY

Rosemary brings together the skills and perspectives of an urban designer, analyst and community builder. She began her career with an Albuquerque-based design-build firm. Her experience in domestic and international sustainable community planning and revitalizing urban neighborhoods led to work in economic revitalization, historic preservation, environmental restoration and transit-oriented development. Rosemary has worked on planning projects for the cities of

Denver, Anchorage and Spokane, and for the American River in Sacramento. Rosemary received a Bachelor of Arts in Architecture from the University of California at Berkeley and a Masters of City Planning from the Massachusetts Institute of Technology.

STANTON JONES

Stan is head of the Department of Landscape Architecture at the University of Oregon, specializing in landscape technologies, urban and community design, and design studios. His focus is equity and justice within the urban environment—how public spaces and management processes can be configured to increase "meaningfulness" and sense of ownership in an inequitably served, multicultural society. Stan received a B.S. degree from the University of Miami, Ohio, a B.S. in Landscape Architecture from the University of California, Davis, and dual Masters in Landscape Architecture and City Planning from the University of California, Berkeley.

JOAN LEON

Joan has a long history of involvement with the Independent Living Movement and is currently Director of Financing for the Ed Roberts Campus. Joan previously served as president of the World Institute of Disability, which she co-founded with Ed Roberts and Judy Heumann. From 1977 to 1983 Joan was the Assistant Director of the California Department of Rehabilitation and prior to that she was Assistant to the Director for the Center for Independent Living. She has also worked as a journalist and editor. In 1995, Joan co-chaired the group of community leaders that developed the concept of the Ed Roberts Campus, becoming Finance Director in 1997.

MUKUL MALHOTRA

Mukul's professional emphasis in the U.S. is designing livable communities through innovative land use planning and pedestrian-friendly streetscapes. He was a senior architect in New Delhi, India, managing the design processes for institutional and industrial buildings. He received awards in the National Architectural Competition for the design of the Shri Shirdi Saibaba Mandir Complex Development in Bombay and in the Low-Cost Housing Design Ideas

Competition in New Delhi. Mukul received a diploma in Architecture from the Sushant School of Art and Architecture in Gurgaon, India, and a Master of Urban Design from the University of California, Berkeley.

SALLY McINTYRE

Sally is director of Parks and Recreation Planning for MIG and a principal of the firm. She focuses on parks and recreation master plans, recreation programming, facility design, strategic planning and communications. Her extensive experience emphasizes involving diverse community members in creating livable neighborhoods, from seniors to children to people with disabilities. Sally co-authored the Vision Insight Planning (VIP) for the California Parks and Recreation Society, a groundbreaking strategic plan for the advancement of the parks and recreation profession. Her work on open space issues involves creating design guidelines and open space system standards for high-density neighborhoods, specific area plans and regional plans. Sally received a Bachelor of Arts degree from San Francisco State University in 1982.

SUSAN McKAY

Susan's practice focuses on collaborative design and planning efforts for school site and park design with an emphasis on incorporating art into public projects. She has broad experience in landscape architecture, leading projects through conceptual design to implementation. While at The Architects Collaborative, Inc., she was the project designer for many projects, including the Bechtel Building Poetry Garden in San Francisco. She received a BA degree in Art from the University of California, Berkeley and is a licensed landscape architect.

ROBIN MOORE

Robin is a founding principal of MIG and an internationally recognized authority on the ecological design of children's play and learning environments, participatory design programming, and user needs in public open space design. He is professor of Landscape Architecture, College of Design at North Carolina State University, Raleigh. Robin has consulted extensively worldwide, serving as a consultant on urban parks for the Chilean government and directing the Argentine segment of the UNESCO study: *Growing Up in Cities*. He has won numerous awards for his contributions to the field of design and has written many books on the topic, including *Natural Learning*, *Plants for Play*, *Childhood's Domain: Play and Place in Child Development* and *Play for All Guidelines*. He was chair of the Environmental Design Research Association and president of the International Association for the Child's Right to Play. Robin holds degrees in architecture from London University and in city and regional planning from the Massachusetts Institute of Technology.

BART NEY

Bart specializes in community participation in transportation and infrastructure planning. As MIG's Public Information Officer, he directed the California Department of Transportation (Caltrans) public outreach program for the Alfred Zampa (Carquinez) Bridge and for the reconstruction of the San Francisco Bay Bridge, connecting the East Bay and San Francisco. Bart received a BS degree in Urban Planning and Real Estate Development from the University of Southern California.

COCO RAYNES

Coco is an internationally known expert in environmental graphics, architectural and industrial design and universal design. Her firm, Coco Raynes Associates, Inc., produces programs for public spaces, airports, universities, hospitals, transportation facilities, parks, museums, hotels, restaurants and visitor centers. The firm's unique accessibility solutions include tactile maps on glass and the Raynes Rail, a Braille and multilingual audio handrail system. Coco's work has been honored by the Industrial Designers Society of America, the Society for Environmental Graphic Design, the United States Access Board, the Art Directors Club of Boston and the American Institute of Graphic Arts.

CHERYL SULLIVAN

Cheryl's work often emphasizes using plants and natural formations to engage the user with surrounding spaces. Her landscape architecture and land planning experience includes urban design and streetscapes, park and bikeway master plans, commercial and residential developments, and riparian systems. Cheryl's award-winning projects include Central Park in Davis, California, and the Putah Creek Corridor Conceptual Master Plan. Cheryl received a degree in Landscape Architecture from the University of California, Davis. One of her first projects was the Davis Central Park.

LAWRENCE WIGHT, ASLA

Larry creates outdoor environments for people of all abilities, from recreation facility assessment, trails and open space planning, to design guidelines and detailed design of award-winning children's play and learning environments. His experience includes natural resource assessment, National Historic Landmark issues, environmental planning studies and impact analysis, and watershed management. Larry received a Bachelor of Landscape Architecture from the University of Oregon and a Master of Landscape Architecture from the University of California, Berkeley. He is MIG's Director of Design and a past president of the Northern California Chapter of the American Society of Landscape Architects.

INDEX

Note: Illustrations are indicated by boldface type.

access, 11, 22–23, 24, 25
  See also accessibility issues; transit-oriented
    development; transportation
accessibility issues
  autistic access, 147
  bridges, 305, 306, 311
  children's zoos, 147, 414, 415–16
  downtowns, 63, 222, 224, 247, 267, 464
  mixed-use facilities, 63, 64, **68, 71,** 179,
    184, 185, 186–87
  museums, 411–12
  parks, 159, 164, 165, 166
  play areas, 418, 419, **420, 421,** 422
  plazas, 423
  regional open spaces, **283, 284,** 285, 287,
    293, 375
  school exteriors, 30, 399, 400, 409–10
  school interiors, 399, 405, **407,** 408, 409
  special schools, 82, 92–93
  trail systems, 425, 426, 427, 431–33
  visually impaired, 98–99, 100, **101,** 102,
    103, 106–7
  See also inclusive design project guidelines;
    specific projects by name
acoustics, 398
activity areas
  dependency courts, 394–95
  Hamill Family Play Zoo and Play Gardens,
    130–47
  landscaping, 420

St. Coletta of Greater Washington, D.C.,
  82–83, 86–93
Tule Elk Park Child Development Center,
  62, 63, 64, 68–72
See also Chase Palm Park; gathering places;
  play area guidelines
ADA (Americans with Disabilities Act),
  98–99, 123–24
See also accessibility issues
ADA Accessibility Guidelines, 425
adventure play. *See* Hamill Family Play Zoo
  and Play Gardens
affordable housing. *See* housing
Alfred Zampa Bridge. *See* Carquinez Bridge
  Retrofit and Replacement
Altman, Andrew, xii–xv, 474
American Association of State Highway and
  Transportation Officials (AASHTO),
  427
Americans with Disabilities Act (ADA),
  98–99, 123–24
See also accessibility issues
Anacostia Waterfront, 10
animal habitats, 421
art
  Carquinez Bridge Retrofit and
    Replacement, **306,** 308–9
  Chase Palm Park, **163,** 169–70
  Davis Central Park, 204–5
  Ed Roberts Campus (ERC), 30
  Edelman Children's Court, **46**
  Edison School/Pacific Park, **181,** 187, **188,**
    191

events, 367
galleries, **364**
Musées des Beaux Arts (Valenciennes and
  Calais, France), 96–109
R Street Corridor, 259–60, **261**
St. Coletta of Greater Washington, D.C.,
  83–84, 88
Tule Elk Park Child Development Center,
  64, 70, 72, **73**
Art Deco (building style), 459
Art Moderne (building style), 459
Art Walk Sector (Sacramento, California
  R Street Corridor), 258–61
assembly areas (schools), 408
audio commentary, 99, 102–3
auditoriums, 408
autism, 147
automobiles. *See* cars
awning signs, 466
awnings, 467–468

Backyard, 145–47
banner signs, 466
barriers, 409
BART (Bay Area Rapid Transit), 21–22,
  29–30
Bay Area. *See* Berkeley, California; Carquinez
  Bridge Retrofit and Replacement; Ed
  Roberts Campus (ERC); Emeryville,
  California; Oakland, California; Presidio
  Trails and Bikeways Master Plan; San
  Jose, California; Tule Elk Park Child
  Development Center

Bay Area Economics, 230

Bay Area Outreach & Research Program (BORP), 19

Bay Area Rapid Transit (BART), 21, 22, 29–30

Beach Access Routes, 430

Beaux Arts (building style), 459

Berkeley, California, 15, 23, 26, **238, 243, 260**

bicycles
    Carquinez Bridge Retrofit and Replacement, 305–6, **308**
    Davis Commons, **217,** 218, 223–24
    Ed Roberts Campus (ERC), 29, 30
    lane markings, 428
    parking, 423–24
    plazas, 423–24
    Presidio Trails and Bikeways Master Plan, 277, **278, 279,** 280–81, 288
    R Street Corridor, 229–30
    safety measures, 427–28
    Spokane Plan for a New Downtown, 345
    urban environments, 462
    See also shared roadway concept

bikeways, 427–28

blind people. *See* accessibility issues; Ed Roberts Campus (ERC); Musées des Beaux Arts (Valenciennes and Calais, France)

boardwalks, 432, 433

BORP (Bay Area Outreach & Research Program), 19

boulevards, 460–61
    See also cars; pedestrian issues; streets; traffic

Braille, 98–99, 102, 103
    See also accessibility issues; signage; wayfinding

bridges. *See* Carquinez Bridge Retrofit and Replacement; Monroe Street Bridge (Spokane, Washington)

Brookfield, Illinois. *See* Hamill Family Play Zoo and Play Gardens

Brookfield Zoo. *See* Hamill Family Play Zoo and Play Gardens

Brookfield Zoo Southeast Section Planning Team (SES), 118–19

Brossard, Alan, 62, 65, 75

brownfield remediation, 246

buildings
    construction materials, 468
    contextual fit, 456–57
    design elements, 456–58
    edges, 454
    exteriors, 388–89
    form, 457–58
    heights, 455–56
    lighting for exterior, 468–69
    roof forms, 458
    signage, 465–67
    styles, 458, 459
    urban environment, 468–69
    urban styles chart, 459
    See also historic building renovation

Business Improvement District (Spokane), 325

CADA (Capitol Area Development Authority, Sacramento), 230, 235–36

cafeterias, 408–9

California Department of Rehabilitation, 17

California Department of Transportation (Caltrans). *See* Carquinez Bridge Retrofit and Replacement

Caltrans (California Department of Transportation). *See* Carquinez Bridge Retrofit and Replacement

Canada Island (Spokane), 356

canopies, 467

Capitol Area Development Authority (CADA), 230, 235–37

Carquinez Bridge Community Advisory Committee (CBCAC), 301–2

Carquinez Bridge Retrofit and Replacement, 294–311
    accessibility features, 305–6, 311
    art, 306, 308–9
    background, 295–96, 298–99
    bypasses, 305
    community outreach, 299–304, 306, **307,** 308–9, 310
    design features, 305–9
    design goals, 298–99
    design process, 299–304
    historic aspects, 309
    history, 296, 298, **304,** 310
    lighting, 306, 308, **311**
    on/off ramp alignments, 305
    opening celebration, 304, **310, 311**
    pedestrian issues, 305–6, 311
    streets, 305
    user feedback, 309–11
    user groups, 299

cars, 229–30
    See also parking; sidewalks; traffic

catalytic sites, 321, 329–32, 356

CBCAC (Carquinez Bridge Community Advisory Committee), 301–2

Center for Accessible Technology (CforAT), 19, 33

Center for Independent Living (CIL), 19

central parks, 446
    See also Davis Central Park

Central Steam Plant (Spokane), **349**

CforAT (Center for Accessible Technology), 19, 33

Chalk Art Festival (Spokane), 367

charettes, 25

   See also community participation (in design process)

Chase Palm Park, 154–71

   accessibility issues, 159, 164, 165, 166

   art, **163,** 169–70

   construction completion, 156

   construction cost, 156

   credits, 156

   design features and settings, 159–66

   design goals, 156

   design process, 158

   as event center, 156

   history, 155–56

   lighthouse, 166–67

   management issues, 168–70

   mural, **163**

   nautilus, **154, 157, 161**

   ocean pathway, 159–60

   operational issues, 168–70

   particulars, 156

   play village, 160, 161, 163, **165**

   programs and activities, 158

   shipwreck playground, **158,** 164–65

   size, 156

   starfish, 160, **162**

   theme, 156, **157,** 158, 159–60, **162, 168**

   tide pool experience, **154,** 160, **161**

   user feedback, 170–71

   user groups, 156

   water elements, 156, 159, **160, 161, 164,** 169

   whales, 159–60, **161, 168**

   wooden pole forest, 165–66, 168

   See also open space guidelines

Chicago School (building style), 459

children. *See* Chase Palm Park; children's zoo guidelines; Davis Central Park; Edelman Children's Court; Edison School/Pacific Park; play area guidelines; school

(K–12) guidelines; Tule Elk Park Child Development Center

Children's Institute International, 35

children's zoo guidelines, 413–16

   approaches, 414

   circulation and pathways, 415

   design parameters, 413

   entrances, 414

   indoor activity settings, 415–16

   indoor/outdoor relationships, 413–14

   outdoor activity settings, 415–16

   sun/shade balance aspects, 416

   wayfinding, 414–15

   See also Hamill Family Play Zoo and Play Gardens

Chronicle Building (Spokane), **348**

CIL (Center for Independent Living), 19

circulation

   children's zoos, 415

   dependency courts, 390

   pedestrian, 461–62

   plazas, 423

   schools (K–12), 400

   See also traffic

cityscape guidelines, 454–69

   design details, 467–68

   gathering spaces, 463–65

   landscaping, 463

   lighting, 468–69

   overview, 454

   signage, 465–67

   site design and layout, 454–58

   transportation and circulation, 458, 460–63

   See also Davenport District Strategic Action Plan; Downtown Spokane Zoning Ordinance & Design Guidelines; R Street Corridor; Spokane Plan for a New Downtown

classrooms, 404–8

   computers, 406

   flooring and surfaces, 405

   lighting, 405

   safety equipment, 409

   special subject area, 406–8

   visual cues, 405

   windows, 405–6

   See also Edison School/Pacific Park; school (K–12) guidelines; St. Coletta of Greater Washington, D.C.

color

   Edelman Children's Court, 47

   Edison School/Pacific Park, **190, 191**

   R Street Corridor, 266

   St. Coletta of Greater Washington, D.C., 84

   urban, 467–68

communications links (interior), 398

community centers. *See* Davenport District Strategic Action Plan; Davis Central Park; Davis Commons; Edison School/Pacific Park; Tule Elk Park Child Development Center

community parks, 443, **445**

   See also Chase Palm Park; Davis Central Park; Edison School/Pacific Park

community participation (in design process)

   Carquinez Bridge Retrofit and Replacement, 299–304

   Chase Palm Park, 158

   Davenport District Strategic Action Plan, 325–26

   Davis Central Park, 200–201

   Davis Commons, 217–18

   Ed Roberts Campus (ERC), 25–26

   Edelman Children's Court, 38–43

   Edison School/Pacific Park, 181, 184–86

   The Great Spokane River Gorge Strategic Master Plan, 326

Hamill Family Play Zoo and Play Gardens, 118–19, 121–22
Musées des Beaux Arts (Valenciennes and Calais, France), 98–100, 104–5
North Bank Development Plan, 325
Presidio Trails and Bikeways Master Plan, 283–85
R Street Corridor, 235–37
Riverfront Park Master Plan, 325
Spokane Plan for a New Downtown, 321–25
St. Coletta of Greater Washington, D.C., 78–79
Tule Elk Park Child Development Center, 67–68
Computer Technologies Program (CTP), 19
computers, 406
connectivity (downtown/neighborhood), 321
   See also housing; neighborhoods; North Bank Development Plan; Riverfront Park Master Plan; Spokane Plan for a New Downtown
context sensitivity, 6
   See also specific project examples
contextual fit (buildings), 456–57
Contra Costa County, California. *See* Carquinez Bridge Retrofit and Replacement
cooking areas (classroom), 407
corridors (exterior). *See* R Street Corridor; streets; traffic; transportation
corridors (interior), 390
courtrooms. *See* hearing rooms
courts. *See* Edelman Children's Court
courtyards, 29
creeklets, 163–64
Crockett, California. *See* Carquinez Bridge Retrofit and Replacement
CTP (Computer Technologies Program), 19
cultural meaning, 11–12

cut-away corners, 455
cyclists. *See* bicycles

Dardik, Calib, 16
Davenport District Arts Board (DDAB), 325, 366, 367, 380
Davenport District Strategic Action Plan, 360–68
   American West Bank, **367**
   art galleries, **364**
   arts events and programs, 367
   background, 338
   Davenport Hotel, **362,** 363
   design guidelines, **367**
   design process, 325–26
   Fox Theater, 363
   housing, **367**
   management issues, 379–80
   marketing and communications strategies, 367
   Met Theater, **360,** 362
   Montvale Hotel, **365**
   Odd Fellows Hall, 363
   operational issues, 379–80
   organizations, 325
   performance measures, 368
   preferred business categories, 362–63
   private investment and development, 360, 362–63
   regulations and incentives, 367–68
   restaurants and entertainment, **364**
   Spokane Transit Authority Plaza, 366
   See also cityscape guidelines
Davis, California. *See* Davis Central Park; Davis Commons
Davis Central Park, 192–209
   art, 204–5
   carousel, 205–6
   children's play areas, 205–6, 208
   collaborative nature, 200–201

   design features, 201–8
   design process, 200–201
   farmers market, **195, 196,** 197
   functions and purposes, 197–99
   garden, 206, **207**
   grove, **194,** 206
   history, 193–95
   landscaping, **194, 198, 202, 204, 206, 207**
   management issues, 208–9
   multi-use aspects, 199, 200–201
   operational issues, 208–9
   user feedback, 209
   user groups, 200
   See also cityscape guidelines; open space guidelines
Davis Commons
   accessibility features, 222, 224
   background, 211–12
   design process, 215, 217–18
   history, 211–12
   housing, 212, 217
   landscaping, **213, 215, 218,** 219–23, **225**
   management issues, 225–26
   mixed-use aspects, 212, 214, 217, 226–27
   operational issues, 225–26
   parking, 217, 218, 223, 224–25, 226
   site plan, **216,** 217
   traffic, 218, 223–24
   user feedback, 226–27
   See also cityscape guidelines
Davis Education Association, 205
DDAB (Davenport District Arts Board), 366, 367, 380, 383
decentralization, xi
defensible space, 455
Demonstration Lawn, 146
Department of Rehabilitation for the State of California, 17
dependency court guidelines, 388–98
   acoustics, 398

amenities, 397
building appearance, 389
circulation, 390
communications links, 398
corridors, 390
eating areas (public), 397
entrances, 392, 394
hearing rooms, 392–93
inclusive design guidelines, 388–98
interview rooms (family), 396
lighting, 398
lobby, 389, 390
shelter care, 393–96
ventilation, 398
See also Edelman Children's Court
design charettes, 25
See also community participation (in design process)
design guidelines. *See* design guidelines and process under each specific project name; inclusive design project guidelines
developers, 12
directional signs, 466
See also signage; wayfinding
directories, 105–106
See also wayfinding
Disability Rights Education and Defense Fund (DREDF), 19, 33
downtown/neighborhood connectivity, 321
See also R Street Corridor; Riverfront Park Master Plan; Spokane Plan for a New Downtown
Downtown Seattle Association, 8
Downtown Spokane Partnership (DSP), 322–323, 325, 340–41, 380, 381–82, 383
Downtown Spokane Ventures Association, 339

Downtown Spokane Zoning Ordinance & Design Guidelines, 322, 346
Downtown Vision Workshop, 324
Downtowns, 321, 324
See also cityscape guidelines; Davis Commons; Downtown Spokane Zoning Ordinance & Design Guidelines; R Street Corridor; Riverfront Park Master Plan; Spokane Plan for a New Downtown
drainage control, 431
DREDF (Disability Rights Education and Defense Fund, 19, 33
DSP (Downtown Spokane Partnership), 322–323, 325, 340–41, 380, 381–82, 383
Dudley, Rosemary, 474–475

Earth Play Garden, 147
East End District (Spokane), 333–34
East Havermale Island (Spokane), 355
ecological requirements, 4–5
Economic Development Council (Spokane), 338–39
economic development fundamentals, 10
Ed Roberts, 15–17, **16**
Ed Roberts Campus (ERC), 14–33
community participation, 25
design charettes, 25
design process, 22–25, **32**
early iterations, 25
entrances, **23, 24–25**
floor plan entrance detail, **28**
funding, 25–26
inclusive design features and settings, 29–32
international aspects, 21
landscape buffer, **31**
lobby, **21,** 29
location, 21

model, **26**
opening, 19
partner organizations, 19, 21
plaza, **20, 26, 27,** 29
purpose, 21
requirements, 19
site plan, **27**
transit access orientation, 21–22, 29–30
University of California, Berkeley, 21
user design input, 22–25, **32**
user feedback, 32–33
user groups, 19
EDC (Economic Development Council) (Spokane), 338–339
Edelman Children's Court, 34–59
as catalyst for functional change, 55, 57
challenges, 36
child-friendly design principles, 38–39
design mission, 36
design process, 38–43
entrance/lobby, 43–47
exteriors, **43, 48**
family visiting rooms, 49–50
function, 35–36
hearing room design iterations, **40–41**
hearing rooms, 50–51
interview rooms, 49
management issues, 55, 57
mediation rooms, 49
operational issues, 55, 57
outdoor area, **56–57**
Shelter Care area, 51, **52–53, 54,** 55
user feedback, 57–59
user groups, 36, **39** (table)
user groups and survey methods (chart), 39
waiting areas, **36, 37,** 48–49, 51, **52–53, 54**
wayfinding, 47–48
See also dependency court guidelines

edged walkways, 409
Edison School/Pacific Park, 172–91
   accessibility features, 179, **184, 185,**
      186–87
   art, **180, 181, 188, 191**
   buildings, **174, 175, 181, 185,** 187–88,
      190–91
   collaborative nature, 181, 184–86, 191
   community center, **174**
   design features, 186–89
   design goals, 175–79
   design process, 181, 184–86
   environment, **177**
   functions and purposes, 173, 175
   interiors, **177, 179, 184,** 187–88
   landscaping, **176, 180, 182–83, 184, 186**
   library, **174**
   management issues, 189–90
   master plan, 177
   mixed-use aspects, 177–79, 188–89, 191
   operational issues, 189–90
   population served, 175
   school facilities, **175**
   user feedback, 191
   user groups, 179
   See also open space guidelines; school
      (K–12) guidelines
education, 9, 11
   See also Edison School/Pacific Park;
      Musées des Beaux Arts (Valenciennes
      and Calais, France); Tule Elk Park Child
      Development Center
Edwards, Mike, 381–82
Emeryville, California, **251**
enclosures, 419
   See also activity areas; landscaping; play
      area guidelines
entrances
   children's zoos, 414
   Davis Commons, 222–23

dependency courts, 388–89, 392, 394
Ed Roberts Campus (ERC), **23, 24–25**
Edelman Children's Court, 43–47
The Great Spokane River Gorge Strategic
   Master Plan, **378**
Hamill Family Play Zoo and Play Gardens,
   12, 124–26, **125, 127**
Musées des Beaux Arts (Valenciennes and
   Calais, France), 102
play areas, 418
plazas, 423
Riverfront Park Master Plan, 353
Envision Spokane (community newsletter),
   324
equitable impacts, 6–7
   See also specific project examples
ERC. *See* Ed Roberts Campus (ERC)
Explore! A Child's Nature. *See* Hamill Family
   Play Zoo and Play Gardens
exterior environments. *See* connectivity
   (downtown/neighborhood); entrances;
   landscaping; parks; specific projects by
   name; trail system guidelines

fareless public transit zone, 8
FCI Cleveland Bridge, 296
Federal Access Board (Regulatory
   Negotiation Committee 1999), 425
Féderation du Nord de la France des Sociétés
   d'Amis des Musées, 100
fences, 419
flooring and surfaces
   Chase Palm Park, 159–60
   classrooms, 405
   Hamill Family Play Zoo and Play Gardens,
      415
   hardscape, 463
   markings, 411
   play areas, 422

trails, 426–27
   See also accessibility issues; wayfinding
Flour Mill buildings (Spokane), 359–360
flush-mounted signs, 465
FOF (Friends of the Falls, Spokane), 326,
   371, 380
France. *See* Musées des Beaux Arts
   (Valenciennes and Calais, France)
Friends of the Davenport, 325
Friends of the Falls (FOF), 326, 371, 380
Fruitvale Transit Village, 7
functionality, 5–6, 7
   See also specific project examples
furniture
   dependency courts, 391, 392, 395, 396
   exterior, 410
   school classrooms, 404, 405, 406, 407,
      408, 409

Gallagher Building (Spokane), **333**
gardens, 401–2, 420
   See also Davis Central Park; Davis
      Commons; landscaping; Riverfront Park
      Master Plan; Tule Elk Park Child
      Development Center
gateways, 463
gathering places
   Davis Central Park, 192–209
   Davis Commons, 210–27
   Edison School/Pacific Park, 172–91
   fundamental principles and aspects, 12
   play areas, 422
   schools, 402–3
   urban, 463–65
   See also performance places; plaza guide-
      lines; promenades
Glendale, California. *See* Edison
   School/Pacific Park
Goltsman, Susan M., 473

Gothic Revival (building style), 459
graphic signs, 466
Graves, Michael, 78, 84
The Great Spokane River Gorge Loop Trail, **374,** 375
The Great Spokane River Gorge Strategic Master Plan, 368–78
  bicycle features, 375
  Centennial Trail, 375
  Confluence Area Visitor Arrival Point, 372
  connectivity with neighborhoods, 371
  description, 368
  design process, 326
  economic development, 377, 378
  entrances, **378**
  environmental impact aspects, 377
  Green Infrastructure Zones, 378
  habitat preservation and restoration, 377, 378
  High Bridge Park, 371
  history, 368
  interpretive facilities and program, 371–72, **373**
  Lower Falls, 371
  management issues, 380–81
  Monroe Street Bridge, **343–45,** 371, **375**
  Native Americans, 371, 372, 383
  neighborhoods, 368, 371
  North Point Overlook, 372
  operational issues, 380–81
  organizations, 326
  Peaceful Valley neighborhood, **368,** 383
  pedestrian features, 375
  recreation aspects, 375–76, 383–84
  signage, 371–72, **373**
  Spokane Park Board, 368
  transportation improvement, 373–74
  wayfinding, 371–72, **373**

West Central neighborhood, 371
  See also open space guidelines; trail system guidelines
Greek Revival (building style), 459
green infrastructure, 436, 448–50
Green Infrastructure Zones, 378
green streets network (Spokane), 341, **342,** 343
greenways, 436, 450–51
ground covering, 422
  See also flooring and surfaces; landscaping guidelines. *See* design guidelines under each specific project name; inclusive design project guidelines
gymnasiums (school), 408

habitat protection, 11–12, 377
Hamill Family Play Zoo and Play Gardens, 110–53
  autistic access, 147
  Backyard section, 145–47
  design goals, 118–19
  design process, 119–22
  design requirements, 122–24
  entrances, 124–26
  greenhouse gardens, 137–39
  indoor pedestrian settings, 126
  management issues, 148–49
  master plans, **114, 115**
  mission, 111
  operational issues, 148–49
  Parent Resource Areas, 139–40
  Play Partners, 146, 148, 149
  prototyping program for developing, 121–22
  quiet alcoves, 140
  settings charts, **120**
  signage, 124
  size, 112

special communication tools, 147
user feedback, 111, 151–53
user groups, 118
wayfinding, 126–29
Zoo-At-Home, 135–37
Zoo Play Gardens, 140
Zoo-Within-A-Zoo, 130–34
  See also children's zoo guidelines
hanging or "blade" signs, 465
hard court areas, 403
hardscape elements, 463
Hattie Weber Museum, 199
hearing rooms, **40–41,** 42–43, 50–51, 392–93
High Bridge Park (Spokane), 371
high-density residential, 8–9
  See also housing
high-speed connectivity hot zone, 338
historic building renovation
  American Legion Building (Spokane), 346
  Davenport Hotel (Spokane), **362**
  Fox Theater (Spokane), 363
  Holley-Mason Hardware Building (Spokane), **348**
  Lewis & Clark High School (Spokane), 346, **347**
  Montvale Hotel (Spokane), **365,** 382–83
  Odd Fellows Hall (Spokane), **363**
  Old Spokane Flour Mill (Spokane), 359, **360**
  West Central neighborhood (Spokane), 371
historic character enhancement, 238, 246–52
  See also historic building renovation
Historic Industrial Sector (Sacramento, California, R Street Corridor), 247–52
historic preservation, 321
  See also Davenport District Strategic Action Plan; historic building renovation;

R Street Corridor; Riverfront Park
Master Plan
history (leading to inclusive design
principles), 1–4
home economics classrooms, 406–7
horizontal rhythms (building design
element), 457
"hot zones" (Spokane), 338
housing
builder fees, 8
Davis Commons, 212, 214, **216,** 217
downtown connectivity, 321
Fruitvale Transit Village, 7
fundamentals, 10
Oakland, California, 7
principles, 10
R Street Corridor, 234, 240–241, **247,**
252, 253, 262
Seattle, Washington, 8
Spokane Plan for a New Downtown, 327,
328, 332, 333, 340–41, 351–53
University of California in San Francisco
project, 9–10
Vancouver, BC, Canada, 8–9
Howard Street Corridor (Spokane), 351, 353

Iacofano, Daniel, 473–74
icon signs, 466
identities (for districts), 321
IMAX theater (Spokane), 355, 356
inappropriate signs, 466–67
inclusive city
context sensitivity and, 6
definition of, xi
design project guidelines for, 12–13
ecological requirements of, 4–5
economic imperative of, xii
entrepreneurial models for, xiii
equitable impacts in, 6–7
framework for, xiv

functionality and, 5–6
need for, xi
planning considerations for, 4–7
policy framework for, 10–12
project design criteria, 5–7
urban exclusivity and segregation reality,
xi–xii
See also specific projects by name
inclusive design, 10–13, 116–18, 387
See also community participation (in design
process); inclusive design project guidelines
inclusive design project guidelines, 12–13,
385–469
children's zoos, 413–16
cityscapes, 454–69
dependency courts, 388–98
museums, 411–12
open spaces, 435–53
play areas, 417–22
plazas, 423–24
schools (K–12), 399–410
trail systems, 425–34
See also specific projects
Independent Living Movement, 15, 16–19
industrial area conversions
Berkeley, California, **238, 243, 260**
Emeryville, California, **251**
encouragement policies, 246
Portland, Oregon, **239, 240, 241, 246**
R Street Corridor, 232–35, **237,** 238, **245,**
247, **248**
San Jose, California, **242, 264**
industrial areas, **228,** 232–35
See also industrial area conversions
industrial building renovation, **333**
See also historic building renovation; indus-
trial area conversions
International (building style), 459
Interstate Highway system, 2, 9

interview rooms, 396

Jacobs, Jane, 3
Japanese Garden (Spokane), 355
Jones, Stanton, 475
Jordan, Susan, 163
Juarez, Lynn, 62
Juvenile Dependency Court for the County
of Los Angeles. *See* Edelman Children's
Court

"Kid's Council," 121
kindergarten and pre-school areas, 404
See also play area guidelines
kiosks, 351
Krumholz, Norman, x

lab stations (classroom), 407
land forms, 420
See also landscaping
landscaping, **31,** 409, **410,** 423, 463–65
See also gardens; gathering places; parks;
public open space
large size neighborhood parks, 443, **444**
Leon, Joan, 475
library/media centers (schools), 409
The Death and Life of Great American Cities
(Jacobs), 3
light rail, 233–34
lighted signs, 466
lighting, 45, 398, 410, 468, 469
Lions Club International District, 100
lobbies, 43–45, 388–89
Long Beach, California, 9
Los Angeles County, California. *See* Edelman
Children's Court; Edison School/Pacific
Park
Lower Falls (Spokane), 371
Lynch, Kevin, 1, 3, 6, 387

Malhotra, Mukul, 475–76

Market Green sector (Sacramento, California R Street Corridor), 262–65

McIntyre, Sally, 476

McKay, Susan, 476

medium size neighborhood parks, **442,** 443

Met Theater (Spokane), **360,** 362

Michael Graves, architect, 78

MIG, Inc.
    Carquinez Bridge Retrofit and Replacement, 296
    Chase Palm Park, 156
    Davis Central Park, 194
    Ed Roberts Campus (ERC), 16
    Edelman Children's Court, 36
    Edison School/Pacific Park, 174
    Hamill Family Play Zoo and Play Gardens, 112
    Presidio Trails and Bikeways Master Plan, 274
    R Street Corridor, 230
    Spokane, Washington projects, 314
    St. Coletta of Greater Washington, D.C., 78
    Tule Elk Park Child Development Center, 62

mixed-use facilities, 177
    See also pedestrian issues; specific projects

Mixed-Use Transit Hub Sector (Sacramento, California R Street Corridor), 240, 241–46, **247–48,** 252–56, **257**

"mixed-use urban village," 327

mobility, 11
    See also accessibility issues

Mobius at Michael Anderson Plaza (Spokane), 359

Mobius Children's Museum (Spokane), 331

Monroe Street Bridge (Spokane), 343, 343–345, 371, **375**

Monterey Park, California. *See* Edelman Children's Court

Montvale Hotel (Spokane), **365,** 382–83

Moore, Rex, 212

Moore, Robin, 476–77

multi-use. *See* mixed-use facilities; specific projects

Mumford, Lewis, 3

Musée des Beaux Arts (Valenciennes, France)
    design features and settings, 105–6
    design process, 104–5
    directory, **106**
    map, **105**
    purpose, 104
    signage, **105,** 107
    staircases and floor markings, 107

Musée des Beaux Arts et de la Dentelle (Calais, France), 100–103
    audio commentary, 102–3
    descriptive information, 103
    design process, 100
    entrance, 102
    inclusive design features, 102–3
    plan, **101**
    wayfinding, 102

Musées des Beaux Arts (Valenciennes and Calais, France), 96–109
    design goals, 98–99
    operational issues, 107
    user feedback, 107–9
    user groups, 99

"Museum at Your Fingertips" program, 96–109

museum guidelines, 411–12
    See also Musée des Beaux Arts

music rooms (school), 406

National Environmental Policy Act (NEPA), 283, 285

National Park Service (NPS), 280

National Park Service/Presidio Trust, 274

Native Americans, 371, 372, 383

navigational aids, 411
    See also accessibility issues; signage; wayfinding

NEC Foundation of America, 26

neighborhood/downtown connectivity, 321
    See also North Bank Development Plan; Riverfront Park Master Plan; Spokane Plan for a New Downtown

neighborhood greens, 437, 452–53

neighborhood unification, 238–40

neighborhoods, 10
    See also housing

Neoclassicism (building style), 459

NEPA (National Environmental Policy Act), 283, 285

New Urbanism, 3–4

Ney, Bart, 477

North Bank Development Plan (Spokane), 356–60
    concept diagram, **358**
    design process, 325
    Flour Mill buildings, 359–360
    management issues, 379
    Mobius at Michael Anderson Plaza, 359
    operational issues, 379
    outdoor attractions, 359–60
    overview, 322
    purposes, 356
    Science Technology Center, 356, 359
    site design, **357**

North Bank District (Spokane), 334
    See also North Bank Development Plan

North Point Overlook (Spokane), 372

NPS (National Park Service), 280

Oakland, California, 7

Odd Fellows Hall (Spokane), 363

Old Spokane Flour Mill (Spokane), **360**

Olmsted Brothers, 316, 368

on-street parking, 462

open areas. *See* gathering places; open space guidelines; parks

open space guidelines, 435–53
  accessibility, 437
  block size, 437
  connectivity, 437
  corridors, 437
  elements, 436–37
  framework, 437–38
  green infrastructure, 436, 448–50
  greenways, 436, 450–51
  location, 437
  multi-use corridors, 437
  neighborhood greens, 437, 452–53
  overview, 435
  parks, 436, 440–46
  pattern for framework creation, process, 438–39
  regional trails, 436
  relationships, 437
  safety, 437
  sustainability, 437
  variety, 437

opening proportions (buildings), 457

The Organization Man (Whyte), 2

outdoor areas. *See* children's zoo guidelines; gathering places; landscaping; open space guidelines; parks; trail system guidelines

outdoor classrooms (schools), 401–2

outdoor eating areas (schools), 402

Outdoor Recreation Access Routes, 430

outsloping, 431

overlooks, 429

Pacific Park. *See* Edison School/Pacific Park

palette. *See* color

Parent Resource Areas, 139–40

parking
  bicycles, 423–24
  buildings, 454
  lot placement and design, 456
  on-street, 462
  plazas, 423–24
  schools (K–12), 400
  signage, 466
  urban, 456, 462

parks
  Chase Palm Park, 154–71
  Davis Central Park, 192–209
  Davis Commons, 210–27
  Edison School/Pacific Park, 172–91
  general design criteria, 440–41
  general system guidelines, 440
  park types, 441–46
  See also Hamill Family Play Zoo and Play Gardens; open space guidelines; Tule Elk Park Child Development Center

pathways, 415, 418–19
  See also The Great Spokane River Gorge Strategic Master Plan; Presidio Trails and Bikeways Master Plan

Paulsen Building (Spokane), **348**

Peaceful Valley neighborhood, 383

Pearl District (Portland, Oregon), **230**

pedestals, 412

pedestrian issues
  accessibility, 222, 230, 247, **249,** 259
  bridges, 305, **308**
  circulation, 223, 264, 373–74, 461–62
  landscaping, 219
  links, 333
  mixed-use streets, **264, 265**
  pedestrian-friendly streets, 241–45, **255,** 256, **257, 258,** 259, 457
  reclamation of neighborhood streets, 229–30
  safety, 419, 460

street orientation, 458, 460

trails, 425–27

transit-oriented development, 240, 260

See also bicycles; mixed-use facilities; Presidio Trails and Bikeways Master Plan; shared roadway concept

people with disabilities. *See* accessibility issues; ADA (Americans with Disabilities Act); Ed Roberts Campus (ERC); Independent Living Movement; Musées des Beaux Arts (Valenciennes and Calais, France)

people with visual impairment. *See* accessibility issues; Ed Roberts Campus (ERC); Musées des Beaux Arts (Valenciennes and Calais, France)

performance places, 422
  See also gathering places

physical planning models, 3, 4

Pioneer Courthouse Square (Portland, Oregon), 8

play area guidelines, 417–22
  accessibility issues, 418, 419, **420, 421,** 422
  animal habitats, 421
  child design participation, 418
  entrances, 418
  equipment, 419–20
  fences and enclosures, 419
  gardens, 420
  gathering areas, 422
  ground covering and safety surfacing, 422
  loose parts, 422
  multipurpose, 420
  overview, 417
  pathways, 418–19
  performance places, 422
  public participation in design, 417–18
  sand play, 421–22
  settings, 418

signage, 419

social accessibility, 418

storage, 422

topography, 420

vegetation, 420

water play, 421

wheeled toys, 418, 422

    See also Chase Palm Park; children's zoo
        guidelines; Davis Central Park; Edelman
        Children's Court; Edison School/Pacific
        Park; Hamill Family Play Zoo and Play
        Gardens; Tule Elk Park Child
        Development Center

play equipment, 419–20

Play Partners, 116, **117,** 146, 148, 149

playgrounds. *See* parks; play area guidelines

plaza guidelines, 423–24, 464

    See also gathering places

pocket parks, 464

policy framework, 10–12

    See also specific projects

Portland, Oregon, 8, **230, 239, 240, 241,
    246**

Postmodern (building style), 459

pre-school and kindergarten areas, 404

    See also play area guidelines

preservation (of historic sites.) *See* Davenport
    District Strategic Action Plan; The Great
    Spokane River Gorge Strategic Master
    Plan; historic building renovation;
    Riverfront Park Master Plan

Presidio Trails and Bikeways Master Plan,
    272–93

accessibility, **283, 284,** 285, 286, 287, 293

aerial view, **276–77**

background, 274–75, 277

bikeways, **279,** 288

design features, 285–89

design goals, 277, 288

design process, 283, 285

historic aspects, 274, 291–93

location, 273–74, **275, 286**

overlooks, **274, 280, 286,** 288, **292–93**

site plans, **278, 279**

trailheads, 288

trails, **278,** 286–87

user feedback, 291–93

user groups, 280–81

    See also open space guidelines; trail system
        guidelines

Presidio Trust, 280–81

promenades, 464

public open space, 9, 116

    See also Davis Commons; gathering places;
        The Great Spokane River Gorge
        Strategic Master Plan; landscaping;
        mixed use facilities; open space guide-
        lines; parks; plaza guidelines; Presidio
        Trails and Bikeways Master Plan;
        promenades

public realm, 11–12, 240–46, 247

public transit, 8

    See also transit-oriented development

Queen Anne (building style), 459

Quiet Alcoves, 139–140

R Street Corridor, 228–71

accessibility, 267

Art Walk sector, 259–61

bicycles, 245

corridor sector design concept, **247**

design goals, 238–46

design palette, 266

design process, 235–37

Design Strategy Framework, **237**

historic character enhancement, 238

historic industrial sector, 247–52

historical significance, 232–33

infrastructure development, 268

location, 230, **231**

management issues, 268–269

Market Green sector, 262–65

mixed-use aspects, 240, 241–43, 245–46,
    247, 248

multi-use nature, 232, 233–35

neighborhood unification, 238–40

operational issues, 268–269

pedestrian issues, 240–45, **249, 251**

program management, 269

project goals, 232–35

public agency/private business
    cooperation, 268

public realm reclamation, 240–46

size, 230

street maintenance, 268

streetscape elements, **266–67**

traffic, 241–42, 245

transit hub sector, 252–56, **253, 254, 255,
    257**

transit-oriented development encourage-
    ment, 240

universal design elements, 267

user feedback, 269–270

user groups, 235

    See also cityscape guidelines

R Street Urban Design and Development
    Plan. *See* R Street Corridor

Raimo, Sharon, 80, 95

Raynes, Coco, 477

Raynes Rail, 99, 102

recreation, 9

    See also Chase Palm Park; Davis Central
        Park; Presidio Trails and Bikeways Master
        Plan; Spokane, Washington projects; Tule
        Elk Park Child Development Center

regional parks, 446

regional trails, 446–48

reinforcement (surface), 431–32

residences. *See* housing; neighborhoods

restrooms, 395–96

Revival (building style), 459

Richardsonian Romanesque (building style), 459

river crossings, 343–45

River Park Square, 317, 318, **329,** 331

Riverfront Park district (Spokane), 335–36

Riverfront Park Master Plan, 350–56

    Canada Island, 356

    design process, 325

    East Havermale Island, 355

    entries, 353

    gondola, 350

    Howard Street Corridor, 351, 353

    IMAX building, 355

    Japanese Garden, 355

    kiosks, 351

    management issues, 379

    operational issues, 379

    Pavilion area, 354–55

    purposes, 350

    signage, 353

    site, **351**

    south entry to park, **352**

    Spokane Falls Skyride, 350

    wayfinding, 351, 353

    See also cityscape guidelines; open space guidelines

Riverside Neighborhood Council (Spokane), 325

Riverview Condominiums (Spokane), **333**

road sharing concept, **285**

    See also bicycles; pedestrian issues

rolling grade dips, 431

roof forms, 458

Rotary Riverfront Fountain (Spokane), **353**

Sacramento, California. *See* R Street Corridor

Sacramento Regional Transit, 233

sacred spaces, 424

safety equipment, 408

safety surfacing, 422

San Francisco, California. *See* Presidio Trails and Bikeways Master Plan; Tule Elk Park Child Development Center

San Francisco Bay Area. *See* Berkeley, California; Carquinez Bridge Retrofit and Replacement; Ed Roberts Campus (ERC); Emeryville, California; Oakland, California; Presidio Trails and Bikeways Master Plan; San Jose, California; Tule Elk Park Child Development Center

San Jose, California, **242, 264**

sand features, 421–22

Santa Barbara, California, 154–71

Santa Barbara Parks and Recreation Department, 158

Santana Row (San Jose, California), **242, 264**

Saranac Hotel (Spokane), 334

Save Open Space (SOS), 195

school (K–12) guidelines, 399–410

    accessibility issues, 399

    assembly areas, 408

    auditoriums, 408

    cafeterias, 408–09

    circulation (building), 400

    exterior environment, 399

    garden outdoor classrooms, 401–2

    interior settings, 404–9

    landscape elements, 409–10

    libraries/media centers, 409

    outdoor environments, 400–404

    overview, 399

    parking, 400

    science labs, 407–8

site access, 399

    See also Edison School/Pacific Park; St. Coletta of Greater Washington, D.C.; Tule Elk Park Child Development Center

schoolyard settings, 400–404, 409–10

    classroom patios, 400–401

    eating areas, 402

    garden outdoor classrooms, 401–2

    gathering areas, 402–3

    hard court areas, 403

    kindergarten and pre-school areas, 404

    multi-purpose outdoor classrooms, 401

    natural area outdoor classrooms, 402

    turf fields, 403–4

Science Technology Center (Spokane), 356, 359

sculpture. *See* art

seating, 423

    See also furniture; waiting areas

Seattle, Washington, 8

Second Empire (building style), 459

service equipment, 468

shared roadway concept, **254, 255, 258, 263, 264, 265,** 460

    See also accessibility issues; bicycles; pedestrian issues

Shelter Care, 393–96

sidewalks, 230

    See also accessibility issues; bicycles; pedestrian issues; wayfinding

signage

    banners, 366

    children's zoos, 414

    The Great Spokane River Gorge Strategic Master Plan, 371–72, **373**

    Hamill Family Play Zoo and Play Gardens, **112, 119,** 124, **128, 129, 139**

    lighted, 466

museums, 411–12

play areas, 419

Presidio Trails and Bikeways Master Plan, **286, 290**

Riverfront Park Master Plan (Spokane), 353

schools (K–12), 399

trail systems, 429–30

urban, 465–67

visually impaired, 107

See also wayfinding

SkyWest magazine, 338

slopes, 426

small neighborhood parks, 441–43

social planning model, 3

SOS (Save Open Space), 195

South Side district (Spokane), 334–35

spatial organization, 411

Special Districts (Spokane), 336–38

Spokane, Washington projects, 312–84

achievements, 319

background, 318–19

City of Spokane, 380

colors, 378

component plans and projects, 314

Davenport District Strategic Action Plan, 360–68

design features, 326–50

design process, 322–26

Downtown Spokane Zoning Ordinance & Design Guidelines, 322

goals, 320–22

The Great Spokane River Gorge Strategic Master Plan, 368–78

history, 313–17

investment amount, 314

management issues, 379–81

operational issues, 379–81

palette, 378

Riverfront Park Master Plan, 350–56

specific area plans, 321–22

Spokane Plan for a New Downtown, 326–50

statistics, 319

user feedback, 381–84

user groups, 322

See also specific component projects

Spokane Plan for a New Downtown, 326–50

action strategies and elements, 326–27

bicycles, 345

community outreach award, 325

community participation, 323–25

design process, 322–25

districts, 329–36, **330**

Downtown Core district, 329–32

East End district, 333–34

economic development, 338–39

green streets network, **342**

historic preservation, 346–48

"hot zones," 338

housing, 340–41

land use, 327, **328**

management issues, 379

neighborhood economic development, 348, 350

North Bank district, 334

operational issues, 379

organizations, 338–39

overview, 321–22

pedestrian circulation, 343

river crossings, 343–45

Riverfront Park district, 335–36

South Side district, 334–35

Special Districts, 336–38

technology zone, 338

Terabyte Triangle, 338

transportation and circulation, 341–46

vision statement, 326

West End district, 333

See also cityscape guidelines

Spokane River Gorge Coalition (SRGC), 380–81

Spokane Transit Authority (STA) Plaza, 366

sports parks, 443, 446

sprawl, xii, 2–3

SRGC (Spokane River Gorge Coalition), 380–81

St. Coletta of Greater Washington, D.C., 76–95

accessibility features, 82, 92–93

art, 83, 88, 95

building elevations, **91**

campus overview, **89**

classroom environments, 80, 81, 82, 84, 86, 87

community involvement activities, 88

community relations, 77–81

construction completion, 78

construction cost, 78

curriculum, 80–81, 87–88

design process, 81–82

exterior view, **85**

functional purposes, 79–81

history, 77–80

inclusive design features, **81,** 82–93

management issues, 93

mission statement, 77

multi-functional nature, 82–83

operational issues, 93

original vision, 78

outdoor environment, 84, **85,** 86, 87–93, **94**

site elements, 83–84

statistics, 79

student activities, **78, 79, 93**

transit aspect, 79

user feedback, 95

user groups, 81

village green, 86

See also school (K–12) guidelines

street trees, 463
streets, 457, 458, 460–61, 469
    See also bicycles; parking; pedestrian issues;
        traffic; transit-oriented development
subsurface grids, 433–34
suburbs, 2–3
Sullivan, Cheryl, 478
surface reinforcing, 431–32
surfaces, 431–34
    See also flooring and surfaces
sustainable design, 30–32

tactile program, 97–98
Tauscher, Ellen, 22
tax service, 10
"Technology and Universal Design
    Assessment of the Ed Roberts Campus
    (ERC)" (NEC Foundation of America),
    26
teen centers, 203–4
Terabyte Triangle (Spokane, Washington), 338
A Theory of Good City Form (Lynch), 1, 3
Through the Looking Glass (TLG), 19, 33
Time magazine, 338
TLG (Through the Looking Glass), 19, 33
topography, 420, 427–28
    See also landscaping
traffic, 240–45
trail edge protection, 430
trail guides, 430
trail markers, 430
trail systems guidelines, 425–34
    above-grade trails, 432–33, 435
    accessibility issues, 425
    bikeways, 427–28
    drainage control, 431
    grades, 427–28
    multi-use, 426–427
    obstacles, 427
    other access routes, 430

overlooks, 429
parking, 429
pedestrian, 425–26
sandy soils, 433–34
slopes, 426
surfaces, 426–427
trail edge protection, 430
trailheads, 428–29
wayfinding, 429–30
wet areas, 431–32
    See also The Great Spokane River Gorge
        Strategic Master Plan; North Bank
        Development Plan; Presidio Trails and
        Bikeways Master Plan; Riverfront Park
        Master Plan
trailheads, 428–29
transit. See public transit
transit-oriented development, 21–22, 240
transit plazas, 465
transportation, 341–46, 373–74, 458,
    460–63
    See also public transit; transit-oriented
        development; transit plazas
trees, 463
    See also green streets network (Spokane,
        Washington); greenways; landscaping
Tribal Cultural Center, 372, 373
Tule Elk Park Child Development Center,
    60–75
    accessibility features, 63, 64, **68,** 71
    amphitheater, 69
    art, **64, 70, 72, 73**
    construction area, 70
    construction completion, 62
    construction cost, 62
    credits, 62
    design process, 67–68
    dining area, 72
    function and purposes, 61, 63, 64–67
    garden areas, **63, 66,** 69–70, **69**

indoor/outdoor transition patios, 68
management issues, 72, 74
multipurpose nature, 64, 65–67, 69, 72,
    74
operational issues, 72, 74
original vision for, 61
particulars, 62
play areas, **62, 64,** 68, 70–71, **72**
site plan, **62**
size, 62
user feedback, 75
    See also school (K–12) guidelines
turf fields, 403–4

UC Berkeley (University of California,
    Berkeley), 15, 17, 21
UC Davis (University of California, Davis),
    212
UC Davis Office of Development, 212
UCSF (University of California, San
    Francisco), 9–10
Universal Design Tool, 26
University of California, Berkeley (UC
    Berkeley), 15, 17, 21
University of California, Davis (UC Davis),
    212
University of California, San Francisco
    (UCSF), 9–10
urban building materials, 468
urban color usage, 467–68
urban outdoor areas, 454–55
urban renaissance, xi
Urban Renewal, 3
urban transportation, 458, 460–61
    See also transit-oriented development;
        transportation
U.S. Department of Transportation, 21
U.S. House of Representatives Committee
    on Education and the Workforce, 22

U.S. House of Representatives Committee on Transportation and Infrastructure, 22
user survey methodologies, **39** (chart)

Vallejo, California. *See* Carquinez Bridge Retrofit and Replacement
values, xii
Vancouver, BC, Canada, 8–9
ventilation, 398
"Vision for Growing an Inclusive City," 10
visiting rooms, 395
visual cues, 405

waiting areas, **37, 38,** 390–92
walking. *See* accessibility issues; bicycles; pedestrian issues; wayfinding
warehouses. *See* industrial area conversions
Washington, D.C., 10
water features, 416, 421
wayfinding
    children's zoos, 414, 415
    directories, 105
    Ed Roberts Campus (ERC), 29
    Edelman Children's Court, 47–48
    The Great Spokane River Gorge Strategic Master Plan, 371–72, **373**
    Hamill Family Play Zoo and Play Gardens, 126–29
    Howard Street corridor (Spokane, Washington), 351, 353

kiosks, 351
museums, 411–12
Presidio Trails and Bikeways Master Plan, 277, 286, 288
trail systems, 429–30
trailheads, 428–29
visually impaired, 102
See also accessibility issues; signage
West End, 333
wheel channel, 30
Whirlwind Wheelchair International (WWI), 19, 32–33
Whyte, William, 2
WID (World Institute on Disability), 19
Wight, Lawrence, 478
Williams, Anthony A., xiii
windows, classroom, 405–6
World Institute on Disability (WID), 19
WWI (Whirlwind Wheelchair International), 19, 32–33

Zampa, Alfred, 302, 304
    See also Carquinez Bridge Retrofit and Replacement
zoning laws, 2
Zoo Play Gardens, 140
Zoos. *See* children's zoo guidelines; Hamill Family Play Zoo and Play Gardens